INTERNATIONAL LIBRARY OF
AFRO-AMERICAN LIFE AND HISTORY

Langston Hughes with his Aunt "Toy" Harper

INTERNATIONAL LIBRARY OF
**AFRO-AMERICAN
LIFE**
AND HISTORY

AN INTRODUCTION
TO BLACK LITERATURE
IN AMERICA

From 1746 to the Present

Compiled and Edited with an Introduction by
LINDSAY PATTERSON

THE PUBLISHERS AGENCY, INC.
CORNWELLS HEIGHTS, PENNSYLVANIA
under the auspices of
THE ASSOCIATION FOR THE STUDY OF AFRO-AMERICAN LIFE AND HISTORY

Copyright © 1976

THE ASSOCIATION FOR THE STUDY OF AFRO-AMERICAN LIFE AND HISTORY

Copyright © 1968, 1969, 1970

THE ASSOCIATION FOR THE STUDY OF NEGRO LIFE AND HISTORY

A NON-PROFIT ORGANIZATION

LIBRARY OF CONGRESS CATALOG CARD NO. 68-56838

INTERNATIONAL STANDARD BOOK NUMBER 0-87781-209-8

PRINTED IN THE UNITED STATES OF AMERICA

REVISED EDITION

EXCLUSIVE WORLD-WIDE DISTRIBUTION BY

THE LIBRARY COMPANY, INC., WASHINGTON, D.C.

To

HERSCHEL *and* JANE SHOHAN

Preface

THE Association for the Study of Afro-American Life and History joins with Pubco Corporation in presenting this new series of volumes which treat in detail the cultural and historical backgrounds of black Americans. This Association, a pioneer in the area of Afro-American History, was founded on September 9, 1915, by Dr. Carter G. Woodson, who remained its director of research and publications until his death in 1950.

In 1916 Dr. Woodson began publishing the quarterly *Journal of Negro History*. In 1926 Negro History Week was launched, and since that time it has been held annually in February, encompassing the birth dates of Abraham Lincoln and Frederick Douglass. The *Negro History Bulletin* was first published in 1937 to serve both schools and families by making available to them little-known facts about black life and history.

During its sixty-one years of existence, the Association for the Study of Afro-American Life and History has supported many publications dealing with the contributions of Afro-Americans to the growth and development of this country. Its activities have contributed to the increasing interest in the dissemination of factual studies which are placing the Afro-American in true perspective in the mainstream of American history.

We gratefully acknowledge the contributions of previous scholars, which have aided us in the preparation of this *International Library of Afro-American Life and History*.

Our grateful acknowledgment is also expressed to Charles W. Lockyer, president of Pubco Corporation, whose challenging approach has made possible this library.

Though each of the volumes in this set can stand as an autonomous unit, and although each author has brought his own interpretation to the area with which he is dealing, together these books form a comprehensive picture of the Afro-American experience in America. The three history volumes give a factual record of a people who were brought from Africa in chains and who today are struggling to cast off the last vestiges of these bonds. The anthologies covering music, art, the theatre and literature provide a detailed account of the black American's contributions to these fields—including those contributions which are largely forgotten today. Achievement in the sports world is covered in another volume. The volume on the Afro-American in medicine is a history of the black American's struggle for equality as a medical practitioner and as a patient. The selected black leaders in the biography book represent the contributions and achievements of many times their number. The documentary history sums up the above-mentioned material in the words of men and women who were themselves a part of black history.

CHARLES H. WESLEY

Washington, D.C.

Editor's Note

I WISH to thank Emily Evershed, a great editor in every sense of the word, and one that a lucky few meet in a lifetime.

LINDSAY PATTERSON

New York City

Acknowledgments

WE are grateful for permission to use the following material in this book.

"The Childhood of an Ex-Colored Man," from *The Autobiography of an Ex-Colored Man*, by James Weldon Johnson. Copyright 1912 by Sherman, French and Co. Reissued 1927 by Alfred A. Knopf, Inc. Reprinted by permission of Alfred A. Knopf, Inc.

"The Negro Renaissance: Jean Toomer and the Harlem Writers of the 1920's," by Arna Bontemps. Copyright 1966 by the author. Reprinted by permission of the author.

"Esther," from *Cane*, by Jean Toomer. Copyright 1923 by the author. Reprinted by permission of Liveright Publishers.

"The Return," from *Their Eyes Were Watching God*, by Zora Neale Hurston. Copyright 1937 by the author. Reprinted by permission of the author's estate.

"Salvation," from *The Big Sea*, by Langston Hughes. Copyright 1940 by the author. "Color Problems," from *Simple's Uncle Sam*. Copyright 1965 by Hill and Wang, Inc. Reprinted by permission of the author's estate.

"Contemporary Negro Poetry: 1914–1936," by Sterling A. Brown. Copyright 1944 by the author. Reprinted by permission of the author.

"I Want To Die While You Love Me," "Common Dust," by Georgia Douglas Johnson. Copyright 1919, 1962 by the author. Reprinted by permission of the author's estate.

"Letter to My Sister," "Lines to a Nasturtium: A Lover Muses," by Anne Spencer. Copyright 1949, 1949 by the author. Reprinted by permission of the author.

"The White House," "Outcast," "Flame-Heart," by Claude McKay. Copyright 1937, 1937, 1922 by the author. Reprinted by permission of the author's estate.

"Harvest Song," "Conversion," "Prayer," by Jean Toomer. Copyright 1923, 1923, 1923 by the author. Reprinted by permission of the author's estate.

"Kid Stuff" by Frank Horne. Copyright 1942 by the author. Reprinted by permission of the author.

"Yet Do I Marvel," "Incident," "Simon the Cyrenian Speaks," by Countee Cullen. Copyright 1925 by the author. Reprinted by permission of the author's estate.

"Harlem," "Merry-Go-Round," "When Sue Wears Red," "Feet o' Jesus," "My People," "Troubled Woman," "The Negro Speaks of Rivers," "One-Way Ticket," "Mother to Son," "Border Line," "I, Too, Sing America," by Langston Hughes. Copyright 1951, 1942, 1926, 1927, 1932, 1926, 1926, 1942, 1926, 1943 and 1926 by the author. Reprinted by permission of the author's estate.

"Threnody," "Finis," by Waring Cuney. Copyright 1930, 1930 by the author. Reprinted by permission of the author's estate.

"A Black Man Talks of Reaping," "Southern Mansion," "Idolatry" by Arna Bontemps. Copyright 1926, 1926, 1926 by the author. Reprinted by permission of the author.

"Challenge," "Return," by Sterling A. Brown. Copyright 1932, 1932 by the author. Reprinted by permission of the author.

"Fate and Bigger Thomas," from *Native Son*, by Richard Wright. Copyright 1940 by the author. Reprinted by permission of the author's estate.

Table of Contents

xiv

Introduction

IT HAS BEEN traditional for intellectuals to dismiss almost entirely the whole body of Afro-American literature as inconsequential and insignificant. When compared with world literature, a great deal of black writing does suffer, not bceause of technical incompetence but because too often the black writer is imprisoned in his own alienation, which ultimately restricts his scope and limits his subject matter. This is not his fault, for the writer has to contend with everyday problems like every other Afro-American, and it would take a superhuman ego to detach himself completely and examine his "soul" and that of his fellow man without bitterness or rancor and with an unimpassioned eye. James Baldwin, recognizing this built-in trap for the black writer, fled to Paris for several years, Richard Wright's politics offered for a time the detachment he needed, and Langston Hughes used humor.

Baldwin, Wright and Hughes, like almost every other black fiction writer, grappled only with their contemporary societies. Few have attempted to use the distant past as a means of achieving objectivity. Perhaps it is because there were no black writers of the stature of Emerson, Thoreau or Hawthorne with whom they could identify, but there are many just as important historically as John Smith, Cotton Mather and Jonathan Edwards, whom black writers could employ to gain a perspective to the present. These early writers are not represented in any standard American literature books but continue to rot virtually undisturbed in the rare book sections of a few libraries. Thus the black writer has been cheated out of a wellspring; but more than that, he has been made to feel that his ancestors contributed only a "shuffling" stereotype to the literary developments in this country.

The present-day black writer, in his search for a positive identity, would do well to ferret out hundreds of pre-Civil War tracts, letters, sermons and narratives for investigation. There are writers such as Venture Smith, James W. C. Pennington, William Craft, Samuel E. Cornish, Martin Delany, David Ruggles, Henry Bibb, James Meachum, Robert Purvis, William C. Nell, Henry Box Brown, Richard Allen, William Wells Brown, Benjamin Banneker and Hosea Eaton, who reveal a version of life in early America completely omitted or distorted in our literature and history books.

Also, it is not enough to have literature books for just one particular ethnic group. If we are to survive as a nation, every American should become acquainted with every other American's contribution. This is a point, I think, that cannot be stressed enough. And it is a sad fact that graduates of our finest institutions of higher learning leave their campuses without any knowledge of American history as it really is. These are the people who head, for the most part, the social and economic institutions in our country. And if they are not aware, how can we expect the man in the street to change his attitudes?

This book is more or less an introduction to black literature, from the earliest prose and poetry the black writer has produced to the latest. The selections are placed chronologically, and should be helpful in aiding students and scholars in tracing the history, thought and status of the black man in this country since his arrival.

LINDSAY PATTERSON

New York City

xvii

The Eighteenth Century
1746–1799

Absalom Jones

Phillis Wheatley

Benjamin Banneker

Richard Allen

Gustavus Vassa

NEGRO NARRATIVES, which had their beginnings in the late 1700's, were a popular form of literature. Many were slave narratives, instigated by Northern abolitionists who discovered in these chronicles a powerful weapon with which to buttress their arguments against slavery as an institution. The first few black authors, however, dealt with religion, making very little or no mention of slavery.

Briton Hammon was the first black prose writer of record, with *A Narrative of the Uncommon Sufferings and Surprizing Deliverance of Briton Hammon, a Negro Man,* in 1760. The first poet was Lucy Terry, with "Bars Fight" in 1746.

Two eighteenth-century works that were of uncommon interest then and should be today are *A Narrative of the Lord's Wonderful Dealings with J. Marrant, a Black* (1785), and *The Interesting Narrative of the Life of Olaudah Equiano, or Gustavus Vassa, the African* (1789).

In its day, *The Interesting Narrative of the Life of Olaudah Equiano, or Gustavus Vassa,* was a bestseller. Vassa, born in Benin, Nigeria, in 1745, and abducted into slavery as an adolescent, was one of the few writers to recall in detail his early childhood in Africa, remembering all the sights, sounds and attitudes of his village as well as the social and political structures. He recalled also the manner of his abduction and the bewilderment that followed. He had a naturally inquisitive mind which even under chains could not be bridled. His curiosity was boundless and, coupled with his African view of things, produced a narrative unique in its imaginative blending of fantasy and fact.

Vassa remained in slavery only a few years, having the good fortune to be purchased by a kindly sea captain who tutored him. After manumission, he became a seaman and eventually a British subject.

His narrative suggests a very plausible conclusion: Had the African been schooled, he would have (as he has in music) brought a priceless inventiveness and vitality to American letters which it lacked then and lacks now.

A Narrative of the Lord's Wonderful Dealings with J. Marrant, a Black, dispels somewhat the myth that religion is intrinsic to the black. Marrant, in passing a white church service, became curious, attended, and was seized with the "holy spirit." He became an object of ridicule to his family—so much so that he ran away from home.

Benjamin Banneker was a man of many interests and talents. He was among other things an inventor, writer and mathematician. He is probably best known for serving on the commission that surveyed our nation's capital. "A Plan of Peace Office for the United States" (1792) was an early foreshadowing of the United Nations; however, there is some doubt as to the plan's authorship by Banneker.

One of the most prolific poets of the eighteenth century was Jupiter Hammon, a slave. Hammon had no formal education and, because of his lack of a strong stand against slavery, had little popularity among blacks. Phillis Wheatley, on the other hand, wrote little or nothing about slavery but enjoyed wide popularity in her day. She was brought to this country from Senegal at the age of about eight and purchased by the Wheatley family of Boston. The family, recognizing her genius, encouraged her to read and write, and sixteen months after having arrived on these shores she had completely mastered the English language. "An Elegiac Poem, on the Death of George Whitefield" (1770) was her first published poem. Much of her poetry can be called occasional verse—that is, it was written for some specific occasion, as a birth, or the death of a friend or a member of the family.

A Narrative of the Uncommon Sufferings and Surprizing Deliverance of Briton Hammon, a Negro Man

Briton Hammon

To the Reader

As my Capacities and Condition of Life are very low, it cannot be expected that I should make those Remarks on the Sufferings I have met with, or the kind Providence of a good GOD for my Preservation, as one in a higher Station, but shall leave that to the Reader as he goes along, and so I shall only relate Matters of Fact as they occur to my Mind.

On Monday, 25th Day of December, 1747, with the leave of my Master, I went from Marshfield, with an Intention to go a Voyage to Sea, and the next Day, the 26th, got to Plymouth, where I immediately ship'd myself on board of a Sloop, Capt. John Howland, Master, bound to Jamaica and the Bay. We sailed from Plymouth in a short Time, and after a pleasant Passage of about 30 Days, arrived at Jamaica; we was detain'd at Jamaica only 5 Days, from whence we sailed for the Bay, where we arrived safe in 10 Days. We loaded our Vessel with Logwood, and sailed from the Bay the 25th Day of May following, and the 15th Day of June we were cast away on Cape-Florida, about 5 Leagues from the Shore; being now destitute of every Help, we knew not what to do or what Course to take in this our sad Condition. The Captain was advised, intreated, and beg'd on, by every Person on board, to heave over but only 20 Ton of the Wood, and we should get clear, which if he had done, might have sav'd his Vessel and Cargo, and not only so, but his own Life, as well as the Lives of the Mate and Nine Hands, as I shall presently relate.

After being upon this Reef two Days, the Captain order'd the Boat to be hoisted out, and then ask'd who were willing to tarry on board. The whole Crew was for going on Shore at this Time, but as the Boat would not carry 12 Persons at once, and to prevent any Uneasiness, the Captain, a Passenger, and one Hand tarry'd on board, while the Mate, with Seven Hands besides myself, were order'd to go on Shore in the Boat, which as soon as we had reached, one half were to be Landed and the other four to return to the Sloop to fetch the Captain and the others on Shore. The Captain order'd us to take with us our Arms, Ammunition, Provisions and Necessaries for Cooking, as also a Sail to make a Tent of, to shelter us from the Weather; after having left the Sloop we stood towards the Shore, and being within Two Leagues of the same, we espy'd a Number of Canoes, which we at first took to be Rocks, but soon found our Mistake, for we perceiv'd they moved towards us; we presently saw an English Colour hoisted in one of the Canoes, at the Sight of which we were not a little rejoiced, but on our advancing yet nearer, we found them, to our very great Surprize, to be Indians, of which there were Sixty.

Being now so near them we could not possibly make our Escape; they soon came up with and boarded us, took away all our Arms, Ammunition and Provision. The whole Number of Canoes (being about Twenty) then made for the Sloop, except Two which they left to guard us, who order'd us to follow on with them; the Eighteen which made for the Sloop went so much faster than we that they got on board above Three Hours before we came along side, and had kill'd Captain Howland, the Passenger and the other hand. We came to the Larboard side of the Sloop, and they order'd us round to the Starboard, and as we were passing round the Bow, we saw the whole Number of Indians advancing forward and loading their Guns, upon which the Mate said, "My Lads, we are all dead Men," and before we had got round, they discharged their Small Arms upon us, and kill'd Three of our hands, viz. Reuben Young of Cape-Cod, Mate, Joseph Little and Lemuel Doty of Plymouth, upon which I immediately jump'd overboard, chusing rather to be drowned than to be kill'd by those barbarous and inhuman Savages. In three or four Minutes after, I heard another Volley which dispatched the other five, viz. John Nowland and Nathaniel Rich, both belonging to Plymouth, and Elkanah Collymore and James Webb, Strangers, and Moses Newmock, Molatto.

As soon as they had kill'd the whole of the People, one of the Canoes padled after me, and soon came up with me, hawled me into the Canoe, and beat me most terribly with a Cutlass; after that they ty'd me down, then this Canoe stood for the Sloop again and as soon as she came along side, the Indians on board the Sloop betook themselves to their Canoes, then set the Vessel on Fire, making a prodigious shouting and hallowing like so many Devils. As soon as the Vessel was burnt down to the Water's edge, the Indians stood for the Shore, together with our Boat, on board of which they put 5 hands.

After we came to the Shore, they led me to their Hutts, where I expected nothing but immediate Death, and as they spoke broken English, were often telling me, while coming from the Sloop to the Shore, that they intended to roast me alive. But the Providence of God order'd it otherways, for He appeared for my Help in this Mount of Difficulty, and they were better to me then my Fears, and soon unbound me, but set a Guard over me every Night.

They kept me with them about five Weeks, during which Time they us'd me pretty well, and gave me boil'd Corn, which was what they often eat themselves. The Way I made my Escape from these Villains was this: a Spanish Schooner arriving there from St. Augustine, the Master of which, whose Name was Romond, asked the Indians to let me go on board his Vessel, which they granted, and the Captain [1] knowing me very well, weigh'd Anchor and carry'd me off to the Havanna, and after being there four Days the Indians came after me, and insisted on having me again, as I was their Prisoner. They made Application to the Governor, and demanded me again from him, in answer to which the Governor told them that, as they had put the whole Crew to Death, they should not have me again, and so paid them Ten Dollars for me, adding that he would not have them kill any Person hereafter, but take as many of them as they could of those that should be cast away, and bring them to him, for which he would pay them Ten Dollars a head.

At the Havanna I lived with the Governor in the Castle about a Twelvemonth, where I was walking thro' the Street, I met with a Press-Gang who immediately prest me, and put me into Gaol; and with a Number of others I was confin'd till next Morning, when we were all brought out and ask'd who would go on board the King's Ships, four of which, having been lately built, were bound to Old-Spain, and on my refusing to serve on board they put me in a close Dungeon, where I was confin'd Four Years and seven months, during which Time I often made application to the Governor, by Persons who came to see the Prisoners, but they never acquainted him with it, nor did he know all this Time what became of me, which was the means of my being confin'd there so long.

But kind Providence so order'd it, that after I had been in this Place so long as the Time mention'd above, the Captain of a Merchantman belonging to Boston, having sprung a Leak, was obliged to put into the Havanna to refit, and while he was at Dinner at Mrs. Betty Howard's, she told the Captain of my deplorable Condition, and said she would be glad if he could by some means or other relieve me. The Captain told Mrs. Howard he would use his best Endeavours for my Relief and Enlargement.

Accordingly, after Dinner, [he] came to the Prison, and ask'd the Keeper if he might see me; upon his Request I was brought out of the Dungeon, and after the Captain had Interrogated me [he] told me he would intercede with the Governor for my Relief out of that miserable Place, which he did, and the next Day the Governor sent an Order to release me. I lived with the Governor about a Year after I was delivered from the Dungeon, in which Time I endeavour'd three Times to make my Escape, the last of which proved effectual. The first Time I got on board of Captain Marsh, an English Twenty Gun Ship, with a Number of others, and lay on board conceal'd that Night; and the next Day the Ship being under sail, I thought myself safe, and so made my Appearance upon Deck, but as soon as we were discovered the Captain ordered the Boat out, and sent us all on Shore. I intreated the Captain to let me, in particular, tarry on board, begging, and crying to him, to commiserate my unhappy Condition, and added that I had been confin'd almost five Years in a close Dungeon, but the Captain would not hearken to any Intreaties, for fear of having the Governor's Displeasure, and so I was obliged to go on Shore.

After being on Shore another Twelvemonth, I endeavour'd to make my Escape the second Time by trying to get on board of a Sloop bound to Jamaica, and as I was going from the City to the Sloop, was unhappily taken by the Guard and ordered back to the Castle and there confined. However, in a short Time I was set at Liberty and order'd with a Number of others to carry the Bishop[2] from the Castle thro' the Country to confirm the old People, baptize Children, etc., for which he receives large Sums of Money. I was employ'd in this Service about Seven Months, during which Time I lived very well, and then returned to the Castle again, where I had my Liberty to walk about the City and do Work for my self. The *Beaver*, an English Man of War, then lay in the Harbour, and having been informed by some of the Ship's Crew that she was to sail in a few Days, I had nothing now to do but to seek an Opportunity how I should make my Escape.

Accordingly one Sunday Night the Lieutenant of the Ship with a Number of the Barge Crew were in a Tavern, and Mrs. Howard, who had before been a Friend to me, interceded with the Lieutenant to carry me on board. The Lieutenant said he would with all his Heart, and immediately I went on board in the Barge. The next Day the Spaniards came along side the *Beaver* and demanded me again, with a Number of others who had made their Escape from them, and got on board the Ship but just before I did; but the Captain, who was a true Englishman, refus'd them, and said he could not answer it, to deliver up any Englishmen under English Colours. In a few Days we set Sail for Jamaica, where we arrived safe, after a short and pleasant Passage.

After being at Jamaica a short Time, we sail'd for London as convoy to a Fleet of Merchantmen, who all arrived safe in the Downs. I was turned over to another Ship, the *Arcenceil*, and there remained about a Month. From this Ship I went on board the *Sandwich*, of 90 Guns; on board the *Sandwich* I tarry'd 6 Weeks, and then was order'd on board the *Hercules*, Capt. John Porter, a 74 Gun Ship. We sail'd on a Cruize and met with a French 84 Gun Ship, and had a very smart Engagement[3] in which about 70 of our Hands were Kill'd and Wounded; the Captain lost his Leg in the Engagement, and I was Wounded in the Head by a small Shot. We should have taken this Ship if they had not cut away the most of our Rigging; however, in about three Hours after, a 64 Gun Ship came up with and took her. I was discharged from the *Hercules* the 12th Day of May, 1759 (having been on board of that Ship 3 Months), on account of my being disabled in the Arm and render'd incapable of Service, after being honourably paid the Wages due to me. I was put into the Greenwich Hospital, where I stay'd and soon recovered. I then ship'd myself a Cook on board Captain Martyn, an arm'd Ship in the King's Service. I was on board this Ship almost Two Months, and after being paid my Wages, was discharg'd in the Month of October.

After my discharge from Captain Martyn, I was taken sick in London of a Fever and was confin'd about 6 Weeks, where I expended all my Money and left in very poor Circumstances; and, unhappy for me, I knew nothing of my good Master's being in London at this my very difficult Time.

After I got well of my sickness, I ship'd myself on board of a large Ship bound to Guinea, and being in a publick House one Evening, I overheard a Number of Persons talking about Rigging a Vessel bound to New-England. I ask'd them to what part of New-England this Vessel was bound. They told me to Boston, and having ask'd them who was Commander, they told me Capt. Watt. In a few Minutes after this the Mate of the Ship came in, and I ask'd him if Captain Watt did not want a Cook, who told me he did, and that the Captain would be in, in a few Minutes; and in about half an Hour the Captain came in, and then I ship'd myself at once, after begging off from the Ship bound to Guinea.

I work'd on board Captain Watt's Ship almost Three Months, before she sail'd, and one Day, being at Work in the Hold, I overheard some Persons on board mention the Name of Winslow, at the Name of which I was very inquisitive, and having ask'd what Winslow they were talking about, they told me it was General Winslow, and that he was one of the Passengers. I ask'd them what General Winslow, for I never knew my good Master by that Title before; but after enquiring more particularly I found it must be Master, and in a few Days Time the Truth was joyfully verify'd by a happy Sight of his Person, which so overcome me that I could not speak to him for some Time. My good Master was exceeding glad to see me, telling me that I was like one arose from the Dead, for he thought I had been Dead a great many Years, having heard nothing of me for almost Thirteen Years.

I think I have not deviated from Truth in any particular of this my Narrative, and tho' I have omitted a great many Things, yet what is wrote may suffice to convince the Reader that I have been most grievously afflicted, and yet, thro' the Divine Goodness, as miraculously preserved, and delivered out of many Dangers, of which I desire to retain a grateful Remembrance as long as I live in the World.

And now That in the Providence of that GOD, who delivered his Servant David out of the Paw of the Lion and out of the Paw of the Bear, I am freed from a long and dreadful Captivity, among worse Savages than they, and am return'd to my own Native Land, to Shew how Great Things the Lord hath done for Me, I would call upon all Men, and Say: "O Magnifie the Lord with Me, and let us Exalt His Name together! O that Men would Praise the Lord for His Goodness, and for His Wonderful Works to the Children of Men!"

—1760

Author's Reference Notes

[1] The Way I came to know this Gentleman was by his being taken last War by an English Privateer and brought into Jamaica, while I was there.

[2] He is carried (by Way of Respect) in a large Two-arm Chair; the Chair is lin'd with crimson Velvet and supported by eight Persons.

[3] A particular Account of this Engagement has been Publish'd in the Boston News-Papers.

The Kidnapping and Enslavement of Olaudah Equiano, or Gustavus Vassa, the African

Gustavus Vassa

I HOPE the reader will not think I have trespassed on his patience in introducing myself to him, with some account of the manners and customs of my country. They had been implanted in me with great care and made an impression on my mind which time could not erase, and which all the adversity and variety of fortune I have since experienced served only to rivet and record; for, whether the love of one's country be real or imaginary, or a lesson of reason, or an instinct of nature, I still look back with pleasure on the first scenes of my life, though that pleasure has been for the most part mingled with sorrow.

I have already acquainted the reader with the time and place of my birth. My father, besides many slaves, had a numerous family, of which seven lived to grow up, including myself and a sister, who was the only daughter. As I was the youngest of the sons, I became, of course, the greatest favorite with my mother and was always with her; and she used to take particular pains to form my mind. I was trained up from my earliest years in the arts of agriculture and war: my daily exercise was shooting and throwing javelins, and my mother adorned me with emblems, after the manner of our greatest warriors. In this way I grew up till I was turned the age of eleven, when an end was put to my happiness in the following manner.

Generally, when the grown people in the neighborhood were gone far in the fields to labor, the children assembled together in some of the neighbors' premises to play; and commonly some of us used to get up a tree to look out for any assailant or kidnapper that might come upon us; for they sometimes took those opportunities of

our parents' absence to attack and carry off as many as they could seize. One day as I was watching at the top of a tree in our yard I saw one of those people come into the yard of our next neighbor but one, to kidnap, there being many stout young people in it. Immediately, on this, I gave the alarm of the rogue, and he was surrounded by the stoutest of them, who entangled him with cords so that he could not escape till some of the grown people came and secured him. But alas! ere long, it was my fate to be thus attacked and to be carried off, when none of our grown people were nigh. One day when all our people were gone out to their works as usual, and only I and my dear sister were left to mind the house, two men and a woman got over our walls and in a moment seized us both; and without giving us time to cry out or make resistance, they stopped our mouths and ran off with us into the nearest wood. Here they tied our hands and continued to carry us as far as they could till night came on, when we reached a small house where the robbers halted for refreshment and spent the night. We were then unbound but were unable to take any food and, being quite overpowered by fatigue and grief, our only relief was some sleep, which allayed our misfortune for a short time.

The next morning we left the house and continued traveling all the day. For a long time we had kept the woods, but at last we came into a road which I believed I knew. I now had some hopes of being delivered, for we had advanced but a little way when I discovered some people at a distance, on which I began to cry out for their assistance; but my cries had no other effect than to make them tie me faster and stop my mouth, and then they put me into a large sack. They also stopped my sister's mouth and tied her hands; and in this manner we proceeded till we were out of the sight of these people.

When we went to rest the following night they offered us some victuals, but we refused them; and the only comfort we had was in being in one another's arms all that night and bathing each other with our tears. But alas! we were soon deprived of even the small comfort of weeping together. The next day proved a day of greater sorrow than I had yet experienced, for my sister and I were then separated while we lay clasped in each other's arms. It was in vain that we besought them not to part us; she was torn from me and immediately carried away, while I was left in a state of distraction not to be described. I cried and grieved continually, and for several days did not eat anything but what they forced into my mouth.

At length, after many days' traveling, during which I had often changed masters, I got into the hands of a chieftain in a very pleasant country. This man had two wives and some children, and they all used me extremely well and did all they could to comfort me—particularly the first wife, who was something like my mother. Although I was a great many days' journey from my father's house, yet these people spoke exactly the same language with us. This first master of mine, as I may call him, was a smith, and my principal employment was working his bellows, which was the same kind as I had seen in my vicinity. They were in some respects not unlike the stoves here in gentlemen's kitchens and were covered over with leather; and in the middle of that leather a stick was fixed, and a person stood up and worked it in the same manner as is done to pump water out of a cask with a hand pump. I believe it was gold he worked, for it was of a lovely bright yellow color and was worn by the women on their wrists and ankles.

I was there I suppose about a month, and they at last used to trust me some little distance from the house. This liberty I used in embracing every opportunity to inquire the way to my own home; and I also sometimes, for the same purpose, went with the maidens in the cool of the evenings to bring pitchers of water from the springs for the use of the house. I had also remarked where the sun rose in the morning and set in the evening, as I had traveled along; and I had observed that my father's house was towards the rising of the sun. I therefore determined to seize the first opportunity of making my escape and to shape my course for that quarter, for I was quite oppressed and weighed down by grief after my mother and friends, and my love of liberty, ever great, was strengthened by the mortifying circumstance of not daring to eat with the freeborn children, although I was mostly their companion.

While I was projecting my escape one day, an unlucky event happened which quite disconcerted my plan and put an end to my hopes. I used to be sometimes employed in assisting an elderly woman slave to cook and take care of the poultry, and one morning while I was feeding some chickens I happened to toss a small pebble at one of them, which hit it on the middle and directly killed it. The old slave, having soon after missed the chicken, inquired after it; and on my relating the accident (for I told her the truth because my mother would never suffer me to tell a lie), she flew into a violent passion, threatened that I should suffer for it and, my master being out, she immediately went and told her mistress what I had done. This alarmed me very much and I expected an instant flogging, which to me was uncommonly dreadful, for I had seldom been beaten at home. I therefore resolved to fly, and accordingly I ran into a thicket that was hard by and hid myself in the bushes.

Soon afterwards my mistress and the slave returned, and, not seeing me, they searched all the house, but not finding me, and I not making answer when they called to me, they thought I had run away, and the whole neighborhood was raised in the pursuit of me. In that part of the country (as well as ours) the houses and villages were skirted with woods or shrubberies, and the bushes were so thick that a man could readily conceal himself in them so as to elude the strictest search. The neighbors continued the whole day looking for me, and several times many of them came within a few yards of the place where I lay hid. I expected every moment, when I heard a rustling among the trees, to be found out and punished by my master; but they never discovered me, though they were often so near that I even heard their conjectures as they were looking about for me, and I now learned from them that any attempt to return home would be hopeless. Most of them supposed I had fled towards home, but the distance was so great and the way so intricate that they thought I could never reach it and that I should be lost in the woods. When I heard this I was seized with a violent panic and abandoned myself to despair. Night, too, began to approach and aggravated all my fears. I had before entertained hopes of getting home and had determined when it should be dark to make the attempt, but I was now convinced that it was fruitless, and began to consider that if possibly I could escape all other animals, I could not those of the human kind, and that, not knowing the way, I must perish in the woods. Thus was I like the hunted deer:

> Ev'ry leaf, and ev'ry whisp'ring breath
> Convey'd a foe, and ev'ry foe a death.

I heard frequent rustlings among the leaves, and being pretty sure they were snakes, I expected every instant to be stung by them. This increased my anguish, and the horror of my situation became now quite insupportable. I at length quitted the thicket, very faint and hungry, for I had not eaten or drank anything all the day, and crept to my master's kitchen, from whence I set out at first, and which was an open shed, and laid myself down in the ashes with an anxious wish for death to relieve me from all my pains. I was scarcely awake in the morning when the old woman slave, who was the first up, came to light the fire and saw me in the fireplace. She was very much surprised to see me and could scarcely believe her own eyes. She now promised to intercede for me and went for her master, who soon after came and, having lightly reprimanded me, ordered me to be taken care of and not ill treated.

Soon after this, my master's only daughter and child by his first wife sickened and died, which affected him so much that for some time he was almost frantic, and really would have killed himself had he not been watched and prevented. However, in a small time afterwards he recovered and I was again sold. I was now carried to the left of the sun's rising, through many dreary wastes and dismal woods, amidst the hideous roaring of wild beasts. The people I was sold to used to carry me very often when I was tired, either on their shoulders or on their backs. I saw many convenient well-built sheds along the road, at proper distances, to accommodate the merchants and travelers who lay in those buildings, along with their wives, who often accompany them (and they always go well armed).

From the time I left my own nation I always found somebody that understood me, till I came to the seacoast. The languages of different nations did not totally differ, nor were they so copious as those of the Europeans, particularly the English. They were therefore easily learned; and while I was journeying thus through Africa, I acquired two or three different tongues. In this manner I had been traveling for a considerable time, when one evening, to my great surprise, whom should I see brought to the house where I was but my dear sister? As soon as she saw me she gave a loud shriek and ran into my arms. I was quite overpowered: neither of us could speak but, for a considerable time, clung to each other in mutual embraces, unable to do anything but weep. Our meeting affected all who saw us; and indeed I must acknowledge, in honor of those sable destroyers of human rights, that I never met with any ill treatment, or saw any offered to their slaves, except tying them when necessary to keep them from running away. When these people knew we were brother and sister, they indulged us to be together, and the man to whom I supposed we belonged lay with us, he in the middle, while she and I held one another by the hands across his breast all night. And thus for a while we forgot our misfortunes in the joy of being together; but even this small comfort was soon to have an end, for scarcely had the fatal morning appeared, when she was again torn from me forever!

I was now more miserable, if possible, than before. The small relief which her presence gave me from pain was gone, and the wretchedness of my situation was redoubled by my anxiety after her fate and my apprehensions lest her sufferings should be greater than mine when I could not be with her to alleviate them. Yes, thou dear partner of my childish sports! thou sharer of my joys and sorrows! happy should I have ever esteemed myself to encounter every misery for you, and to procure your freedom by the sacrifice of my own! Though you were early forced from my arms, your image has been always riveted in my heart, from which neither *time nor fortune* have been able to remove it, so that, while the thoughts of your suffering have dampened my prosperity, they have mingled with adversity and increased its bitterness. To that heaven which protects the weak from the strong, I commit the care of your innocence and virtues, if they have not already received their full reward, and if your youth and delicacy have not long since fallen victims to the violence of the African trader, the pestilential stench of a Guinea ship, the seasoning in the European colonies or the lash and lust of a brutal and unrelenting overseer.

I did not long remain after my sister. I was again sold, and carried through a number of places, till after traveling a considerable time I came to a town called Tinmah, in the most beautiful country I had yet seen in Africa. It was extremely rich, and there were many rivulets which flowed through it and supplied a large pond in the center of the town, where the people washed. Here I first saw and tasted cocoa nuts, which I thought superior to any nuts I had ever tasted before; and the trees, which were loaded, were also interspersed among the houses, which had commodious shades adjoining and were in the same manner as ours, the insides being neatly plastered and whitewashed. Here I also saw and tasted for the first time sugar cane. Their money consisted of little white shells the size of the fingernail. I was sold here for one hundred and seventy-two of them, by a merchant who lived and brought me there.

I had been about two or three days at his house when a wealthy widow, a neighbor of his, came there one evening and brought with her an only son, a young gentleman about my own age and size. Here they saw me, and having taken a fancy to me, I was bought of the merchant and went home with them. Her house and premises were situated close to one of those rivulets I have mentioned, and were the

finest I ever saw in Africa: they were very extensive, and she had a number of slaves to attend her. The next day I was washed and perfumed, and when mealtime came I was led into the presence of my mistress, and ate and drank before her with her son. This filled me with astonishment, and I could scarce help expressing my surprise that the young gentleman should suffer me, who was bound, to eat with him who was free—and not only so, but that he would not at any time either eat or drink till I had taken first, because I was the eldest, which was agreeable to our custom. Indeed, everything here, and all their treatment of me, made me forget that I was a slave. The language of these people resembled ours so nearly that we understood each other perfectly. They had also the same customs as we. There were likewise slaves daily to attend us, while my young master and I, with other boys, sported with our darts and bows and arrows, as I had been used to do at home. In this resemblance to my former happy state I passed about two months, and I now began to think I was to be adopted into the family, and was beginning to be reconciled to my situation and to forget by degrees my misfortunes, when all at once the delusion vanished; for, without the least previous knowledge, one morning early, while my dear master and companion was still asleep, I was awakened out of my reverie to fresh sorrow, and hurried away even amongst the uncircumcised.

Thus, at the very moment I dreamed of the greatest happiness, I found myself most miserable; and it seemed as if fortune wished to give me this taste of joy only to render the reverse more poignant. The change I now experienced was as painful as it was sudden and unexpected. It was a change indeed from a state of bliss to a scene which is inexpressible by me, as it discovered to me an element I had never before beheld and till then had no idea of, and wherein such instances of hardship and cruelty occurred as I can never reflect on but with horror.

All the nations and people I had hitherto passed through resembled our own in their manners, customs and language; but I came at length to a country, the inhabitants of which differed from us in all those particulars. I was very much struck with this difference, especially when I came among a people who did not circumcise and ate without washing their hands. They cooked also in iron pots, and had European cutlasses and crossbows, which were unknown to us, and fought with their fists among themselves. Their women were not so modest as ours, for they ate and drank and slept with their men. But, above all, I was amazed to see no sacrifices or offerings among them. In some of these places the people ornamented themselves with scars, and likewise filed their teeth very sharp. They wanted sometimes to ornament me in the same manner, but I would not suffer them, hoping that I might some time be among a people who did not thus disfigure themselves, as I thought they did.

At last I came to the banks of a large river which was covered with canoes, in which the people appeared to live with their household utensils and provisions of all kinds. I was beyond measure astonished at this, as I had never before seen any water larger than a pond or a rivulet; and my surprise was mingled with no small fear when I was put into one of these canoes, and we began to paddle and move along the river. We continued going on thus till night, when we came to land and made fires on the banks, each family by themselves. Some dragged their canoes on shore; others stayed and cooked in theirs, and laid in them all night. Those on the land had mats, of which they made tents, some in the shape of little houses; in these we slept, and after the morning meal we embarked again and proceeded as before. I was often very much astonished to see some of the women, as well as the men, jump into the water, dive to the bottom, come up again and swim about.

Thus I continued to travel, sometimes by land, sometimes by water, through different countries and various nations till, at the end of six or seven months after I had been kidnapped, I arrived at the seacoast. It would be tedious and uninteresting to relate all the incidents which befell me during this journey and which I have not yet forgotten—of the various hands I passed through, and the manners and customs of all the different people among whom I lived. I shall therefore only observe that, in all the places where I was, the soil was exceedingly rich; the pumpkins, eadas, plaintains, yams, etc., were in great abundance and of incredible size. There were also vast quantities of different gums, though not used for any purpose, and everywhere a great deal of tobacco. The cotton even grew quite wild, and there was plenty of redwood. I saw no mechanics whatever in all the way, except such as I have mentioned. The chief employment in all these countries was agriculture, and both the males and females, as with us, were brought up to it, and trained in the arts of war.

The first object which saluted my eyes when I arrived on the coast was the sea, and a slave ship which was then riding at anchor and waiting for its cargo. These filled me with astonishment, which was soon converted into terror when I was carried on board. I was immediately handled, and tossed up to see if I were sound, by some of the crew; and I was now persuaded that I had gotten into a world of bad spirits and that they were going to kill me. Their complexions, too, differing so much from ours, their long hair, and the language they spoke (which was very different from any I had ever heard), united to confirm me in this belief. Indeed, such were the horrors of my views and fears at the moment that, if ten thousand worlds had been my own, I would have freely parted with them all to have exchanged my condition with that of the meanest slave in my own country. When I looked round the ship, too, and saw a large furnace of copper boiling, and a multitude of black people of every description chained together, every one of their countenances expressing dejection and sorrow, I no longer doubted of my fate; and quite overpowered with horror and anguish, I fell motionless on the deck and fainted.

When I recovered a little, I found some black people about me, who I believed were some of those who had brought me on board and had been receiving their pay. They talked to me in order to cheer me, but all in vain. I asked them if we were not to be eaten by those white men with horrible looks, red faces and long hair. They told me I was not, and one of the crew brought me a small portion of spirituous liquor in a wine glass, but, being afraid of him, I would not take it out of his hand. One of the blacks, therefore, took it from him and gave it to me, and I took a little down my palate, which, instead of reviving me as they thought it would, threw me into the greatest consternation at the strange feeling it produced, having never tasted any such liquor before. Soon after this, the blacks who brought me on board went off and left me abandoned to despair.

I now saw myself deprived of all chance of returning to my native country, or even the least glimpse of hope of gaining the shore, which I now considered as friendly; and I even wished for my former slavery in preference to my present situation, which was filled with horrors of every kind, still heightened by my ignorance of what I was to undergo. I was not long suffered to indulge my grief. I was soon put down under the decks, and there I received such a salutation in my nostrils as I had never experienced in my life, so that, with the loathsomeness of the stench and crying together, I became so sick and low that I was not able to eat, nor had I the least desire to taste anything. I now wished for the last friend, death, to relieve me. But soon, to my grief, two of the white men offered me eatables, and, on my refusing to eat, one of them held me fast by the hands and laid me across, I think, the windlass, and tied my feet, while the other flogged me severely. I had never experienced anything of this kind before, and although not being used to the water I naturally feared that element the first time I saw it, yet nevertheless, could I have got over the nettings, I would have jumped over the side, but I could not; and besides, the crew used to watch us very closely who were not chained down to the decks, lest we should leap into the water. And I have seen some of these poor African prisoners most severely cut for attempting to do so, and hourly whipped for not eating. This indeed was often the case with myself.

In a little time after, amongst the poor chained men, I found some of my own nation, which in a small degree gave ease to my mind. I inquired of these what was to be done with us. They gave me to understand we were to be carried to these white people's country to work for them. I then was a little revived, and thought if it were no worse than working my situation was not so desperate; but still I feared I should be put to death, the white people looked and acted, as I thought, in so savage a manner. For I had never seen among any people such instances of brutal cruelty, and this not only shown towards us blacks, but also to some of the whites themselves. One white man in particular I saw, when we were permitted to be on deck, flogged so unmercifully with a large rope near the foremast, that he died in consequence of it, and they tossed him over the side as they would have done a brute. This made me fear these people the more, and I expected nothing less than to be treated in the same manner.

I could not help expressing my fears and apprehensions to some of my countrymen. I asked them if these people had no country, but lived in this hollow place (the ship). They told me they did not, but came from a distant one. "Then," said I, "how comes it in all our country we never heard of them?" They told me because they lived so very far off. I then asked where were their women. Had they any like themselves? I was told they had. "And why," said I, "do we not see them?" They answered, because they were left behind. I asked how the vessel could go. They told me they could not tell, but that there was cloth put upon the masts by the help of the ropes I saw, and then the vessel went on; and the white men had some spell or magic they put in the water when they liked in order to stop the vessel. I was exceedingly amazed at this account and really thought they were spirits. I therefore wished much to be from amongst them, for I expected they would sacrifice me; but my wishes were vain, for we were so quartered that it was impossible for any of us to make our escape.

While we stayed on the coast I was mostly on deck; and one day, to my great astonishment, I saw one of these vessels coming in with the sails up. As soon as the whites saw it they gave a great shout, at which we were amazed—and the more so as the vessel appeared larger by approaching nearer. At last she came to an anchor in my sight, and, when the anchor was let go, I and my countrymen who saw it were lost in astonishment to observe the vessel stop—and were now convinced it was done by magic. Soon after this the other ship got her boats out, and they came on board of us, and the people of both ships seemed very glad to see each other. Several of the strangers also shook hands with us black people and made motions with their hands, signifying, I suppose, we were to go to their country, but we did not understand them.

At last, when the ship we were in had got in all her cargo, they made ready with many fearful noises, and we were all put under deck so that we could not see how they managed the vessel. But this disappointment was the least of my sorrow. The stench of the hold while we were on the coast was so intolerably loathsome that it was dangerous to remain there for any time, and some of us had been permitted to stay on the deck for the fresh air; but now that the whole ship's cargo were confined together, it became absolutely pestilential. The closeness of the place and the heat of the climate, added to the number in the ship—which was so crowded that each had scarcely room to turn himself—almost suffocated us. This produced copious perspirations, so that the air soon became unfit for respiration from a variety of loathsome smells, and brought on a sickness among the slaves, of which many died —thus falling victims to the improvident avarice, as I may call it, of their purchasers. This wretched situation was again aggravated by the falling of the chains—now become insupportable—and the filth of the necessary tubs, into which the children often fell and were almost suffocated. The shrieks of the women and the groans of the dying rendered the whole a scene of horror almost inconceivable. Happily perhaps, for myself, I was soon reduced so low here that it was thought necessary to keep me almost always on deck; and from my extreme youth I was not put in fetters. In this situation I expected every hour to share the fate of my companions, some of whom were almost daily brought upon the deck at the point of death, which I began to hope would soon put an end to my miseries. Often did I think many of the inhabitants of the deep much more happy than myself. I envied them the freedom they enjoyed, and as often wished I could change my condition for theirs. Every circumstance I met with served only to render my state more painful, and heightened my apprehensions and my opinion of the cruelty of the whites.

One day they had taken a number of fishes, and when they had killed and satisfied themselves with as many as they thought fit, to our astonish-ment, who were on deck, rather than give any of them to us to eat, as we expected, they tossed the remaining fish into the sea again, although we begged and prayed for some as well as we could, but in vain; and some of my countrymen, being pressed by hunger, took an opportunity, when they thought no one saw them, of trying to get a little privately. But they were discovered, and the attempt procured them some very severe floggings.

One day, when we had a smooth sea and moderate wind, two of my wearied countrymen who were chained together (I was near them at the time), preferring death to such a life of misery, somehow made through the nettings and jumped into the sea: immediately, another quite dejected fellow who on account of his illness was suffered to be out of irons, also followed their example; and I believe many more would very soon have done the same if they had not been prevented by the ship's crew, who were instantly alarmed. Those of us that were the most active were in a moment put down under the deck, and there was such a noise and confusion amongst the people of the ship as I never heard before, to stop her and get the boat out to go after the slaves. However, two of the wretches were drowned, but they got the other, and afterwards flogged him unmercifully for thus attempting to prefer death to slavery. In this manner we continued to undergo more hardships than I can now relate—hardships which are inseparable from this accursed trade. Many a time we were near suffocation from the want of fresh air, which we were often without for whole days together. This and the stench of the necessary tubs carried off many.

During our passage, I first saw flying fishes, which surprised me very much; they used frequently to fly across the ship, and many of them fell on the deck. I also now first saw the use of the quadrant. I had often with astonishment seen the mariners make observations with it, and I could not think what it meant. They at last took notice of my surprise, and one of them, willing to increase it as well as to gratify my curiosity, made me one day look through it. The clouds appeared to me to be land, which disappeared as they passed along. This heightened my wonder, and I was now more persuaded than ever that I was in another world and that everything about me was magic.

At last we came in sight of the island of Barbadoes, at which the whites on board gave a great shout and made many signs of joy to us. We did not know what to think of this, but as the vessel drew nearer we plainly saw the harbor and other ships of different kinds and sizes, and we soon anchored amongst them, off Bridgetown. Many merchants and planters now came on board, though it was in the evening. They put us in separate parcels and examined us attentively. They also made us jump, and pointed to the land, signifying we were to go there. We thought by this we should be eaten by these ugly men, as they appeared to us; and, when soon after we were all put down under the deck again, there was much dread and trembling among us and nothing but bitter cries to be heard all the night from these apprehensions, insomuch that at last the white people got some old slaves from the land to pacify us. They told us we were not to be eaten, but to work, and were soon to go on land, where we should see many of our country people. This report eased us much. And sure enough, soon after we were landed, there came to us Africans of all languages.

We were conducted immediately to the merchant's yard, where we were all pent up together, like so many sheep in a fold, without regard to sex or age. As every object was new to me, everything I saw filled me with surprise. What struck me first was that the houses were built with bricks and [in] stories, and [were] in every other respect different from those I had seen in Africa; but I was still more astonished on seeing people on horseback. I did not know what this could mean, and, indeed, I thought these people were full of nothing but magical arts. While I was in this astonishment, one of my fellow prisoners spoke to a countryman of his about the horses, who said they were the same kind they had in their country. I understood them, though they

were from a distant part of Africa, and I thought it odd I had not seen any horses there. But afterwards, when I came to converse with different Africans, I found they had many horses amongst them, and much larger than those I then saw.

We were not many days in the merchant's custody before we were sold after their usual manner, which is this: on a signal given (as the beat of a drum), the buyers rush at once into the yard where the slaves are confined and make choice of that parcel they like best. The noise and clamor with which this is attended, and the eagerness visible in the countenance of the buyers, serve not a little to increase the apprehension of terrified Africans, who may well be supposed to consider them as the ministers of that destruction to which they think themselves devoted. In this manner, without scruple, are relations and friends separated, most of them never to see each other again. I remember in the vessel in which I was brought over, in the men's apartment, there were several brothers who, in the sale, were sold in different lots, and it was very moving on this occasion to see and hear their cries at parting. O ye nominal Christians! might not an African ask you: "Learned you this from your God, who says unto you, 'Do unto all men as you would men should do unto you'? Is it not enough that we are torn from our country and friends, to toil for your luxury and lust of gain? Must every tender feeling be likewise sacrificed to your avarice? Are the dearest friends and relations, now renderd more dear by their separation from their kindred, still to be parted from each other and thus prevented from cheering the gloom of slavery with the small comfort of being together and mingling their sufferings and sorrows? Why are parents to lose their children, brothers their sisters, or husbands their wives? Surely this is a new refinement in cruelty which, while it has no advantage to atone for it, thus aggravates distress and adds fresh horrors even to the wretchedness of slavery."

—1789

From *The Interesting Narrative of the Life of Olaudah Equiano, or Gustavus Vassa, the African*

A Plan of Peace Office for the United States

Benjamin Banneker

AMONG the many defects which have been pointed out in the federal Constitution by its antifederal enemies, it is much to be lamented that no person has taken notice of its total silence upon the subject of an office of the utmost importance to the welfare of the United States, that is, an office for promoting and preserving perpetual peace in our country.

It is to be hoped that no objection will be made to the establishment of such an office while we are engaged in a war with the Indians, for as the War Office of the United States was established in time of peace, it is equally reasonable that a Peace Office should be established in time of war.

The plan of this office is as follows:

I. Let a Secretary of Peace be appointed to preside in this office, who shall be perfectly free from all the present absurd and vulgar European prejudices upon the subject of government; let him be a genuine republican and a sincere Christian, for the principles of republicanism and Christianity are no less friendly to universal and perpetual peace than they are to universal and equal liberty.

II. Let a power be given to this Secretary to establish and maintain free schools in every city, village and township of the United States; and let him be made responsible for the talents, principles and morals of all his schoolmasters. Let the youth of our country be carefully instructed in reading, writing and arithmetic, and in the doctrines of a religion of some kind; the Christian religion should be preferred to all others, for it belongs to this religion exclusively to teach us not only to cultivate peace with all men, but to forgive, nay more—to love our very enemies. It belongs to it further to teach us that the Supreme Being alone possesses a power to take away human life, and that we rebel against his laws whenever we undertake to execute death in any way whatever upon any of his creatures.

III. Let every family in the United States be furnished at the public expense, by the Secretary of this office, with a copy of an American edition of the Bible. This measure has become the more necessary in our country since the banishment of the Bible as a schoolbook from most of the schools in the United States. Unless the price of this book be paid for by the public, there is reason to fear that in a few years it will be met with only in courts of justice or in magistrates' offices; and should the absurd mode of establishing truth by kissing this sacred book fall into disuse, it may probably, in the course of the next generation, be seen only as a curiosity on a shelf in Mr. Peale's museum.[1]

IV. Let the following sentences [*sic*] be inscribed in letters of gold over the door of every home in the United States:

THE SON OF MAN CAME INTO THE WORLD, NOT TO DESTROY MEN'S LIVES, BUT TO SAVE THEM.

V. To inspire a veneration for human life and an horror at the shedding of human blood, let all those laws be repealed which authorize juries, judges, sheriffs or hangmen to assume the resentments of individuals, and to commit murder in cold blood in any case whatever. Until this reformation in our code of penal jurisprudence takes place, it will be in vain to attempt to introduce universal and perpetual peace in our country.

VI. To subdue that passion for war which education, added to human depravity, has made universal, a familiarity with the instruments of death, as well as all military shows, should be carefully avoided. For which reason militia laws should everywhere be repealed and military dresses and military titles should be laid aside: reviews tend to lessen the horrors of a battle by connecting them with the charms of order; militia laws generate idleness and vice, and thereby produce the wars they are said to prevent; military dresses fascinate the mind of young men, and lead them from serious and useful professions—were there no uniforms, there would probably be no armies; lastly, military titles feed vanity and keep up ideas in the mind which lessen a sense of the folly and miseries of war.

In the seventh and last place, let a large room, adjoining the federal hall, be appointed for transacting the business and preserving all the records of this office. Over the door of this room let there be a sign on which the figures of a lamb, a dove and an olive branch should be painted, together with the following inscriptions in letters of gold:

PEACE ON EARTH—GOODWILL TO MAN.
AH! WHY SHOULD MEN FORGET
THAT THEY ARE BRETHREN?

Within this apartment let there be a collection of plowshares and pruning hooks made out of swords and spears, and on each of the walls of the apartment the following pictures as large as life:

1. A lion eating straw with an ox, and an adder playing upon the lips of a child.

2. An Indian boiling his venison in the same pot with a citizen of Kentucky.

3. Lord Cornwallis and Tippo Saib under the shade of a sycamore tree in the East Indies, drinking Madeira wine out of the same decanter.[2]

4. A group of French and Austrian soldiers dancing, arm in arm, under a bower erected in the neighborhood of Mons.[3]

5. A St. Domingo planter, a man of color, and a native of Africa legislating together in the same colonial assembly.

To complete the entertainment of this delightful apartment, let a group of young ladies clad in white robes assemble every day at a certain hour, in a gallery to be erected for the purpose, and sing odes and hymns and anthems in praise of the blessings of peace.

One of these songs should consist of the following beautiful lines of Mr. Pope:

Peace o'er the world her olive wand extends,
And white-rob'd innocence from heaven descends;
All crimes shall cease, and ancient frauds shall fail,
Returning justice lifts aloft her scale.

—1792

Editor's Reference Notes

[1] Charles Willson Peale (1741–1827) was an American painter born in Maryland. He studied with John Singleton Copley in Boston and with Benjamin West in London. In the course of the Revolutionary War he painted portraits of Washington and other officers and leaders. In 1782 he opened a museum of art and natural history, and later, in 1805, he founded the Pennsylvania Academy of Fine Arts—the first in the United States.

[2] Tippoo Sahib (1753–1799), Sultan of Mysore, fought the British in India for many years. After suffering a defeat by Cornwallis in the 1790's, Tippoo had to make reparations of both land and money.

[3] In April 1792, France had declared war on Austria and Prussia. In November of that year a very bloody battle was fought at Jemappes, near Mons, in Belgium, between the French and the Austrian army of the Netherlands. Although the French were victorious, the slaughter was severe for both sides.

The Conversion of a Young Musician

John Marrant

I JOHN MARRANT, born June 15th, 1755, in New-York, in North-America, wish these gracious dealings of the Lord with me to be published in hopes they may be useful to others, to encourage the fearful, to confirm the wavering and to refresh the hearts of true believers. My father died when I was little more than four years of age, and before I was five my mother removed from New-York to St. Augustine, about seven hundred miles from that city. Here I was sent to school and taught to read and spell. After we had resided here about eighteen months, it was found necessary to remove to Georgia, where we remained; and I was kept to school until I had attained my eleventh year. The Lord spoke to me in my early days, by these removes, if I could have understood Him, and said, "Here we have no continuing city."

We left Georgia and went to Charles-Town [Charleston, S.C.], where it was intended I should be put apprentice to some trade. Some time after I had been in Charles-Town, as I was walking one day, I passed by a school and heard music and dancing, which took my fancy very much, and I felt a strong inclination to learn the music. I went home and informed my sister that I had rather learn to play upon music than go to a trade. She told me she could do nothing in it until she had acquainted my mother with my desire. Accordingly she wrote a letter concerning it to my mother, which, when she read, the contents were disapproved of by her, and she came to Charles-Town to prevent it. She persuaded me much against it, but her persuasions were fruitless. Disobedience either to God or man, being one of the fruits of sin, grew out from me in early

buds. Finding I was set upon it and resolved to learn nothing else, she agreed to it and went with me to speak to the man and to settle upon the best terms with him she could. He insisted upon twenty pounds down, which was paid, and I was engaged to stay with him eighteen months, and my mother to find me everything during that term. The first day I went to him he put the violin into my hand, which pleased me much, and, applying close, I learned very fast, not only to play but to dance also, so that in six months I was able to play for the whole school. In the evenings after the scholars were dismissed, I used to resort to the bottom of our garden, where it was customary for some musicians to assemble to blow the French horn.

Here my improvement was so rapid that in a twelvemonth's time I became master both of the violin and of the French horn and was much respected by the gentlemen and ladies whose children attended the school, as also by my master. This opened to me a large door of vanity and vice, for I was invited to all the balls and assemblies that were held in the town and met with the general applause of the inhabitants. I was a stranger to want, being supplied with as much money as I had any occasion for, which my sister observing, said, "You have now no need of a trade." I was now in my thirteenth year, devoted to pleasure and drinking in iniquity like water—a slave to every vice suited to my nature and to my years.

The time I had engaged to serve my master being expired, he persuaded me to stay with him, and offered me anything, or any money, not to leave him. His intreaties proving ineffectual, I quitted his service and visited my mother in the country. With her I staid two months, living without God or hope in the world, fishing and hunting on the sabbath-day. Unstable as water, I returned to town and wished to go to some trade. My sister's husband being informed of my inclination provided me with a master, on condition that I should serve him one year and a half on trial and afterwards be bound, if he approved of me. Accordingly I went, but every evening I was sent for to play on music somewhere or another; and I often continued out very late, sometimes all night, so as to render me incapable of attending my master's business the next day. Yet in this manner I served him a year and four months and was much approved of by him. He wrote a letter to my mother to come and have me bound, and whilst my mother was weighing the matter in her own mind, the gracious purposes of God respecting a perishing sinner were now to be disclosed.

One evening I was sent for in a very particular manner to go and play for some gentlemen, which I agreed to do, and was on my way to fulfil my promise; and passing by a large meeting-house I saw many lights in it, and crouds of people going in. I enquired what it meant, and was answered by my companion that a crazy man was hallooing there; this raised my curiosity to go in, that I might hear what he was hallooing about. He persuaded me not to go in, but in vain. He then said, "If you will do one thing I will go in with you." I asked him what that was. He replied, "Blow the French horn among them." I liked the proposal well enough but expressed my fears of being beaten for disturbing them; but upon his promising to stand by and defend me, I agreed. So we went, and with much difficulty got within the doors. I was pushing the people to make room, to get the horn off my shoulder to blow it, just as Mr. Whitefield was naming his text, and looking round and, as I thought, directly upon me, and pointing with his finger, he uttered these words: *"Prepare to meet thy God, O Israel."* The Lord accompanied the word with such power that I was struck to the ground and lay both speechless and senseless near half an hour.

When I was come a little too [*sic*], I found two men attending me and a woman throwing water in my face and holding a smelling-bottle to my nose; and, when something more recovered, every word I heard from the minister was like a parcel of swords thrust into me and, what added to my distress, I thought I saw the Devil on every side of me. I was constrained in the bitterness of my spirit to halloo out in the midst of the congregation, which disturbing them, they took me away; but finding I could neither walk or stand, they carried me as far as the vestry, and there I remained till the service was over. When the people were dismissed Mr. Whitefield came into the vestry, and being told of my condition he came immediately, and the first word he said to me was, *"Jesus Christ has got thee at last."* He asked where I lived, intending to come and see me the next day; but recollecting he was to leave the town the next morning, he said he could not come himself but would send another minister. He desired them to get me home, and then, taking his leave of me, I saw him no more.

When I reached my sister's house, being carried by two men, she was very uneasy to see me in so distressed a condition. She got me to bed and sent for a doctor, who came immediately, and after looking at me he went home and sent me a bottle of mixture and desired her to give me a spoonful every two hours; but I could not take anything the doctor sent, nor indeed keep in bed. This distressed my sister very much and she cried out, "The lad will surely die." She sent for two other doctors, but no medicine they prescribed could I take. No, no; it may be asked, a wounded spirit who can cure, as well as who can bear?

In this distress of soul I continued for three days without any food, only a little water now and then. On the fourth day the minister Mr. Whitefield had desired to visit me came to see me (Mr. Hall, a Baptist minister at Charles-Town), and being directed upstairs, when he entered the room I thought he made my distress much worse.

He wanted to take hold of my hand but I durst not give it to him. He insisted upon taking hold of it, and I then got away from him on the other side of the bed; but being very weak I fell down, and before I could recover he came to me and took me by the hand and lifted me up, and after a few words desired to go to prayer. So he fell upon his knees and pulled me down also. After he had spent some time in prayer, he rose up and asked me now how I did; I answered, "Much worse." He then said, "Come, we will have the old thing over again"; and so we kneeled down a second time, and after he had prayed earnestly we got up, and he said again, "How do you do now?" I replied, "Worse and worse," and asked him if he intended to kill me. "No, no," said he, "you are worth a thousand dead men; let us try the old thing over again." And so falling upon our knees, he continued in prayer a considerable time, and near the close of his prayer the Lord was pleased to set my soul at perfect liberty, and being filled with joy I began to praise the Lord immediately; my sorrows were turned into peace and joy and love. The minister said, "How is it now?" I answered, "All is well, all happy." He then took his leave of me but called every day for several days afterwards, and the last time he said, "Hold fast that thou hast already obtained, till Jesus Christ come."

—1785

From *A Narrative of the Lord's Wonderful Dealings with J. Marrant, a Black*

A Narrative of the Proceedings of the Black People during the Late Awful Calamity in Philadelphia in the Year 1793

Absalom Jones and Richard Allen

IN CONSEQUENCE of a partial representation of the conduct of the people who were employed to nurse the sick in the calamitous state of the city of Philadelphia, we were solicited by a number of those who felt themselves injured thereby, and by the advice of several respectable citizens, to step forward and declare facts as they really were—and seeing that from our situation, on account of the charge we took upon us, we had it more fully and generally in our power to know and observe the conduct and behavior of those that were so employed.[1]

Early in September, a solicitation appeared in the public papers to the people of color to come forward and assist the distressed, perishing and neglected sick, with a kind of assurance that people of our color were not liable to take the infection[2]—upon which we and a few others met and consulted how to act on so truly alarming and melancholy an occasion. After some conversation, we found a freedom to go forth, confiding in Him who can preserve in the midst of a burning, fiery furnace. Sensible that it was our duty to do all the good we could to our suffering fellow mortals, we set out to see where we could be useful.

The first we visited was a man in Elmsley's Alley who was dying, and his wife lay dead at the time in the house. There were none to assist but two poor helpless children. We administered what relief we could and applied to the overseers of the poor to have the woman buried. We visited upwards of twenty families that day. They were scenes of woe indeed! The Lord was pleased to strengthen us and remove all fear from us, and disposed our hearts to be as useful as possible.

In order the better to regulate our conduct, we called on the mayor next day to consult with him how to proceed so as to be most useful. The first object he recommended was a strict attention to the sick and the procuring of nurses. This was attended to by Absalom Jones and William Gray; and in order that the distressed might know where to apply, the mayor advertised the public that upon application to them they would be supplied. Soon after, the mortality increasing, the difficulty of getting a corpse taken away was such that few were willing to do it when offered great rewards. The colored people were looked to. We then offered our services in the public papers, by advertising that we would remove the dead and procure nurses.

Our services were the production of real sensibility; we sought not fee nor reward, until the increase of the disorder rendered our labor so arduous that we were not adequate to the service we had assumed. The mortality increasing rapidly obliged us to call in the assistance of five hired men in the awful charge of interring the dead. They, with great reluctance, were prevailed upon to join us. It was very uncommon at this time to find anyone that would go near, much more handle, a sick or dead person.

When the sickness became general, and several of the physicians died and most of the survivors were exhausted by sickness or fatigue, that good man Dr. Rush[3] called us more immediately to attend upon the sick, knowing that we could both bleed. He told us that we could increase our utility by attending to his instructions, and according directed us where to procure medicine duly prepared, with proper directions how to administer them, and at what stages of the disorder to bleed, and when we found ourselves incapable of judging what was proper to be done, to apply to him and he would, if able, attend them himself or send Edward Fisher, his pupil, which he often did; and Mr. Fisher manifested his humanity by an affectionate attention for their relief. This has been no small satisfaction to us, for we think that when a physician was not attainable we have been the instruments in the hands of God for saving the lives of some hundreds of our suffering fellow mortals.

We feel ourselves sensibly aggrieved by the censorious epithets of many who did not render the least assistance in the time of necessity, yet are liberal of their censure of us for the prices paid for our services, when no one knew how to make a proposal to anyone they wanted to assist them. At first we made no charge but left it to those we served in removing their dead to give what they thought fit. We set no price until the reward was fixed by those we had served. After paying the people we had to assist us, our compensation was much less than many will believe.

We do assure the public that all the money we received for burying and for coffins, which we ourselves purchased and procured, has not defrayed the expense of wages which we had to pay those whom we employed to assist us.

*   *   *   *   *   *

We feel ourselves hurt most by a partial, censorious paragraph in Mr. Carey's [4] second edition of his account of the sickness, etc., in Philadelphia, pages 76 and 77, where he asperses the blacks alone for having taken the advantage of the distressed situation of the people.

That some extravagant prices were paid we admit; but how came they to be demanded? The reason is plain. It was with difficulty persons could be had to supply the wants of the sick as nurses. Applications became more and more numerous; the consequence was, when we procured them at six dollars per week and called upon them to go where they were wanted, we found they were gone elsewhere. Here was a disappointment. Upon inquiring the cause, we found they had been allured away by others, who offered greater wages, until they got from two to four dollars per day. We had no restraint upon the people. It was natural for people in low circumstances to accept a voluntary, bounteous reward—especially under the loathsomeness of many of the sick, when nature shuddered at the thought of the infection, and the task assigned was aggravated by lunacy and being left much alone with them. . . .

The great prices paid did not escape the observation of that worthy and vigilant magistrate Matthew Clarkson, mayor of the city and president of the committee. He sent for us and requested we would use our influence to lessen the wages of the nurses. But on informing him of the cause, i.e. that of the people overbidding one another, it was concluded unnecessary to attempt anything on that head; therefore it was left to the people concerned.

That there were some few colored people guilty of plundering the distressed we acknowledge; but in that they only are pointed out and made mention of, we esteem partial and injurious. We know as many whites who were guilty of it, but this is looked over, while the blacks are held up to censure. Is it a greater crime for a black to pilfer than for a white to privateer?

We wish not to offend, but when an unprovoked attempt is made to make us blacker than we are, it becomes less necessary to be overcautious on that account; therefore we shall take the liberty to tell of the conduct of some of the whites.

We know that six pounds was demanded by and paid to a white woman for putting a corpse into a coffin, and forty dollars was demanded and paid to four white men for bringing it down the stairs.

Mr. and Mrs. Taylor both died in one night. A white woman had the care of them. After they were dead she called on Jacob Servoss, Esq., for her pay, demanding six pounds for laying them out. Upon seeing a bundle with her, he suspected she had pilfered. On searching her, Mr. Taylor's buckles were found in her pocket, with other things.

An elderly lady, Mrs. Malony, was given into the care of a white woman. She died. We were called to remove the corpse. When we came, the woman was lying so drunk that she did not know what we were doing, but we knew that she had one of Mrs. Maloney's [sic] rings on her finger.

It is unpleasant to point out the bad and unfeeling conduct of any color; yet the defense we have undertaken obliges us to remark that, although hardly any of good character at that time could be procured, yet only two colored women were at that time in the hospital, and they were retained and the others discharged when it was reduced to order and good government.

The bad consequences many of our color apprehend from a partial relation of our conduct are that it will prejudice the minds of the people in general against us, because it is impossible that one individual can have knowledge of all. Therefore, at some future day, when some of the most virtuous that were upon most praiseworthy motives induced to serve the sick may fall into the service of a family that are strangers to him or her, and it is discovered that it is one of those stigmatized wretches, what may we suppose will be the consequence? Is it not reasonable to think the person will be abhorred, despised and perhaps dismissed from employment, to their great disadvantage? Would not this be hard? And have we not therefore sufficient reason to seek for redress?

We can with certainty assure the public that we have seen more humanity, more real sensibility, from the poor colored than from the poor whites. When many of the former, of their own accord, rendered services where extreme necessity called for it, the general part of the poor white people were so dismayed that instead of attempting to be useful they, in a manner, hid themselves. A remarkable instance of this: a poor, afflicted, dying man stood at his chamber window, praying and beseeching everyone that passed by to help him to a drink of water. A number of white people passed, and instead of being moved by the poor man's distress they hurried, as fast as they could, out of the sound of his cries, until at length a gentleman who seemed to be a foreigner came up. He could not pass by but had not resolution enough to go into the house. He held eight dollars in his hand and offered it to several as a reward for giving the poor man a drink of water, but was refused by everyone until a poor colored man came up. The gentleman offered the eight dollars

to him if he would relieve the poor man with a little water. "Master," replied the good-natured fellow, "I will supply the gentleman with water, but surely I will not take your money for it," nor could he be prevailed upon to accept his bounty. He went in, supplied the poor object with water, and rendered him every service he could.

A poor colored man named Sampson went constantly from house to house where distress was, and no assistance, without fee or reward. He was smitten with the disorder and died. After his death his family were neglected by those he had served.

Sarah Bass, a colored widow woman, gave all the assistance she could in several families, for which she did not receive anything, and when anything was offered her she left it to the option of those she served.

A colored woman nursed Richard Mason and son. They died. Richard's widow, considering the risk the poor woman had run and from observing the fears that sometimes rested on her mind, expected she would have demanded something considerable, but upon asking her what she demanded, her reply was, "Fifty cents per day." Mrs. Mason intimated it was not sufficient for her attendance. She replied that it was enough for what she had done, and would take no more. Mrs. Mason's feelings were such that she settled an annuity of six pounds a year on her for life. Her name was Mary Scott.

An elderly colored woman nursed ——— with great diligence and attention. When recovered, he asked what he must give her for her services. She replied, "A dinner, master, on a cold winter's day." And thus she went from place to place, rendering every service in her power without an eye to reward.

A young colored woman was requested to attend one night upon a white man and his wife who were very ill. No other person could be had. Great wages were offered her. She replied, "I will not go for money. If I go for money, God will see it and may make me take the disorder and die; but if I go and take no money he may spare my life." She went about nine o'clock, and found them both on the floor. She could procure no candle or other light, but staid with them about two hours and then left them. They both died that night. She was afterwards very ill with the fever. Her life was spared.

Cæsar Cranchal, a man of color, offered his services to attend the sick and said, "I will not take your money; I will not sell my life for money." It is said he died with the flux.

A colored lad at the widow Gilpin's was entrusted with his young master's keys on his leaving the city, and transacted his business with the greatest honesty and dispatch, having unloaded a vessel for him in the time and loaded it again.

A woman that nursed David Bacon charged with exemplary moderation and said she would not have any more.

It may be said in vindication of the conduct of those who discovered ignorance or incapacity in nursing that it is, in itself, a considerable art, derived from experience as well as the exercise of the finer feelings of humanity. This experience nine-tenths of those employed, it is probable, were wholly strangers to.

* * * * * *

It has been alleged that many of the sick were neglected by the nurses. We do not wonder at it, considering their situation; in many instances [they were] up night and day, without anyone to relieve them. Worn down with fatigue and want of sleep, they could not . . . render that assistance which was needful.

Where we visited, the causes of complaint on this score were not numerous. The case[s] of the nurses, in many instances, were deserving of commiseration—the patient raging and frightful to behold. It has frequently required two persons to hold them from running away. Others have made attempts to jump out of a window; in many chambers they were nailed down and the door kept locked, to prevent them from running away or breaking their necks. Others lay vomiting blood and screaming enough to chill them with horror. Thus were many of the nurses circumstanced, alone, until the patient died—then called away to another scene of distress, and thus have been, for a week or ten days, left to do the best they could without any sufficient rest, many of them having some of their dearest connections sick at the time and suffering for want, while their husband, wife, father, mother, etc.,

have been engaged in the service of the white people. We mention this to show the difference between this and nursing in common cases.

We have suffered equally with the whites; our distress hath been very great, but much unknown to the white people. Few have been the whites that paid attention to us, while the colored persons were engaged in others' service. We can assure the public that we have taken four and five colored people in a day to be buried. In several instances, when they have been seized with the sickness while nursing, they have been turned out of the house, wandering and destitute, until they found shelter wherever they could (as many of them would not be admitted to their former homes); they have languished alone, and we know of one who even died in a stable. Others [white people] acted with more tenderness; when their nurses were taken sick they had proper care taken of them at their houses. We know of two instances of this.

It is even to this day a generally received opinion in this city that our color was not so liable to the sickness as the whites. We hope our friends will pardon us for setting this matter in its true state. The public were informed that, in the West Indies and other places where this terrible malady had been, it was observed that the blacks were not affected with it. Happy would it have been for you, and much more so for us, if this observation had been verified by our experience.

When the people of color had the sickness and died, we were imposed upon and told it was not with the prevailing sickness, until it became too notorious to be denied; then we were told some few died, but not many. Thus were our services extorted at the peril of our lives. Yet you accuse us of extorting a little money from you. . . .

Perhaps it may be acceptable to the reader to know how we found the sick affected by the sickness. Our opportunities of hearing and seeing them have been very great. They were taken with a chill, a headache, a sick stomach, with pains in their limbs and back. This was the way the sickness in general began; but all were not affected alike. Some appeared but slightly affected with some of those symptoms. What confirmed us in the opinion of a person being smitten was the color of their eyes. In some it raged more furiously than in others. Some have languished for seven and ten days, and appeared to get better the day—or some hours before—they died, while others were cut off in one, two or three days; but their complaints were similar. Some lost their reason and raged with all the fury madness could produce, and died in strong convulsions; others retained their reason to the last, and seemed rather to fall asleep than die. We could not help remarking that the former were of strong passions and the latter of a mild temper. Numbers died in a kind of dejection; they concluded they must go (so the phrase for dying was), and therefore in a kind of fixed, determined state of mind went off.

It struck our minds with awe to have application made by those in health to take charge of them in their sickness, and of their funeral. . . . Many appeared as though they thought they must die and not live; some have lain on the floor to be measured for their coffins and graves.

A gentleman called one evening to request a good nurse might be got for him when he was sick, and to superintend his funeral, and gave particular directions how he would have it conducted. It seemed a surprising circumstance, for the man appeared at the time to be in perfect health; but calling two or three days after to see him, [we] found a woman dead in the house and the man so far gone that to administer anything for his recovery was needless. He died that evening.

We mention this as an instance of the dejection and despondence that took hold on the minds of thousands, and are of opinion that it aggravated the case of many; while others, who bore up cheerfully, got up again, that probably would otherwise have died.

When the mortality came to its greatest stage, it was impossible to procure sufficient assistance; therefore many, whose friends and relations had left them, died unseen and unassisted. We have found them in various situations: some lying on the floor, as bloody as if they had been dipped in it, without any appearance of their having had even a drink of water for their relief; others lying on a bed with their clothes on, as if they had come in fatigued and lain down to rest; some appeared as if they had fallen dead on the floor, from the position we found them in.

Surely our task was hard; yet through mercy we were enabled to go on.

*   *   *   *   *   *

We have found reports spread of our taking between one and two hundred beds from houses where people died. Such slanderers as these, who propagate such willful lies, are dangerous, although unworthy, and we wish, if any person hath the least suspicion of us, they would endeavor to bring us to the punishment which such atrocious conduct must deserve; and by this means the innocent will be cleared from reproach and the guilty known.

We shall now conclude with the following proverb, which we think applicable to those of our color who exposed their lives in the late afflicting dispensation:

> God and a soldier all men do adore
> In time of war and not before;
> When the war is over, and all things righted,
> God is forgotten, and the soldier slighted.

—1794

Editor's Reference Notes

[1] The sickness referred to here was the very severe epidemic of yellow fever in Philadelphia in 1793.

[2] Later on in the epidemic it became evident that Negroes were as susceptible as white people to the fever.

[3] This was Benjamin Rush (1745–1813), the leading American physician of his day—a signer of the Declaration of Independence and one of the organizers of the first antislavery society in America.

[4] Mathew Carey (1760–1839) was a publisher of periodicals in Philadelphia, a pamphleteer, and an economist.

Lucy Terry

Bars Fight

AUGUST 'twas the twenty-fifth
Seventeen hundred forty-six,[1]
The Indians did in ambush lay
Some very valient men to slay,
The names of whom I'll not leave out.
Samuel Allen like a hero fout,
And though he was so brave and bold
His face no more shall we behold.
Eleazer Hawks was killed outright
Before he had time to fight,
Before he did the Indians see
Was shot and killed immediately.
Oliver Amsden he was slain,
Which caused his friends much grief and pain.
Samuel Amsden they found dead
Not many rods off from his head.
Adonijah Gillet we do hear
Did lose his life which was so dear.
John Saddler fled across the water
And so excaped the dreadful slaughter.
Eunice Allen see the Indians comeing
And hoped to save herself by running,
And had not her petticoats stopt her
The awful creatures had not cotched her
And tommyhawked her on the head
And left her on the ground for dead.
Young Samuel Allen, Oh! lack-a-day!
Was taken and carried to Canada.

—1746

Jupiter Hammon

An Evening Thought: Salvation by Christ, with Penitential Cries

SALVATION comes by Christ alone,
    The only Son of God;
Redemption now to every one,
    That love His holy Word.

Dear Jesus, we would fly to Thee,
    And leave off every sin,
Thy tender mercy will agree;
    Salvation from our King.

Salvation comes now from the Lord,
    Our victorious King.
His holy name be well ador'd,
    Salvation surely bring.

Dear Jesus, give Thy Spirit now,
    Thy grace to every nation,
That han't the Lord to whom we bow,
    The Author of Salvation.

Dear Jesus, unto Thee we cry,
    Give us the preparation;
Turn not away Thy tender eye;
    We seek Thy true salvation.

Salvation comes from God we know,
    The true and only One;
It's well agreed and certain true,
    He gave His only Son.

Lord, hear our penitential cry:
    Salvation from above;
It is the Lord that doth supply,
    With His redeeming love.

Dear Jesus, by Thy precious blood,
    The world redemption have:
Salvation now comes from the Lord,
    He being thy captive slave.

Dear Jesus, let the nations cry,
    And all the people say,
Salvation comes from Christ on high,
    Haste on Tribunal Day.

We cry as sinners to the Lord,
    Salvation to obtain;
It is firmly fixt, His holy Word,
    Ye shall not cry in vain.

Dear Jesus, unto Thee we cry,
  And make our lamentation:
O let our prayers ascend on high;
  We felt Thy salvation.

Lord, turn our dark benighted souls;
  Give us a true motion,
And let the hearts of all the world,
  Make Christ their salvation.

Ten thousand angels cry to Thee,
  Yea, louder than the ocean.
Thou art the Lord, we plainly see;
  Thou art the true salvation.

Now is the day, excepted[2] time;
  The day of salvation;
Increase your faith, do not repine:
  Awake ye, every nation.

Lord, unto whom now shall we go,
  Or seek a safe abode?
Thou hast the Word salvation, too,
  The only Son of God.

Ho! every one that hunger hath,
  Or pineth after me,
Salvation be Thy leading staff,
  To set the sinner free.

Dear Jesus, unto Thee we fly;
  Depart, depart from sin,
Salvation doth at length supply
  The glory of our King.

Come, ye blessed of the Lord,
  Salvation greatly given;
O turn your hearts, accept the Word,
  Your souls are fit for heaven.

Dear Jesus, we now turn to Thee,
  Salvation to obtain;
Our hearts and souls do meet again,
  To magnify Thy name.

Come, Holy Spirit, Heavenly Dove,
  The object of our care;
Salvation doth increase our love;
  Our hearts hath felt Thy fear.

Now glory be to God on high,
  Salvation high and low;
And thus the soul on Christ rely,
  To heaven surely go.

Come, Blessed Jesus, Heavenly Dove,
  Accept repentance here;
Salvation give, with tender love;
  Let us with angels share. *Finis*.

—1760

Phillis Wheatley

On the Death of a Young Lady of Five Years of Age

FROM dark abodes to fair ethereal light
Th' enraptur'd innocent has wing'd her flight;
On the kind bosom of eternal love
She finds unknown beatitude above.
This known, ye parents, nor her loss deplore;
She feels the iron hand of pain no more;
The dispensations of unerring grace
Should turn your sorrows into grateful praise;
Let then no tears for her henceforward flow,
No more distress'd in our dark vale below.

  Her morning sun, which rose divinely bright,
Was quickly mantled with the gloom of night;
But hear in heav'n's blest bow'rs your Nancy fair,
And learn to imitate her language there.
"Thou, Lord, whom I behold with glory crown'd,
By what sweet name, and in what tuneful sound
Wilt Thou be prais'd? Seraphic pow'rs are faint
Infinite love and majesty to paint.
To Thee let all their grateful voices raise,
And saints and angels join their songs of 'praise.'"

  Perfect in bliss she from her heav'nly home
Looks down, and smiling beckons you to come;
Why then, fond parents, why these fruitless groans?
Restrain your tears, and cease your plaintive moans.
Freed from a world of sin, and snares, and pain,
Why would you wish your daughter back again?
No—bow resign'd. Let hope your grief control,
And check the rising tumult of the soul.
Calm in the prosperous, and adverse, day,
Adore the God who gives and takes away;
Eye Him in all, His holy name revere,
Upright your actions, and your hearts sincere,
Till having sail'd through life's tempestuous sea,
And from its rocks and boist'rous billows free,
Yourselves, safe landed on the blissful shore,
Shall join your happy babe to part no more.

—1773

To S. M., a Young African Painter,
on Seeing His Works[3]

To show the lab'ring bosom's deep intent,
And thought in living characters to paint,
When first thy pencil did those beauties give,
And breathing figures learnt from thee to live,
How did those prospects give my soul delight,
A new creation rushing on my sight?
Still, wond'rous youth! each noble path pursue,
On deathless glories fix thine ardent view:
Still may the painter's and the poet's fire
To aid thy pencil, and thy verse conspire!
And may the charms of each seraphic theme
Conduct thy footsteps to immortal fame!
High to the blissful wonders of the skies
Elate thy soul, and raise thy wishful eyes.
Thrice happy, when exalted to survey
That splendid city, crown'd with endless day,

Whose twice six gates on radiant hinges ring:
Celestial Salem[4] blooms in endless spring.

Calm and serene thy moments glide along,
And may the muse inspire each future song!
Still, with the sweets of contemplation bless'd,
May peace with balmy wings your soul invest!
But when these shades of time are chas'd away,
And darkness ends in everlasting day,
On what seraphic pinions shall we move,
And view the landscapes in the realms above?
There shall thy tongue in heav'nly murmurs flow,
And there my muse with heav'nly transport glow:
No more to tell of Damon's tender sighs,
Or rising radiance of Aurora's eyes,
For nobler themes demand a nobler strain,
And purer language on th' ethereal plain.
Cease, gentle muse! the solemn gloom of night
Now seals the fair creation from my sight.

—1773

Editor's Reference Notes to Poetry

[1] The poem refers to an attack by Indians on the town of Deerfield, Massachusetts.

[2] Accepted.

[3] Benjamin Brawley, in *The Negro in Literature and Art in the United States* (New York, 1929), suggests that "S. M." was Scipio Moorhead, a servant of the Rev. John Moorhead of Boston. Scipio Moorhead showed considerable artistic ability.

[4] Salem here is "Jerusalem" (heaven).

The Nineteenth Century

1800–1899

1. Albery A. Whitman
2. James McCune Smith
3. Frederick Douglass
4. Moses Roper
5. Paul Laurence Dunbar
6. William Wells Brown
7. Alexander Crummell
8. Booker T. Washington
9. Frances Ellen Watkins Harper

ONE CAN UNDERSTAND fully from the *Narrative of the Adventures and Escape of Moses Roper, from American Slavery* (1837) the cruelty of slavery. Roper's troubles began early: "I was born in North Carolina, in Caswell County, I am not able to tell in what month or year. What I shall now relate, is what was told me by my mother and grandmother. A few months before I was born my father married my mother's young mistress. As soon as my father's wife heard of my birth, she sent one of my mother's sisters to see whether I was white or black, and when my Aunt had seen me, she returned back as soon as she could, and told her mistress that I was white, and resembled Mr. Roper very much. Mr. Roper's wife not being pleased with this report, she got a large club-stick and knife, and hastened to the place in which my mother was confined. She went into my mother's room with a full intention to murder me with her knife and club, but as she was going to stick the knife into me, my grandmother happening to come in, caught the knife and saved my life." Soon afterwards, Moses and his mother were sold. Upon the death of their second owner a few years later, they were sold again, but this time separately— Moses to a psychotic owner from whom he repeatedly escaped only to be recaptured and treated each time to more cruel and longer punishments.

Another narrative which offers a penetrating and unusual insight into the nineteenth century is William G. Allen's *The American Prejudice against Color: An Authentic Narrative, Showing How Easily the Nation Got into an Uproar* (1853).

The epoch from 1800 to 1859 was one of the most fertile periods in America for black writing. The narrative reached the height of its popularity during this period, and, increasingly, political thought began to emerge in black writing. By this time there were substantial colonies of free blacks in Northern cities who sought to protect with letters and tracts their rights as human beings. One such writer was James Forten, who authored a series of letters to the Pennsylvania legislature protesting a bill seeking to stop the migration of free blacks into Philadelphia.

In 1853 the first novel by a black appeared— William Wells Brown's *Clotel: Or the President's Daughter*. It was published first in England (as many previous works by blacks had been) and in 1867 was brought out in the United States in a much emasculated version.

The *Anglo-African*, the first literary magazine, published in 1859 and 1860, contained some of the best writing by blacks in the nineteenth century. Many of the leading black writers and intellectuals, such as James McCune Smith, William C. Nell and James W. C. Pennington, contributed to the magazine. The first short story by a black author, "The Two Offers" by Frances Ellen Watkins Harper, appeared in the magazine.

Two of the most prolific writers, of course, were Booker T. Washington and Frederick Douglass. There were others, such as Alexander Crummell, less well known to the general public, who in their speeches and essays touched on every aspect of Negro life in our society.

For a long time in many parts of our republic it was a crime for anyone to teach the black man to read and write. Naturally this stifled his intellectual development, forcing him to lean heavily on his oral tradition, and thus out of repression the spirituals were born. These developed into other forms, such as the work songs, ballads, blues and street cries. In all of these musical forms, the words were as important as the music.

Before and after the Civil War many blacks began to find formal poetry a pungent way of expressing their anguish. Paul Laurence Dunbar was perhaps the most accomplished poet of this period and the best known. There were other less famous but outstanding poets such as George Moses Horton, James Edwin Campbell and Albery A. Whitman.

Letters from a Man of Color: On a Late Bill before the Senate of Pennsylvania

James Forten

Letter I

WE HOLD THIS TRUTH to be self-evident, that God created all men equal, and [it] is one of the most prominent features in the Declaration of Independence, and in that glorious fabric of collected wisdom, our noble Constitution. This idea embraces the Indian and the European, the savage and the saint, the Peruvian and the Laplander, the white man and the African, and whatever measures are adopted subversive of this inestimable privilege are in direct violation of the letter and spirit of our Constitution, and become subject to the animadversion of all, particularly those who are deeply interested in the measure.

These thoughts were suggested by the promulgation of a late bill, before the Senate of Pennsylvania, to prevent the emigration of people of color into this state. It was not passed into a law at this session and must in consequence lay over until the next, before when we sincerely hope the white men, whom we should look upon as our protectors, will have become convinced of the inhumanity and impolicy of such a measure, and forbear to deprive us of those inestimable treasures, liberty and independence.

This is almost the only state in the Union wherein the African race have justly boasted of rational liberty and the protection of the laws, and shall it now be said they have been deprived of that liberty, and publicly exposed for sale to the highest bidder? Shall colonial inhumanity, that has marked many of us with shameful stripes, become the practice of the people of Pennsylvania, while Mercy stands weeping at the miserable spectacle? People of Pennsylvania, descendants of the immortal Penn, doom us not to the unhappy fate of thousands of our countrymen in the Southern states and the West Indies; despise the traffic in blood, and the blessing of the African will forever be around you.

Many of us are men of property, for the security of which we have hitherto looked to the laws of our blessed state, but should this become a law, our property is jeopardized, since the same power which can expose to sale an unfortunate fellow creature can wrest from him those estates which years of honest industry have accumulated. Where shall the poor African look for protection, should the people of Pennsylvania consent to oppress him?

We grant there are a number of worthless men belonging to our color, but there are laws of sufficient rigor for their punishment, if properly and duly enforced. We wish not to screen the guilty from punishment, but with the guilty do not permit the innocent to suffer. If there are worthless men, there are also men of merit among the African race, who are useful members of society. The truth of this let their benevolent institutions and the numbers clothed and fed by them witness. Punish the guilty man of color to the utmost limit of the laws, but sell him not to slavery! If he is in danger of becoming a public charge, prevent him! If he is too indolent to labor for his own subsistence, compel him to do so; but sell him not to slavery. By selling him you do not make him better, but commit a wrong, without benefiting the object of it or society at large. Many of our ancestors were brought here more than one hundred years ago; many of our fathers, many of ourselves, have fought and bled for the independence of our country. Do not then expose us to sale. Let not the spirit of the father behold the son robbed of that liberty which he died to establish, but let the motto of our legislators be: "The Law knows no distinction."

These are only a few desultory remarks on the subject, and [I] intend to succeed this effervescence of feeling by a series of essays tending to prove the impolicy and unconstitutionality of the law in question.

For the present, I leave the public to the consideration of the above observations, in which I hope they will see so much truth that they will never consent to sell to slavery

A MAN OF COLOR

Letter II

Those patriotic citizens who—after resting from the toils of an arduous war, which achieved our independence and laid the foundation of the only reasonable republic upon earth—associated together, and for the protection of those inestimable rights for the establishment of which they had exhausted their blood and treasure, framed the constitution of Pennsylvania, have by the ninth article declared that "all men are born equally free and independent, and have certain inherent and indefeasible rights, among which are those of enjoying life and liberty." Under the restraint of wise and well administered laws, we cordially unite in the above glorious sentiment, but by the bill upon which we have been remarking, it appears as if the committee who drew it up mistook the sentiment expressed in this article and do not consider us as men, or that those enlightened statesmen who formed the constitution upon the basis of experience intended to exclude us from its blessings and protection. If the former, why are we not to be considered as men? Has the God who made the white man and the black left any record declaring us a different species? Are we not sustained by the same power, supported by the same food, hurt by the same wounds, wounded by the same wrongs, pleased with the same delights and propagated by the same means? And should we not then enjoy the

same liberty and be protected by the same laws?

We wish not to legislate, for our means of information and the acquisition of knowledge are, in the nature of things, so circumscribed that we must consider ourselves incompetent to the task; but let us, in legislation, be considered as men. It cannot be that the authors of our Constitution intended to exclude us from its benefits, for, just emerging from unjust and cruel mancipation, their souls were too much affected with their own deprivations to commence the reign of terror over others. They knew we were deeper skinned than they were, but they acknowledged us as men, and found that many an honest heart beat beneath a dusky bosom. They felt that they had no more authority to enslave us than England had to tyrannize over them. They were convinced that, if amenable to the same laws in our actions, we should be protected by the same laws in our rights and privileges. Actuated by these sentiments they adopted the glorious fabric of our liberties, and declaring "all men" free, they did not particularize white and black, because they never supposed it would be made a question whether *we were men or not.* . . .

It seems almost incredible that the advocates of liberty should conceive the idea of selling a fellow creature to slavery. It is like the heroes of the French Revolution, who cried "Vive la Republic [*sic*]," while the decapitated nun was precipitated into the general reservoir of death, and the palpitating embryo decorated the point of the bayonet. Ye who should be our protectors, do not destroy. We will cheerfully submit to the laws and aid in bringing offenders against them of every color to justice; but do not let the laws operate so severely, so degradingly, so unjustly against us alone.

Let us put a case, in which the law in question operates peculiarly hard and unjust: I have a brother, perhaps, who resides in a distant part of the Union, and after a separation of years, actuated by the same fraternal affection which beats in the bosom of a white man, he comes to visit me. Unless that brother be registered in twenty-four hours after, and be able to produce a certificate to that effect, he is liable, according to the second and third sections of the bill, to a fine of twenty dollars, to arrest, imprisonment and sale. Let the unprejudiced mind ponder upon this, and then pronounce it the justifiable act of a free people, if he can. To this we trust our cause, without fear of the issue. The unprejudiced must pronounce any act tending to deprive a free man of his right, freedom and immunities, as not only cruel in the extreme but decidedly unconstitutional both as regards the letter and spirit of that glorious instrument. The same power which protects the white man should protect

A MAN OF COLOR

Letter III

The evils arising from the bill before our legislature, so fatal to the rights of freemen and so characteristic of European despotism, are so numerous that to consider them all would extend these numbers further than time or my talent will permit me to carry them. The concluding paragraph of my last number states a case of peculiar hardship, arising from the second section of this bill, upon which I cannot refrain from making a few more remarks. The man of color receiving as a visitor any other person of color is bound to turn informer, and rudely report to the Register that a friend and brother has come to visit him for a few days, whose name he must take within twenty-four hours or forfeit a sum which the iron hand of the law is authorized to rend from him, partly for the benefit of the *Register*. Who is this Register? A man, and exercising an office where ten dollars is the fee for each delinquent, will probably be a cruel man and find delinquents where they really do not exist. The poor black is left to the merciless gripe of an avaricious Register, without an appeal, in the event, from his tyranny or oppression!

O miserable race! Born to the same hopes, created with the same feeling and destined for the same goal, you are reduced by your fellow creatures below the brute. The dog is protected and pampered at the board of his master, while the poor African and his descendant, whether a saint or a felon, is branded with infamy, registered as a slave, and we may expect shortly to find a law to prevent their increase by taxing them according to numbers and authorizing the constables to seize and confine every one who

dare to walk the streets without a collar on his neck!

What have the people of color been guilty of, that they, more than others, should be compelled to register their houses, lands, servants and *children*? Yes, ye rulers of the black man's destiny, reflect upon this: our *children* must be registered and bear about them a certificate, or be subject to imprisonment and fine. You who are perusing this effusion of feeling, are you a parent? Have you children around whom your affections are bound by those delightful bonds which none but a parent can know? . . . By your verdict will we stand or fall—by your verdict live slaves or freemen.

It is said that the bill does not extend to children, but the words of the bill are: "Whether as an *inmate, visitor, hireling, or tenant, in his or her house or room.*" Whether this does not embrace every soul that can be in a house, the reader is left to judge; and whether the father should be bound to register his child, even within the twenty-four hours after it is brought into the world, let the father's feelings determine. This is the fact, and our children sent on our lawful business, not having sense enough to understand the meaning of such proceedings, must show their certificate of registry or be borne to prison. The bill specifies neither age nor sex—designates neither the honest man or the vagabond—but like the fretted porcupine, his quills aim its deadly shafts promiscuously at all.

For the honor and dignity of our native state, we wish not to see this bill pass into a law, as well as for its degrading tendency towards us; for although oppressed by those to whom we look for protection, our grievances are light compared with the load of reproach that must be heaped upon our commonwealth. The story will fly from the North to the South, and the advocates of slavery, the traders in human blood, will smile contemptuously at the once boasted moderation and humanity of Pennsylvania! What, that place, whose institutions for the prevention of slavery are the admiration of surrounding states and of Europe, become the advocate of mancipation and wrong, and the oppressor of the free and innocent! *Tell it not in Gath! publish it not in the streets of Askelon! lest the daughters of the Philistines rejoice, lest the children [sic] of the uncircumcized triumph!*

It is to be hoped that in our legislature there is patriotism, humanity and mercy sufficient to crush this attempt upon the civil liberty of freemen, and to prove that the enlightened body who have hitherto guarded their fellow creatures, without regard to the color of the skin, will still stretch forth the wings of protection to that race whose persons have been the scorn, and whose calamities have been the jest, of the world for ages. We trust the time is at hand when this obnoxious bill will receive its death warrant, and freedom still remain to cheer the bosom of

A MAN OF COLOR

Letter IV

I proceed again to the consideration of the bill of *unalienable* rights belonging to black men, the passage of which will only tend to show that the advocates of emancipation can enact laws more degrading to the freeman, and more injurious to his feelings, than all the tyranny of slavery or the shackles of infatuated despotism. And let me here remark that this unfortunate race of humanity, although protected by our laws, are already subject to the fury and caprice of a certain set of men who regard neither humanity, law nor privilege. They are already considered as a different species, and little above the brute creation. They are thought to be objects fit for nothing else than lordly men to vent the effervescence of their spleen upon, and to tyrannize over, like the bearded Musselman over his horde of slaves. Nay, the Musselman thinks more of his horse than the generality of people do of the despised black! Are not men of color sufficiently degraded? Why then increase their degradation?

It is a well known fact that black people, upon certain days of public jubilee, dare not be seen after twelve o'clock in the day upon the field to enjoy the times; for no sooner do the fumes of that potent devil liquor mount into the brain, than the poor black is assailed like the destroying hyena or the avaricious wolf! I allude particularly to the Fourth of July! Is it not wonderful that the day set apart for the festival of liberty should be abused by the advocates of freedom, in endeavor-

ing to sully what they profess to adore? If men, though they know that the law protects all, will dare, in defiance of law, to execute their hatred upon the defenseless black, will they not by the passage of this bill believe him still more a mark for their venom and spleen? Will they not believe him completely deserted by authority, and subject to every outrage brutality can inflict? Too surely they will, and the poor wretch will turn his eyes around to look in vain for protection. Pause, ye rulers of a free people, before you give us over to despair and violation. We implore you, for the sake of humanity, to snatch us from the pinnacle of ruin, from that gulf which will swallow our rights, as fellow creatures; our privileges, as citizens; and our liberties, as men!

There are men among us of reputation and property, as good citizens as any men can be, and who, for their property, pay as heavy taxes as any citizens are compelled to pay. All taxes, except personal, fall upon them, and still even they are not exempted from this degrading bill. The villainous part of the community, of all colors, we wish to see punished and retrieved as much as any people can. Enact laws to punish them severely, but do not let them operate against the innocent as well as the guilty. Can there be any generosity in this? Can there be any semblance of justice, or of that enlightened conduct which is ever the boasted pole star of freedom? By no means. This bill is nothing but the ignis fatuus of mistaken policy!

I could write for ages on the subject of this unrighteous bill, but as I think enough has already been said to convince every unprejudiced mind of its unjust, degrading, undeserved tendency, one more number shall conclude the letters from

A MAN OF COLOR

Letter V

A few more remarks upon the bill which has been the subject of my preceding numbers shall conclude these letters, which have been written in my own cause as an individual, and my brethren as a part of the community. They are the simple dictates of nature and need no apology. They are not written in the gorgeous style of a scholar, nor dressed in the garments of literary perfection. They are the impulse of a mind formed, I trust, for feeling, and smarting under all the rigors which the bill is calculated to produce.

By the third section of this bill, which is its peculiar hardship, the police officers are authorized to apprehend any black, whether a vagrant or a man of reputable character, who cannot produce a certificate that he has been registered. He is to be arrayed before a justice, who is thereupon to commit him to prison! The jailer is to advertise a freeman, and at the expiration of six months, if no owner appear for this degraded black, he is to be *exposed to sale*, and if not sold to be confined at hard labor for seven years! Man of feeling, read this! No matter who, no matter where.

The constable, whose antipathy generally against the black is very great, will take every opportunity of hurting his feelings! Perhaps he sees him at a distance, and having a mind to raise the boys in hue and cry against him, exclaims, "Halloa! Stop the Negro!" The boys, delighting in the sport, immediately begin to hunt him, and immediately from a hundred tongues is heard the cry: "Hoa, Negro, where is your certificate?" Can anything be conceived more degrading to humanity? Can anything be done more shocking to the principles of civil liberty?

A person arriving from another state, ignorant of the existence of such a law, may fall a victim to its cruel oppression. But he is to be advertised, and if no owner appear (how can an owner appear for a man who is free and belongs to no one?)—if no owner appear, he is exposed for sale! Oh, inhuman spectacle: found in no unjust act, convicted of no crime, he is barbarously sold, like the produce of the soil, to the highest bidder, or what is still worse, for no crimes, without the inestimable privilege of a trial by his peers, doomed to the dreary walls of a prison for the term of seven tedious years! . . .

The fifth section of this bill is also peculiarly hard, inasmuch as it prevents freemen from living where they please. Pennsylvania has always been a refuge from slavery, and to this state the Southern black, when freed, has flown for safety. Why does he this? When masters in many of the Southern states, which they frequently do, free a particular black, unless the black leaves the state in so many hours any person resident of the said state can have him arrested and again sold to slavery. The hunted black is obliged to flee or remain and be again a slave. I have known persons of this description sold three times after being first emancipated. Where shall he go? Shut every state against him and, like Pharaoh's kine, drive him into the sea. Is there no spot on earth that will protect him? Against their inclination, his ancestors were forced from their homes by traders in human flesh, and even under such circumstances the wretched offspring are denied the protection you afford to brutes.

It is in vain that we are forming societies of different kinds to ameliorate the condition of our unfortunate brethren, to correct their morals and to render them not only honest but useful members to society. All our efforts, by this bill, are despised, and we are doomed to feel the lash of oppression. As well may we be outlawed, as well may the glorious privileges of the Gospel be denied us, and all endeavors used to cut us off from happiness hereafter as well as here! The case is similar, and I am much deceived if this bill does not destroy the morals it is intended to produce.

I have done. My feelings are acute, and I have ventured to express them without intending either accusation or insult to anyone. An appeal to the heart is my intention, and if I have failed, it is my great misfortune not to have had a power of eloquence sufficient to convince. But I trust the eloquence of nature will succeed, and that the lawgivers of this happy commonwealth will yet remain the blacks' friend and the advocates of freemen, is the sincere wish of

A MAN OF COLOR
—1813

A Final Escape from American Slavery

Moses Roper

IN THE YEAR 1834, Mr. Beveridge, who was now residing in Appalachicola [*sic*], a town in west Florida, became a bankrupt, when all his property was sold, and I fell into the hands of a very cruel master, Mr. Register, a planter in the same state—of whom, knowing his savage character, I always had a dread. Previously to his purchasing me, he had frequently taunted me by saying, "You have been a gentleman long enough, and whatever may be the consequences, I intend to buy you," to which I remarked that I would on no account live with him if I could help it. Nevertheless, intent upon his purpose, in the month of July 1834, he bought me—after which I was so exasperated that I cared not whether I lived or died. In fact, whilst I was on my passage from Appalachicola, I procured a quart bottle of whiskey for the purpose of so intoxicating myself that I might be able either to plunge myself into the river or so enrage my master that he should dispatch me forthwith. I was, however, by a kind Providence, prevented from committing this horrid deed by an old slave on board, who, knowing my intention, secretly took the bottle from me, after which my hands were tied and I was led into the town of Ochesa, to a warehouse, where my master was asked by the proprietor of the place the reason of his confining my hands—in answer to which Mr. Register said that he had purchased me. The proprietor, however, persuaded him to untie me, after which my master, being excessively drunk, asked for a cowhide, intending to flog me, from which the proprietor dissuaded him, saying that he had known me for some time and he was sure that I did not require to be flogged.

From this place we proceeded about midday on our way. He placed me on the bare back of a half-starved old horse which he had purchased, and upon which sharp surface he kindly intended I should ride about eighty miles, the distance we were then from his home. In this unpleasant situation I could not help reflecting upon the prospects before me, not forgetting that I had heard my new master had been in the habit of stealing cattle and other property, and among other things a slave woman; and that I had said, as it afterwards turned out, in the hearing of someone who communicated the saying to my master, that I had been accustomed to live with a gentleman and not with a rogue; and finding that he had been informed of this, I had the additional dread of a few hundred lashes for it on my arrival at my destination.

About two hours after we started it began to rain very heavily and continued to do so until we arrived at Marianna, about twelve at night, when we were to rest till morning. My master here questioned me as to whether I intended to run away or not; and I, not then knowing the sin of lying, at once told him that I would not. He then gave me his clothes to dry. I took them to the kitchen for that purpose, and he retired to bed, taking a bag of clothes belonging to me with him as a kind of security, I presume, for my safety. In an hour or two afterwards I took his clothes to him dried, and found him fast asleep. I placed them by his side and said that I would then take my own to dry too, taking care to speak loud enough to ascertain whether he was asleep or not —knowing that he had a dirk and pistol by his side, which he would not have hesitated using against me if I had attempted secretly to have procured them. I was glad to find that the effects of his drinking the day before had caused his sleeping very soundly, and I immediately resolved on making my escape, and without loss of time started with my few clothes into the woods, which were in the immediate neighborhood. And after running many miles, I came up to the river Chapoli [Chipola], which is very deep and so beset with alligators that I dared not attempt to swim across.

I paced up and down this river, with the hope of finding a conveyance across, for a whole day, the succeeding night, and till noon on the following day, which was Saturday. About twelve o'clock on that day I discovered an Indian canoe, which had not, from all appearance, been used for some time. This, of course, I used to convey myself across, and after being obliged to go a little way down the river, by means of a piece of wood I providentially found in the boat, I landed on the opposite side. Here I found myself surrounded by planters looking for me, in consequence of which I hid myself in the bushes until night, when I again traveled several miles to the farm of a Mr. Robinson—a large sugar and cotton planter—where I rested till morning in a field.

Afterwards I set out, working my way through the woods about twenty miles towards the east. This I knew by my knowledge of the position of the sun at its rising. Having reached the Chattahoochee River, which divides Florida from Georgia, I was again puzzled to know how to cross. It was about three o'clock in the day, when a number of persons were fishing. Having walked for some hours along the banks, I at last, after dark, procured a ferryboat, which, not being able from the swiftness of the river to steer direct across, I was carried many miles down the river, landing on the Georgian side, from whence I proceeded on through the woods two or three miles and came to a little farmhouse about twelve o'clock at night. At a short distance from the house I found an old slave hut, into which I went, and informed the old man, who appeared seventy or eighty years old, that I had had a very bad master from whom I run away, and asked him if he could give me something to eat, having had no suitable food for three or four days. He told

me he had nothing but a piece of dry Indian bread, which he cheerfully gave me. Having eaten it, I went on a short distance from the hut and laid down in the wood to rest for an hour or two.

All the following day (Monday) I continued traveling through the woods and was greatly distressed for want of water to quench my thirst, it being a very dry country, till I came to Spring Creek, which is a wide, deep stream, and with some of which I gladly quenched my thirst. I then proceeded to cross the same by a bridge close by, and continued my way until dusk. I came to a gentleman's house in the woods, where I inquired how far it was to the next house, taking care to watch an opportunity to ask some individual whom I could master and get away from if any interruption to my progress was attempted. I went on for some time, it being a very fine moonlight night, and was presently alarmed by the howling of a wolf near me, which, I concluded, was calling others to join him in attacking me—having understood that they always assemble in numbers for such a purpose. The howling increased and I was still pursued, and the numbers were evidently increasing fast. But I was happily rescued from my dreadful fright by coming to some cattle, which attracted—as I supposed—the wolves and saved my life; for I could not get up the trees for safety, they being very tall pines, the lowest branches of which were at least forty or fifty feet from the ground, and the trunks very large and smooth.

About two o'clock I came to the house of a Mr. Cherry, on the borders of the Flint River. I went up to the house and called them up to beg something to eat; but having nothing cooked, they kindly allowed me to lie down in the porch, where they made me a bed. In conversation with this Mr. Cherry I discovered that I had known him before, having been in a steamboat, the *Versailles*, some months previous, which sunk very near the house, but which I did not at first discern to be the same. I then thought it would not be prudent for me to stop there and therefore told them I was in a hurry to get on and must start very early again, he having no idea who I was; and I gave his son six cents to take me across the river, which he did when the sun was about half an hour high, and unfortunately landed me where there was a man building a boat, who knew me very well and my former master too. He, calling me by name, asked me where I was going.

I was very much frightened at being discovered, but summoned up courage and said that my master had gone to Tallyhassa [Tallahassee] by the coach, and that there was not room for me and I had to walk round to meet him. I then asked the man to put me in the best road to get there, which, however, I knew as well as he did, having traveled there before. He directed me the best way, but I, of course, took the contrary direction, wanting to get on to Savannah. By this hasty and wicked deception I saved myself from going to Bainbridge prison, which was close by, and to which I should certainly have been taken had it been known that I was making my escape.

Leaving Bainbridge, I proceeded about forty miles, traveling all day under a scorching sun, through the woods, in which I saw many deer and serpents, until I reached Thomas Town [Thomasville] in the evening. I there inquired the way to Augusta of a man whom I met, and also asked where I could obtain lodgings, and was told there was a poor minister about a mile from the place who would give me lodgings. I accordingly went, and found them in a little log-house, where, having awakened the family, I found them all lying on the bare boards, where I joined them for the remainder of the night.

In the morning the old gentleman prayed for me, that I might be preserved on my journey. He had previously asked me where I was going, and knowing that if I told him the right place, any that inquired of him for me would be able to find me, asked the way to Augusta instead of Savannah, my real destination. I also told him that I was partly Indian and partly white. But I am also partly African, but this I omitted to tell him, knowing if I did I should be apprehended. After I had left this hut I again inquired for Augusta, for the purpose of misleading my pursuers, but I afterwards took my course through the woods and came into a road called the Coffee Road (which General Jackson cut down for his troops at the time of the war between the Americans and Spaniards, in Florida), in which road there are

but few houses, and which I preferred for the purpose of avoiding detection.

After several days I left this road and took a more direct way to Savannah, where I had to wade through two rivers before I came to the Alatamah [Altamaha], which I crossed in a ferry-boat, about a mile below the place where the rivers Oconee and Ocmulgee run together into one river, called the Alatamah. I here met with some cattle drovers who were collecting cattle to drive to Savannah. On walking on before them, I began to consider in what way I could obtain a passport for Savannah and determined on the following plan.

I called at a cottage, and after I had talked some time with the wife, who began to feel greatly for me in consequence of my telling her a little of my history (her husband being out hunting), I pretended to show her my passport. Feeling for it everywhere about my coat and hat and not finding it, I went back a little way, pretending to look for it, but came back saying I was very sorry but I did not know where it was. At last the man came home, carrying a deer upon his shoulders, which he brought into the yard, and began to dress it. The wife then went out to tell him my situation, and after long persuasion he said he could not write but that if I could tell his son what was in my passport he would write me one. Knowing that I should not be able to pass through Savannah without one, and having heard several free colored men read theirs, I thought I could tell the boy what to write.

The lad sat down and wrote what I told him, nearly filling a large sheet of paper for the passport, and another with recommendations. These being completed, I was invited to partake of the fresh venison which the woman of the house had prepared for dinner, and having done so, and feeling grateful for their kindness, I proceeded on my way. Going along, I took my papers out of my pocket, and looking at them, although I could not read a word, I perceived that the boy's writing was very unlike other writing that I had seen, and was greatly blotted besides. Consequently I was afraid that these documents would not answer my purpose and began to consider what other plan I could pursue to obtain another pass.

I had now to wade through another river to

which I came, and which I had great difficulty in crossing in consequence of the water overflowing the banks of several rivers to the extent of upwards of twenty miles. In the midst of the water, I passed one night upon a small island, and the next day I went through the remainder of the water. On many occasions I was obliged to walk upon my toes—and consequently found the advantage of being six feet two inches high (I have grown three inches since)—and at other times was obliged to swim. In the middle of this extremity, I felt it would be imprudent for me to return; for if my master was in pursuit of me, my safest place from him was in the water, if I could keep my head above the surface. I was, however, dreadfully frightened at the crocodiles and most earnestly prayed that I might be kept from a watery grave, and resolved that if again I landed I would spend my life in the service of God.

Having, through mercy, again started on my journey, I met with the drovers; and having, whilst in the waters, taken the pass out of my hat and so dipped it in the water as to spoil it, I showed it to the men and asked them where I could get another. They told me that in the neighborhood there lived a rich cotton merchant who would write me one. They took me to him and gave their word that they saw the passport before it was wet (for I had previously showed it to them), upon which the cotton planter wrote a free pass and a recommendation, to which the cow drovers affixed their marks.

The recommendation was as follows:

> John Roper, a very interesting young lad whom I have seen and traveled with for eighty or ninety miles on his road from Florida, is a free man, descended from Indian and white. I trust he will be allowed to pass on without interruption, being convinced, from what I have seen, that he is free, and, though dark, is not an African. I had seen his papers before they were wetted.

These cow drovers, who procured me the passport and recommendation from the cotton planter, could not read; and they were intoxicated when they went with me to him. I am part African, as well as Indian and white—my father being a white man, Henry Roper, Esq., Caswell County, North Carolina, U.S., a very wealthy slaveholder, who sold me when quite a child, for the strong resemblance I bore him. My mother is part Indian, part African; but I dared not disclose that, or I should have been taken up.

I then had eleven miles to go to Savannah, one of the greatest slaveholding cities in America, and where they are always looking out for runaway slaves. When at this city, I had traveled about five hundred miles. It required great courage to pass through this place. I went through the main street with apparent confidence, though much alarmed; did not stop at any house in the city, but went down immediately to the docks and inquired for a berth as a steward to a vessel to New York. I had been in this capacity before on the Appalachicola [sic] River.

The person whom I asked to procure me a berth was steward of one of the New York packets. He knew Captain Deckay of the schooner Fox, and got me a situation on board that vessel in five minutes after I had been at the docks. The schooner Fox was a very old vessel, twenty-seven years old, laden with lumber and cattle for New York; she was rotten and could not be insured. The sailors were afraid of her; but I ventured on board, and five minutes after, we dropped from the docks into the river. My spirits then began to revive, and I thought I should get to a free country directly. We cast anchor in the stream to keep the sailors on, as they were so dissatisfied with the vessel, and lay there four days, during which time I had to go into the city several times, which exposed me to great danger, as my master was after me and I dreaded meeting him in the city.

Fearing the Fox would not sail before I should be seized, I deserted her and went on board a brig sailing to Providence, that was towed out by a steamboat, and got thirty miles from Savannah. During this time I endeavored to persuade the steward to take me as an assistant, and hoped to have accomplished my purpose; but the captain had examined me attentively and thought I was a slave. He therefore ordered me, when the steamboat was sent back, to go on board her to Savannah, as the fine for taking a slave from that city to any of the free states is five hundred dollars.

I reluctantly went back to Savannah, among

slaveholders and slaves. My mind was in a sad state and I was under strong temptation to throw myself into the river. I had deserted the schooner *Fox* and knew that the captain might put me into prison till the vessel was ready to sail. If this happened, and my master had come to jail in search of me, I must have gone back to slavery. But when I reached the docks at Savannah the first person I met was the captain of the *Fox*, looking for another steward in my place. He was a very kind man, belonging to the free states, and inquired if I would go back to his vessel. This usage was very different to what I expected, and I gladly accepted his offer. This captain did not know that I was a slave. In about two days we sailed from Savannah to New York.

I am unable to express the joy I . . . felt (August 1834). I never was at sea before, and after I had been out about an hour was taken with sea-sickness, which continued five days. I was scarcely able to stand up, and one of the sailors was obliged to take my place. The captain was very kind to me all this time; but even after I recovered, I was not sufficiently well to do my duty properly and could not give satisfaction to the sailors, who swore at me and asked me why I shipped as I was not used to the sea. We had a very quick passage; and in six days after leaving Savannah we were in the harbor at Staten Island, where the vessel was quarantined for two days, six miles from New York.

The captain went to the city but left me aboard with the sailors, who had most of them been brought up in the slaveholding states, and were very cruel men. One of the sailors was particularly angry with me, because he had to perform the duties of my place; and while the captain was in the city the sailors called me to the fore hatch, where they said they would treat me. I went, and while I was talking they threw a rope round my neck and nearly choked me. The blood streamed from my nose profusely. They also took up ropes with large knots and knocked me over the head. They said I was a Negro. They despised me; and I expected they would have thrown me into the water. When we arrived at the city, these men who had so ill-treated me ran away, that they might escape the punishment which would otherwise have been inflicted on them.

When I arrived in the city of New York I thought I was free, but learned I was not and could be taken there. I went out into the country several miles and tried to get employment but failed, as I had no recommendation. I then returned to New York, but finding the same difficulty there to get work as in the country, I went back to the vessel, which was to sail eighty miles up the Hudson River, to Poughkeepsie.

When I arrived I obtained employment at an inn, and after I had been there about two days was seized with the cholera, which was at that place. The complaint was, without doubt, brought on by having subsisted on fruit only for several days while I was in the slave states. The landlord of the inn came to me when I was in bed suffering violently from cholera, and told me he knew I had that complaint and, as it had never been in his house, I could not stop there any longer. No one would enter my room except a young lady who appeared very pious and amiable and had visited persons with the cholera. She immediately procured me some medicine at her own expense and administered it herself; and whilst I was groaning with agony, the landlord came up and ordered me out of the house directly. Most of the persons in Poughkeepsie had retired for the night, and I lay under a shed on some cotton bales. The medicine relieved me, having been given so promptly; and next morning I went from the shed and laid on the banks of the river below the city. Towards evening, I felt must better and went on in a steamboat to the city of Albany, about eighty miles. When I reached there I went into the country and tried for three or four days to procure employment, but failed.

At that time I had scarcely any money and lived upon fruit. So I returned to Albany, where I could get no work as I could not show the recommendations I possessed, which were only from slave states, and I did not wish anyone to know I came from them. After a time, I went up the western canal as steward in one of the boats. When I had gone about three hundred and fifty miles up the canal, I found I was going too much towards the slave states, in consequence of which I returned to Albany and went up the northern canal into one of the New England States—

Vermont. The distance I had traveled, including the three hundred and fifty miles I had to return from the west and the hundred to Vermont, was two thousand three hundred miles. When I reached Vermont I found the people very hospitable and kind. They seemed opposed to slavery, so I told them I was a runaway slave. I hired myself to a firm in Sudbury.

After I had been in Sudbury some time, the neighboring farmers told me that I had hired myself for much less money than I ought. I mentioned it to my employers, who were very angry about it. I was advised to leave by some of the people around, who thought the gentleman I was with would write to my former master, informing him where I was, and obtain the reward fixed upon me. Fearing I should be taken, I immediately left and went into the town of Ludlow, where I met with a kind friend, Mr. ———,[1] who sent me to school for several weeks.

At this time I was advertised in the papers and was obliged to leave. I went a little way out of Ludlow to a retired place and lived two weeks with a Mr. ———, deacon of a Baptist church at Ludlow.

At this place I could have obtained education, had it been safe to have remained. From there I went to New Hampshire, where I was not safe, so went to Boston, Massachusetts, with the hope of returning to Ludlow, a place to which I was much attached. At Boston I met with a friend who kept a shop and took me to assist him for several weeks.

Here I did not consider myself safe, as persons from all parts of the country were continually coming to the shop, and I feared some might come who knew me. I now had my head shaved and bought a wig, and engaged myself to a Mr. Perkins of Brookline, three miles from Boston, where I remained about a month. Some of the family discovered that I wore a wig and said that I was a runaway slave. But the neighbors all around

From *Narrative of the Adventures and Escape of Moses Roper, from American Slavery*

thought I was a white, to prove which I have a document in my possession to call me to military duty. The law is that no slave or colored person performs this, but every other person in America of the age of twenty-one is called upon to perform military duty once or twice in the year, or pay a fine.

COPY OF THE DOCUMENT

MR. MOSES ROPER,

You being duly enrolled as a soldier in the company, under the command of Captain Benjamin Bradley, are hereby notified and ordered to appear at the Town House, in Brookline, on Friday, 28th instant, at three o'clock, P.M., for the purpose of filling the vacancy in the said company, occasioned by the promotion of Lieut. Nathaniel M. Weeks, and of filling any other vacancy which may then and there occur in the said company, and then wait further orders.

By order of the Captain,
F. P. WENTWORTH, *Clerk.*

BROOKLINE, August 14th, 1835.

I then returned to the city of Boston, to the shop where I was before. Several weeks after I had returned to my situation, two colored men informed me that a gentleman had been inquiring for a person whom, from the description, I knew to be myself, and [had] offered them a considerable sum if they would disclose my place of abode. But they, being much opposed to slavery, came and told me, upon which information I secreted myself till I could get off.

I went into the Green Mountains for several weeks, from thence to the city of New York, and remained in secret several days till I heard of a ship, the *Napoleon*, sailing to England; and on the eleventh of November, 1835, I sailed, taking my letters of recommendation to the Drs. Morrison and Raffles and the Rev. Alexander Fletcher. The time I first started from slavery was in July 1834, so that I was nearly sixteen months in making my escape.

—1837

Author's Reference Note

[1] It would not be proper to mention any names, as a person in any of the states in America found harboring a slave would have to pay a heavy fine.

A Freeman's Flight from the South

William G. Allen

I WAS BORN in Virginia, but not in slavery. The early years of my life were spent partly in the small village of Urbanna, on the banks of the Rappahannock, partly in the city of Norfolk, near the mouth of the James River, and partly in the Fortress of Monroe, on the shores of the Chesapeake. I was eighteen years in Virginia. My father was a white man, my mother a mulattress, so that I am what is generally termed a quadroon. Both parents died when I was quite young, and I was then adopted by another family, whose name I bear. My parents by adoption were both colored, and possessed a flourishing business in the Fortress of Monroe.

I went to school a year and a half in Norfolk. The school was composed entirely of colored children and was kept by a man of color, a Baptist minister, who was highly esteemed, not only as a teacher but as a preacher of rare eloquence and power. His color did not debar him from taking an equal part with his white brethren in matters pertaining to their church.

But the school was destined to be of short duration. In 1831 Nathaniel Turner, a slave, having incited a number of his brethren to avenge their wrongs in a summary manner, marched by night with his comrades upon the town of Southampton, Virginia, and in a few hours put to death about one hundred[1] of the white inhabitants. This act of Turner and his associates struck such terror into the hearts of the whites throughout the state that they immediately, as an act of retaliation or vengeance, abolished every colored school within their borders, and having dispersed the pupils, ordered the teachers to leave the state forthwith, and never more to return.

I now went to the Fortress of Monroe, but soon found that I could not get into any school there. For, though being a military station, and therefore under the sole control of the federal government, it did not seem that this place was free from the influence of slavery, in the form of prejudice against color. But my parents had money, which always and everywhere has a magic charm. I was also of a persevering habit; and what therefore I could not get in the schools, I sought among the soldiers in the garrison and succeeded in obtaining. Many of the rank and file of the American Army are highly educated foreigners— some of them political refugees who have fled to America and become unfortunate, oftentimes from their own personal habits. I now learned something of several languages, and considerable music. My German teacher, a common soldier, was, by all who knew him, reputed to be both a splendid scholar and musician. I also now and then bought the services of other teachers, which greatly helped to advance me.

Many of the slaveholders aided my efforts. This seems like a paradox; but, to the credit of humanity, be it said that the bad are not always bad. One kindhearted slaveholder, an army officer, gave me free access to his valuable library; and another slaveholder, a naval officer who frequented the garrison, presented me, as a gift, with a small but well selected library, which formerly belonged to a deceased son.

My experience, therefore, in the state of Virginia is, in many respects, quite the opposite of that which others of my class have been called to undergo.

Could I forget how often I have stood at the

foot of the market in the city of Norfolk and heard the cry of the auctioneer: "What will you give for this man? What for this woman? What for this child?"—could I forget that I have again and again stood upon the shores of the Chesapeake and, while looking out upon that splendid bay, beheld ships and brigs carrying into unutterable misery and woe men, women and children, victims of the most cruel slavery that ever saw the sun; could I forget the innumerable scenes of cruelty I have witnessed, and blot out the remembrance of the degradation, intellectual, moral and spiritual, which everywhere surrounded me—making the country like unto a den of dragons and pool of waters—my reminiscence of Virginia were indeed a joy and not a sorrow.

Some things I do think of with pleasure. A grand old state is Virginia. Nowhere else, in America at least, has nature revealed herself on a more munificent scale. Lofty mountains, majestic hills, beautiful valleys, magnificent rivers cover her bosom. A genial clime warms her heart. Her resources are exhaustless. Why should she not move on? Execrated forever be this wretched slavery—this disturbing force. It kills the white man—kills the black man—kills the master—kills the slave—kills everybody and everything. Liberty is, indeed, the first condition of human progress and the especial handmaiden of all that in human life is beautiful and true.

I attained my eighteenth year. About this time the Rev. W. H—— of New York City visited the Fortress of Monroe and opened a select school. He was a white man, and of a kind and benevolent nature. He could not admit me into his school; nevertheless he took a deep interest in my welfare. He aided my studies in such ways as he could and, on his return to the state of New York (he remained but a short time in Virginia), acquainted the Honorable Gerrit Smith of Peterboro with my desires.[2] Mr. Smith's sympathies were immediately touched on my behalf. He requested the Rev. W. H—— to write to me at once and extend to me an invitation to visit the state of New York, enter college and graduate at his expense—if need be.

I have to remark just here that at the time of the visit of the Rev. W. H—— to the Fortress of Monroe, my parents were in greatly reduced circumstances, owing to a destructive fire which had recently taken place and burned to the ground a most valuable property. The fire was supposed to be the work of incendiaries—low whites of the neighborhood, who had become envious of my parents' success. There was no insurance on the property. Under these circumstances I gladly accepted the kind offer of Mr. Smith. His generous nature then and there turned towards me in friendship; and I am happy to be able to add, he has ever continued my friend from that day to this.

Mr. Smith is one of the noblest men that America has ever produced, and is especially remarkable for his profound appreciation of that sublime command of our Savior, "All things whatsoever ye would that men should do to you, do ye even so to them." Where he treads, no angel of sorrow follows.

He is a man of vast estates—a millionaire. He is also what in America is termed a land reformer. He believes that every man should possess an inviolable homestead. He himself possesses by inheritance millions of acres in the Northern and Eastern states of America, and shows his sincerity and consistency by parceling off from time to time such portions of these lands as are available, in lots of forty or fifty acres each, and presenting the deeds thereof, free of charge, to the deserving landless men, white or black, in the region where the lands in question are located. He also long since vacated the splendid Peterboro mansion, into possession of which he came on the death of his father, and now resides, himself and family, in a simple cottage near Peterboro, with only forty acres attached. His sympathies are not bounded by country or clime. He sent into Ireland, during the famine of 1847, the largest single donation that reached the country from abroad.

He was elected to the United States Congress a few years ago, as one of the members for New York, but resigned his seat after holding it only a year—probably feeling outraged by the manners and morals, not to say superlative wickedness, of so many of his associates. Whatever may have been the cause which induced him to resign, he did well to give up his post. Nature had evidently not set him to the work. Of great ability, winning eloquence and undoubted moral courage, his heart and temper were too soft and apologetic to deal with the blustering tyrants who fill too many of the seats of both houses of Congress.

Mr. Smith is truly a great orator. He has in an eminent degree the first qualification thereof —a great heart. His voice is a magnificent bass, deep, full, sonorous; and being as melodious as deep, it gives him enviable power over the hearts and sympathies of men.

In personal appearance he is extremely handsome—large and noble in stature, with a face not only beautiful, but luminous with the reflection of every Christian grace.

He is now engaged in the care of his vast estates and in his private enterprises—scarcely private, since they are all for the public good. He is sixty-two years of age. A true Christian in every exalted sense of the term, long may he live an honor and a blessing to his race.

Having accepted the invitation of this gentleman, I prepared to leave the South. On making arrangements for a passage from Norfolk to Baltimore, I found that the "Free Papers" which every man of color in a slave state must possess in order to be able to prove, in case of his being apprehended at any time, that he is not an absconding slave, were of very little avail. I must needs have a "Pass" as well, or I could not leave. However, I obtained this document without much trouble, and as it is a curious specimen of American literature, I will give it. It does not equal, to be sure, the "charming pages" of Washington Irving, but it is certainly quite as illustrative in its way:

From *A Short Personal Narrative by William G. Allen*

NORFOLK, Oct. 1839.

The bearer of this, William G. Allen, is permitted to leave Norfolk by the Steam Boat Jewess, Capt. Sutton, for Baltimore.
Signed,   J. F. HUNTER,
Agent, Baltimore Steam Packet Company.

This document was also countersigned by one of the justices of the peace. Really, there is something preposterous about these slaveholders. They make all sorts of attempts to drive the free colored people out of their borders; but when a man of this class wishes to go of his own accord, he must then be permitted!

I reached Baltimore in safety, but now found that neither "Free Papers" nor "Pass" were of any further use. I desired to take the train to Philadelphia en route to New York. I must this time get a white man to testify to my freedom, or further I could not go. Or, worse still, if no such man could be found, I must be detained in Baltimore and lodged in jail! By no means a pleasant prospect. There was no time to be lost. My previous experience had taught me this truth: the more we trust, the more we are likely to find to trust. Acting upon this principle, and putting in practice my studies in physiognomy, I presently found a friend among the crowd, who, being satisfied with my statements and the documents I presented, kindly gave the desired testimony. The ticket seller then recorded my name, age and personal appearance in his book, and delivered me my ticket. I now had no further trouble, and reached the college (in the state of New York) in safety.

—1860

Editor's Reference Notes

[1] The number of inhabitants killed was later found to be about half of the figure given here.

[2] Gerrit Smith (1797–1874), a noted reformer and philanthropist, was an active supporter of the antislavery movement.

The German Invasion

James McCune Smith

IN 1853, the Irish population of New York City was 110,000; the German, 55,000.

Their relative mortality in the same city was:

	IRISH		GERMAN	
1851	4,326	1 in 25	1,044	1 in 40
1852	4,135		1,265	

The Irish mortality was 37½ per cent greater than the German. In the year 1858, the mortality in New York City was as high as one in twenty-seven, which a leading daily attributes to the increased unhealthiness of said city; the truth is, that this mortality is largely due to Ward's Island Hospital, where the feeble and emaciated and disabled emigrants of two years' standing are sent.

The Irish emigrants either linger about large cities or spread over the country, cutting canals and railroads, and exposed to malaria from Michigan to Texas. The German emigrants, already well informed by numerous books on the United States published in Germany, seek in their new homes the healthiest localities and betake themselves to husbandry.

Of all the invaders of our land, the Germans pre-eminently maintain their nationality; the southwest and northeast portions of New York City are rapidly assuming the appearance of a German city, and almost every week a new cellar is opened in the mid-regions of the metropolis with *Wirthschaft* [sic], *Gasthaus* or *Lager Bier* [1] emblazoned above it in staring red or blue German text. Their newspapers, too, are a significant element in the maintenance of their nationality. It was the boast of Tucker, in his *Progress of the United States*, that in a population of seventeen millions the United States had 130 daily and 1,142 weekly newspapers, "such a diffusion of intelligence and information as had never existed in any other age or country." [2]

In the city of New York there are ten dailies to 500,000 of Anglo-American population, or one to 50,000; in the same city the Germans have four dailies to 55,000, or one to 14,000, whilst the Irish have not one daily to their 110,000, and only three or four weeklies, and those largely supported by officeholders at the bid of our Democratic Executive at Washington.

In 1853, in the whole United States, the American people had one daily to 130,769 population; the Germans had one daily to 61,800 population; the Americans had one newspaper to 13,655 population; the Germans had one newspaper to 6,866 population.

In other words, taking newspapers as indices of intelligence, activity and movement, the German population excel us 100 per cent!

Such is the material of the German invasion, a persistent vitality, strong nationality, intelligence and a capacity for organized effort; let us glance at the character or idiosyncrasies which this powerful element is introducing into our midst.

The thrift of the Germans is proverbial. We flesh-devouring Americans, twenty-five years ago, jeered at the Irish emigrant who fed on buttermilk and potatoes while performing hard labor; now the Irish furiously declare that "the Dutch live on nothing, grow fat and make money."

This example of thrift is one which we need very much as a set-off to our extravagant habits and rapid living.

There is, moreover, a truthfulness in the German character, strongly exemplified in their deportment and dealing—a truthfulness which comes like a precious manna among a people whose boasted principles of liberty are hourly contradicted and belied by their combined maintenance of a most cruel system of chattel slavery.

A love of rational enjoyment, and the practice of holidays, are two other elements in the German character, whose refining, not to say hallowing, influences are already felt, and in the future will be largely imitated by us. The *Sanger bands* and *Turner verein* [sic] [3] are institutions, more especially the latter, entirely new to us, and of the most admirable character. The prevailing beauty of them is their ideality; they meet and sing, and utter myriad harmonies, for the very love of music itself—and of companionship and social union.

There is nothing in our national makeup which at all compares with these stated reunions, in all that softens the manners and polishes away the rust of barbarism. Neither in our Christmas feast, with its solemn rituals, nor our New Year's Day, in which the highest meed is due to him who can walk the fastest, eat the greatest number of indigestible substances, drink the widest variety of alcoholic compounds, be in the greatest hurry and earn the most violent headache, for the beginning of the year—nor on the Fourth of July, in which the loudest cannon, the loudest pistols, the loudest bragging and self-laudation, indicate our short remove from the savage state—nor when, on the other hand, the vile desecration of the pulpit to the begging of alms to remove from our midst our sable brother shows how little of Christian love dwells amongst us—nor in our Thanksgiving Day, in which, characteristically enough, we set ourselves up to a certain measure of enjoyment, under the pretense of *fasting* and prayer. No, none of these at all compare with those vast gatherings, in the month of May or June, on the banks of the Hudson, beneath the grand old trees and the grander canopy above them, when these German men and women and children, happiest of all, "sing . . . a new song . . . sing . . . with the harp. . . . With trumpets and sound of cornet, make a joyful noise . . . ," and like the floods "clap their hands . . . ," and like the hills are "joyful together."

Another element in the character of our Ger-

man invaders worthy of thoughtful attention is the position which woman holds in their social fabric. The man and his wife are the warp and woof not only of their domestic, but also of their social, relations; in his house, in his business and in his amusements, in laying out his plans of life and in executing the same, his *Vrow* [sic] is, in old Scripture language, "a helpmeet" for the German man.

This is not a new element in the German character; it has been part and parcel of their institutions in the *Vaterland* for nearly two thousand years. In that fine passage in which Tacitus speaks of the noble simplicity of the German marriages, he tells us that:

> . . . the bride offers not a dowry to the husband, but the husband to the bride. Parents and relatives are present to approve the gifts; gifts not intended as female toys, nor to be consumed at the nuptials—but oxen, and a bridled horse, and a shield with javelin and sword . . . and she in turn presents a few arms. This do they regard as the highest bond, these are the sacred arcana, these the household gods. Nor does the woman regard herself as without the pale of bravery, nor the hap of war; she is admonished by the very ceremonies of marriage that she comes into a compact of difficulties and dangers; alike in peace and in war to suffer and to dare! . . . Thus they live, thus they die.[4]

Tempora mutantur: the times are changed, but in the eighteen centuries that have rolled over their heads since these words were written, and though they have passed through all the phases of society that intervene between barbarism and the highest culture, the relation between the German man and his wife remains the same in all things except . . . to do and dare in battle.

And the noisy things we call mass meetings, and the furious vortices we call political meetings, and the popinjay martial shows in which citizen soldiers show how nearly they can imitate in dress, in step and in music the standing armies which tyrants alone require—all these mannish, but hardly manly, exhibitions are in painful contrast with—and, let us trust, will be gradually exchanged for—the more humanizing influences of the pleasure gardens and fetes in which the German and his wife and prattling children quietly enjoy the songs and the dances of the fatherland. But Tacitus also says of this people: "Frequent fights, rarely with noise, often with murder and wounds, occur, as they will among wine drinkers." [5]

The Germans still drink, but their beer fights are now confined to the students at their universities at home; for there is a mildness about their *Lager Bier*, altogether different from the fiery fluid which excited them in the savage state; but the worst of it is that not content with drinking thus moderately themselves, they offer "firewaters" of the most poisonous quality to the people whom they invade on this continent. It is the same way that our fathers conquered and destroyed the red man, and unless the majesty of the law be interposed, we cannot avoid a similar fate.

In painful contrast to all that is admirable and desirable in the German character appears the fact that in a recent state election sharp-witted politicians secured the German vote in the metropolis for men whom they declared, in handbills printed in that language, to be practical opponents of the Maine liquor law. And fitting commentary on this fact is the other, that in the city of New York, of the keepers of liquor stores, there are (in 1853):

Americans	1,043	350,000
Irish	2,327 (colored 22)	100,000
Germans	3,272	50,000

Every seventeenth German in the city of New York is engaged in selling rum—and the vilest of rum, which festers and poisons the persons of the lowest classes. Men and women too poor to drink themselves to death in the shilling or sixpenny drinks find in the Dutch groceries vile stuff by the three cents' worth, two cents' worth and, more frequently, the one cent's worth! The Dutch grocers, except in rare instances, avoid tasting the poison with which they fill our prisons and our gallows.

The other negative quality in our German invaders is their inertia in relation to rights and government. If Franklin Pierce should, by a coup d'état, declare himself Emperor of all the Americas,[6] our German friends, with few exceptions, would take the matter quietly, except so far as it might affect the price of groceries, or produce,

or *Lager Bier*! And by consequence there is a like inertia in regard to the question of liberty or slavery. Of the 180 newspapers published by them in this land, only one recently started is antislavery—the *National Democrat*, published in Washington by Frederick Schmidt.

* * * * * *

I have said nothing of German culture, for German culture has not yet mingled in the flood of emigration—probably never will. Bonn and Heidelburgh [sic], Berlin and Göttingen, cannot be transported into our midst. No Genie of the Lamp has the power, in a moment, in a year, nor in a century, to remove to this side of the Atlantic those hoary seats of learning which are the growth of a long and patient and unremitting toil, through generation after generation, and which have penetrated to the verge of human thought in all ages and nations. The very noise and hurry of our times would frighten from amongst us such seats of learning, even if they came.

We may buy with our money the library of Neander,[7] the chisels of Thorwaldsen,[8] or the easel of Michael Angelo [sic], yet there remains behind a something which gold cannot purchase—the genius loci, the charmed atmosphere, that has blazed with so many lamps of science, has been brilliant with so many lights of genius, and in which there still lingers the spirits of the great departed, breathing their divine afflatus upon those who there come after them, and who are thus enabled to put on the armor and wield the weapons of the giants who have gone before them.

We cannot, then, import German culture, nor will it seek our land; a portion of it will doubtless reach us through the multitude of our young men seeking to complete their studies at the German universities, but we cannot have the German culture in our midst—nor do we want it. If we live—and God grant that we may—we must have a culture of our own, a culture grand beyond all European example because the result of a larger combination of the varied intellect of the human race—a culture the foundation stones of whose altars are not yet laid, whose priests have not yet begun their novitiate.

In conclusion, I have endeavored to lay before you what facts I could cull relative to this, the most important, perhaps the best, invasion or immigration we have received in the nineteenth century.

They come among us, a thrifty, docile, law-abiding people—for the code of Justinian [9] has entered the very marrow of their being, and from the difference of their language and their intense nationality, they must amalgamate slowly.

Whilst we receive and cherish the good that they bring us, we must not be slow, in return, to give them back the complementary elements of character which are ours and not theirs. We must awaken them from the hazy dream of physical content which beams from their countenances; we must talk to them of liberty and justice, and their guarantee—eternal vigilance. We must not permit them to sleep on, nor lie dumb while the chains clank and the lash resounds, and women shriek for help and freedom.

—1860

Editor's Reference Notes

[1] *Wirtschaft:* inn, hotel, tavern; *Gasthaus:* inn, tavern; *Lagerbier:* beer made for storage.

[2] George Tucker, *Progress of the United States* (Boston, 1843).

[3] *Sängerbanden:* choral groups; *Turnvereine:* gymnastic clubs.

[4] Tacitus, *Germania.*

[5] *Ibid.*

[6] This article was written in 1853, during Pierce's presidency. It was revised and was published in 1860.

[7] Johann August Wilhelm Neander (1789–1850), German writer and scholar, and noted church historian.

[8] Bertel Thorwaldsen, or Thorvaldsen (1768 or 1770–1844), the famous Danish sculptor of the early nineteenth century.

[9] Under Justinian I, the great Eastern Roman Emperor from 527 to 565, the Roman law was codified. This codification, the *Corpus Juris Civilis*, was studied extensively in the Middle Ages, and modern European civil law is based on it.

Colored American Patriots

William C. Nell

THE DECISION of Judge Taney[1] that colored men have no rights that white men are bound to respect, and the recent campaign speeches of Senator Douglas,[2] claiming that this government rested solely upon a white basis—are alike appeals to white Americans to ignore many of the prominent and significant facts in the early history of their country; and it is a most humiliating but true statement that the national administration, and also too many of the state governments, are shaping their legislation to practically enforce the atrocious doctrine.

Waiving all arguments that might be urged from many a standpoint against the unrighteous "decision" and alike gratuitous "sentiment," it is sufficient for present purposes to state a few simple facts of colored Americans' patriotism and loyalty to their country—and facts which, if narrated of white Americans, would be accepted by the nation as their passports to perennial fame.

It was a colored American, Crispus Attucks, who on the fifth of March, 1770, led on the American force in King Street, Boston, against the British guard, being himself the first to attack, and fell pierced by two musket balls, one in each breast—the first martyr on that day which history has selected as the dawn of the American Revolution.

It was a colored American, Peter Salem, who shot Major Pitcairn on the seventeenth of June, 1775, on Bunker Hill, and thus turned the tide of battle on that memorable day. A number of other colored Americans took prominent part in the same scenes, and also shared the labors of Lexington, Dorchester Heights, Brandywine, Princeton, Monmouth, Stony Point, Fort Moultrie, Greenbank, Croton Heights, Catskill, Bennington and Yorktown, besides signal services at New Orleans, and naval exploits on the lakes in the War of 1812 (which war was undertaken because of the impressment of three seamen, two of whom were colored)—satisfactory proof at least that they were American citizens. Confirmation of colored citizenship has been made by five presidents of the United States, and which [*sic*] it will take more than the potency of Judge Taney and Senator Douglas to offset. In convoking the Congress of the fourth of September, 1774, there was not a word said about color.[3] At a subsequent meeting, Congress met again to get in readiness twelve thousand men to act in any emergency; to the same time, a request was forwarded to Connecticut, New Hampshire and Rhode Island to increase this army to twenty thousand men. Now it is well known that hundreds of the men of which this army was composed were colored men, and recognized by Congress as Americans.

Facts could be piled Olympus high in proof that the colored American has ever proved loyal, and ready to die, if need be, at Freedom's shrine. The *amor patriæ* has always burned vividly on the altar of his heart. He loves

> . . . his native land,
> Its hills, and mountains green.

—1860

Editor's Reference Notes

[1] Roger B. Taney (1777–1864), Chief Justice of the Supreme Court at the time of the Dred Scott case.

[2] Stephen A. Douglas (1813–1861), senator from Illinois, against whom Lincoln ran in the 1858 campaign.

[3] The First Continental Congress of the American colonies.

Crispus Attucks

William Wells Brown

THE PRINCIPLE that taxation and representation were inseparable was in accordance with the theory, the genius and the precedents of British legislation; and this principle was now, for the first time, intentionally invaded. The American colonies were not represented in Parliament, yet an act was passed by that body the tendency of which was to invalidate all right and title to their property. This was the Stamp Act of March 23, 1765, which ordained that no sale, bond, note of hand nor other instrument of writing should be valid unless executed on paper bearing the stamp prescribed by the home government. The intelligence of the passage of the Stamp Act at once roused the indignation of the liberty-loving portion of the people of the colonies, and meetings were held at various points to protest against this high-handed measure.

Massachusetts was the first to take a stand in opposition to the mother country. The merchants and traders of Boston, New York and Philadelphia entered into nonimportation agreements, with a view of obtaining a repeal of the obnoxious law. Under the pressure of public sentiment, the Stamp Act officers gave in their resignations. The eloquence of William Pitt[1] and the sagacity of Lord Camden[2] brought about a repeal of the Stamp Act in the British Parliament. A new ministry, in 1767, succeeded in getting through the House of Commons a bill to tax the tea[3] imported into the American colonies, and it received the royal assent. Massachusetts again took the lead in opposing the execution of this last act, and Boston began planning to take the most conspicuous part in the great drama. The agitation in the colonies provoked the home government,

and power was given to the governor of Massachusetts to take notice of all persons who might offer any treasonable objections to these oppressive enactments, that the same might be sent home to England to be tried there. Lord North[4] was now at the head of affairs, and no leniency was to be shown to the colonies. The concentration of British troops in large numbers at Boston convinced the people that their liberties were at stake, and they began to rally.

A crowded and enthusiastic meeting, held in Boston in the latter part of the year 1769, was addressed by the ablest talent that the progressive element could produce. Standing in the back part of the hall, eagerly listening to the speakers, was a dark mulatto man, very tall, rather good-looking, and apparently about fifty years of age. This was Crispus Attucks. Though taking no part in the meeting, he was nevertheless destined to be conspicuous in the first struggle in throwing off the British yoke. Twenty years previous to this, Attucks was the slave of William Brouno, Esq., of Framingham, Massachusetts; but his was a heart beating for freedom and not to be kept in the chains of mental or bodily servitude.

From the *Boston Gazette* of Tuesday, November 20, 1750, I copy the following advertisement:

> Ran away from his master William Brouno Framingham, on the 30th of Sept., last, a Molatto Fellow, about 27 years of Age named Crispus, well set, six feet 2 inches high, short curl'd Hair, knees nearer together than common; had on a light coloured Bearskin Coat, brown Fustian jacket, new Buckskin Breeches, blew yarn Stockins and Checkered Shirt. Whoever shall take up said Runaway, and convey

him to his above said Master at Framingham, shall have Ten Pounds, old Tenor Reward and all necessary charges paid.

The above is a *verbatim et literatim* advertisement for a runaway slave one hundred and twenty-two years ago. Whether Mr. Brouno succeeded in recapturing Crispus or not, we are left in the dark.

Ill feeling between the mother country and her colonial subjects had been gaining ground while British troops were concentrating at Boston. On the fifth of March, 1770, the people were seen early congregating at the corners of the principal streets, at Dock Square, and near the Custom House. Captain Preston, with a body of redcoats, started out for the purpose of keeping order in the disaffected town and was hissed at by the crowds in nearly every place where he appeared. The day passed off without any outward manifestation of disturbance, but all seemed to feel that something would take place after nightfall. The doubling of the guard in and about the Custom House showed the authorities felt an insecurity that they did not care to express. The lamps in Dock Square threw their light in the angry faces of a large crowd who appeared to be waiting for the crisis, in whatever form it should come. A part of Captain Preston's company was making its way from the Custom House, when they were met by the crowd from Dock Square, headed by the black man Attucks, who was urging them to meet the redcoats and drive them from the streets. "These rebels have no business here," said he, "let's drive them away." The people became enthusiastic; their brave leader grew more daring in his language and attitude, while the soldiers under Captain Preston appeared to give way. "Come on! Don't be afraid!" cried Attucks. "They dare not shoot; and, if they dare, let them do it."

From *The Rising Son*

Stones and sticks, with which the populace were armed, were freely used, to the great discomfiture of the English soldiers. "Don't hesitate! Come on! We'll drive these rebels out of Boston!" were the last words heard from the lips of the colored man, for the sharp crack of muskets silenced his voice, and he fell weltering in his blood. Two balls had pierced his sable breast. Thus died Crispus Attucks, the first martyr to American liberty and the inaugurator of the Revolution that was destined to take from the crown of George III its brightest star. An immense concourse of citizens followed the remains of the hero to its last resting place, and his name was honorably mentioned in the best circles. The last words, the daring and the death of Attucks gave spirit and enthusiasm to the Revolution, and his heroism was imitated by both whites and blacks. His name was a rallying cry for the brave colored men who fought at the Battle of Bunker's [sic] Hill. In the gallant defense of Red Bank, where four hundred blacks met and defeated fifteen hundred Hessians headed by Count Donop, the thought of Attucks filled them with ardor. When Colonel Green fell at Groton, surrounded by his black troops who perished with him, they went into the battle feeling proud of the opportunity of imitating the first martyr of the American Revolution.

No monument has yet been erected to him. An effort was made in the legislature of Massachusetts a few years since, but without success. Five generations of accumulated prejudice against the Negro had excluded from the American mind all inclination to do justice to one of her bravest sons. Now that slavery is abolished, we may hope, in future years, to see a monument raised to commemorate the heroism of Crispus Attucks.

—1874

Editor's Reference Notes

[1] The elder William Pitt (1708–1778), First Earl of Chatham, who championed the colonies against the repressive measures taken by the British government.

[2] Charles Pratt (1713–1793), First Earl Camden, who was Lord Chancellor at that time.

[3] Certain other items were also taxed.

[4] Frederick North (1732–1792), Second Earl of Guilford and Eighth Baron North, was Prime Minister from 1770 to 1782. He was a strong supporter of the tax bill referred to here.

The Black Woman of the South: Her Neglects and Her Needs

Alexander Crummell

IT IS AN AGE clamorous everywhere for the dignities, the grand prerogatives, and the glory, of woman. There is not a country in Europe where she has not risen somewhat above the degradation of centuries and pleaded successfully for a new position and a higher vocation. As the result of this new reformation we see her, in our day, seated in the lecture rooms of ancient universities, rivaling her brothers in the field of literature—the grand creator of ethereal art, the participant in noble civil franchises, the moving spirit in grand reformations and the guide, agent or assistant in all the noblest movements for the civilization and regeneration of man.

In these several lines of progress the American woman has run on in advance of her sisters in every other quarter of the globe. The advantage she has received, the rights and prerogatives she has secured for herself, are unequaled by any other class of women in the world. It will not be thought amiss, then, that I come here today to present to your consideration the one grand exception to this general superiority of women, viz., *the black woman of the South*.

In speaking today of the "black woman," I must needs make a very clear distinction. The African race in this country is divided into two classes, that is—the *colored people* and the *Negro population*. In the census returns of 1860 this whole population was set down at 4,500,000. Of these, the colored numbered 500,000, the black or Negro population at 4,000,000. But notice these other broad lines of demarkation between them. The colored people, while indeed but *one-eighth* of the number of the blacks, counted more men and women who could read

and write than the whole 4,000,000 of their brethren in bondage. A like disparity showed itself in regard to their material condition. The 500,000 colored people were absolutely richer in lands and houses than the many millions of their degraded kinsmen.

The causes of these differences are easily discovered. The colored population received, in numerous cases, the kindness and generosity of their white kindred—white fathers and relatives. Forbidden by law to marry the Negro woman, very many slaveholders took her as the wife, despite the law; and when children were begotten every possible recognition was given those children, and they were often cared for, educated and made possessors of property. Sometimes they were sent to Northern schools, sometimes to France or England. Not unfrequently whole families, nay, at times whole colonies, were settled in Western or Northern towns and largely endowed with property. The colored population, moreover, was, as compared with the Negro, the urban population. They were brought in large numbers to the cities, and thus partook of the civilization and refinement of the whites. They were generally the domestic servants of their masters, and thus, brought in contact with their superiors, they gained a sort of education which never came to the field hands living in rude huts on the plantations. All this, however casual it may seem, was a merciful providence, by which some gleams of light and knowledge came indirectly to the race in this land.

The rural or plantation population of the South was made up almost entirely of people of pure Negro blood. And this brings out also the other disastrous fact—namely, that this large black population has been living from the time of their introduction into America, a period of more than two hundred years, in a state of unlettered rudeness. The Negro all this time has been an intellectual starveling. This has been more especially the condition of the black woman of the South. Now and then a black man has risen above the debased condition of his people. Various causes would contribute to the advantage of the men: the relation of servants to superior masters; attendance at courts with them; their presence at political meetings; listening to table talk behind their chairs; traveling as valets; the privilege of books and reading in great houses and with indulgent masters. All these served to lift up a black man here and there to something like superiority. But no such fortune fell to the lot of the plantation woman. The black woman of the South was left perpetually in a state of hereditary darkness and rudeness. Since the day of Phillis Wheatley no Negress in this land (that is, in the South) has been raised above the level of her sex. The lot of the black man on the plantation has been sad and desolate enough; but the fate of the black woman has been awful! Her entire existence from the day she first landed, a naked victim of the slave trade, has been degradation in its extremest forms.

In her girlhood all the delicate tenderness of her sex has been rudely outraged. In the field, in the rude cabin, in the pressroom, in the factory, she was thrown into the companionship of coarse and ignorant men. No chance was given her for delicate reserve or tender modesty. From her childhood she was the doomed victim of the grossest passions. All the virtues of her sex were utterly ignored. If the instinct of chastity asserted itself, then she had to fight like a tigress for the ownership and possession of her own person, and, ofttimes, had to suffer pains and lacerations for her virtuous self-assertion. When she reached maturity all the tender instincts of her womanhood were ruthlessly violated. At the age of marriage—always prematurely anticipated under slavery—she was mated, as the stock of the plantation were mated, not to be the companion of a loved and chosen husband, but to be the breeder of human cattle for the field or the auction block.

With that mate she went out, morning after morning, to toil as a common field hand. As it was his, so likewise was it her lot to wield the heavy hoe, or to follow the plow, or to gather in the crops. She was a "hewer of wood and a drawer of water." She was a common field hand. She had to keep her place in the gang from morn till eve, under the burden of a heavy task, or under the stimulus or the fear of a cruel lash. She was a picker of cotton. She labored at the sugar mill and in the tobacco factory. When, through weariness or sickness, she has fallen behind her allotted task, then came, as punishment, the fearful stripes upon her shrinking, lacerated flesh.

Her home life was of the most degrading nature. She lived in the rudest huts, and partook of the coarsest food, and dressed in the scantiest garb, and slept in multitudinous cabins upon the hardest boards!

Thus she continued a beast of burden down to the period of those maternal anxieties which, in ordinary civilized life, give repose, quiet and care to expectant mothers. But under the slave system few such relaxations were allowed. And so it came to pass that little children were ushered into this world under conditions which many cattle raisers would not suffer for their flocks or herds. Thus she became the mother of children.

But even then there was for her no suretyship of motherhood, or training, or control. Her own offspring were not her own. She and husband and children were all the property of others. All these sacred ties were constantly snapped and cruelly sundered. *This* year she had one husband; and next year, through some auction sale, she might be separated from him and mated to another. There was no sanctity of family, no binding tie of marriage, none of the fine felicities and the endearing affections of home. None of these things were the lot of Southern black women. Instead thereof a gross barbarism, which tended to blunt the tender sensibilities, to obliterate feminine delicacy and womanly shame, came down as her heritage from generation to generation; and it seems a miracle of providence and grace that, notwithstanding these terrible circumstances, so much struggling virtue lingered amid these rude cabins, that so much womanly worth and sweetness abided in their bosoms, as slave-holders themselves have borne witness to.

But some of you will ask: "Why bring up these sad memories of the past? Why distress us with these dead and departed cruelties?" Alas, my friends, these are not dead things. Remember that

The evil that men do lives after them.[1]

The evil of gross and monstrous abominations, the evil of great organic institutions, crop out long after the departure of the institutions themselves. If you go to Europe you will find not only the roots, but likewise many of the deadly fruits, of the old feudal system still surviving in several of its old states and kingdoms. So, too, with slavery. The eighteen years of freedom have not obliterated all its deadly marks from either the souls or bodies of the black woman. The conditions of life, indeed, have been modified since emancipation; but it still maintains that the black woman is the pariah woman of this land!

We have, indeed, degraded women immigrants from foreign lands. In their own countries some of them were so low in the social scale that they were yoked with the cattle to plow the fields. They were rude, unlettered, coarse and benighted. But when they reach *this* land there comes an end to their degraded condition:

They touch our country, and their shackles fall.[2]

As soon as they become grafted into the stock of American life they partake at once of all its large gifts and its noble resources.

Not so with the black woman of the South. Freed legally she has been; but the act of emancipation had no talismanic influence to reach to and alter and transform her degrading social life. . . .

The truth is, Emancipation Day found her a prostrate and degraded being; and, although it has brought numerous advantages to her sons, it has produced but the simplest changes in her social and domestic condition. She is still the crude, rude, ignorant mother. Remote from cities, the dweller still in the old plantation hut, neighboring to the sulky, disaffected master class who still think her freedom was a personal robbery of themselves—none of the "fair humanities" have visited her humble home.

The light of knowledge has not fallen upon her eyes. The fine domesticities which give the charm to family life and which, by the refinement and delicacy of womanhood, preserve the civilization of nations, have not come to her. She has still the rude, coarse labor of men. With her rude husband she still shares the hard service of a field hand. Her house, which shelters perhaps some six or eight children, embraces but two rooms. Her furniture is of the rudest kind. The clothing of the household is scant and of the coarsest material, has ofttimes the garniture of rags, and for herself and offspring is marked, not seldom, by the absence of both hats and shoes. She has rarely been taught to sew, and the field labor of slavery times has kept her ignorant of the habitudes of neatness and the requirements of order. Indeed, coarse food, coarse clothes, coarse living, coarse manners, coarse companions, coarse surroundings, coarse neighbors, both black and white—yea, everything coarse, down to the coarse, ignorant, senseless religion, which excites her sensibilities and starts her passions—go to make up the life of the masses of black women in the hamlets and villages of the rural South.

This is the state of black womanhood. Take the girlhood of this same region, and it presents the same aspect, save that in large districts the white man has not forgotten the olden times of slavery and with, indeed, the deepest sentimental abhorrence of "amalgamation," still thinks that the black girl is to be perpetually the victim of his lust! In the larger towns and in cities our girls, in common schools and academies, are receiving superior culture. Of the fifteen thousand colored school teachers in the South, more than half are colored young women, educated since emancipation. But even these girls, as well as their more ignorant sisters in rude huts, are followed and tempted and insulted by the ruffianly element of Southern society, who think that black men have no rights which white men should regard, and black women no virtue which white men should respect!

And now look at the vastness of this degradation. If I had been speaking of the population of a city or a town, or even a village, the tale would be a sad and melancholy one. But I have brought before you the condition of millions of women.

According to the census of 1880 there were, in the Southern states, 3,327,678 females of all ages of the African race. Of these there were 674,365 girls between twelve and twenty, 1,522,696 [women] between twenty and eighty. . . . And when you think that the masses of these women live in the rural districts, that they grow up in rudeness and ignorance, that their former masters are using few means to break up their hereditary degradation, you can easily take in the pitiful condition of this population and forecast the inevitable future to multitudes of females unless a mighty special effort is made for the improvement of the black womanhood of the South.

I know the practical nature of the American mind; I know how the question of values intrudes itself into even the domain of philanthropy, and hence I shall not be astonished if the query suggests itself whether special interest in the black woman will bring any special advantage to the American nation.

Let me dwell for a few moments upon this phase of the subject. Possibly the view I am about suggesting has never before been presented to the American mind. But, Negro as I am, I shall make no apology for venturing the claim that the Negress is one of the most interesting of all the classes of women on the globe. I am speaking of her not as a perverted and degraded creature, but in her natural state, with her native instincts and peculiarities.

Let me repeat just here the words of a wise, observing, tenderhearted philanthropist, whose name and worth and words have attained celebrity. It is fully forty years ago since the celebrated Dr. Channing said: [3]

> We are holding in bondage one of the best races of the human family. The Negro is among the mildest, gentlest of men. He is singularly susceptible of improvement from abroad. . . . His nature is affectionate, easily touched, and hence he is more open to religious improvement than the white man. . . . The African carries with him much more than *we* the genius of a meek, long-suffering, loving virtue.

* * * * * *

Humble and benighted as she is, the black woman of the South is one of the queens of womanhood. If there is any other woman on this earth who in native aboriginal qualities is her superior, I know not where she is to be found, for, I do say, that in tenderness of feeling, in genuine native modesty, in large disinterestedness, in sweetness of disposition and deep humility, in unselfish devotedness and in warm, motherly assiduities, the Negro woman is unsurpassed by any other woman on this earth.

The testimony to this effect is almost universal —our enemies themselves being witnesses. You know how widely and how continuously, for generations, the Negro has been traduced, ridiculed, derided. Some of you may remember the journals and the hostile criticisms of Coleridge and Trollope and Burton, West Indian and African travelers.[4] Very many of you may remember the philosophical disquisitions of the ethnological school of 1847, the contemptuous dissertations of Hunt and Gliddon.[5] But it is worthy of notice in all these cases that the sneer, the contempt, the bitter gibe, have been invariably leveled against the black man—never against the black woman! On the contrary, she has . . . everywhere been extolled and eulogized. . . .

Everywhere, even in the domains of slavery, how tenderly has the Negress been spoken of! She has been the nurse of childhood. To her all the cares and heart-griefs of youth have been entrusted. Thousands and tens of thousands in the West Indies and in our Southern states have risen up and told the tale of her tenderness, of her gentleness, patience and affection. No other woman in the world has ever had such tributes to a high moral nature, sweet, gentle love and unchanged devotedness. And by the memory of my own mother and dearest sisters I can declare it to be true!

Hear the tribute of Michelet: [6]

> The Negress, of all others, is the most loving, the most generating; and this, not only because of her youthful blood, but we must also admit, for the richness of her heart. She is loving among the loving, good among the good (ask the travelers whom she has so often saved). Goodness is creative, it is fruitfulness, it is the very benediction of a holy act. The fact that woman is so fruitful I attribute to her treasures of tenderness, to that ocean of goodness which permeates her heart. . . . Africa is a woman. Her races are feminine. . . . In many of the

black tribes of Central Africa the women rule, and they are as intelligent as they are amiable and kind.

The reference in Michelet to the generosity of the African woman to travelers brings to mind the incident in Mungo Park's travels,[7] where the African women fed, nourished and saved him. The men had driven him away. They would not even allow him to feed with the cattle; and so, faint, weary and despairing, he went to a remote hut and lay down on the earth to die. One woman, touched with compassion, came to him, brought him food and milk, and at once he revived. Then he tells us of the solace and the assiduities of these gentle creatures for his comfort. I give you his own words:

> The rites of hospitality thus performed toward a stranger in distress, my worthy benefactress, pointing to the mat, and telling me that I might sleep there without apprehension, called to the female part of her family which had stood gazing on me all the while in fixed astonishment, to resume the task of spinning cotton, in which they continued to employ themselves a great part of the night. They lightened their labors by songs, one of which was composed extempore, for I was myself the subject of it. It was sung by one of the young women, the rest joining in a sort of chime. The air was sweet and plaintive, and the words, literally translated, were these: "The winds roared and the rains fell; the poor white man, faint and weary, came and sat under our tree. He has no mother to bring him milk, no wife to grind his corn. Let us pity the white man, no mother has he."

Perhaps I may be pardoned the intrusion, just here, on my own personal experience. During a residence of nigh twenty years in West Africa, I saw the beauty and felt the charm of the native female character. I saw the native woman in her heathen state, and was delighted to see, in numerous tribes, that extraordinary sweetness, gentleness, docility, modesty, and especially those maternal solicitudes which make every African boy both gallant and [a] defender of his mother.

I saw her in her civilized state in Sierra Leone —saw precisely the same characteristics, but heightened, dignified, refined and sanctified by the training of the schools, the refinements of civilization and the graces of Christian sentiment

and feeling. Of all the memories of foreign travel there are none more delightful than those of the families and the female friends of Freetown.

A French traveler speaks with great admiration of the black ladies of Hayti. "In the towns," he says, "I met all the charms of civilized life. The graces of the ladies of Port-au-Prince will never be effaced from my recollections." [8]

It was, without doubt, the instant discernment of these fine and tender qualities which prompted the touching sonnet of Wordsworth, written in 1802, on the occasion of the cruel exile of Negroes from France by the French government: [9]

> Driven from the soil of France, a female came
>   From Calais with us, brilliant in array,
>   A Negro woman, like a lady gay,
> Yet downcast as a woman fearing blame;
> Meek, destitute, as seemed, of hope or aim
>   She sat, from notice turning not away,
>   But on all proffered intercourse did lay
> A weight of languid speech—or at the same
> Was silent, motionless in eyes and face.
>   Meanwhile those eyes retained their tropic fire,
> That, burning independent of the mind,
>   Joined with the lustre of her rich attire
> To mock the outcast—O ye heavens, be kind!
> And feel, thou earth, for this afflicted race!

But I must remember that I am to speak not only of the neglects of the black woman, but also of her needs. And the consideration of her needs suggests the remedy which should be used for the uplifting of this woman from a state of brutality and degradation.

I have two or three plans to offer which, I feel assured, if faithfully used, will introduce widespread and ameliorating influences amid this large population.

The first of these is specially adapted to the adult female population of the South, and is designed for more immediate effect. I ask for the equipment and the mission of "sisterhoods" to the black women of the South. I wish to see large numbers of practical Christian women—women of intelligence and piety, women well trained in domestic economy, women who combine delicate sensibility and refinement with industrial acquaintance—scores of such women to go South, to enter every Southern state, to visit "Uncle Tom's Cabin," to sit down with "Aunt Chloe" and her daughters, to show and teach them the ways and habits of thrift, economy, neatness and order, to gather them into "mothers' meetings" and sewing schools, and by both lectures and "talks" guide these women and their daughters into the modes and habits of clean and orderly housekeeping.

There is no other way, it seems to me, to bring about this domestic revolution. We cannot postpone this reformation to another generation. Postponement is the reproduction of the same evils in numberless daughters now coming up into life, imitators of the crude and untidy habits of their neglected mothers and the perpetuation of plantation life to another generation. No, the effect must be made immediately, in *this* generation, with the rude, rough, neglected women of the times.

And it is to be done at their own homes, in their own huts. In this work all theories are useless. This is a practical need, and as personal as practical. It is emphatically a personal work. It is to be done by example. The "sister of mercy," putting aside all fastidiousness, is to enter the humble and, perchance, repulsive cabin of her black sister and, gaining her confidence, is to lead her out of the crude, disordered and miserable ways of her plantation life into neatness, cleanliness, thrift and self-respect.

In every community women could be found who would gladly welcome such gracious visitations and instructors and seize with eagerness their lessons and teachings. Soon their neighbors would seek the visitations which had lifted up friends and kinsfolk from inferiority and wretchedness. And then, erelong, whole communities would crave the benediction of these inspiring sisterhoods, and thousands and tens of thousands would hail the advent of these missionaries in their humble cabins. And then, the seed of a new and orderly life planted in a few huts and localities, it would soon spread abroad, through the principle of imitation, and erelong, like the banyan tree, the beneficent work would spread far and wide through large populations.

Doubtless they would be received, first of all, with surprise, for neither they nor their mothers, for two hundred years, have known the solicitudes of the great and cultivated for their domestic comfort. But surprise would soon give way

to joy and exultation. Mrs. Fanny Kemble Butler,[10] in her work *Journal of a Residence on a Georgian Plantation in 1838–1839* [New York, 1863], tells us of the amazement of the wretched slave women on her husband's plantation when she went among them and tried to improve their quarters and to raise them above squalor, and then of their immediate joy and gratitude.

There is nothing original in the suggestion I make for the "sisters of mercy." It is no idealistic and impractical scheme I am proposing, no new-fangled notion that I put before you. The Roman Catholic church has, for centuries, been employing the agency of women in the propagation of her faith and as dispensers of charity. The Protestants of Germany are noted for the effective labors of holy women, not only in the Fatherland but in some of the most successful missions among the heathen in modern times. The Church of England, in that remarkable revival which has lifted her up, as by a tidal wave, from the dead passivity of the last century to an apostolic zeal and fervor never before known in her history, has shown as one of her main characteristics the wonderful power of sisterhoods, not only in the conversion of reprobates, but in the reformation of whole districts of abandoned men and women. This agency has been one of the most effective instrumentalities in the hands of that special school of devoted men called "Ritualists." [11]

Women of every class in that church, many of humble birth and as many more from the ranks of the noble, have left home and friends and the choicest circles of society and given up their lives to the lowliest service of the poor and miserable. They have gone down into the very slums of her great cities, among thieves and murderers and harlots, amid filth and disease and pestilence, and for Christ's sake served and washed and nursed the most repulsive wretches —and then have willingly laid [*sic*] down and died, either exhausted by their labors or poisoned by infectious disease. Anyone who will read the life of "Sister Dora" and of Charles Lowder[12] will see the glorious illustrations of my suggestion. Why cannot this be done for the black women of the South?

My second suggestion is as follows, and it reaches over to the future. I am anxious for a permanent and uplifting civilization to be engrafted on the Negro race in this land. And this can only be secured through the womanhood of a race. If you want the civilization of a people to reach the very best elements of their being, and then, having reached them, there to abide as an indigenous principle, you must imbue the womanhood of that people with all its elements and qualities. Any movement which passes by the female sex is an ephemeral thing. Without them, no true nationality, patriotism, religion, cultivation, family life or true social status is a possibility. In *this* matter it takes two to make one: mankind is a duality. The male may bring, as an exotic, a foreign graft, say of a civilization, to a new people. But what then? Can a graft live or thrive of itself? By no manner of means. It must get vitality from the stock into which it is put; and it is the women who give the sap to every human organization which thrives and flourishes on earth.

I plead, therefore, for the establishment of at least one large "industrial school" in every Southern state for the black girls of the South. I ask for the establishment of schools which may serve especially the home life of the rising womanhood of my race. I am not soliciting for these girls scholastic institutions, seminaries for the cultivation of elegance, conservatories of music and schools of classical and artistic training. I want such schools and seminaries for the women of my race as much as any other race; and I am glad that there are such schools and colleges, and that scores of colored women are students within their walls.

But this higher style of culture is not what I am aiming after for *this* great need. I am seeking something humbler, more homelike and practical, in which the education of the land and the use of the body shall be the specialties, and where the intellectual training will be the incident.

Let me state just here definitely what I want for the black girls of the South:

1. I want boarding schools for the *industrial training* of one hundred and fifty or two hundred of the poorest girls, of the ages of twelve to eighteen years.

2. I wish the *intellectual* training to be limited to reading, writing, arithmetic and geography.

3. I would have these girls taught to do accurately all domestic work, such as sweeping floors, dusting rooms, scrubbing, bedmaking, washing and ironing, sewing, mending and knitting.

4. I would have the trades of dressmaking, millinery, straw-plaiting, tailoring for men, and such like, taught them.

5. The art of cooking should be made a specialty, and every girl should be instructed in it.

6. In connection with these schools, garden plots should be cultivated, and every girl should be required daily to spend at least an hour in learning the cultivation of small fruits, vegetables and flowers.

I am satisfied that the expense of establishing such schools would be insignificant. As to their maintenance, there can be no doubt that, rightly managed, they would in a brief time be self-supporting. Each school would soon become a hive of industry and a source of income. But the good they would do is the main consideration. Suppose that the time of a girl's schooling be limited to three, or perchance to two years. It is hardly possible to exaggerate either the personal family or society influence which would flow from these schools. Every class, yea, every girl in an outgoing class, would be a missionary of thrift, industry, common sense and practicality. They would go forth, year by year, a leavening power into the houses, towns and villages of the Southern black population—girls fit to be thrifty wives of the honest peasantry of the South, the worthy matrons of their numerous households.

I am looking after the domestic training of the *masses*, for the raising up [of] women meet to be the helpers of *poor* men, the *rank and file* of black society, all through the rural districts of the South. The city people and the wealthy can seek more ambitious schools and should pay for them.

Ladies and gentlemen, since the day of emancipation millions of dollars have been given by the generous Christian people of the North for the intellectual training of the black race in this land. Colleges and universities have been built in the South, and hundreds of youth have been gathered within their walls. . . . The complement to all this generous and ennobling effort is the elevation of the black woman.

Up to this day and time, your noble philanthropy has touched, for the most part, the male population of the South, given them superiority and stimulated them to higher aspirations. But a true civilization can only then be attained when the life of woman is reached—her whole being permeated by noble ideas, her fine taste enriched by culture, her tendencies to the beautiful gratified and developed, her singular and delicate nature lifted up to its full capacity; and then, when all these qualities are fully matured, cultivated and sanctified, all their sacred influences shall circle around ten thousand firesides, and the cabins of the humblest freedmen shall become the homes of Christian refinement and of domestic elegance through the . . . uplifted and cultivated black woman of the South!

—1881

Editor's Reference Notes

[1] Shakespeare, *Julius Caesar*, Act III, scene 2.

[2] William Cowper, *The Task*, Book II. The passage reads:

> Slaves cannot breathe in England, if their lungs
> Receive our air, that moment they are free;
> They touch our country, and their shackles fall.

[3] This was the Rev. William Ellery Channing (1780–1842), of Boston, the famous author and Unitarian minister. Although Dr. Channing was not actually a member of an abolitionist group, his writings and sermons furthered the antislavery cause. This passage is from: Channing, "Emancipation," *Works* (Boston, 1875).

[4] This refers to: Henry Nelson Coleridge (1798–1843), nephew of the English poet Samuel Taylor Coleridge and author of the book *Six Months in the West Indies in 1825* (London, 1826); Anthony Trollope (1815–1882), the English novelist, who traveled in the West Indies and North America; and Sir Richard Burton (1821–1890), the English explorer and traveler, and translator of the *Arabian Nights*, who spent much time in Africa.

[5] Dr. James Hunt, president of the Anthropological Society of London, in November 1863 read a paper to the society in which he referred to the Negro's supposed inferiority ("The Negro's Place in Nature," *Memoirs of the Anthropological Society*, I [London, 1863]). George B. Gliddon, an American, collaborated with Dr. Josiah Clark Nott in the latter's writings on racial types.

[6] Jules Michelet (1798–1874), the great French historian, in his work *Woman* (*La Femme* [Paris, 1859]).

[7] Mungo Park (1771–1806), a Scotsman, was an early explorer of Africa, who in 1799 published his *Travels in the Interior of Africa*.

[8] John Bigelow, *Jamaica in 1850* (New York, 1851).

[9] William Wordsworth, sonnet known as "September 1, 1802."

[10] Fanny Kemble (1809–1893), the English actress, daughter of the actor Charles Kemble, married Pierce Butler, an American who owned an estate in Georgia. She was horrified by the circumstances in which her husband's slaves lived, and did what little she could to improve their condition. Eventually she parted with her husband. During the Civil War, Fanny Kemble lived in England, where her writing against slavery appeared in *The Times*.

[11] This was a term applied to those members of the Church of England who followed the Oxford Movement, which from about 1833 onward advocated a return to High Anglican rituals and institutions.

[12] "Sister Dora" (Dorothy Wyndlow Pattison [1832–1878]), an Englishwoman and the daughter of a clergyman, entered a sisterhood in 1864. She studied nursing and devoted herself to hospital work among the miners and factory workers. In 1875 she had charge of Walsall Epidemic Hospital, in Birmingham, England, in which the major illness was smallpox. Charles Fuge Lowder (1820–1880), a London clergyman, who worked among poor parishioners and who advocated High Church rituals at a time when they were unpopular, won his flock over by his devoted work among them—particularly during the cholera epidemic of the 1860's.

The Future of the Negro

Frederick Douglass

IT WOULD require the ken of a statesman and the vision of a prophet combined to tell with certainty what will be the ultimate future of the colored people of the United States, and to neither of these qualifications can I lay claim. We have known the colored man long as a slave, but we have not known him long as a freeman and as an American citizen. What he was as a slave we know; what he will be in his new relation to his fellowmen, time and events will make clear. One thing, however, may safely be laid down as probable, and that is that the Negro, in one form and complexion or another, may be counted upon as a permanent element of the population of the United States. He is now seven millions, has doubled his number in thirty years and is increasing more rapidly than the more favored population of the South. The idea of his becoming extinct finds no support in this fact. But will he emigrate? No! Individuals may, but the masses will not. Dust will fly, but the earth will remain. The expense of removal to a foreign land, the difficulty of finding a country where the conditions of existence are more favorable than here, attachment to native land, gradual improvement in moral surroundings, increasing hope of a better future, improvement in character and value by education, impossibility of finding any part of the globe free from the presence of white men —all conspire to keep the Negro here and compel him to adjust himself to American civilization.

In the face of history I do not deny that a darker future than I have indicated may await the black man. Contact of weak races with strong has not always been beneficent. The weak have been oppressed, persecuted, driven out and destroyed. The Hebrews in Egypt, the Moors in Spain, the Caribs in the West Indies, the Picts in Scotland, the Indians and Chinese in our own country, show what may happen to the Negro. But happily he has a moral and political hold upon this country, deep and firm—one which in some measure destroys the analogy between him and other weak peoples and classes.

His religion and civilization are in harmony with those of the people among whom he lives. He worships with them in a common temple and at a common altar, and to drag him away is to destroy the temple and tear down the altar. Drive out the Negro and you drive out Christ, the Bible and American liberty with him. The thought of setting apart a state or territory and confining the Negro within its borders is a delusion. If the North and South could not live separately in peace, and without bloody and barbarous border wars, the white and black cannot. If the Negro could be bottled up, who could or would bottle up the irrepressible white man? What barrier has been strong enough to confine him? Plainly enough, migration is no policy for the Negro. He would invite the fate of the Indian and be pushed away before the white man's bayonet.

Nor do I think that the Negro will become more distinct as a class. Ignorant, degraded and repulsive as he was during his two hundred years of slavery, he was sufficiently attractive to make possible an intermediate race of a million, more or less. If this has taken place in the face of those odious barriers, what is likely to occur when the colored man puts away his ignorance and degradation and becomes educated and prosperous? The tendency of the age is unification, not isolation—not to clans and classes, but to human brotherhood. It was once degradation intensified for a Norman to associate with a Saxon; but time and events have swept down the barriers between them, and Norman and Saxon have become Englishmen. The Jew was once despised and hated in Europe, and is so still in some parts of that continent; but he has risen, and is rising to higher consideration, and no man is now degraded by association with him anywhere. In like manner the Negro will rise in social scale.

For a time the social and political privileges of the colored people may decrease. This, however, will be apparent rather than real. An abnormal condition, born of war, carried him to an altitude unsuited to his attainments. He could not sustain himself there. He will now rise naturally and gradually and hold onto what he gets, and will not drop from dizziness. He will gain both by concession and by self-assertion. Shrinking cowardice wins nothing from either meanness or magnanimity. Manly self-assertion and eternal vigilance are essential to Negro liberty, not less than to that of the white man.

—1884

A Slave among Slaves

Booker T. Washington

I WAS BORN a slave on a plantation in Franklin County, Virginia. I am not quite sure of the exact place or exact date of my birth, but at any rate I suspect I must have been born somewhere and at some time. As nearly as I have been able to learn, I was born near a crossroads post office called Hale's Ford, and the year was 1858 or 1859. I do not know the month or the day. The earliest impressions I can now recall are of the plantation and the slave quarters—the latter being the part of the plantation where the slaves had their cabins.

My life had its beginning in the midst of the most miserable, desolate and discouraging surroundings. This was so, however, not because my owners were especially cruel, for they were not, as compared with many others. I was born in a typical log cabin, about fourteen by sixteen feet square. In this cabin I lived with my mother and a brother and sister till after the Civil War, when we were all declared free.

Of my ancestry I know almost nothing. In the slave quarters, and even later, I heard whispered conversations among the colored people of the tortures which the slaves, including, no doubt, my ancestors on my mother's side, suffered in the middle passage of the slave ship while being conveyed from Africa to America. I have been unsuccessful in securing any information that would throw any accurate light upon the history of my family beyond my mother. She, I remember, had a half-brother and a half-sister. In the days of slavery not very much attention was given to family history and family records—that is, black family records. My mother, I suppose, attracted the attention of a purchaser who was afterward my owner and hers. Her addition to the slave family attracted about as much attention as the purchase of a new horse or cow.

Of my father I know even less than of my mother. I do not even know his name. I have heard reports to the effect that he was a white man who lived on one of the nearby plantations. Whoever he was, I never heard of his taking the least interest in me or providing in any way for my rearing. But I do not find especial fault with him. He was simply another unfortunate victim of the institution which the nation unhappily had engrafted upon it at that time.

The cabin was not only our living place, but was also used as the kitchen for the plantation. My mother was the plantation cook. The cabin was without glass windows; it had only openings in the side which let in the light, and also the cold, chilly air of winter. There was a door to the cabin—that is, something that was called a door—but the uncertain hinges by which it was hung and the large cracks in it, to say nothing of the fact that it was too small, made the room a very uncomfortable one. In addition to these openings there was, in the lower right-hand corner of the room, the "cat-hole"—a contrivance which almost every mansion or cabin in Virginia possessed during the antebellum period. The cat-hole was a square opening, about seven by eight inches, provided for the purpose of letting the cat pass in and out of the house at will during the night. In the case of our particular cabin I could never understand the necessity for this convenience, since there were at least a half-dozen other places in the cabin that would have accommodated the cats.

There was no wooden floor in our cabin, the naked earth being used as a floor. In the center of the earthen floor there was a large, deep opening covered with boards, which was used as a place in which to store sweet potatoes during the winter. An impression of this potato-hole is very distinctly engraved upon my memory, because I recall that during the process of putting the potatoes in or taking them out I would often come into possession of one or two, which I roasted and thoroughly enjoyed. There was no cooking-stove on our plantation, and all the cooking for the whites and slaves my mother had to do over an open fireplace, mostly in pots and "skillets." While the poorly built cabin caused us to suffer with cold in the winter, the heat from the open fireplace in summer was equally trying.

The early years of my life, which were spent in the little cabin, were not very different from those of thousands of other slaves. My mother, of course, had little time in which to give attention to the training of her children during the day. She snatched a few moments for our care in the early morning before her work began and at night after the day's work was done. One of my earliest recollections is that of my mother cooking a chicken late at night and awakening her children for the purpose of feeding them. How or where she got it I do not know. I presume, however, it was procured from our owner's farm. Some people may call this theft. If such a thing were to happen now, I should condemn it as theft myself. But taking place at the time it did, and for the reason that it did, no one could ever make me believe that my mother was guilty of thieving. She was simply a victim of the system of slavery.

I cannot remember having slept in a bed until after our family was declared free by the Emancipation Proclamation. Three children—John, my older brother, Amanda, my sister, and myself—had a pallet on the dirt floor, or, to be more correct, we slept in and on a bundle of filthy rags laid upon the dirt floor.

I was asked not long ago to tell something about the sports and pastimes that I engaged in during my youth. Until that question was asked it had never occurred to me that there was no period of my life that was devoted to play. From the time that I can remember anything, almost every day of my life has been occupied in some kind of labor, though I think I would now be a more useful man if I had had time for sports. During the period that I spent in slavery I was not large enough to be of much service; still I was occupied most of the time in cleaning the yards, carrying water to the men in the fields, or going to the mill, to which I used to take the corn once a week to be ground. The mill was about three miles from the plantation.

This work I always dreaded. The heavy bag of corn would be thrown across the back of the horse and the corn divided about evenly on each side; but in some way, almost without exception, on these trips the corn would shift as to become unbalanced and would fall off the horse, and often I would fall with it. As I was not strong enough to reload the corn upon the horse, I would have to wait, sometimes for many hours, till a chance passerby came along who would help me out of my trouble. The hours while waiting for someone were usually spent in crying.

The time consumed in this way made me late in reaching the mill, and by the time I got my corn ground and reached home it would be far into the night. The road was a lonely one and often led through dense forests. I was always frightened. The woods were said to be full of soldiers who had deserted from the army, and I had been told that the first thing a deserter did to a Negro boy when he found him alone was to cut off his ears. Besides, when I was late in getting home I knew I would always get a severe scolding or a flogging.

I had no schooling whatever while I was a slave, though I remember on several occasions I went as far as the schoolhouse door with one of my young mistresses to carry her books. The picture of several dozen boys and girls in a schoolroom engaged in study made a deep impression upon me, and I had the feeling that to get into a schoolhouse and study in this way would be about the same as getting into paradise.

So far as I can now recall, the first knowledge that I got of the fact that we were slaves, and that freedom of the slaves was being discussed, was early one morning before day, when I was awakened by my mother kneeling over her children and fervently praying that Lincoln and his armies might be successful and that one day she and her children might be free.

In this connection I have never been able to understand how the slaves throughout the South, completely ignorant as were the masses so far as books or newspapers were concerned, were able to keep themselves so accurately and completely informed about the great national questions that were agitating the country. From the time that Garrison,[1] Lovejoy[2] and others began to agitate for freedom, the slaves throughout the South kept in close touch with the progress of the movement. Though I was a mere child during the preparation for the Civil War and during the War itself, I now recall the many late-at-night whispered discussions that I heard my mother and the other slaves on the plantation indulge in. These discussions showed that they understood the situation and that they kept themselves informed of events by what was termed the "grapevine telegraph."

During the campaign when Lincoln was first a candidate for the Presidency, the slaves on our far-off plantation, miles from any railroad or large city or daily newspaper, knew what the issues involved were. When war was begun between the North and the South, every slave on our plantation felt and knew that, though other issues were discussed, the primal one was that of slavery. Even the most ignorant members of my race on the remote plantations felt in their hearts, with a certainty that admitted of no doubt, that the freedom of the slaves would be the one great result of the War, if the Northern armies conquered. Every success of the federal armies and every defeat of the Confederate forces was watched with the keenest and most intense interest. Often the slaves got knowledge of the results of great battles before the white people received it. This news was usually gotten from the colored man who was sent to the post office for the mail.

In our case the post office was about three miles from the plantation and the mail came once or twice a week. The man who was sent to the office would linger about the place long enough to get the drift of the conversation from the group of white people who naturally congregated there, after receiving their mail, to discuss the latest news. The mail-carrier on his way back to our master's house would as naturally retail the news that he had secured among the slaves, and in this way they often heard of important events before the white people at the "big house," as the master's house was called.

I cannot remember a single instance during my childhood or early boyhood when our entire family sat down to the table together, and God's blessing was asked, and the family ate a meal in a civilized manner. On the plantation in Virginia, and even later, meals were gotten by the children very much as dumb animals get theirs. It was a piece of bread here and a scrap of meat there. It was a cup of milk at one time and some potatoes at another. Sometimes a portion of our family would eat out of the skillet or pot, while someone would eat from a tin plate held on the knees, and often using nothing but the hands with which to hold the food.

When I had grown to sufficient size, I was required to go to the big house at mealtimes to fan the flies from the table by means of a large set of paper fans operated by a pulley. Naturally much of the conversation of the white people turned upon the subject of freedom and the War, and I absorbed a good deal of it. I remember that at one time I saw two of my young mistresses and some lady visitors eating ginger-cakes in the yard. At that time those cakes seemed to me to be absolutely the most tempting and desirable things that I had ever seen; and I then and there resolved that, if I ever got free, the height of my ambition would be reached if I could get to the point where I could secure and eat ginger-cakes in the way that I saw those ladies doing.

Of course, as the War was prolonged, the white people in many cases often found it difficult to secure food for themselves. I think the slaves felt the deprivation less than the white, because the usual diet for the slaves was corn bread and pork, and these could be raised on the plantation; but coffee, tea, sugar and other articles which the whites had been accustomed to use could not be raised on the plantation, and the conditions brought about by the War frequently made it impossible to secure these things. The whites were often in great straits. Parched corn was used for coffee, and a kind of black molasses was used instead of sugar. Many times nothing was used to sweeten the so-called tea and coffee.

The first pair of shoes that I recall wearing were wooden ones. They had rough leather on the top, but the bottoms, which were about an inch thick, were of wood. When I walked they made a fearful noise, and besides this they were very inconvenient, since there was no yielding to the natural pressure of the foot. In wearing them one presented an exceedingly awkward appearance.

The most trying ordeal that I was forced to endure as a slave boy, however, was the wearing of a flax shirt. In the portion of Virginia where I lived it was common to use flax as part of the clothing for the slaves. That part of the flax from which our clothing was made was largely the refuse, which of course was the cheapest and roughest part. I can scarcely imagine any torture, except, perhaps, the pulling of a tooth, that is equal to that caused by putting on a new flax shirt for the first time. It is almost equal to the feeling that one would experience if he had a dozen or more chestnut burrs, or a hundred small pin-points, in contact with his flesh. Even to this day I can recall accurately the tortures that I underwent when putting on one of these garments. The fact that my flesh was soft and tender added to the pain. But I had no choice. I had to wear the flax shirt or none; and had it been left to me to choose, I should have chosen to wear no covering. In connection with the flax shirt, my brother John, who is several years older than I am, performed one of the most generous acts that I ever heard of one slave relative doing for another. On several occasions when I was being forced to wear a new flax shirt, he generously agreed to put it on in my stead and wear it for several days till it was "broken in." Until I had grown to be quite a youth this single garment was all that I wore.

One may get the idea from what I have said that there was bitter feeling toward the white people on the part of my race, because of the fact that most of the white population was away fighting in a war which would result in keeping the Negro in slavery if the South was successful. In the case of the slaves on our place this was

not true, and it was not true of any large portion of the slave population in the South where the Negro was treated with anything like decency. During the Civil War one of my young masters was killed, and two were severely wounded. I recall the feeling of sorrow which existed among the slaves when they heard of the death of "Mars' Billy." It was no sham sorrow but real. Some of the slaves had nursed Mars' Billy; others had played with him when he was a child. Mars' Billy had begged for mercy in the case of others when the overseer or master was thrashing them. The sorrow in the slave quarter was only second to that in the big house.

When the two young masters were brought home wounded, the sympathy of the slaves was shown in many ways. They were just as anxious to assist in the nursing as the family relatives of the wounded. Some of the slaves would even beg for the privilege of sitting up at night to nurse their wounded masters.

This tenderness and sympathy on the part of those held in bondage was a result of their kindly and generous nature. In order to defend and protect the women and children who were left on the plantations when the white males went to war, the slaves would have laid down their lives. The slave who was selected to sleep in the big house during the absence of the males was considered to have the place of honor. Anyone attempting to harm "young Mistress" or "old Mistress" during the night would have had to cross the dead body of the slave to do so. I do not know how many have noticed it, but I think that it will be found to be true that there are few instances, either in slavery or freedom, in which a member of my race has been known to betray a specific trust.

As a rule, not only did the members of my race entertain no feelings of bitterness against the whites before and during the War, but there are many instances of Negroes tenderly caring for their former masters and mistresses who for some reason have become poor and dependent since the War. I know of instances where the former masters of slaves have for years been supplied with money by their former slaves to keep them from suffering. I have known of still other cases in which the former slaves have assisted in the education of the descendants of their former owners.

I know of a case on a large plantation in the South in which a young white man, the son of the former owner of the estate, has become so reduced in purse and self-control by reason of drink that he is a pitiable creature; and yet, notwithstanding the poverty of the colored people themselves on this plantation, they have for years supplied this young white man with the necessities of life. One sends him a little coffee or sugar, another a little meat, and so on. Nothing that the colored people possess is too good for the son of "old Mars' Tom," who will perhaps never be permitted to suffer while any remain on the place who knew directly or indirectly of old Mars' Tom.

I have said that there are few instances of a member of my race betraying a specific trust. One of the best illustrations of this which I know of is in the case of an ex-slave from Virginia whom I met not long ago in a little town in the state of Ohio. I found that this man had made a contract with his master two or three years previous to the Emancipation Proclamation, to the effect that the slave was to be permitted to buy himself by paying so much per year for his body; and while he was paying for himself, he was to be permitted to labor where and for whom he pleased. Finding that he could secure better wages in Ohio, he went there.

When freedom came, he was still in debt to his master some three hundred dollars. Notwithstanding that the Emancipation Proclamation freed him from any obligation to his master, this black man walked the greater portion of the distance back to where his old master lived in Virginia and placed the last dollar, with interest, in his hands. In talking to me about this, the man told me that he knew that he did not have to pay the debt but that he had given his word to his master, and his word he had never broken. He felt that he could not enjoy his freedom till he had fulfilled his promise.

From some things that I have said one may get the idea that some of the slaves did not want freedom. This is not true. I have never seen one who did not want to be free, or one who would return to slavery.

I pity from the bottom of my heart any nation or body of people that is so unfortunate as to get entangled in the net of slavery. I have long since ceased to cherish any spirit of bitterness against the Southern white people on account of the enslavement of my race. No one section of our country was wholly responsible for its introduction, and, besides, it was recognized and protected for years by the general government. Having once got its tentacles fastened onto the economic and social life of the Republic, it was no easy matter for the country to relieve itself of the institution.

Then, when we rid ourselves of prejudice or racial feeling and look facts in the face, we must acknowledge that notwithstanding the cruelty and moral wrong of slavery, the ten million Negroes inhabiting this country who themselves or whose ancestors went through the school of American slavery are in a stronger and more hopeful condition materially, intellectually, morally and religiously than is true of an equal number of black people in any other portion of the globe. This is so to such an extent that Negroes in this country who themselves or whose forefathers went through the school of slavery, are constantly returning to Africa as missionaries to enlighten those who remained in the fatherland.

This I say not to justify slavery—on the other hand, I condemn it as an institution, as we all know that in America it was established for selfish and financial reasons, and not from a missionary motive—but to call attention to a fact, and to show how Providence so often uses men and institutions to accomplish a purpose. When persons ask me in these days how, in the midst of what sometimes seem hopelessly discouraging conditions, I can have such faith in the future of my race in this country, I remind them of the wilderness through which and out of which a good Providence has already led us.

Ever since I have been old enough to think for myself I have entertained the idea that, notwithstanding the cruel wrongs inflicted upon us, the black man got nearly as much out of slavery as the white man did. The hurtful influences of the institution were not by any means confined to the Negro. This was fully illustrated by the life upon our own plantation. The whole machinery of slavery was so constructed as to cause labor, as a rule, to be looked upon as a badge of degradation, of inferiority. Hence labor was something that both races on the slave plantation sought to escape.

The slave system on our place, in a large measure, took the spirit of self-reliance and self-help out of the white people. My old master had many boys and girls, but not one, so far as I know, ever mastered a single trade or special line of productive industry. The girls were not taught to cook, sew or to take care of the house. All of this was left to the slaves. The slaves, of course, had little personal interest in the life of the plantation, and their ignorance prevented them from learning how to do things in the most improved and thorough manner. As a result of the system, fences were out of repair, gates were hanging half off the hinges, doors creaked, window-panes were out, plastering had fallen but was not replaced, weeds grew in the yard.

As a rule there was food for whites and blacks, but inside the house, and on the dining room table, there was wanting that delicacy and refinement of touch and finish which can make a home the most convenient, comfortable and attractive place in the world. Withal, there was a waste of food and other materials which was sad.

When freedom came, the slaves were almost as well fitted to begin life anew as the master, except in the matter of book-learning and ownership of property. The slaveowner and his sons had mastered no special industry. They unconsciously had imbibed the feeling that manual labor was not the proper thing for them. On the other hand, the slaves in many cases had mastered some handicraft, and none were ashamed and few unwilling to labor.

Finally the War closed, and the day of freedom came. It was a momentous and eventful day to all upon our plantation. We had been expecting it. Freedom was in the air and had been for months. Deserting soldiers returning to their homes were to be seen every day. Others, who had been discharged or whose regiments had been paroled, were constantly passing near our place. The grapevine telegraph was kept busy night and day. The news and mutterings of great events were swiftly carried from one plantation to another. In the fear of "Yankee" invasions, the silverware and other valuables were taken from the big house, buried in the woods and guarded by trusted slaves. Woe be to anyone who would have attempted to disturb the buried treasure. The slaves would give the Yankee soldiers food, drink, clothing—anything but that which had been specifically entrusted to their care and honor.

As the great day drew nearer, there was more singing in the slave quarters than usual. It was bolder, had more ring and lasted later into the night. Most of the verses of the plantation songs had some reference to freedom. True, they had sung those same verses before, but they had been careful to explain that the "freedom" in these songs referred to the next world and had no connection with life in this world. Now they gradually threw off the mask and were not afraid to let it be known that the freedom in their songs meant freedom of the body in this world.

The night before the eventful day, word was sent to the slave quarters to the effect that something unusual was going to take place at the big house the next morning. There was little, if any, sleep that night. All was excitement and expectancy. Early the next morning word was sent to all the slaves, old and young, to gather at the house. In company with my mother, brother and sister, and a large number of other slaves, I went to the master's house. All of our master's family were either standing or seated on the veranda of the house, where they could see what was to take place and hear what was said. There was a feeling of deep interest, or perhaps sadness, on their faces, but not bitterness. As I now recall the impression they made upon me, they did not at the moment seem to be sad because of the loss of property, but rather because of parting with those whom they had reared and who were in many ways very close to them. The most distinct thing that I now recall in connection with the scene was that some man who seemed to be a stranger (a United States officer, I presume) made a little speech and then read a rather long paper—the Emancipation Proclamation, I think.

After the reading we were told that we were all free and could go when and where we pleased. My mother, who was standing by my side, leaned over and kissed her children, while tears of joy ran down her cheeks. She explained to us what it all meant, that this was the day for which she had been so long praying, but fearing that she would never live to see.

For some minutes there was great rejoicing and thanksgiving, and wild scenes of ecstasy. But there was no feeling of bitterness. In fact there was pity among the slaves for our former owners. The wild rejoicing on the part of the emancipated colored people lasted but for a brief period, for I noticed that by the time they returned to their cabins there was a change in their feelings. The great responsibility of being free, of having charge of themselves, of having to think and plan for themselves and their children, seemed to take possession of them. It was very much like suddenly turning a youth of ten or twelve years out into the world to provide for himself. In a few hours the great questions with which the Anglo-Saxon race had been grappling for centuries had been thrown upon these people to be solved. . . . the questions of a home, a living, the rearing of children, education, citizenship

From *Up from Slavery*

and the establishment and support of churches.

Was it any wonder that within a few hours the wild rejoicing ceased and a feeling of deep gloom seemed to pervade the slave quarters? To some it seemed that now that they were in actual possession of it freedom was a more serious thing than they had expected to find it. Some of the slaves were seventy or eighty years old; their best days were gone. They had no strength with which to earn a living in a strange place and among strange people, even if they had been sure where to find a new place of abode. To this class the problem seemed especially hard. Besides, deep down in their hearts there was a strange and peculiar attachment to "old Marster" and "old Missus" and to their children, which they found it hard to think of breaking off. With these they had spent in some cases nearly a half-century, and it was no light thing to think of parting. Gradually, one by one, stealthily at first, the older slaves began to wander from the slave quarters back to the big house to have a whispered conversation with their former owners as to the future.

—1900

Editor's Reference Notes

[1] William Lloyd Garrison (1805–1879), the abolitionist, editor of the *Liberator*.

[2] Elijah Parish Lovejoy (1802–1837), who edited a journal in St. Louis and later in Alton, Illinois, took a forthright stand against slavery, despite repeated threats of violence. His press was destroyed several times, and eventually he was killed by a mob.

Clotel in Slavery

William Wells Brown

The Negro Sale

WITH THE growing population of slaves in the Southern states of America, there is a fearful increase of half whites, most of whose fathers are slaveowners and their mothers slaves. Society does not frown upon the man who sits with his mulatto child upon his knee whilst its mother stands a slave behind his chair. The late Henry Clay, some years since, predicted that the abolition of Negro slavery would be brought about by the amalgamation of the races. John Randolph, a distinguished slaveholder of Virginia, and a prominent statesman, said in a speech in the legislature of his native state that "the blood of the first American statesmen coursed through the veins of the slave of the South." In all the cities and towns of the slave states, the real Negro, or clear black, does not amount to more than one in every four of the slave population. This fact is, of itself, the best evidence of the degraded and immoral condition of the relation of master and slave in the United States of America.

In all the slave states the law says:

> Slaves shall be deemed, sold, taken, reputed, and adjudged in law to be chattels personal in the hands of their owners and possessors, and their executors, administrators and assigns, to all intents, constructions, and purposes whatsoever.

A slave is one who is in the power of a master to whom he belongs. The master may sell him, dispose of his person, his industry and his labor. He can do nothing, possess nothing, nor acquire anything but what must belong to his master. The slave is entirely subject to the will of his master, who may correct and chastise him, though not with unusual rigor, or so as to maim and mutilate him, or expose him to the danger of loss of life, or to cause his death. The slave, to remain a slave, must be sensible that there is no appeal from his master.

Where the slave is placed by law entirely under the control of the man who claims him, body and soul, as property, what else could be expected than the most depraved social condition? The marriage relation, the oldest and most sacred institution given to man by his Creator, is unknown and unrecognized in the slave laws of the United States. Would that we could say that the moral and religious teaching in the slave states were better than the laws; but alas! we cannot. A few years since, some slaveholders became a little uneasy in their minds about the rightfulness of permitting slaves to take to themselves husbands and wives while they still had others living, and applied to their religious teachers for advice; and the following will show how this grave and important subject was treated:

> Is a servant, whose husband or wife has been sold by his or her master into a distant country, to be permitted to marry again?

The query was referred to a committee, who made the following report, which, after discussion, was adopted:

> That, in view of the circumstances in which servants in this country are placed, the committee are unanimous in the opinion that it is better to permit servants thus circumstanced to take another husband or wife.

Such was the answer from a committee of the Shiloh Baptist Association; and instead of receiving light, those who asked the question were plunged into deeper darkness!

A similar question was put to the Savannah River Association, and the answer, as the following will show, did not materially differ from the one we have already given:

Whether, in a case of involuntary separation, of such a character as to preclude all prospect of future intercourse, the parties ought to be allowed to marry again.

Answer:

That such separation among persons situated as our slaves are, is civilly a separation by death; and they believe that, in the sight of God, it would be so viewed. To forbid second marriages in such cases would be to expose the parties, not only to stronger hardships and strong temptation, but to church-censure for acting in obedience to their masters, who cannot be expected to acquiesce in a regulation at variance with justice to the slaves, and to the spirit of that command which regulates marriage among Christians. The slaves are not free agents; and a dissolution by death is not more entirely without their consent, and beyond their control, than by such separation.

Although marriage, as the above indicates, is a matter which the slaveholders do not think is of any importance or of any binding force with their slaves, yet it would be doing that degraded class an injustice not to acknowledge that many of them do regard it as a sacred obligation, and show a willingness to obey the commands of God on this subject. Marriage is, indeed, the first and most important institution of human existence—the foundation of all civilization and culture—the root of church and state. It is the most intimate covenant of heart formed among mankind, and, for many persons, the only relation in which they feel the true sentiments of humanity. It gives scope for every human virtue, since each of these is developed from the love and confidence which here predominate. It unites all which ennobles and beautifies life—sympathy, kindness of will and deed, gratitude, devotion and every delicate, intimate feeling. As the only asylum for true education, it is the first and last sanctuary of human culture. As husband and wife through each other become conscious of complete humanity, and every human feeling and every human virtue, so children, at their first awakening in the fond covenant of love between parents, both of whom are tenderly concerned for the same object, find an image of complete humanity leagued in free love. The spirit of love which prevails between them acts with creative power upon the young mind and awakens every germ of goodness within it. This invisible and incalculable influence of parental life acts more upon the child than all the efforts of education, whether by means of instruction, precept or exhortation. If this be a true picture of the vast influence for good of the institution of marriage, what must be the moral degradation of that people to whom marriage is denied? Not content with depriving them of all the higher and holier enjoyments of this relation, by degrading and darkening their souls the slaveholder denies to his victim even that slight alleviation of his misery which would result from the marriage relation being protected by law and public opinion. Such is the influence of slavery in the United States, that the ministers of religion, even in the so-called free states, are the mere echoes, instead of the correctors, of public sentiment.

We have thought it advisable to show that the present system of chattel slavery in America undermines the entire social condition of man, so as to prepare the reader for the following narrative of slave life in that otherwise happy and prosperous country.

In all the large towns in the Southern states there is a class of slaves who are permitted to hire their time of their owners, and for which they pay a high price. These are mulatto women, or quadroons, as they are familiarly known, and are distinguished for their fascinating beauty. The handsomest usually pays the highest price for her time. Many of these women are the favorites of persons who furnish them with the means of paying their owners, and not a few are dressed in the most extravagant manner. Reader, when you take into consideration the fact that amongst the slave population no safeguard is thrown around virtue, and no inducement held out to slave women to be chaste, you will not be surprised when we tell you that immorality and vice pervade the cities of the Southern states in a manner unknown in the cities and towns of the Northern states. Indeed, most of the slave women have no higher aspiration than that of becoming the finely dressed mistress of some white man. And at Negro balls and parties, this class of women usually cut the greatest figure.

At the close of the year ———, the following advertisement appeared in a newspaper published in Richmond, the capital of the state of Virginia:

Notice: Thirty-eight negroes will be offered for sale on Monday, November 10th, at twelve o'clock, being the entire stock of the late John Graves, Esq. The negroes are in good condition, some of them very prime; among them are several mechanics, able-bodied field hands, plow-boys, and women with children at the breast, and some of them very prolific in their generating qualities, affording a rare opportunity to anyone who wishes to raise a strong and healthy lot of servants for their own use. Also several mulatto girls of rare personal qualities: two of them very superior. Any gentleman or lady wishing to purchase, can take any of the above slaves on trial for a week, for which no charge will be made.

Amongst the above slaves to be sold were Currer and her two daughters, Clotel and Althesa; the latter were the girls spoken of in the advertisement as "very superior." Currer was a bright mulatto, and of prepossessing appearance, though then nearly forty years of age. She had hired her time for more than twenty years, during which time she had lived in Richmond. In her younger days Currer had been the housekeeper of a young slaveholder, but of later years had been a laundress or washerwoman, and was considered to be a woman of great taste in getting up linen. The gentleman for whom she had kept house was Thomas Jefferson, by whom she had two daughters. Jefferson being called to Washington to fill a government appointment, Currer was left behind, and thus she took herself to the business of washing, by which means she paid her master, Mr. Graves, and supported herself and two children.

At the time of the decease of her master, Currer's daughters, Clotel and Althesa, were aged respectively sixteen and fourteen years, and both, like most of their own sex in America, were well grown. Currer early resolved to bring her daughters up as ladies, as she termed it, and therefore imposed little or no work upon them. As her daughters grew older, Currer had to pay a stipulated price for them; yet her notoriety as a laundress of the first class enabled her to put an extra price upon her charges, and thus she and her daughters lived in comparative luxury. To bring up Clotel and Althesa to attract attention, and especially at balls and parties, was the great aim of Currer. Although the term "Negro ball" is applied to most of these gatherings, yet a majority of the attendants are often whites. Nearly all the Negro parties in the cities and towns of the Southern states are made up of quadroon and mulatto girls, and white men. These are democratic gatherings, where gentlemen, shopkeepers, and their clerks all appear upon terms of perfect equality. And there is a degree of gentility and decorum in these companies that is not surpassed by similar gatherings of white people in the Slave states.

It was at one of these parties that Horatio Green, the son of a wealthy gentleman of Richmond, was first introduced to Clotel. The young man had just returned from college, and was in his twenty-second year. Clotel was sixteen, and was admitted by all to be the most beautiful girl, colored or white, in the city. So attentive was the young man to the quadroon during the evening, that it was noticed by all and became a matter of general conversation—while Currer appeared delighted beyond measure at her daughter's conquest. From that evening, young Green became the favorite visitor at Currer's house. He soon promised to purchase Clotel as speedily as it could be effected, and make her mistress of her own dwelling; and Currer looked forward with pride to the time when she should see her daughter emancipated and free.

It was a beautiful moonlight night in August, when all who reside in tropical climes are eagerly gasping for a breath of fresh air, that Horatio Green was seated in the small garden behind Currer's cottage, with the object of his affections by his side. And it was here that Horatio drew from his pocket the newspaper, wet from the press, and read the advertisement for the sale of the slaves to which we have alluded—Currer and her two daughters being of the number. At the close of the evening's visit, and as the young man was leaving, he said to the girl, "You shall soon be free and your own mistress."

As might have been expected, the day of sale brought an unusually large number together to compete for the property to be sold. Farmers who make a business of raising slaves for the market were there; slave traders and speculators were also numerously represented. And in the midst of this throng was one who felt a deeper interest in the result of the sale than any other of the by-standers; this was young Green. True to his prom-ise, he was there with a blank bank check in his pocket, awaiting with impatience to enter the list as a bidder for the beautiful slave. The less val-uable slaves were first placed upon the auction block, one after another, and sold to the highest bidder. Husbands and wives were separated with a degree of indifference that is unknown in any other relation of life except that of slavery. Brothers and sisters were torn from each other, and mothers saw their children leave them for the last time on this earth.

It was late in the day, when the greatest num-ber of persons were thought to be present, that Currer and her daughters were brought forward to the place of sale. Currer was first ordered to ascend the auction stand, which she did with a trembling step. The slave mother was sold to a trader. Althesa, the youngest, and who was scarcely less beautiful than her sister, was sold to the same trader for one thousand dollars. Clotel was the last and, as was expected, com-manded a higher price than any that had been offered for sale that day.

The appearance of Clotel on the auction block created a deep sensation amongst the crowd. There she stood, with a complexion as white as most of those who were waiting with a wish to become her purchasers—her features as finely defined as any of her sex of pure Anglo-Saxon, her long, black, wavy hair done up in the neatest manner, her form tall and graceful and her whole appearance indicating one superior to her posi-tion. The auctioneer commenced by saying that Miss Clotel had been reserved for the last, be-cause she was the most valuable. "How much,

gentlemen? Real albino, fit for a fancy girl for anyone. She enjoys good health and has a sweet temper. How much do you say?"

"Five hundred dollars."

"Only five hundred for such a girl as this? Gen-tlemen, she is worth a deal more than that sum; you certainly don't know the value of the article you are bidding upon. Here, gentlemen, I hold in my hand a paper certifying that she has a good moral character."

"Seven hundred."

"Ah, gentlemen, that is something like. This paper also states that she is very intelligent."

"Eight hundred."

"She is a devoted Christian and perfectly trust-worthy."

"Nine hundred."

"Nine fifty."

"Ten."

"Eleven."

"Twelve hundred."

Here the sale came to a dead stand. The auctioneer stopped, looked around, and began in a rough manner to relate some anecdotes rela-tive to the sale of slaves, which, he said, had come under his own observation. At this juncture the scene was indeed strange. Laughing, joking, swearing, smoking, spitting and talking kept up a continual hum and noise amongst the crowd, while the slave girl stood with tears in her eyes, at one time looking towards her mother and sister and at another towards the young man whom she hoped would become her purchaser.

"The chastity of this girl is pure; she has never been from under her mother's care; she is a virtu-ous creature."

"Thirteen."

"Fourteen."

"Fifteen."

"Fifteen hundred dollars!" cried the auctioneer, and the maiden was struck for that sum.

This was a Southern auction, at which the bones, muscles, sinews, blood and nerves of a young lady of sixteen were sold for five hundred dollars; her moral character for two hundred; her improved intellect for one hundred; her Chris-tianity for four hundred; and her chastity and virtue for three hundred dollars more. And this, too, in a city thronged with churches, whose tall spires look like so many signals pointing to heaven, and whose ministers preach that slavery is a God-ordained institution!

What words can tell the inhumanity, the atrocity and the immorality of that doctrine which, from exalted office, commends such a crime to the favor of enlightened and Christian people? What indignation from all the world is not due to the government and people who put forth all their strength and power to keep in existence such an institution? Nature abhors it; the age repels it, and Christianity needs all her meekness to forgive it.

Clotel was sold for fifteen hundred dollars, but her purchaser was Horatio Green. Thus closed a Negro sale, at which two daughters of Thomas Jefferson, the writer of the Declaration of American Independence, and one of the presidents of the great republic, were disposed of to the highest bidder!

* * * * * *

Today a Mistress, Tomorrow a Slave

Let us return for a moment to the home of Clotel. While she was passing lonely and dreary hours with none but her darling child, Horatio Green was trying to find relief in that insidious enemy of man, the intoxicating cup. Defeated in politics, forsaken in love by his wife, he seemed to have lost all principle of honor, and was ready to nerve himself up to any deed, no matter how unprincipled. Clotel's existence was now well known to Horatio's wife, and . . . [she] and her father demanded that the beautiful quadroon and her child should be sold and sent out of the state.

To this proposition he at first turned a deaf ear; but when he saw that his wife was about to return to her father's roof, he consented to leave the matter in the hands of his father-in-law. The result was that Clotel was immediately sold to the slave trader Walker, who, a few years previous, had taken her mother and sister to the far South. But, as if to make her husband drink of the cup of humiliation to its very dregs, Mrs. Green resolved to take his child under her own roof for a servant. Mary was, therefore, put to the meanest work that could be found, and al-

though only ten years of age, she was often compelled to perform labor which under ordinary circumstances would have been thought too hard for one much older.

One condition of the sale of Clotel to Walker was that she should be taken out of the state, which was accordingly done. Most quadroon women who are taken to the lower countries to be sold are either purchased by gentlemen for their own use or sold for waiting-maids; and Clotel, like her sister, was fortunate enough to be bought for the latter purpose. The town of Vicksburg stands on the left bank of the Mississippi and is noted for the severity with which slaves are treated. It was here that Clotel was sold to Mr. James French, a merchant.

Mrs. French was severe in the extreme to her servants. Well dressed, but scantily fed, and overworked, were all who found a home with her. The quadroon had been in her new home but a short time ere she found that her situation was far different from what it was in Virginia. What social virtues are possible in a society of which injustice is the primary characteristic? In a society which is divided into two classes, masters and slaves? Every married woman in the far South looks upon her husband as unfaithful and regards every quadroon servant as a rival. Clotel had been with her new mistress but a few days when she was ordered to cut off her long hair. The Negro, constitutionally, is fond of dress and outward appearance. He that has short woolly hair combs it and oils it to death. He that has long hair would sooner have his teeth drawn than lose it. However painful it was to the quadroon, she was soon seen with her hair cut as short as any of the full-blooded Negroes in the dwelling.

Even with her short hair, Clotel was handsome. Her life had been a secluded one, and though now nearly thirty years of age, she was still beautiful. At her short hair, the other servants laughed.

"Miss Clo needn't strut round so big; she got short nappy har well as I," said Nell, with a broad grin that showed her teeth.

"She tinks she white, when she come here wid dat long har of hers," replied Mill.

"Yes," continued Nell, "missus make her take down her wool so she no put it up today."

The fairness of Clotel's complexion was regarded with envy, as well by the other servants as by the mistress herself. This is one of the hard features of slavery. Today the woman is mistress of her own cottage; tomorrow she is sold to one who aims to make her life as intolerable as possible. And be it remembered, that the house servant has the best situation which a slave can occupy.

Some American writers have tried to make the world believe that the condition of the laboring classes of England is as bad as [that of] the slaves of the United States. The English laborer may be oppressed; he may be cheated, defrauded, swindled, and even starved; but it is not slavery under which he groans. He cannot be sold; in point of law he is equal to the prime minister. It is easy to captivate the unthinking and the prejudiced, by eloquent declamation about the oppression of English operatives being worse than that of American slaves, and by exaggerating the wrongs on one side and hiding them on the other. But all informed and reflecting minds . . . [know] that bad as are the social evils of England, those of slavery are immeasurably worse.

But the degradation and harsh treatment that Clotel experienced in her new home was nothing compared with the grief she underwent at being separated from her dear child. Taken from her without scarcely a moment's warning, she knew not what had become of her. The deep and heartfelt grief of Clotel was soon perceived by her owners and, fearing that her refusal to take food would cause her death, they resolved to sell her. Mr. French found no difficulty in getting a purchaser for the quadroon woman, for such are usually the most marketable kind of property. Clotel was sold at private sale to a young man for a housekeeper. . . .

*   *   *   *   *

The Arrest

It was late in the evening when the coach arrived at Richmond and Clotel [disguised as a gentleman] once more alighted in her native city. She had intended to seek lodgings somewhere in the outskirts of the town, but the lateness of the hour compelled her to stop at one of the principal hotels for the night. She had scarcely entered the inn when she recognised among the numerous black servants one to whom she was well known, and her only hope was that her disguise would keep her from being discovered. The imperturbable calm and entire forgetfulness of self which induced Clotel to visit a place from which she could scarcely hope to escape, to attempt the rescue of a beloved child, demonstrate that overwillingness of woman to carry out the promptings of the finer feelings of her heart. True to woman's nature, she had risked her own liberty for another.

She remained in the hotel during the night, and the next morning, under the plea of illness, she took her breakfast alone. That day the fugitive slave paid a visit to the suburbs of the town and once more beheld the cottage in which she had spent so many happy hours. It was winter, and the clematis and passionflower were not there; but there were the same walks she had so often pressed with her feet, and the same trees which had so often shaded her as she passed through the garden at the back of the house. Old remembrances rushed upon her memory and caused her to shed tears freely.

Clotel was now in her native town and near her daughter; but how could she communicate with her? How could she see her? To have made herself known would have been a suicidal act; betrayal would have followed, and she [would have been] arrested. Three days had passed away, and Clotel still remained in the hotel at which she had first put up; and yet she had got no tidings of her child. Unfortunately for Clotel, a disturbance had just broken out amongst the slave population in the state of Virginia, and all strangers were eyed with suspicion.

The evils consequent on slavery are not lessened by the incoming of one or two rays of light. If the slave only becomes aware of his condition and conscious of the injustice under which he suffers, if he obtains but a faint idea of these things, he will seize the first opportunity to possess himself of what he conceives to belong to him. The infusion of Anglo-Saxon with African blood has created an insurrectionary feeling among the slaves of America hitherto unknown. Aware of their blood connection with their owners, these mulattoes labor under the sense of their personal and social injuries and tolerate, if they do not encourage in themselves, low and vindictive passions. On the other hand, the slaveowners are aware of their critical position and are ever watchful, always fearing an outbreak. . . .

True, the free states are equally bound with the slave states to suppress any insurrectionary movement that may take place among the slaves. The Northern freemen are bound by their constitutional obligations to aid the slaveholder in keeping his slaves in their chains. Yet there are, at the time we write, four millions of bond slaves in the United States. The insurrection to which we now refer was headed by a full-blooded Negro who had been born and brought up a slave. He had heard the twang of the driver's whip, and saw the warm blood streaming from the Negro's body; he had witnessed the separation of parents and children, and was made aware, by too many proofs, that the slave could expect no justice at the hand of the slaveowner. He went by the name of Nat Turner. He was a preacher amongst the Negroes, and distinguished for his eloquence, respected by the whites, and loved and venerated by the Negroes. On the discovery of the plan for the outbreak, Turner fled to the swamps, followed by those who had joined in the insurrection. Here the revolted Negroes numbered some hundreds, and for a time bade defiance to their oppressors.

The Dismal Swamps cover many thousands of acres of wild land and a dense forest, with wild animals and insects such as are unknown in any other part of Virginia. Here runaway Negroes usually seek a hiding place, and some have been known to reside here for years. The revolters were joined by one of these. He was a large, tall, full-blooded Negro with a stern and savage countenance; the marks on his face showed that he was from one of the barbarous tribes in Africa and claimed that country as his native land. His only covering was a girdle around his loins, made of skins of wild beasts which he had killed; his only token of authority among those that he led was a pair of epaulettes made from the tail of a fox and tied to his shoulder by a cord.

Brought from the coast of Africa when only fifteen years of age to the island of Cuba, he was smuggled from thence into Virginia. He had been two years in the swamps and considered it his future home. He had met a Negro woman who was also a runaway, and, after the fashion of his native land, had gone through the process of oiling her as the marriage ceremony. They had built a cave on a rising mound in the swamp; this was their home.

His name was Picquilo. His only weapon was a sword, made from the blade of a scythe which he had stolen from a neighboring plantation. His dress, his character, his manners, his mode of fighting, were all in keeping with the early training he had received in the land of his birth. He moved about with the activity of a cat, and neither the thickness of the trees nor the depth of the water could stop him. He was a bold, turbulent spirit, and from revenge imbrued his hands in the blood of all the whites he could meet. Hunger, thirst, fatigue and loss of sleep he seemed made to endure as if by peculiarity of constitution. His air was fierce, his step oblique, his look sanguinary. Such was the character of one of the leaders in the Southampton insurrection.

All Negroes were arrested who were found beyond their master's threshold, and all strange whites watched with a great degree of alacrity.

Such was the position in which Clotel found affairs when she returned to Virginia in search of her Mary. Had not the slaveowners been watchful of strangers, owing to the outbreak, the fugitive could not have escaped the vigilance of the police, for advertisements announcing her escape and offering a large reward for her arrest had been received in the city previous to her arrival, and the officers were therefore on the lookout for the runaway slave.

It was on the third day, as the quadroon was seated in her room at the inn, still in the disguise of a gentleman, that two of the city officers entered the room and informed her that they were authorized to examine all strangers, to assure the authorities that they were not in league with the revolted Negroes. With trembling heart the fugitive handed the key of her trunk to the officers. To their surprise, they found nothing but woman's apparel in the box, which raised their curiosity and caused a further investigation that resulted in the arrest of Clotel as a fugitive slave. She was immediately conveyed to prison, there to await the orders of her master. For many days, uncheered by the voice of kindness, alone, hopeless, desolate, she waited for the time to arrive when the chains were to be placed on her limbs, and she returned to her . . . unfeeling owner.

The arrest of the fugitive was announced in all the newspapers but created little or no sensation. The inhabitants were too much engaged in putting down the revolt among the slaves, and although all the odds were against the insurgents, the whites found it no easy matter, with all their caution. Every day brought news of fresh outbreaks. Without scruple and without pity, the whites massacred all blacks found beyond their owners' plantations: the Negroes, in return, set fire to houses, and put those to death who attempted to escape from the flames. Thus carnage was added to carnage, and the blood of the whites flowed to avenge the blood of the blacks.

These were the ravages of slavery. No graves were dug for the Negroes; their dead bodies became food for dogs and vultures, and their bones, partly calcined by the sun, remained scattered about, as if to mark the mournful fury of servitude and lust of power.

—1853

From *Clotel: Or the President's Daughter*

The Two Offers

Frances Ellen Watkins Harper

WHAT IS the matter with you, Laura, this morning? I have been watching you this hour, and in that time you have commenced a half-dozen letters and torn them all up. What matter of such grave moment is puzzling your dear little head, that you do not know how to decide?"

"Well, it is an important matter: I have two offers for marriage, and I do not know which to choose."

"I should accept neither, or to say the least, not at present."

"Why not?"

"Because I think a woman who is undecided between two offers has not love enough for either to make a choice; and in that very hesitation, indecision, she has a reason to pause and seriously reflect, lest her marriage, instead of being an affinity of souls or a union of hearts, should only be a mere matter of bargain and sale, or an affair of convenience and selfish interest."

"But I consider them both very good offers, just such as many a girl would gladly receive. But to tell you the truth, I do not think that I regard either as a woman should the man she chooses for her husband. But then if I refuse, there is the risk of being an old maid, and that is not to be thought of."

"Well, suppose there is? Is that the most dreadful fate that can befall a woman? Is there not more intense wretchedness in an ill-assorted marriage, more utter loneliness in a loveless home, than in the lot of the old maid who accepts her earthly mission as a gift from God and strives to walk the path of life with earnest and unfaltering steps?"

"Oh! what a little preacher you are. I really believe that you were cut out for an old maid—that when nature formed you she put in a double portion of intellect to make up for a deficiency of love; and yet you are kind and affectionate. But I do not think that you know anything of the grand, overmastering passion, or the deep necessity of woman's heart for loving."

"Do you think so?" resumed the first speaker, and bending over her work she quietly applied herself to the knitting that had lain neglected by her side during this brief conversation. But as she did so, a shadow flitted over her pale and intellectual brow, a mist gathered in her eyes, and a slight quivering of the lips revealed a depth of feeling to which her companion was a stranger.

But before I proceed with my story, let me give you a slight history of the speakers. They were cousins who had met life under different auspices. Laura Lagrange was the only daughter of rich and indulgent parents who had spared no pains to make her an accomplished lady. Her cousin, Janette Alston, was the child of parents rich only in goodness and affection. Her father had been unfortunate in business and, dying before he could retrieve his fortunes, left his business in an embarrassed state. His widow was unacquainted with his business affairs, and when the estate was settled, hungry creditors had brought their claims and the lawyers had received their fees, she found herself homeless and almost penniless, and she, who had been sheltered in the warm clasp of loving arms, found them too powerless to shield her from the pitiless pelting storms of adversity. Year after year she struggled with poverty and wrestled with want, till her toilworn hands became too feeble to hold the shattered chords of existence, and her tear-dimmed eyes grew heavy with the slumber of death.

Her daughter had watched over her with untiring devotion, had closed her eyes in death and gone out into the busy, restless world, missing a precious tone from the voices of earth, a beloved step from the paths of life. Too self-reliant to depend on the charity of relations, she endeavored to support herself by her own exertions, and she had succeeded. Her path for a while was marked with struggle and trial, but instead of uselessly repining she met them bravely, and her life became not a thing of ease and indulgence, but of conquest, victory and accomplishments.

At the time when this conversation took place, the deep trials of her life had passed away. The achievements of her genius had won her a position in the literary world, where she shone as one of its bright particular stars. And with her fame came a competence of worldly means, which gave her leisure for improvement and the riper development of her rare talents. And she, that pale, intellectual woman, whose genius gave life and vivacity to the social circle and whose presence threw a halo of beauty and grace around the charmed atmosphere in which she moved, had at one period of her life known the mystic and solemn strength of an all-absorbing love. Years faded into the misty past had seen the kindling of her eye, the quick flushing of her cheek and the wild throbbing of her heart at tones of a voice long since hushed to the stillness of death. Deeply, wildly, passionately, she had loved. . . . This love quickened her talents, inspired her genius and threw over her life a tender and spiritual earnestness.

And then came a fearful shock, a mournful waking from that "dream of beauty and delight." A shadow fell around her path; it came between her and the object of her heart's worship. First a few cold words, estrangement, and then a painful separation: the old story of woman's pride. . . . And thus faded out from that young heart her bright, brief and saddened dream of life. Faint and spirit-broken, she turned from the scenes associated with the memory of the loved and lost. She tried to break the chain of sad associations that bound her to the mournful past; and so . . .

her genius gathered strength from suffering, and wondrous power and brilliancy from the agony she hid within the desolate chambers of her soul . . . and turning, with an earnest and shattered spirit, to life's duties and trials, she found a calmness and strength that she had only imagined in her dreams of poetry and song.

We will now pass over a period of ten years, and the cousins have met again. In that calm and lovely woman, in whose eyes is a depth of tenderness tempering the flashes of her genius, whose looks and tones are full of sympathy and love, we recognize the once smitten and stricken Janette Alston. The bloom of her girlhood had given way to a higher type of spiritual beauty, as if some unseen hand had been polishing and refining the temple in which her lovely spirit found its habitation. . . .

Never in the early flush of womanhood, when an absorbing love had lit up her eyes and glowed in her life, had she appeared so interesting as when, with a countenance which seemed overshadowed with a spiritual light, she bent over the deathbed of a young woman just lingering at the shadowy gates of the unseen land.

"Has he come?" faintly but eagerly exclaimed the dying woman. "Oh! how I have longed for his coming, and even in death he forgets me."

"Oh, do not say so, dear Laura. Some accident may have detained him," said Janette to her cousin; for on that bed, from whence she will never rise, lies the once beautiful and light-hearted Laura Lagrange, the brightness of whose eyes had long since been dimmed with tears, and whose voice had become like a harp whose every chord is tuned to sadness—whose faintest thrill and loudest vibrations are but the variations of agony. A heavy hand was laid upon her once warm and bounding heart, and a voice came whispering through her soul that she must die. But to her the tidings was a message of deliverance—a voice hushing her wild sorrows to the calmness of resignation and hope.

Life had grown so weary upon her head—the future looked so hopeless—she had no wish to tread again the track where thorns had pierced her feet and clouds overcast her sky, and she hailed the coming of death's angel as the footsteps of a welcome friend. And yet, earth had one object so very dear to her weary heart. It was her absent and recreant husband; for, since that conversation [ten years earlier], she had accepted one of her offers and become a wife. But before she married she learned that great lesson of human experience and woman's life—to love the man who bowed at her shrine, a willing worshipper.

He had a pleasing address, raven hair, flashing eyes, a voice of thrilling sweetness and lips of persuasive eloquence; and being well versed in the ways of the world, he won his way to her heart and she became his bride, and he was proud of his prize. Vain and superficial in his character, he looked upon marriage not as a divine sacrament for the soul's development and human progression, but as the title deed that gave him possession of the woman he thought he loved. But alas for her, the laxity of his principles had rendered him unworthy of the deep and undying devotion of a pure-hearted woman. But, for a while, he hid from her his true character, and she blindly loved him, and for a short period was happy in the consciousness of being beloved. Though sometimes a vague unrest would fill her soul, when, overflowing with a sense of the good, the beautiful and the true, she would turn to him but find no response to the deep yearnings of her soul—no appreciation of life's highest realities, its solemn grandeur and significant importance. Their souls never met, and soon she found a void in her bosom that his earthborn love could not fill. He did not satisfy the wants of her mental and moral nature: between him and her there was no affinity of minds, no intercommunion of souls.

Talk as you will of woman's deep capacity for loving—of the strength of her affectional nature. I do not deny it. But will the mere possession of any human love fully satisfy all the demands of her whole being? You may paint her in poetry or fiction as a frail vine, clinging to her brother man for support and dying when deprived of it, and all this may sound well enough to please the imaginations of schoolgirls, or lovelorn maidens. But woman—the true woman—if you would render her happy, it needs more than the mere development of her affectional nature. Her con-

science should be enlightened, her faith in the true and right established, and scope given to her heaven-endowed and God-given faculties. The true aim of female education should be, not a development of one or two, but all the faculties of the human soul, because no perfect womanhood is developed by imperfect culture. Intense love is often akin to intense suffering, and to trust the whole wealth of a woman's nature on the frail bark of human love may often be like trusting a cargo of gold and precious gems to a bark that has never battled with the storm or buffeted the waves. Is it any wonder, then, that so many life-barks . . . are stranded on the shoals of existence, mournful beacons and solemn warnings for the thoughtless, to whom marriage is a careless and hasty rushing together of the affections? Alas, that an institution so fraught with good for humanity should be so perverted, and [that] that state of life which should be filled with happiness [should] become so replete with misery. And this was the fate of Laura Lagrange.

For a brief period after her marriage her life seemed like a bright and beautiful dream, full of hope and radiant with joy. And then there came a change: he found other attractions that lay beyond the pale of home influences. The gambling saloon had power to win him from her side; he had lived in an element of unhealthy and unhallowed excitements, and the society of a loving wife, the pleasures of a well-regulated home, were enjoyments too tame for one who had vitiated his tastes by the pleasures of sin. There were charmed houses of vice, built upon dead men's loves, where, amid a flow of song, laughter, wine and careless mirth, he would spend hour after hour, forgetting the cheek that was paling through his neglect, heedless of the tear-dimmed eyes peering anxiously into the darkness, waiting or watching his return.

The influence of old associations was upon him. In early life, home had been to him a place of ceilings and walls, not a true home built upon goodness, love and truth. It was a place where velvet carpets hushed his tread, where images of loveliness and beauty, invoked into being by painter's art and sculptor's skill, pleased the eye and gratified the taste, where magnificence surrounded his way and costly clothing adorned his person; but it was not the place for the true culture and right development of his soul. His father had been too much engrossed in making money and his mother in spending it, in striving to maintain a fashionable position in society and shining in the eyes of the world, to give the proper direction to the character of their wayward and impulsive son. His mother put beautiful robes upon his body but left ugly scars upon his soul; she pampered his appetite but starved his spirit. . . .

That parental authority which should have been preserved as a string of precious pearls, unbroken and unscattered, was simply the administration of chance. At one time obedience was enforced by authority, at another time by flattery and promises, and just as often it was not enforced. . . . His early associations were formed as chance directed, and from his want of home training, his character received a bias, his life a shade, which ran through every avenue of his existence and darkened all his future hours. . . .

Before a year of his married life had waned, his young wife had learned to wait and mourn his frequent and uncalled-for absence. More than once had she seen him come home from his midnight haunts, the bright intelligence of his eye displaced by the drunkard's stare, and his manly gait changed to the inebriate's stagger; and she was beginning to know the bitter agony that is compressed in the mournful words "a drunkard's wife."

And then there came a bright but brief episode in her experience. The angel of life gave to her existence a deeper meaning and loftier significance: she sheltered in the warm clasp of her loving arms a dear babe, a precious child whose love filled every chamber of her heart. . . . How many lonely hours were beguiled by its winsome ways, its answering smiles and fond caresses! How exquisite and solemn was the feeling that thrilled her heart when she clasped the tiny hands together and taught her dear child to call God "Our Father"!

What a blessing was that child! The father paused in his headlong career, awed by the strange beauty and precocious intellect of his child; and the mother's life had a better expression through her ministrations of love. And then there came hours of bitter anguish, shading the

sunlight of her home and hushing the music of her heart. The angel of death bent over the couch of her child and beckoned it away. Closer and closer the mother strained her child to her wildly heaving breast and struggled with the heavy hand that lay upon its heart. Love and agony contended with death. . . .

But death was stronger than love and mightier than agony, and won the child for the land of crystal founts and deathless flowers, and the poor stricken mother sat down beneath the shadow of her mighty grief, feeling as if a great light had gone out from her soul and that the sunshine had suddenly faded around her path. She turned in her deep anguish to the father of her child, the loved and cherished dead. For a while his words were kind and tender, his heart seemed subdued and his tenderness fell upon her worn and weary heart like rain on perishing flowers, or cooling waters to lips all parched with thirst and scorched with fever. But the change was evanescent; the influence of unhallowed associations and evil habits had vitiated and poisoned the springs of his existence. They had bound him in their meshes, and he lacked the moral strength to break his fetters and stand erect in all the strength and dignity of a true manhood, making life's highest excellence his ideal and striving to gain it.

And yet moments of deep contrition would sweep over him, when he would resolve to abandon the wine cup forever, when he was ready to forswear the handling of another card, and he would try to break away from the associations that he felt were working his ruin. But when the hour of temptation came his strength was weakness, his earnest purposes were cobwebs, his well-meant resolutions ropes of sand—and thus passed year after year of the married life of Laura Lagrange. She tried to hide her agony from the public gaze, to smile when her heart was almost breaking. But year after year her voice grew fainter and sadder, her once light and bounding step grew slower and faltering.

Year after year she wrestled with agony and strove with despair, till the quick eyes of her brother read, in the paling of her cheek and the dimming eye, the secret anguish of her worn and weary spirit. On that wan, sad face he saw the death tokens, and he knew the dark wing of the mystic angel swept coldly around her path.

"Laura," said her brother to her one day, "you are not well, and I think you need our mother's tender care and nursing. You are daily losing strength, and if you will go I will accompany you."

At first she hesitated; she shrank almost instinctively from presenting that pale, sad face to the loved ones at home. . . . But then a deep yearning for home sympathy woke within her a passionate longing for love's kind words, for tenderness and heart support, and she resolved to seek the home of her childhood and lay her weary head upon her mother's bosom, to be folded again in her loving arms, to lay that poor, bruised and aching heart where it might beat and throb closely to the loved ones at home.

A kind welcome awaited her. All that love and tenderness could devise was done to bring the bloom to her cheek and the light to her eye. But it was all in vain; hers was a disease that no medicine could cure, no earthly balm would heal. It was a slow wasting of the vital forces, the sickness of the soul. The unkindness and neglect of her husband lay like a leaden weight upon her heart. . . .

And where was he that had won her love and then cast it aside as a useless thing, who rifled her heart of its wealth and spread bitter ashes upon its broken altars? He was lingering away from her when the death damps were gathering on her brow, when his name was trembling on her lips! Lingering away! when she was watching his coming, though the death films were gathering before her eyes and earthly things were fading from her vision.

"I think I hear him now," said the dying woman, "surely that is his step," but the sound died away in the distance.

Again she started from an uneasy slumber: "That is his voice! I am so glad he has come."

Tears gathered in the eyes of the sad watchers by that dying bed, for they knew that she was deceived. He had not returned. For her sake they wished his coming. Slowly the hours waned away, and then came the sad, soul-sickening thought that she was forgotten, forgotten in the last hour of human need, forgotten when the spirit, about to be dissolved, paused for the last time on the threshold of existence, a weary watcher at the gates of death.

"He has forgotten me," again she faintly murmured, and the last tears she would ever shed on earth sprung to her mournful eyes, and . . . a few broken sentences issued from her pale and quivering lips. They were prayers for strength, and earnest pleading for him who had desolated her young life by turning its sunshine to shadows, its smiles to tears.

"He has forgotten me," she murmured again, "but I can bear it; the bitterness of death is passed, and soon I hope to exchange the shadows of death for the brightness of eternity, the rugged paths of life for the golden streets of glory, and the care and turmoils of earth for the peace and rest of heaven."

Her voice grew fainter and fainter; they saw the shadows that never deceive flit over her pale and faded face and knew that the death angel waited to soothe their weary one to rest, to calm the throbbing of her bosom and cool the fever of her brain. And amid the silent hush of their grief the freed spirit, refined through suffering and brought into divine harmony through the spirit of the living Christ, passed over the dark waters of death as on a bridge of light, over whose radiant arches hovering angels bent. They parted the dark locks from her marble brow, closed the waxen lids over the once bright and laughing eye and left her to the dreamless slumber of the grave.

Her cousin turned from that deathbed a sadder and wiser woman. She resolved more earnestly than ever to make the world better by her example, gladder by her presence, and to kindle the fires of her genius on the altars of universal love and truth. She had a higher and better object in all her writings than the mere acquisition of gold or acquirement of fame. She felt that she had a high and holy mission on the battlefield of existence—that life was not given her to be frittered away in nonsense or wasted away in trifling pursuits. She would willingly espouse an unpopular cause, but not an unrighteous one.

In her the downtrodden slave found an earnest advocate; the flying fugitive remembered her kindness as he stepped cautiously through our Republic to gain his freedom in a monarchial land, having broken the chains on which the rust of centuries had gathered. Little children learned to name her with affection; the poor called her blessed as she broke her bread to the pale lips of hunger.

Her life was like a beautiful story, only it was clothed with the dignity of reality and invested with the sublimity of truth. True, she was an old maid; no husband brightened her life with his love or shaded it with his neglect. No children nestling lovingly in her arms called her mother. No one appended Mrs. to her name.

She was indeed an old maid, not vainly striving to keep up an appearance of girlishness when "departed" was written on her youth, not vainly pining at her loneliness and isolation. The world was full of warm, loving hearts, and her own beat in unison with them. Neither was she always sentimentally sighing for something to love; objects of affection were all around her, and the world was not so wealthy in love that it had no use for hers. In blessing others she made a life and benediction, and as old age descended peacefully and gently upon her, she had learned one of life's most precious lessons: that true happiness consists not so much in the fruition of our wishes as in the regulation of desires and the full development and right culture of our whole natures.

—1859

The Goophered Grapevine

Charles Waddell Chesnutt

WE ALIGHTED from the buggy, walked about the yard for a while, and then wandered off into the adjoining vineyard. Upon Annie's complaining of weariness I led the way back to the yard, where a pine log lying under the spreading elm afforded a shady though somewhat hard seat. One end of the log was already occupied by a venerable-looking colored man. He held on his knees a hat full of grapes, over which he was smacking his lips with great gusto; and a pile of grapeskins near him indicated that the performance was no new thing. We approached him at an angle from the rear, and were close to him before he perceived us. He respectfully rose as we drew near, and was moving away, when I begged him to keep his seat.

"Don't let us disturb you," I said. "There is plenty of room for us all."

He resumed his seat with some embarrassment. While he had been standing, I had observed that he was a tall man, and though slightly bowed by the weight of years, apparently quite vigorous. He was not entirely black, and this fact, together with the quality of his hair, which was about six inches long and very bushy, except on the top of his head, where he was quite bald, suggested a slight strain of other than Negro blood. There was a shrewdness in his eyes, too, which was not altogether African, and which, as we afterwards learned from experience, was indicative of a corresponding shrewdness in his character. He went on eating his grapes, but did not seem to enjoy himself quite so well as he had apparently done before he became aware of our presence.

"Do you live around here?" I asked, anxious to put him at his ease.

"Yas, suh. I lives des ober yander, behine de nex' san'hill, on de Lumberton plank-road."

"Do you know anything about the time when this vineyard was cultivated?"

"Lawd bless you, suh, I knows all about it. Dey ain' na'er a man in dis settlement w'at won' tell you ole Julius McAdoo 'uz bawn en raise' on dis yer same plantation. Is you de Norv'n gemman w'at's gwine ter buy de ole vimya'd?"

"I am looking at it," I replied, "but I don't know that I shall care to buy unless I can be reasonably sure of making something out of it."

"Well, suh, you is a stranger ter me, en I is a stranger ter you, en we is bofe strangers ter one anudder, but 'f I 'uz in yo' place, I wouldn' buy dis vimya'd."

"Why not?" I asked.

"Well, I dunno whe'r you b'lieves in conj'in' er not—some er de w'ite folks doan, er says dey doan—but de truf er de matter is dat dis yer ole vimya'd is goophered."

"Is what?" I asked, not grasping the meaning of this unfamiliar word.

"Is goophered—cunju'd, bewitch'."

He imparted this information with such solemn earnestness and with such an air of confidential mystery that I felt somewhat interested, while Annie was evidently much impressed and drew closer to me.

"How do you know it is bewitched?" I asked.

"I wouldn' spec' fer you ter b'lieve me 'less you know all 'bout de fac's. But ef you en young miss dere doan min' lis'nin' ter a ole nigger run on a minute er two w'ile you er restin', I kin 'splain to you how it all happen'."

We assured him that we would be glad to hear

how it all happened, and he began to tell us. At first the current of his memory—or imagination—seemed somewhat sluggish; but as his embarrassment wore off, his language flowed more freely, and the story acquired perspective and coherence. As he became more and more absorbed in the narrative, his eyes assumed a dreamy expression, and he seemed to lose sight of his auditors and to be living over again in monologue his life on the old plantation.

"Ole Mars Dugal' McAdoo," he began, "bought dis place long many years befo' de Wah, en I 'member well w'en he sot out all dis yer part er de plantation in scuppernon's. De vimes growed monst'us fas', en Mars Dugal' made a thousan' gallon er scuppernon' wine eve'y year.

"Now, ef dey's an'thing a nigger lub, nex' ter 'possum, en chick'n, en watermillyums, its scuppernon's. Dey ain' nuffin dat kin stan' up side'n de scuppernon' fer sweetness; sugar ain' a suckumstance ter scuppernon'. W'en de season is nigh 'bout ober, en de grapes begin ter swivel up des a little wid de wrinkles er ole age—w'en de skin git sof' en brown—den de scuppernon' make you smack yo' lip en roll yo' eye en wush fer mo'; so I reckon it ain' very 'stonishin' dat niggers lub scuppernon'.

"Dey wuz a sight er niggers in de naberhood er de vimya'd. Dere wuz ole Mars Henry Brayboy's niggers, en ole Mars Jeems McLean's niggers, en Mars Dugal's own niggers; den dey wuz a settlement er free niggers en po' buckrahs down by de Wim'l'ton Road, en Mars Dugal' had de only vimya'd in de naberhood. I reckon it ain' so much so nowadays, but befo' de Wah, in slab'ry times, a nigger didn' mine goin' fi' er ten mile in a night w'en dey wuz sump'n good ter eat at de yuther een'.

"So atter a w'ile Mars Dugal' begin ter miss his scuppernon's. Co'se he 'cuse' de niggers er it, but dey all 'nied it ter de las'. Mars Dugal' sot spring guns en steel traps, en he en de oberseah sot up nights once't or twice't, tel one night Mars Dugal'—he 'uz a monst'us keerless man—got his leg shot full er cowpeas. But somehow er nudder dey couldn' nebber ketch none er de niggers. I dunner how it happen, but it happen des like I tell you, en de grapes kep' on a-goin' des de same.

"But bimeby ole Mars Dugal' fix' up a plan ter stop it. Dey wuz a cunjuh 'oman livin' down 'mongs' de free niggers on de Wim'l'ton Road, en all de darkies fum Rockfish ter Beaver Crick wuz feared er her. She could wuk de mos' powerfulles' kin' er goopher—could make people hab fits, er rheumatiz, er make 'em des dwinel away en die; en dey say she went out ridin' de niggers at night, fer she wuz a witch 'sides bein' a cunjuh 'oman. Mars Dugal' hearn 'bout Aun' Peggy's doin's, en begun ter 'flect whe'r er no he couldn' git her ter he'p 'im keep de niggers off'n de grapevimes. One day in de spring er de year, ole miss pack' up a basket er chick'n en poun'cake, en a bottle er scuppernon' wine, en Mars Dugal' tuk it in his buggy en driv ober ter Aun' Peggy's cabin. He tuk de basket in, en had a long talk wid Aun' Peggy.

"De nex' day Aun' Peggy come up ter de vimya'd. De niggers seed her slippin' roun', en dey soon foun' out w'at she 'uz doin' dere. Mars Dugal' had hi'ed her ter goopher de grapevimes. She sa'ntered 'roun' 'mongs' de vimes, en tuk a leaf fum dis one, en a grape-hull fum dat one, en den a little twig fum here, en a little pinch er dirt fum dere—en put it all in a big black bottle, wid a snake's toof en a speckle hen's gall en some ha'rs fum a black cat's tail, en den fill' de bottle wid scuppernon' wine. W'en she got de goopher all ready en fix', she tuk 'n went out in de woods en buried it under de root uv a red oak tree, en den come back en tole one er de niggers she done goopher de grapevimes, en a'er a nigger w'at eat dem grapes 'ud be sho ter die inside'n twel' mont's.

"Atter dat de niggers let de scuppernon's 'lone, en Mars Dugal' didn' hab no 'casion ter fine no mo' fault; en de season wuz mos' gone, w'en a strange gemman stop at de plantation one night ter see Mars Dugal' on some business; en his coachman, seein' de scuppernon's growin' so nice en sweet, slip 'roun' behine de smokehouse en et all de scuppernon's he could hole. Nobody didn' notice it at de time, but dat night, on de way home, de gemman's hoss runned away en kill' de coachman. W'en we hearn de noos, Aun' Lucy, de cook, she up 'n' say she seed de strange nigger eat'n' er de scuppernon's behine de smokehouse, en den we knowed de goopher had be'en er wukkin'. Den one er de nigger chilluns runned away fum de quarters one day, en got in de scuppernon's, en died de nex' week. W'ite folks say he die' er de fevuh, but de niggers knowed it wuz de goopher. So you k'n be sho de darkies didn' hab much ter do wid dem scuppernon' vimes.

"W'en de scuppernon' season 'uz ober fer dat year, Mars Dugal' foun' he had made fifteen hund'ed gallon er wine; en one er de niggers hearn 'im laffin' wid de oberseah fit ter kill, en sayin' dem fifteen hund'ed gallon er wine wuz monst'us good intrus' on de ten dollars he laid out on de vimya'd. So I 'low ez he paid Aun' Peggy ten dollars fer ter goopher de grapevimes.

"De goopher didn' wuk no mo' tel de nex' summer, w'en 'long to'ds de middle er de season one er de fiel' han's died; en ez dat lef' Mars Dugal' sho't er han's, he went off ter town fer ter buy anudder. He fotch de noo nigger home wid 'im. He wuz er ole nigger, er de color er a gingy-cake, en ball ez a hossapple on de top er his head. He wuz a peart ole nigger, do', en could do a big day's wuk.

"Now it happen dat one er de niggers on de nex' plantation, one er ole Mars Henry Bray-boy's niggers, had runned away de day befo', en tuk ter de swamp, en ole Mars Dugal' en some er de yuther nabor w'ite folks had gone out wid dere guns en dere dogs fer ter he'p 'em hunt fer de nigger; en de han's on our own plantation wuz all so flusterated dat we fuhgot ter tell de noo han' 'bout de goopher on de scuppernon' vimes. Co'se he smell de grapes en see de vimes, an atter dahk de fus' thing he done wuz ter slip off ter de grapevimes 'dout sayin' nuffin ter nobody. Nex' mawnin' he tole some er de niggers 'bout de fine bait er scuppernon' he et de night befo'.

"W'en dey tole 'im 'bout de goopher on de grapevimes, he 'uz dat tarrified dat he turn pale en look des like he gwine ter die right in his tracks. De oberseah come up en axed w'at 'uz de matter; en w'en dey tole 'im Henry been eatin' er de scuppernon's, en got de goopher on 'im, he gin Henry a big drink er w'iskey, en 'low dat de nex' rainy day he take 'im ober ter Aun' Peggy's en see ef she wouldn' take de goopher off'n 'im, seein' ez he didn' know nuffin erbout it tel he done et de grapes.

"Sho 'nuff, it rain de nex' day, en de oberseah went ober ter Aun' Peggy's wid Henry. En Aun' Peggy say dat bein' ez Henry didn' know 'bout de goopher, en et de grapes in ign'ance er de conseq'ences, she reckon she mought be able ter take de goopher off'n 'im. So she fotch out er bottle wid some cunjuh medicine in it, en po'd some out in a go'd fer Henry ter drink. He man-age' ter git it down; he say it tas'e like w'iskey wid sump'n bitter in it. She 'lowed dat 'ud keep de goopher off'n 'im tel de spring; but w'en de sap begin ter rise in de grapevimes he ha' ter come en see her ag'in, en she tell 'im w'at he's ter do.

"Nex' spring, w'en de sap commence' ter rise in de scuppernon' vime, Henry tuk a ham one night. Whar'd he git de ham? I doan know; dey wa'n't no hams on de plantation 'cep'n' w'at 'uz in de smokehouse, but I never see Henry 'bout de smokehouse. But ez I wuz a-sayin', he tuk de ham ober ter Aun' Peggy's en Aun' Peggy tole 'im dat w'en Mars Dugal' begin ter prune de grapevimes, he must go en take 'n' scrape off de sap w'at it ooze out'n de cut een's er de vimes, en 'n'int his ball head wid it; en ef he do dat once't a year de goopher wouldn' wuk agin 'im long ez he done it. En bein' ez he fotch her de ham, she fix' it so he kin eat all de scuppernon' he want.

"So Henry 'n'int his head wid de sap out'n de big grapevime des ha'fway 'twix de quarters en de big house, en de goopher nebber wuk agin 'im dat summer. But de beatenes' thing you eber see happen' ter Henry. Up ter dat time he wuz ez ball ez a sweeten' 'tater, but des ez soon ez de young leaves begun ter come out on de grapevimes, de ha' begun ter grow out on Henry's head, en by de middle er de summer he had de bigges' head er ha'r on de plantation. Befo' dat, Henry had tol'able good ha'r 'roun' de aidges, but soon ez de young grapes begun ter come, Henry's ha'r begun to quirl all up in little balls, des like dis yer reg'lar grapy ha'r, en by de time de grapes got ripe his head look des like a bunch er grapes. Combin' it didn' do no good; he wuk at it ha'f de night wid er Jim Crow en think he git it straighten' out, but in de mawnin' de grapes 'ud be dere des de same. So he gin it up, en tried ter keep de grapes down by havin' his ha'r cut sho't.

"But dat wa'n't de quares' thing 'bout de goopher. W'en Henry come ter de plantation, he wuz gittin' a little ole and stiff en de j'ints. But dat summer he got des ez spry en libely ez any young nigger on de plantation; fac', he got so biggity dat Mars Jackson, de oberseah, ha' ter th'eaten ter whip 'im ef he didn' stop cuttin' up his didos en behave hisse'f. But de mos' cur'ouses' thing happen' in de fall, w'en de sap begin ter go down in de grapevimes. Fus', w'en de grapes 'uz gethered, de knots begun ter straighten out'n Henry's ha'r; en w'en de leaves begin ter fall, Henry's ha'r commence' ter drap out; en w'en de vimes 'uz bar', Henry's head wuz baller'n it wuz in de spring, en he begin ter git ole en stiff in de j'ints ag'in, en paid no mo' 'tention ter de gals dyoin' er de whole winter. En nex' spring, w'en he rub de sap on ag'in, he got young ag'in, en so soopl en libely dat none er de young niggers on de plantation couldn' jump, ner dance, ner hoe ez much cotton ez Henry. But in de fall er de year his grapes 'mence' ter straighten out, en his j'ints ter git stiff, en his ha'r drap off, en de rheumatiz begin ter wrastle wid 'im.

"Now, ef you'd 'a' knowed ole Mars Dugal' McAdoo, you'd 'a' knowed dat it ha' ter be a mighty rainy day w'en he couldn' fine sump'n fer his niggers ter do, en it ha' ter be a mighty little hole he couldn' crawl thoo, en ha' ter be a monst'us cloudy night w'en a dollar git by 'im in de dahkness; en w'en he see how Henry git young in de spring en ole in de fall, he 'lowed ter hisse'f ez how he could make mo' money out'n Henry dan by wukkin' 'im in de cotton-fiel'. 'Long de nex' spring, atter de sap 'mence' ter rise, en Henry 'n'int his head en sta'ted fer ter git young en soopl, Mars Dugal' up 'n' tuk Henry ter town, en sole 'im fer fifteen hund'ed dollars. Co'se de man w'at bought Henry didn' know nuffin 'bout de goopher, en Mars Dugal' didn' see no 'casion fer ter tell 'im. Long to'ds de fall, w'en de sap went down, Henry begin ter git ole ag'in same ez yuzhal, en his noo marster begin ter git skeered les'n he gwine ter lose his fifteen-hund'ed-dollar nigger. He sent fer a mighty fine doctor, but de med'cine didn' 'pear ter do no good; de goopher had a good holt. Henry tole de doctor 'bout de goopher, but de doctor des laff at 'im.

"One day in de winter Mars Dugal' went ter town, en wuz santerin' 'long de Main Street w'en who should he meet but Henry's noo marster. Dey said 'Hoddy,' en Mars Dugal' ax 'im ter hab a seegyar; en atter dey run on awhile 'bout de craps en de weather, Mars Dugal' ax 'im, sorter keer-less, like ez ef he des thought of it: 'How you like de nigger I sole you las' spring?'

"Henry's marster shuck his head en knock de ashes off'n his seegyar.

"'Spec' I made a bad bahgin when I bought dat nigger. Henry done good wuk all de summer, but sence de fall set in he 'pears ter be sorter pinin' away. Dey ain' nuffin pertickler de matter wid 'im—leastways de doctor say so—'cep'n' a tech er de rheumatiz; but his ha'r is all fell out, en ef he doan pick up his strenk mighty soon, I spec' I'm gwine ter lose 'im.'

"Dey smoked on awhile, en bimeby ole mars says, 'Well, a bahgin's a bahgin, but you en me is good fren's, en I doan wan' ter see you lose all de money you paid fer dat nigger; en ef w'at you say is so, en I ain' 'sputin' it, he ain' wuf much now. I spec's you wukked 'im too ha'd dis summer, er e'se de swamps down here doan agree wid de san'hill nigger. So you des lemme know, en ef he gits any wusser, I'll be willin' ter gib yer five hund'ed dollars for 'im, en take my chances on his livin'.'

"Sho 'nuff, w'en Henry begun ter draw up wid de rheumatiz en it look like he gwine ter die fer sho, his noo marster sen' fer Mars Dugal', en Mars Dugal' gin 'im w'at he promus, en brung Henry home ag'in. He tuk good keer uv 'im dyoin' er de winter—give 'im w'iskey ter rub his rheumatiz, en terbacker ter smoke, en all he want ter eat—'caze a nigger w'at he could make a thousan' dollars a year off'n didn' grow on eve'y huckleberry bush.

"Nex' spring, w'en de sap rise en Henry's ha'r commence' ter sprout, Mars Dugal' sole 'im ag'in, down in Robeson County dis time; en he kep' dat sellin' business up fer five year er mo'. Henry nebber say nuffin 'bout de goopher ter his noo marsters, 'caze he know he gwine ter be tuk good keer uv de nex' winter, w'en Mars Dugal' buy 'im back. En Mars Dugal' made 'nuff money off'n Henry ter buy anudder plantation ober on Beaver Crick.

"But 'long 'bout de een 'er dat five year dey come a stranger ter stop at de plantation. De fus' day he 'uz dere he went out wid Mars Dugal' en spent all de mawnin' lookin' ober de vimya'd, en atter dinner dey spent all de evenin' playin' kya'ds. De niggers soon 'skivver' dat he wuz a Yankee, en dat he come down ter Norf C'lina fer ter l'arn de w'ite folks how to raise grapes en make wine. He promus Mars Dugal' he c'd make de grapevimes b'ar twice't ez many grapes, en dat de noo winepress he wuz a-sellin' would make mo' d'n twice't ez many gallons er wine. En ole Mars Dugal' des drunk it all in, des 'peared ter be bewitch' wid dat Yankee. W'en de darkies see dat Yankee runnin' 'roun' de vimya'd en diggin' under de grapevimes, dey shuk dere heads, en 'lowed dat dey feared Mars Dugal' losin' his min'. Mars Dugal' had all de dirt dug away fum under de roots er all de scuppernon' vimes, en let 'em stan' dat away fer a week er mo'. Den dat Yankee made de niggers fix up a mixtry er lime en ashes en manyo, en po' it 'roun' de roots er de grapevimes. Den he 'vise Mars Dugal' fer ter trim de vimes close't, en Mars Dugal' tuk 'n' done eve'ything de Yankee tole 'im ter do. Dyoin' all er dis time, mine yer, dis yer Yankee wuz libbin' off'n de fat er de lan', at de big house, en playin' kya'ds wid Mars Dugal' eve'y night; en dey say Mars Dugal' los' mo'n a thousan' dollars dyoin' er de week dat Yankee wuz a-ruinin' de grapevimes.

"W'en de sap ris nex' spring, ole Henry 'n'inted his head ez yuzhal, en his ha'r 'mence' ter grow des de same ez it done eve'y year. De scuppernon' vimes growed monst'us fas', en de leaves wuz greener en thicker dan dey eber be'n dyoin' my rememb'ance; en Henry's ha'r growed out thicker dan eber, en he 'peared ter git younger 'n' younger, en soopler. En seein' ez he wuz sho't er han's dat spring, havin' tuk in consid'able noo groun', Mars Dugal' git de crap in en de cotton chop'. So he kep' Henry on de plantation.

"But 'long 'bout time fer de grapes ter come on de scuppernon' vimes, dey 'peared ter come a change ober 'em; de leaves wither' en swivel' up, en de young grapes turn' yaller, en bimeby eve'ybody on de plantation could see dat de whole vimya'd wuz dyin'. Mars Dugal' tuk 'n' water de vimes en done all he could, but 't wa'n'

no use; dat Yankee had done bus' de watermill-yum. One time de vimes picked up a bit, en Mars Dugal' 'lowed dey wuz gwine ter come out ag'in; but dat Yankee done dug too close under de roots, en prune de branches too close ter de vime, en all dat lime en ashes done burn de life out'n de vimes, en dey des kep' a-with'in' en a-swivelin'.

"All dis time de goopher wuz a-wukkin'. W'en de vimes sta'ted ter wither, Henry 'mence' ter complain er his rheumatiz; en w'en de leaves begin ter dry up, his ha'r 'mence' ter drap out. W'en de vimes fresh' up a bit, Henry'd git peart ag'in, en w'en de vimes wither' ag'in, Henry'd git ole ag'in, en des kep' gittin' mo' fitten fer nuffin. He des pined away, en pined away, en fin'ly tuk ter his cabin; en w'en de big vime whar he got de sap ter 'n'int his head wither' en turn' yaller en died, Henry died too—des went out sorter like a cannel. Dey didn' 'pear ter be nuffin de matter wid 'im, 'cep'n de rheumatiz, but his strenk des dwinel' away 'tel he didn' hab ernuff lef' ter draw his bref. De goopher had got de under holt, en th'owed Henry dat time fer good en all.

"Mars Dugal' tuk on might'ly 'bout losin' his vimes en his nigger in de same year; en he swo' dat ef he could git holt er dat Yankee he'd wear 'im ter a frazzle en den chaw up de frazzle; en he'd done it, too, for Mars Dugal' 'uz a monst'us brash man w'en he once git started. He sot de vimya'd out ober ag'in, but it wuz th'ee er fo' year befo' de vimes got ter b'arin' any scuppernon's.

"W'en de Wah broke out, Mars Dugal' raise' a comp'ny, en went off ter fight de Yankees. He say he wuz mighty glad wah come, en he des want ter kill a Yankee for eve'y dollar he los' 'long er dat grape-raisin' Yankee. En I spec' he would 'a' done it, too, ef de Yankees hadn' s'picioned sump'en en killed 'im fus'. Atter de s'render ole miss move' ter town, de niggers all scattered 'way fum de plantation, en de vimya'd ain' be'n cultervated sence."

"Is that story true?" asked Annie doubtfully, but seriously, as the old man concluded his narrative.

"It's des ez true ez I'm a-settin' here, miss. Dey's a easy way ter prove it: I kin lead de way right ter Henry's grave ober yonder in de plantation buryin'-groun'. En I tell yer w'at, marster, I wouldn' 'vise you to buy dis yer ole vimya'd, 'caze de goopher's on it yit, en dey ain' no tellin' w'en it's gwine ter crap out."

"But I thought you said all the old vines died."

"Dey did 'pear ter die, but a few un 'em come out ag'in, en is mixed in 'mongs' de yuthers. I ain' skeered ter eat de grapes 'caze I knows de old vimes fum de noo ones; but wid strangers dey ain' no tellin' w'at mought happen. I wouldn' 'vise you ter buy dis vimya'd."

I bought the vineyard, nevertheless, and it has been for a long time in a thriving condition, and is often referred to by the local press as a striking illustration of the opportunities open to Northern capital in the development of Southern industries. The luscious scuppernong holds first rank among our grapes, though we cultivate a great many other varieties, and our income from grapes packed and shipped to the Northern markets is quite considerable. I have not noticed any developments of the goopher in the vineyard, although I have a mild suspicion that our colored assistants do not suffer from want of grapes during the season.

I found, when I bought the vineyard, that Uncle Julius had occupied a cabin on the place for many years, and derived a respectable revenue from the produce of the neglected grapevines. This, doubtless, accounted for his advice to me not to buy the vineyard, though whether it inspired the goopher story I am unable to state. I believe, however, that the wages I paid him for his services as coachman, for I gave him employment in that capacity, were more than an equivalent for anything he lost by the sale of the vineyard.

—1887

George Moses Horton

On Liberty and Slavery

ALAS! and am I born for this,
  To wear this slavish chain?
Deprived of all created bliss,
  Through hardship, toil and pain!

How long have I in bondage lain,
  And languished to be free!
Alas! and must I still complain—
  Deprived of Liberty.

Oh, heaven! and is there no relief
  This side the silent grave—
To soothe the pain—to quell the grief
  And anguish of a slave?

Come Liberty, thou cheerful sound,
  Roll through my ravished ears!
Come, let my grief in joys be drowned,
  And drive away my fears.

Say unto foul oppression, "Cease:
  Ye tyrants rage no more,"
And let the joyful trump of peace
  Now bid the vassal soar.

Soar on the pinions of that dove
  Which long has cooed for thee,
And breathed her notes from Afric's grove,
  The sound of Liberty.

Oh, Liberty! thou golden prize,
  So often sought by blood—
We crave thy sacred sun to rise,
  The gift of nature's God!

Bid Slavery hide her haggard face,
  And barbarism fly:
I scorn to see the sad disgrace
  In which enslaved I lie.

Dear Liberty! upon thy breast
  I languish to respire;
And like the swan unto her nest,
  I'd to thy smiles retire.

Oh, blest asylum—heavenly balm!
  Unto thy boughs I flee—
And in thy shades the storm shall calm
  With songs of Liberty!

—1829

Frances Ellen Watkins Harper

The Dying Bondman

LIFE was trembling, faintly trembling,
  On the bondman's latest breath,
And he felt the chilling pressure
  Of the cold, hard hand of Death.

He had been an Afric chieftain,
  Worn his manhood as a crown;
But upon the field of battle
  Had been fiercely stricken down.

He had longed to gain his freedom,
  Waited, watched and hoped in vain,
Till his life was slowly ebbing—
  Almost broken was his chain.

By his bedside stood the master,
  Gazing on the dying one,
Knowing by the dull gray shadows
  That life's sands were almost run.

"Master," said the dying bondman,
  "Home and friends I soon shall see;
But before I reach my country,
  Master, write that I am free;

"For the spirits of my fathers
    Would shrink back from me in pride,
If I told them at our greeting
    I a slave had lived and died.

"Give to me the precious token,
    That my kindred dead may see—
Master! write it, write it quickly!
    Master! write that I am free!"

At his earnest plea, the master
    Wrote for him the glad release,
O'er his wan and wasted features
    Flitted one sweet smile of peace.

Eagerly he grasped the writing;
    "I am free!" at last he said.
Backward fell upon the pillow,
    He was free among the dead.

—1871

Albery A. Whitman

Custer's Last Ride

FORTH on the fatal morn,
Proud as the waves of Horn
Rode the cavalier,
Followed by gallant men,
Far in a rocky glen
To disappear.

"Halt!" bands of Sioux are seen
O'er all the dark ravine,
    Crouched in numbers vast;
"Halt!" and a hush, "Prepare!
Charge!" and the very air
    Starts at the blast.

Long waves of horsemen break,
And hoofy thunders wake
    On the steep glen sides.
Back roll the columns brave,
Back in a smoky grave
    Each hero rides.

"Ready!" their chieftain cries,
Steady his eagle eyes
    Sweep the dark ground o'er.
Slowly the lines re-form,
Slowly returns the storm,
    Yet dreadful more.

"Charge!" is the proud command;
Onward the daring band
    Like a torrent dash;
On heaving gorges long,
On groaning rocks among,
    With tempest crash.

Up from their ferny beds
Dart fields of pluming heads,
    As if hideous earth,
Out of her rocky womb,
Out of an army's tomb,
    Doth give them birth.

"Rally!" but once is heard,
"Rally!" and not a word
    The brave boys, rallying, speak.
Lightnings of valiant steel
Flash fast; the columns reel,
    Bend—reel and break!

"Stand!" cries their Custer proud,
"Stand!" in the battle cloud
    Echoes high around.
Answers the saber's stroke,
Tho' in black waves of smoke
    His fair form's drown'd.

Fierce hordes of painted braves
Melt down, for well behave
    Horse and cavalier,
As round their chief they fall,
Cheered by his clarion call,
    From front to rear.

No more their leader calls,
Pierced 'mid his men he falls,
    But sinks breathing, "Stand!"
And where the hero lies,
Each soldier till he dies
    Fights hand to hand.

—1877

James Edwin Campbell

Negro Serenade

O, DE light'bugs glimmer down de lane,
    Merlindy! Merlindy!
O, de whip'will callin' notes ur pain—
    Merlindy, O, Merlindy!
O, honey lub, my turkle dub,
    Doan' you hyuh my bawnjer ringin'?
While de night-dew falls an' de ho'n owl calls
    By de ol' ba'n gate Ise singin'.

O, Miss 'Lindy, doan' you hyuh me, chil'?
    Merlindy! Merlindy!
My lub fur you des dribe me wil'—
    Merlindy, O, Merlindy!
I'll sing dis night twel broad daylight,
    Ur bu's' my froat wid tryin',
'Less you come down, Miss 'Lindy Brown,
    An' stops dis ha't f'um sighin'!

                                    —1895

Paul Laurence Dunbar

We Wear the Mask

WE wear the mask that grins and lies,
It hides our cheeks and shades our eyes—
This debt we pay to human guile;
With torn and bleeding hearts we smile,
And mouth with myriad subtleties.

Why should the world be overwise
In counting all our tears and sighs?
Nay, let them only see us while
        We wear the mask.

We smile, but, O great Christ, our cries
To Thee from tortured souls arise.
We sing, but oh the clay is vile
Beneath our feet, and long the mile;
But let the world dream otherwise,
        We wear the mask.

                                    —1895

Ships That Pass in the Night

OUT in the sky the great dark clouds are massing;
    I look far out into the pregnant night,
Where I can hear a solemn booming gun
    And catch the gleaming of a random light,
That tells me that the ship I seek is passing, passing.

My tearful eyes my soul's deep hurt are glassing;
    For I would hail and check that ship of ships.
I stretch my hands imploring, cry aloud,
    My voice falls dead a foot from mine own lips,
And but its ghost doth reach that vessel, passing,
    passing.

O Earth, O Sky, O Ocean, both surpassing,
    O heart of mine, O soul that dreads the dark!
Is there no hope for me? Is there no way
    That I may sight and check that speeding bark
Which out of sight and sound is passing, passing?

                                    —1895

When Malindy Sings

G'WAY an' quit dat noise, Miss Lucy—
    Put dat music book away;
What's de use to keep on tryin'?
    Ef you practice twell you're gray,
You cain't sta't no notes a-flyin'
    Lak de ones dat rants and rings
F'om de kitchen to de big woods
    When Malindy sings.

You ain't got de nachel o'gans
    Fu' to make de soun' come right,
You ain't got de tu'ns an' twistin's
    Fu' to make hit sweet an' light.
Tell you one thing now, Miss Lucy,
    An' I'm tellin' you fu' true,
When hit comes to raal right singin',
    'Tain't no easy thing to do.

Easy 'nough fu' folks to hollah,
    Lookin' at de lines an' dots,
When dey ain't no one kin sense it,
    An' de chune comes in, in spots;
But fu' real melojous music,
    Dat jes' strikes yo' hea't and clings,
Jes' you stan' an' listen wif me
    When Malindy sings.

Ain't you nevah hyeahd Malindy?
    Blessed soul, tek up de cross!
Look hyeah, ain't you jokin', honey?
    Well, you don't know whut you los'.
Y'ought to hyeah dat gal a-wa'blin',
    Robins, la'ks, an' all dem things,
Heish dey moufs an' hides dey faces
    When Malindy sings.

Fiddlin' man jes' stop his fiddlin',
    Lay his fiddle on de she'f;
Mockin'bird quit tryin' to whistle,
    'Cause he jes' so 'shamed hisse'f.
Folks a-playin' on de banjo
    Draps dey fingahs on de strings—
Bless yo' soul—fu'gits to move 'em
    When Malindy sings.

She jes' spreads huh mouf and hollahs,
    "Come to Jesus," twell you hyeah
Sinnahs' tremblin' steps and voices,
    Timid-lak a-drawin' neah;
Den she tu'ns to "Rock of Ages,"
    Simply to de cross she clings,
An' you fin' yo' teahs a-drappin'
    When Malindy sings.

Who dat says dat humble praises
　　Wif de Master nevah counts?
Heish yo' mouf, I hyeah dat music,
　　Ez hit rises up an' mounts—
Floatin' by de hills an' valleys,
　　Way above dis buryin' sod,
Ez hit makes hits way in glory
　　To de very gates of God!

Oh, hit's sweetah dan de music
　　Of an edicated band;
An' hit's dearah dan de battle's
　　Song o' triumph in de lan'.
It seems holier dan evenin'
　　When de solemn chu'ch bell rings,
Ez I sit an' ca'mly listen
　　While Malindy sings.

Towsah, stop dat ba'kin', hyeah me!
　　Mandy, mek dat chile keep still;
Don't you hyeah de echoes callin'
　　F'om de valley to de hill?
Let me listen, I can hyeah hit,
　　Th'oo de bresh of angels' wings,
Sof' an' sweet, "Swing low, sweet chariot,"
　　Ez Malindy sings.

　　　　　　　　　—1895

Ere Sleep Comes Down To Soothe the Weary Eyes

ERE sleep comes down to soothe the weary eyes,
Which all the day with ceaseless care have sought
The magic gold which from the seeker flies;
Ere dreams put on the gown and cap of thought,
And make the waking world a world of lies—
Of lies most palpable, uncouth, forlorn,
That say life's full of aches and tears and sighs—
Oh, how with more than dreams the soul is torn,
Ere sleep comes down to soothe the weary eyes.

Ere sleep comes down to soothe the weary eyes,
How all the griefs and heartaches we have known
Come up like pois'nous vapors that arise
From some base witch's caldron, when the crone,
To work some potent spell, her magic plies.
The past which held its share of bitter pain,
Whose ghost we prayed that Time might exorcise,
Comes up, is lived and suffered o'er again,
Ere sleep comes down to soothe the weary eyes.

Ere sleep comes down to soothe the weary eyes,
What phantoms fill the dimly lighted room;
What ghostly shades in awe-creating guise
Are bodied forth within the teeming gloom.

What echoes faint of sad and soul-sick cries,
And pangs of vague inexplicable pain
That pay the spirit's ceaseless enterprise,
Come thronging through the chambers of the brain,
Ere sleep comes down to soothe the weary eyes.

Ere sleep comes down to soothe the weary eyes,
Where ranges forth the spirit far and free?
Through what strange realms and unfamiliar skies
Tends her far course to lands of mystery?
To lands unspeakable—beyond surmise,
Where shapes unknowable to being spring,
Till, faint of wing, the fancy fails and dies
Much wearied with the spirit's journeying,
Ere sleep comes down to soothe the weary eyes.

Ere sleep comes down to soothe the weary eyes,
How questioneth the soul that other soul—
The inner sense which neither cheats nor lies,
But self exposes unto self, a scroll
Full writ with all life's acts unwise or wise,
In characters indelible and known;
So, trembling with the shock of sad surprise,
The soul doth view its awful self alone,
Ere sleep comes down to soothe the weary eyes.

When sleep comes down to seal the weary eyes,
The last dear sleep, whose soft embrace is balm,
And whom sad sorrow teaches us to prize
For kissing all our passions into calm,
Ah, then, no more we heed the sad world's cries,
Or seek to probe th' eternal mystery,
Or fret our souls at long-withheld replies,
At glooms through which our visions cannot see,
When sleep comes down to seal the weary eyes.

　　　　　　　　　—1895

Sympathy

I KNOW what the caged bird feels, alas!
When the sun is bright on the upland slopes;
When the wind stirs soft through the springing grass
And the river flows like a stream of glass;
When the first bird sings and the first bud opes,
And the faint perfume from its chalice steals—
I know what the caged bird feels!

I know why the caged bird beats his wing
Till its blood is red on the cruel bars;
For he must fly back to his perch and cling
When he fain would be on the bough a-swing;
And a pain still throbs in the old, old scars
And they pulse again with a keener sting—
I know why he beats his wing!

I know why the caged bird sings, ah me,
When his wing is bruised and his bosom sore,
When he beats his bars and would be free;
It is not a carol of joy or glee,
But a prayer that he sends from his heart's deep core,
But a plea, that upward to heaven he flings—
I know why the caged bird sings!

—1895

Spirituals

Oh, Mary, Don't You Weep

OH, Mary, don't you weep, don't you moan,
Oh, Mary, don't you weep, don't you moan;
Pharaoh's army got drownded,
Oh, Mary, don't you weep.

One of dese mornings, bright and fair,
Take my wings and cleave de air;
Pharaoh's army got drownded,
Oh, Mary, don't you weep.

One of dese mornings, five o'clock,
Dis ole world gonna reel and rock;
Pharaoh's army got drownded,
Oh, Mary, don't you weep.

Oh, Mary, don't you weep, don't you moan,
Oh, Mary, don't you weep, don't you moan;
Pharaoh's army got drownded,
Oh, Mary, don't you weep.

Go Tell It on the Mountain

Go tell it on the mountain,
Over the hills and everywhere;
Go tell it on the mountain,
That Jesus Christ is born.

When I was a seeker,
I sought both night and day;
I asked the Lord to help me,
And he showed me the way.

He made me a watchman
Upon a city wall,
And if I am a Christian,
I am the least of all.

Go tell it on the mountain,
Over the hills and everywhere;
Go tell it on the mountain,
That Jesus Christ is born.

What You Gonna Name That Pretty Little Baby?

OH, Mary, what you gonna name
That pretty little baby?
Glory, glory, glory
To the newborn King!
"Some will call Him one thing,
But I think I'll call Him Jesus."
Glory, glory, glory
To the newborn King!
"Some will call Him one thing,
But I think I'll say Emmanuel."
Glory, glory, glory
To the newborn King!

Steal Away

STEAL away, steal away, steal away to Jesus,
Steal away, steal away home;
I ain't got long to stay here.

My Lord, He calls me,
He calls me by the thunder,
The trumpet sounds within-a my soul;
I ain't got long to stay here.

Steal away, steal away, steal away to Jesus,
Steal away, steal away home;
I ain't got long to stay here.

Green trees a-bending,
Po' sinner stands a-trembling,
The trumpet sounds within-a my soul;
I ain't got long to stay here.

Steal away, steal away, steal away to Jesus,
Steal away, steal away home;
I ain't got long to stay here.

God's Gonna Set Dis World on Fire

GOD's gonna set dis world on fire,
God's gonna set dis world on fire,
Some o' dese days—God knows it!
God's gonna set dis world on fire,
Some o' dese days.

I'm gonna drink dat healin' water,
I'm gonna drink dat healin' water,
Some o' dese days—God knows it!
I'm gonna drink dat healin' water,
Some o' dese days.

I'm gonna drink and never git thirsty,
I'm gonna drink and never git thirsty,
Some o' dese days—God knows it!
I'm gonna drink and never git thirsty,
Some o' dese days.

I'm gonna walk on de streets of glory,
I'm gonna walk on de streets of glory,
Some o' dese days—God knows it!
I'm gonna walk on de streets of glory,
Some o' dese days.

I Got a Home in Dat Rock

I GOT a home in dat rock,
Don't you see?
I got a home in dat rock,
Don't you see?
Between de earth an' sky,
Thought I heard my Savior cry,
"You got a home in dat rock,"
Don't you see?

Poor man Laz'rus, poor as I,
Don't you see?
Poor man Laz'rus, poor as I,
Don't you see?
Poor man Laz'rus, poor as I,
When he died he found a home on high;
He had a home in dat rock,
Don't you see?

Rich man Dives, he lived so well,
Don't you see?
Rich man Dives, he lived so well,
Don't you see?

Rich man Dives, he lived so well,
When he died he found a home in hell;
He had no home in dat rock,
Don't you see?

God gave Noah de rainbow sign,
Don't you see?
God gave Noah de rainbow sign,
Don't you see?
God gave Noah de rainbow sign,
No more water but fire next time;
Better get a home in dat rock,
Don't you see?

No More Auction Block

No more auction block for me,
No more, no more;
No more auction block for me,
Many thousand gone.

No more peck of corn for me,
No more, no more;
No more peck of corn for me,
Many thousand gone.

No more pint of salt for me,
No more, no more;
No more pint of salt for me,
Many thousand gone.

No more driver's lash for me,
No more, no more;
No more driver's lash for me,
Many thousand gone.

The Twentieth Century
1900–1919
1920–1934
1935–1959
1960's
Critical Commentary

1. Lindsay Patterson
2. John Oliver Killens
3. Waring Cuney
4. Richard Wright
5. Zora Neale Hurston
6. Countee Cullen
7. Henry Van Dyke
8. Gwendolyn Brooks
9. James Weldon Johns
10. Arna Bontemps

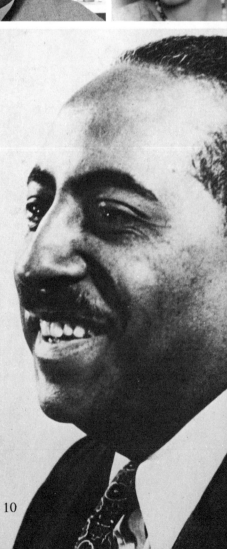

Introduction

IT WAS NOT until the publication of the novels and short stories of Charles Waddell Chesnutt, James Weldon Johnson and others that fiction by blacks came into its own. The flood of black fiction began at the time of the Harlem Renaissance, when such writers as Jean Toomer, Zora Neale Hurston, Countee Cullen and Langston Hughes began publishing.

The black writer has always been in a dilemma as to who and what should be his subject and how to approach this subject. There has never been a purely literary magazine, staffed by tough-minded critics who would dare suggest some direction or provide background. This has caused a great many writers to flounder, taking their cues only from the white establishment—who do not, in many cases, understand their problems and needs.

Whereas many of the writers of a generation ago imitated whites, the young black writer today, without much help from his elders, is finding his own voice. He is breaking away from the decorum of his predecessors.

One young voice of magnitude is that of LeRoi Jones, who has shocked white America into listening, both in his poetry and prose. Jones, who has one of the finest sensibilities of any young writer today, is threatening to let it disintegrate into propaganda before he has completed his full apprenticeship as a craftsman.

The black writer who has had perhaps the greatest impact in the twentieth century is Richard Wright. His books *Native Son* and *Black Boy* have had the largest number of imitators as well as the greatest influence; this is still being felt through almost two generations of writers and only now shows any signs of waning. One reason for this is that Wright, as well as being a good story-teller and craftsman, left a large body of distinguished work.

In 1965, Book Week of the *New York Herald Tribune* polled two hundred prominent authors, critics and editors as to the most important novel since World War II. The overwhelming response was for Ralph Ellison's *Invisible Man*, published in 1952. It won the National Book Award for fiction in 1953.

James Baldwin, with his three collections of essays, *Notes of a Native Son*, *Nobody Knows My Name* and *The Fire Next Time*, is single-handedly credited with reviving the essay form in American letters. Baldwin more than any other black writer has laid his personal life bare, which accounts for much of his power.

It is in the writings of the young that one can see much of the diversity of black life in America. Writers such as Henry Van Dyke are not necessarily concerned with racial themes as much as they are with ordinary human problems. And writers such as Robert Boles, though concerned with race, effectively chart the conflict between the middle class values of the affluent and the values of the poor.

There is no need here to reiterate the beauty and power of the poems by Langston Hughes, Countee Cullen, Sterling Brown, Margaret Walker or Gwendolyn Brooks; they speak for themselves. They, like the younger poets Jay Wright, Mari Evans, David Henderson and Ted Joans, have been concerned with everything involving life, death and hope.

The Scapegoat

Paul Laurence Dunbar

THE LAW is usually supposed to be a stern mistress, not to be lightly wooed, and yielding only to the most ardent pursuit. But even law, like love, sits more easily on some natures than on others.

This was the case with Mr. Robinson Asbury. Mr. Asbury had started life as a bootblack in the growing town of Cadgers. From this he had risen one step and become porter and messenger in a barbershop. This rise fired his ambition, and he was not content until he had learned to use the shears and the razor and had a chair of his own. From this, in a man of Robinson's temperament, it was only a step to a shop of his own, and he placed it where it would do the most good.

Fully one-half of the population of Cadgers was composed of Negroes, and with their usual tendency to colonize, a tendency encouraged, and in fact compelled, by circumstances, they had gathered into one part of the town. Here in alleys, and streets as dirty and hardly wider, they thronged like ants.

It was in this place that Mr. Asbury set up his shop, and he won the hearts of his prospective customers by putting up the significant sign, "Equal Rights Barbershop." This legend was quite unnecessary, because there was only one race about, to patronize the place. But it was a delicate sop to the people's vanity, and it served its purpose.

Asbury came to be known as a clever fellow, and his business grew. The shop really became a sort of club and, on Saturday nights especially, was the gathering place of the men of the whole Negro quarter. He kept the illustrated and race journals there, and those who cared neither to talk nor listen to someone else might see pictured the doings of high society in very short skirts or read in the Negro papers how Miss Boston had entertained Miss Blueford to tea on such and such an afternoon. Also, he kept the policy returns, which was wise, if not moral.

It was his wisdom rather more than his morality that made the party managers after a while cast their glances towards him as a man who might be useful to their interests. It would be well to have a man—a shrewd, powerful man—down in that part of the town who could carry his people's vote in his vest pocket, and who, at any time its delivery might be needed, could hand it over without hesitation. Asbury seemed that man, and they settled upon him. They gave him money, and they gave him power and patronage. He took it all silently and he carried out his bargain faithfully. His hands and his lips alike closed tightly when there was anything within them. It was not long before he found himself the big Negro of the district and, of necessity, of the town. The time came when, at a critical moment, the managers saw that they had not reckoned without their host in choosing this barber of the black district as the leader of his people.

Now, so much success must have satisfied any other man. But in many ways Mr. Asbury was unique. For a long time he himself had done very little shaving—except of notes, to keep his hand in. His time had been otherwise employed. In the evening hours he had been wooing the coquettish Dame Law, and wonderful to say, she had yielded easily to his advances.

It was against the advice of his friends that he

asked for admission to the bar. They felt that he could do more good in the place where he was.

"You see, Robinson," said old Judge Davis, "it's just like this: if you're not admitted, it'll hurt you with the people; if you are admitted, you'll move uptown to an office and get out of touch with them."

Asbury smiled an inscrutable smile. Then he whispered something into the judge's ear that made the old man wrinkle from his neck up with appreciative smiles.

"Asbury," he said, "you are—you are—well, you ought to be white, that's all. When we find a black man like you we send him to state's prison. If you were white, you'd go to the Senate."

The Negro laughed confidently.

He was admitted to the bar soon after, whether by merit or by connivance is not to be told.

"Now he will move uptown," said the black community. "Well, that's the way with a colored man when he gets a start."

But they did not know Robinson Asbury yet. He was a man of surprises, and they were destined to disappointment. He did not move uptown. He built an office in a small open space next to his shop, and there hung out his shingle.

"I will never desert the people who have done so much to elevate me," said Mr. Asbury. "I will live among them and I will die among them."

This was a strong card for the barber-lawyer. The people seized upon the statement as expressing a nobility of an altogether unique brand.

They held a mass meeting and endorsed him. They made resolutions that extolled him, and the Negro band came around and serenaded him, playing various things in varied time.

All this was very sweet to Mr. Asbury, and the party managers chuckled with satisfaction and said, "That Asbury, that Asbury!"

Now there is a fable extant of a man who tried to please everybody, and his failure is a matter of record. Robinson Asbury was not more successful. But be it said that his ill success was due to no fault or shortcoming of his.

For a long time his growing power had been looked upon with disfavor by the colored law firm of Bingo and Latchett. Both Mr. Bingo and Mr. Latchett themselves aspired to be Negro leaders in Cadgers, and they were delivering Emancipation Day orations and riding at the head of processions when Mr. Asbury was blacking boots. Is it any wonder, then, that they viewed with alarm his sudden rise? They kept their counsel, however, and treated with him, for it was best. They allowed him his scope without open revolt until the day upon which he hung out his shingle. This was the last straw. They could stand no more. Asbury had stolen their other chances from them, and now he was poaching upon the last of their preserves. So Mr. Bingo and Mr. Latchett put their heads together to plan the downfall of their common enemy.

The plot was deep and embraced the formation of an opposing faction made up of the best Negroes of the town. It would have looked too much like what it was for the gentlemen to show themselves in the matter, and so they took into their confidence Mr. Isaac Morton, the principal of the colored school, and it was under his ostensible leadership that the new faction finally came into being.

Mr. Morton was really an innocent young man, and he had ideals which should never have been exposed to the air. When the wily confederates came to him with their plan, he believed that his worth had been recognized and at last he was to be what nature destined him for—a leader.

The better class of Negroes—by that is meant those who were particularly envious of Asbury's success—flocked to the new man's standard. But whether the race be white or black, political virtue is always in a minority, so Asbury could afford to smile at the force arrayed against him.

The new faction met together and resolved. They resolved, among other things, that Mr. Asbury was an enemy to his race and a menace to civilization. They decided that he should be abolished; but as they couldn't get out an injunction against him, and as he had the whole undignified but still voting black belt behind him, he went serenely on his way.

"They're after you hot and heavy, Asbury," said one of his friends to him.

"Oh, yes," was the reply, "they're after me, but after a while I'll get so far away that they'll be running in front."

"It's all the best people, they say."

"Yes. Well, it's good to be one of the best people, but your vote only counts one just the same."

The time came, however, when Mr. Asbury's theory was put to the test. The Cadgerites celebrated the first of January as Emancipation Day. On this day there was a large procession, with speechmaking in the afternoon and fireworks at night. It was the custom to concede the leadership of the colored people of the town to the man who managed to lead the procession. For two years past this honor had fallen, of course, to Robinson Asbury, and there had been no disposition on the part of anybody to try conclusions with him.

Mr. Morton's faction changed all this. When Asbury went to work to solicit contributions for the celebration, he suddenly became aware that he had a fight upon his hands. All the better-class Negroes were staying out of it. The next thing he knew was that plans were on foot for a rival demonstration.

"Oh," he said to himself, "that's it, is it? Well, if they want a fight they can have it."

He had a talk with the party managers, and he had another with Judge Davis.

"All I want is a little lift, Judge," he said, "and I'll make 'em think the sky has turned loose and is vomiting niggers."

The judge believed that he could do it. So did the party managers. Asbury got his lift. Emancipation Day came.

There were two parades. At least, there was one parade and the shadow of another. Asbury's, however, was not the shadow. There was a great deal of substance about it—substance made up of many people, many banners and numerous bands. He did not have the best people. Indeed, among his cohorts there were a good many of the pronounced ragtag and bobtail. But he had noise and numbers. In such cases, nothing more is needed. The success of Asbury's side of the affair did everything to confirm his friends in their good opinion of him.

When he found himself defeated, Mr. Silas Bingo saw that it would be policy to placate his rival's just anger against him. He called upon him at his office the day after the celebration.

"Well, Asbury," he said, "you beat us, didn't you?"

"It wasn't a question of beating," said the other calmly. "It was only an inquiry as to who were the people—the few or the many."

"Well, it was well done, and you've shown that you are a manager. I confess that I haven't always thought that you were doing the wisest thing in living down here and catering to this class of people when you might, with your ability, be much more to the better class."

"What do they base their claims of being better on?"

"Oh, there ain't any use discussing that. We can't get along without you, we see that. So I, for one, have decided to work with you for harmony."

"Harmony. Yes, that's what we want."

"If I can do anything to help you at any time, why you have only to command me."

"I am glad to find such a friend in you. Be sure, if I ever need you, Bingo, I'll call on you."

"And I'll be ready to serve you."

Asbury smiled when his visitor was gone. He smiled, and knitted his brow. "I wonder what Bingo's got up his sleeve," he said. "He'll bear watching."

It may have been pride at his triumph, it may have been gratitude at his helpers, but Asbury went into the ensuing campaign with reckless enthusiasm. He did the most daring things for the party's sake. Bingo, true to his promise, was ever at his side ready to serve him. Finally, association and immunity made danger less fearsome; the rival no longer appeared a menace.

With the generosity born of obstacles overcome, Asbury determined to forgive Bingo and give him a chance. He let him in on a deal, and from that time they worked amicably together until the election came and passed.

It was a close election and many things had had to be done, but there were men there ready and waiting to do them. They were successful, and then the first cry of the defeated party was, as usual, "Fraud! Fraud!" The cry was taken up by the jealous, the disgruntled and the virtuous.

Someone remembered how two years ago the registration books had been stolen. It was known upon good authority that money had been freely used. Men held up their hands in horror at the suggestion that the Negro vote had been juggled with, as if that were a new thing. From their pulpits ministers denounced the machine and bade their hearers rise and throw off the yoke of a corrupt municipal government. One of those sudden fevers of reform had taken possession of the town and threatened to destroy the successful party.

They began to look around them. They must purify themselves. They must give the people some tangible evidence of their own yearnings after purity. They looked around them for a sacrifice to lay upon the altar of municipal reform. Their eyes fell upon Mr. Bingo. No, he was not big enough. His blood was too scant to wash the political stains. Then they looked into each other's eyes and turned their gaze away to let it fall upon Mr. Asbury. They really hated to do it. But there must be a scapegoat. The god from the machine commanded them to slay him.

Robinson Asbury was charged with many crimes—with all that he had committed and some that he had not. When Mr. Bingo saw what was afoot he threw himself heart and soul into the work of his old rival's enemies. He was of incalculable use to them.

Judge Davis refused to have anything to do with the matter. But in spite of his disapproval it went on. Asbury was indicted and tried. The evidence was all against him, and no one gave more damaging testimony than his friend Mr. Bingo. The judge's charge was favorable to the defendant, but the current of popular opinion could not be entirely stemmed. The jury brought in a verdict of guilty.

"Before I am sentenced, Judge, I have a statement to make to the court. It will take less than ten minutes."

"Go on, Robinson," said the judge kindly.

Asbury started, in a monotonous tone, a recital that brought the prosecuting attorney to his feet in a minute. The judge waved him down, and sat transfixed by a sort of fascinated horror as the convicted man went on. The before-mentioned attorney drew a knife and started for the prisoner's dock. With difficulty he was restrained. A dozen faces in the courtroom were red and pale by turns.

"He ought to be killed," whispered Mr. Bingo audibly.

Robinson Asbury looked at him and smiled, and then he told a few things of him. He gave the ins and outs of some of the misdemeanors of which he stood accused. He showed who were the men behind the throne. And still, pale and transfixed, Judge Davis waited for his own sentence.

Never were ten minutes so well taken up. It was a tale of rottenness and corruption in high places told simply and with the stamp of truth upon it.

He did not mention the judge's name. But he had torn the mask from the face of every other man who had been concerned in his downfall. They had shorn him of his strength, but they had forgotten that he was yet able to bring the roof and pillars tumbling about their heads.

The judge's voice shook as he pronounced sentence upon his old ally—a year in state's prison.

Some people said it was too light, but the judge knew what it was to wait for the sentence of doom, and he was grateful and sympathetic.

When the sheriff led Asbury away the judge hastened to have a short talk with him.

"I'm sorry, Robinson," he said, "and I want to tell you that you were no more guilty than the rest of us. But why did you spare me?"

"Because I knew you were my friend," answered the convict.

"I tried to be, but you were the first man that I've ever known since I've been in politics who ever gave me any decent return for friendship."

"I reckon you're about right, Judge."

In politics, party reform usually lies in making a scapegoat of someone who is only as criminal as the rest, but a little weaker. Asbury's friends and enemies had succeeded in making him bear the burden of all the party's crimes, but their reform was hardly a success, and their protestations of a change of heart were received with doubt. Already there were those who began to pity the victim and to say that he had been hardly dealt with.

Mr. Bingo was not of these; but he found, strange to say, that his opposition to the idea went but a little way, and that even with Asbury out of his path he was a smaller man than he was before. Fate was strong against him. His poor prosperous humanity could not enter the lists against a martyr. Robinson Asbury was now a martyr.

A year is not a long time. It was short enough to prevent people from forgetting Robinson, and yet long enough for their pity to grow strong as they remembered. Indeed, he was not gone a year. Good behavior cut two months off the time of his sentence, and by the time people had come around to the notion that he was really the greatest and smartest man in Cadgers he was at home again.

He came back with no flourish of trumpets, but quietly, humbly. He went back again into the heart of the black district. His business had deteriorated during his absence, but he put new blood and new life into it. He did not go to work in the shop himself but, taking down the shingle that had swung idly before his office door during his imprisonment, he opened the little room as a news- and cigarstand.

Here anxious, pitying customers came to him and he prospered again. He was very quiet. Uptown hardly knew that he was again in Cadgers, and it knew nothing whatever of his doings.

"I wonder why Asbury is so quiet," they said to one another. "It isn't like him to be quiet." And they felt vaguely uneasy about him.

So many people had begun to say, "Well, he was a mighty good fellow after all."

Mr. Bingo expressed the opinion that Asbury was quiet because he was crushed, but others expressed doubt as to this. There are calms and calms, some after and some before the storm. Which was this?

They waited a while and, as no storm came, concluded that this must be the afterquiet. Bingo, reassured, volunteered to go and seek confirmation of this conclusion.

He went, and Asbury received him with an indifferent, not to say impolite, demeanor.

"Well, we're glad to see you back, Asbury," said Bingo patronizingly. He had variously demonstrated his inability to lead during his rival's absence and was proud of it. "What are you going to do?"

"I'm going to work."

"That's right. I reckon you'll stay out of politics."

"What could I do even if I went in?"

"Nothing now, of course; but I didn't know—"

He did not see the gleam in Asbury's half-shut eyes. He only marked his humility, and he went back swelling with the news.

"Completely crushed—all the run taken out of him," was his report.

The black district believed this, too, and a sullen, smoldering anger took possession of them. Here was a good man ruined. Some of the people whom he had helped in his former days— some of the rude, coarse people of the low quarter who were still sufficiently unenlightened to be grateful—talked among themselves and offered to get up a demonstration for him. But he denied them. No, he wanted nothing of the kind. It would only bring him into unfavorable notice. All he wanted was that they would always be his friends and would stick by him.

They would to the death.

There were again two factions in Cadgers. The schoolmaster could not forget how once on a time he had been made a tool of by Mr. Bingo. So he revolted against his rule and set himself up as the leader of an opposing clique. The fight had been long and strong, but had ended with odds slightly in Bingo's favor.

But Mr. Morton did not despair. As the first of January and Emancipation Day approached, he arrayed his hosts, and the fight for supremacy became fiercer than ever. The schoolteacher brought the schoolchildren in for chorus singing, secured an able orator and the best essayist in town. With all this, he was formidable.

Mr. Bingo knew that he had the fight of his life on his hands, and he entered with fear as well as zest. He, too, found an orator, but he was not sure that he was good as Morton's. There was no doubt but that his essayist was not. He secured a band, but still he felt unsatisfied. He had hardly done enough, and for the schoolmaster to beat him now meant his political destruction.

It was in this state of mind that he was surprised to receive a visit from Mr. Asbury.

"I reckon you're surprised to see me here," said Asbury, smiling.

"I am pleased, I know." Bingo was astute.

"Well, I just dropped in on our business."

"To be sure, to be sure, Asbury. What can I do for you?"

"It's more what I can do for you that I came to talk about," was the reply.

"I don't believe I understand you."

"Well, it's plain enough. They say that the schoolteacher is giving you a pretty hard fight."

"Oh, not so hard."

"No man can be too sure of winning, though. Mr. Morton once did me a mean turn when he started the faction against me."

Bingo's heart gave a great leap and then stopped for the fraction of a second.

"You were in it, of course," pursued Asbury, "but I can look over your part in it in order to get even with the man who started it."

It was true, then, thought Bingo gladly. He did not know. He wanted revenge for his wrongs and upon the wrong man. How well the schemer had covered his tracks! Asbury should have his revenge and Morton would be the sufferer.

"Of course, Asbury, you know that I did what I did innocently."

"Oh, yes, in politics we are all lambs and the wolves are only to be found in the other party. We'll pass that, though. What I want to say is that I can help you to make your celebration an overwhelming success. I still have some influence down in my district."

"Certainly, and very justly, too. Why I should be delighted with your aid. I could give you a prominent position in the procession."

"I don't want it; I don't want to appear in this at all. All I want is revenge. You can have all the credit, but let me down my enemy."

Bingo was perfectly willing, and with their heads close together they had a long and close consultation. When Asbury was gone, Mr. Bingo lay back in his chair and laughed. "I'm a slick duck," he said.

From that hour Mr. Bingo's cause began to take on the appearance of something very like a boom. More bands were hired. The interior of the state was called upon and a more eloquent orator secured. The crowd hastened to array itself on the growing side.

With surprised eyes, the schoolmaster beheld the wonder of it, but he kept to his own pur-

pose with dogged insistence, even when he saw that he could not turn aside the overwhelming defeat that threatened him. But in spite of his obstinacy, his hours were dark and bitter. Asbury worked like a mole, all underground, but he was indefatigable. Two days before the celebration time everything was perfected for the biggest demonstration that Cadgers had ever known. All the next day and night he was busy among his allies.

On the morning of the great day, Mr. Bingo, wonderfully caparisoned, rode down to the hall where the parade was to form. He was early. No one had yet come. In an hour a score of men all told had collected. Another hour passed, and no more had come. Then there smote upon his ear the sound of music. They were coming at last. Bringing his sword to his shoulder, he rode forward to the middle of the street. Ah, there they were. But—but—could he believe his eyes? They were going in another direction and at their head rode—Morton! He gnashed his teeth in fury. He had been led into a trap and betrayed. The procession passing had been his—all his. He heard them cheering, and then, oh! climax of infidelity, he saw his own orator go past in a carriage, bowing and smiling to the crowd.

There was no doubting who had done this thing. The hand of Asbury was apparent in it. He must have known the truth all along, thought Bingo. His allies left him one by one for the other hall, and he rode home in a humiliation deeper than he had ever known before.

Asbury did not appear at the celebration. He was at his little newsstand all day.

In a day or two the defeated aspirant had further cause to curse his false friend. He found that not only had the people defected from him, but that the thing had been so adroitly managed that he appeared to be in fault, and three-fourths of those who knew him were angry at some supposed grievance. His cup of bitterness was full when his partner, a quietly ambitious man, suggested that they dissolve their relations.

His ruin was complete.

The lawyer was not alone in seeing Asbury's hand in his downfall. The party managers saw it too, and they met together to discuss the dangerous factor which, while it appeared to slumber, was so terribly awake. They decided that he must be appeased, and they visited him.

He was still busy at his newsstand. They talked to him adroitly, while he sorted papers and kept an impassive face. When they were all done, he looked up for a moment and replied, "You know, gentlemen, as an ex-convict I am not in politics."

Some of them had the grace to flush.

"But you can use your influence," they said.

"I am not in politics," was his only reply.

And the spring elections were coming on. Well, they worked hard, and he showed no sign. He treated with neither one party nor the other. "Perhaps," thought the managers, "he is out of politics," and they grew more confident.

It was nearing eleven o'clock on the morning of election when a cloud no bigger than a man's hand appeared upon the horizon. It came from the direction of the black district. It grew, and the managers of the party in power looked at it, fascinated by an ominous dread. Finally it began to rain Negro voters, and as one man they voted against their former candidates. Their organization was perfect. They simply came, voted, and left, but they overwhelmed everything. Not one of the party that had damned Robinson Asbury was left in power save old Judge Davis. His majority was overwhelming.

The generalship that had engineered the thing was perfect. There were loud threats against the newsdealer. But no one bothered him except a reporter. The reporter called to see just how it was done. He found Asbury very busy sorting papers. To the newspaperman's questions he had only this reply, "I am not in politics, sir."

But Cadgers had learned its lesson.

—1904

Dreams

W. E. B. Du Bois

NIGHT fell. The red waters of the swamp grew sinister and sullen. The tall pines lost their slimness and stood in wide blurred blotches all across the way, and a great shadowy bird arose, wheeled and melted, murmuring, into the black-green sky.

The boy wearily dropped his heavy bundle and stood still, listening as the voice of crickets split the shadows and made the silence audible. A tear wandered down his brown cheek. They were at supper now, he whispered—the father and old mother, away back yonder beyond the night. They were far away; they would never be as near as once they had been, for he had stepped into the world. And the cat and Old Billy—ah, but the world was a lonely thing, so wide and tall and empty! And so bare, so bitter bare! Somehow he had never dreamed of the world as lonely before; he had fared forth to beckoning hands and luring, and to the eager hum of human voices, as of some great, swelling music.

Yet now he was alone; the empty night was closing all about him here in a strange land, and he was afraid. The bundle with his earthly treasure had hung heavy and heavier on his shoulder; his little horde of money was tightly wadded in his sock, and the school lay hidden somewhere far away in the shadows. He wondered how far it was; he looked and hearkened, starting at his own heartbeats and fearing more and more the long dark fingers of the night.

Then of a sudden up from the darkness came music. It was human music, but of a wildness and a weirdness that startled the boy as it fluttered and danced across the dull red waters of the swamp. He hesitated, then, impelled by some strange power, left the highway and slipped into the forest of the swamp, shrinking, yet following the song hungrily and half forgetting his fear. A harsher, shriller note struck in as of many and ruder voices; but above it flew the first sweet music, birdlike, abandoned, and the boy crept closer. The cabin crouched ragged and black at the edge of black waters. An old chimney leaned drunkenly against it, raging with fire and smoke, while through the chinks winked red gleams of warmth and wild cheer. With a revel of shouting and noise, the music suddenly ceased. Hoarse staccato cries and peals of laughter shook the old hut, and as the boy stood there peering through the black trees, abruptly the door flew open and a flood of light illumined the wood.

Amid this mighty halo, as on clouds of flame, a girl was dancing. She was black, and lithe, and tall, and willowy. Her garments twined and flew around the delicate molding of her dark, young, half-naked limbs. A heavy mass of hair clung motionless to her wide forehead. Her arms twirled and flickered, and body and soul seemed quivering and whirring in the poetry of her motion.

As she danced she sang. He heard her voice as before, fluttering like a bird's in the full sweetness of her utter music. It was no tune nor melody, it was just formless, boundless music. The boy forgot himself and all the world besides. All his darkness was sudden light; dazzled he crept forward, bewildered, fascinated, until with one last wild whirl the elf-girl paused. The crimson light fell full upon the warm and velvet bronze of her face—her midnight eyes were aglow, her full purple lips apart, her half-hid bosom panting and all the music dead. Involuntarily the boy gave a gasping cry and awoke to swamp and night and fire, while a white face, drawn, red-eyed, peered outward from some hidden throng within the cabin.

"Who's that?" a harsh voice cried.

"Where?" "Who is it?" and pale crowding faces blurred the light.

The boy wheeled blindly and fled in terror, stumbling through the swamp, hearing strange sounds and feeling stealthy creeping hands and arms and whispering voices. On he toiled in mad haste, struggling toward the road and losing it, until finally beneath the shadows of a mighty oak he sank exhausted. There he lay a while, trembling, and at last drifted into dreamless sleep.

It was morning when he awoke and threw a startled glance upward to the twisted branches of the oak that bent above, sifting down sunshine on his brown face and close-curled hair. Slowly he remembered the loneliness, the fear and wild running through the dark. He laughed in the bold courage of day and stretched himself.

Then suddenly he bethought him again of that vision of the night—the waving arms and flying limbs of the girl, and her great black eyes looking into the night and calling him. He could hear her now, and hear that wondrous savage music. Had it been real? Had he dreamed? Or had it been some witch-vision of the night, come to tempt and lure him to his undoing? Where was that black and flaming cabin? Where was the girl—the soul that had called him? *She* must have been real; she had to live and dance and sing; he must again look into the mystery of her great eyes. And he sat up in sudden determination, and lo! gazed straight into the very eyes of his dreaming.

She sat not four feet from him, leaning against the great tree, her eyes now languorously abstracted, now alert and quizzical with mischief. She seemed but half-clothed, and her warm, dark flesh peeped furtively through the rent gown; her thick, crisp hair was frowsy and rumpled, and the long curves of her bare young arms gleamed in the morning sunshine, glowing with vigor and life. A little mocking smile came and sat upon her lips.

"What you run for?" she asked, with dancing mischief in her eyes.

"Because—" he hesitated, and his cheeks grew hot.

"I knows," she said, with impish glee, laughing low music.

"Why?" he challenged sturdily.

"You was afeared."

He bridled. "Well, I reckon you'd be afeared if you was caught out in the black dark all alone."

"Pooh!" she scoffed and hugged her knees. "Pooh! I'se stayed out all alone heaps o' nights."

He looked at her with a curious awe.

"I don't believe you," he asserted; but she tossed her head and her eyes grew scornful.

"Who's afeared of the dark? I love night." Her eyes grew soft. He watched her silently, till, waking from her daydream, she abruptly asked, "Where you from?"

"Georgia."

"Where's that?"

He looked at her in surprise, but she seemed matter-of-fact.

"It's away over yonder," he answered.

"Behind where the sun comes up?"

"Oh, no!"

"Then it ain't so far," she declared. "I knows where the sun rises, and I knows where it sets." She looked up at its gleaming splendor glinting through the leaves and, noting its height, announced abruptly, "I'se hungry."

"So 'm I," answered the boy, fumbling at his bundle; and then, timidly: "Will you eat with me?"

"Yes," she said, and watched him with eager eyes.

Untying the strips of cloth, he opened his box and disclosed chicken and biscuits, ham and corn bread. She clapped her hands in glee.

"Is there any water near?" he asked.

Without a word she bounded up and flitted off like a brown bird, gleaming dull-golden in the sun, glancing in and out among the trees, till she paused above a tiny black pool and then came tripping and swaying back with hands held cupwise and dripping with cool water.

"Drink," she cried. Obediently he bent over the little hands that seemed so soft and thin. He took a deep draught; and then to drain the last drop, his hands touched hers and the shock of flesh first meeting flesh startled them both, while the water rained through. A moment their eyes looked deep into each other's—a timid, startled gleam in hers, a wonder in his. Then she said dreamily: "We'se known us all our lives, and—before, ain't we?"

He hesitated. "Ye—es—I reckon," he slowly returned. And then, brightening, he asked gaily, "And we'll be friends always, won't we?"

"Yes," she said at last, slowly and solemnly, and another brief moment they stood still.

Then the mischief danced in her eyes and a song bubbled on her lips. She hopped to the tree.

"Come—eat!" she cried. And they nestled together amid the big black roots of the oak, laughing and talking while they ate.

"What's over there?" he asked, pointing northward.

"Cresswell's big house."

"And yonder to the west?"

"The school."

He started joyfully. "The school! What school?"

"Old Miss' school."

"Miss Smith's school?"

"Yes." The tone was disdainful.

"Why, that's where I'm going. I was afeared it was a long way off; I must have passed it in the night."

"I hate it!" cried the girl, her lips tense.

"But I'll be so near," he explained. "And why do you hate it?"

"Yes—you'll be near," she admitted, "that'll be nice, but—" she glanced westward and the fierce look faded. Soft joy crept to her face again and she sat once more dreaming.

"Yon way's nicest," she said.

"Why, what's there?"

"The swamp," she said mysteriously.

"And what's beyond the swamp?"

She crouched beside him and whispered in eager, tense tones: "Dreams!"

He looked at her, puzzled. "Dreams?" vaguely —"dreams? Why, dreams ain't—nothing."

"Oh, yes they is!" she insisted, her eyes flaming in misty radiance as she sat staring beyond the shadows of the swamp. "Yes they is! There ain't nothing but dreams—that is, nothing much.

"And over yonder behind the swamps is great fields full of dreams, piled high and burning; and right amongst them the sun, when he's tired o' night, whispers and drops red things, 'cept when devils make 'em black."

The boy stared at her; he knew not whether to jeer or wonder.

"How you know?" he asked at last, skeptically.

"Promise you won't tell?"

"Yes," he answered.

She cuddled into a little heap, nursing her knees, and answered slowly.

"I goes there sometimes. I creeps in 'mongst the dreams; they hangs there like big flowers, dripping dew and sugar and blood—red, red blood. And there's little fairies there that hop about and sing, and devils—great ugly devils that grabs at you and roasts and eats you if they gits you; but they don't git me. Some devils is big and white, like ha'nts; some is long and shiny, like creepy, slippery snakes; and some is little and broad and black, and they yells—"

The boy was listening in incredulous curiosity, half minded to laugh, half minded to edge away from the black-red radiance of yonder dusky swamp. He glanced furtively backward, and his heart gave a great bound.

"Some is little and broad and black, and they yells—" chanted the girl. And as she chanted, deep harsh tones came booming through the forest: "Zo-ra! Zo-ra! O—o—oh, Zora!"

He saw far behind him, toward the shadows of the swamp, an old woman—short, broad, black and wrinkled, with fangs and pendulous lips and red, wicked eyes. His heart bounded in sudden fear; he wheeled toward the girl and caught only the uncertain flash of her garments —the wood was silent, and he was alone.

He arose, startled, quickly gathered his bundle, and looked around him. The sun was strong and high, the morning fresh and vigorous. Stamping one foot angrily, he strode jauntily out of the wood toward the big road.

But ever and anon he glanced curiously back. Had he seen a haunt? Or was the elf-girl real? And then he thought of her words:

"We'se known us all our lives."

—1911

From *The Quest of the Silver Fleece*

The Childhood of an Ex-Colored Man

James Weldon Johnson

I KNOW that in writing the following pages I am divulging the great secret of my life, the secret which for some years I have guarded far more carefully than any of my earthly possessions; and it is a curious study to me to analyze the motives which prompt me to do it. I feel that I am led by the same impulse which forces the unfound-out criminal to take somebody into his confidence, although he knows that the act is likely, even almost certain, to lead to his undoing. I know that I am playing with fire, and I feel the thrill which accompanies that most fascinating pastime; and, back of it all, I think I find a sort of savage and diabolical desire to gather up all the little tragedies of my life and turn them into a practical joke on society.

And, too, I suffer a vague feeling of unsatisfaction, of regret, of almost remorse, from which I am seeking relief. . . .

I was born in a little town of Georgia a few years after the close of the Civil War. I shall not mention the name of the town, because there are people still living there who could be connected with this narrative. I have only a faint recollection of the place of my birth. At times I can close my eyes and call up in a dreamlike way things that seem to have happened ages ago in some other world. I can see in this half vision a little house—I am quite sure it was not a large one. I can remember that flowers grew in the front yard, and that around each bed of flowers was a hedge of varicolored glass bottles stuck in the ground neck down. I remember that once, while playing round in the sand, I became curious to know whether or not the bottles grew as the flowers did, and I proceeded to dig them up to find out; the investigation brought me a terrific spanking, which indelibly fixed the incident in my mind.

I can remember, too, that behind the house was a shed under which stood two or three wooden washtubs. These tubs were the earliest aversion of my life, for regularly on certain evenings I was plunged into one of them and scrubbed until my skin ached. I can remember to this day the pain caused by the strong, rank soap's getting into my eyes.

Back from the house a vegetable garden ran, perhaps seventy-five or one hundred feet; but to my childish fancy it was an endless territory. I can still recall the thrill of joy, excitement and wonder it gave me to go on an exploring expedition through it, to find the blackberries, both ripe and green, that grew along the edge of the fence.

I remember with what pleasure I used to arrive at, and stand before, a little enclosure in which stood a patient cow chewing her cud, how I would occasionally offer her through the bars a piece of my bread and molasses and how I would jerk back my hand in half fright if she made any motion to accept my offer.

I have a dim recollection of several people who moved in and about this little house, but I have a distinct mental image of only two: one, my mother, and the other, a tall man with a small dark moustache. I remember that his shoes or boots were always shiny, and that he wore a gold chain and a great gold watch with which he was always willing to let me play. My admiration was almost equally divided between the watch and chain and the shoes. He used to come to the house evenings, perhaps two or three times a week; and it became my appointed duty whenever he came to bring him a pair of slippers and to put the shiny shoes in a particular corner. He often gave me in return for this service a bright coin, which my mother taught me to promptly drop in a little tin bank. I remember distinctly the last time this tall man came to the little house in Georgia. That evening, before I went to bed, he took me up in his arms and squeezed me very tightly; my mother stood behind his chair wiping tears from her eyes. I remember how I sat upon his knee and watched him laboriously drill a hole through a ten-dollar gold piece, and then tie the coin around my neck with a string. I have worn that gold piece around my neck the greater part of my life, and still possess it, but more than once I have wished that some other way had been found of attaching it to me besides putting a hole through it.

On the day after the coin was put around my neck, my mother and I started on what seemed to me an endless journey. I knelt on the seat and watched through the train window the corn- and cotton-fields pass swiftly by until I fell asleep. When I fully awoke, we were being driven through the streets of a large city—Savannah. I sat up and blinked at the bright lights. At Savannah we boarded a steamer which finally landed us in New York. From New York we went to a town in Connecticut, which became the home of my boyhood.

My mother and I lived together in a little cottage which seemed to me to be fitted up almost luxuriously; there were horsehair-covered chairs in the parlor, and a little square piano; there was a stairway with red carpet on it leading to a half second-story; there were pictures on the walls, and a few books in a glass-doored case. My mother dressed me very neatly, and I developed that pride which well-dressed boys generally have. She was careful about my associates, and I myself was quite particular. As I look back now I can see that I was a perfect little aristocrat. My mother rarely went to anyone's house, but she did sewing, and there were a great many ladies coming to our cottage. If I was round they would generally call me and ask me my name and age and tell my mother what a pretty boy I

was. Some of them would pat me on the head and kiss me.

My mother was kept very busy with her sewing; sometimes she would have another woman helping her. I think she must have derived a fair income from her work. I know, too, that at least once each month she received a letter; I used to watch for the postman, get the letter and run to her with it; whether she was busy or not, she would take it and instantly thrust it into her bosom. I never saw her read one of these letters. I knew later that they contained money and what was to her more than money.

As busy as she generally was, she found time, however, to teach me my letters and figures and how to spell a number of easy words. Always on Sunday evenings she opened the little square piano and picked out hymns. I can recall now that whenever she played hymns from the book her tempo was always decidedly largo.

Sometimes on other evenings, when she was not sewing, she would play simple accompaniments to some old Southern songs which she sang. In these songs she was freer, because she played them by ear. Those evenings on which she opened the little piano were the happiest hours of my childhood. Whenever she started toward the instrument, I used to follow her with all the interest and irrepressible joy that a pampered pet dog shows when a package is opened in which he knows there is a sweet bit for him. I used to stand by her side and often interrupt and annoy her by chiming in with strange harmonies which I found on either the high keys of the treble or the low keys of the bass. I remember that I had a particular fondness for the black keys. Always on such evenings, when the music was over, my mother would sit with me in her arms, often for a very long time. She would hold me close, softly crooning some old melody without words, all the while gently stroking her face against my head; many and many a night I thus fell asleep. I can see her now, her great dark eyes looking into the fire, to where? No one knew but her. The memory of that picture has more than once kept me from straying too far from the place of purity and safety in which her arms held me.

At a very early age I began to thump on the

piano alone, and it was not long before I was able to pick out a few tunes. When I was seven years old, I could play by ear all of the hymns and songs that my mother knew. I had also learned the names of the notes in both clefs, but I preferred not to be hampered by notes.

About this time several ladies for whom my mother sewed heard me play, and they persuaded her that I should at once be put under a teacher; so arrangements were made for me to study the piano with a lady who was a fairly good musician. At the same time arrangements were made for me to study my books with this lady's daughter. My music teacher had no small difficulty at first in pinning me down to the notes. If she played my lesson over for me, I invariably attempted to reproduce the required sounds without the slightest recourse to the written characters. Her daughter, my other teacher, also had her worries. She found that in reading, whenever I came to words that were difficult or unfamiliar, I was prone to bring my imagination to the rescue and read from the picture. She has laughingly told me since then that I would sometimes substitute whole sentences and even paragraphs from what meaning I thought the illustrations conveyed. She said she not only was sometimes amused at the fresh treatment I would give an author's subject but, when I gave some new and sudden turn to the plot of the story, often grew interested and even excited in listening to hear what kind of a denouement I would bring about. But I am sure this was not due to dullness, for I made rapid progress in both my music and my books.

And so for a couple of years my life was divided between my music and my schoolbooks. Music took up the greater part of my time. I had no playmates, but amused myself with games—some of them my own invention—which could be played alone. I knew a few boys whom I had met at the church which I attended with my mother, but I had formed no close friendships with any of them.

Then, when I was nine years old, my mother decided to enter me in the public school, so all at once I found myself thrown among a crowd of boys of all sizes and kinds; some of them seemed to me like savages. I shall never forget the bewilderment, the pain, the heartsickness, of that first day at school. I seemed to be the only stranger in the place; every other boy seemed to know every other boy. I was fortunate enough, however, to be assigned to a teacher who knew me; my mother made her dresses. She was one of the ladies who used to pat me on the head and kiss me. She had the tact to address a few words directly to me. This gave me a certain sort of standing in the class and put me somewhat at ease.

Within a few days I had made one staunch friend and was on fairly good terms with most of the boys. I was shy of the girls, and remained so; even now a word or look from a pretty woman sets me all a-tremble. This friend I bound to me with hooks of steel in a very simple way. He was a big awkward boy with a face full of freckles and a head full of very red hair. He was perhaps fourteen years of age—that is, four or five years older than any other boy in the class. This seniority was due to the fact that he had spent twice the required amount of time in several of the preceding classes. I had not been at school many hours before I felt that "Red Head"—as I involuntarily called him—and I were to be friends.

I do not doubt that this feeling was strengthened by the fact that I had been quick enough to see that a big, strong boy was a friend to be desired at a public school; and, perhaps, in spite of his dullness, Red Head had been able to discern that I could be of service to him. At any rate, there was a simultaneous mutual attraction.

The teacher had strung the class promiscuously round the walls of the room for a sort of trial heat for places of rank. When the line was straightened out, I found that by skillful maneuvering I had placed myself third and had piloted Red Head to the place next to me. The teacher began by giving us to spell the words corresponding to our order in the line. "Spell *first*." "Spell *second*." "Spell *third*."

I rattled off: "T-h-i-r-d, third," in a way which said, "Why don't you give us something hard?" As the words went down the line, I could see how lucky I had been to get a good place together with an easy word. As young as I was, I felt

impressed with the unfairness of the whole pro-
ceeding when I saw the tail-enders going down
before *twelfth* and *twentieth*, and I felt sorry for
those who had to spell such words in order to
hold a low position.

"Spell *fourth*." Red Head, with his hands
clutched tightly behind his back, began bravely:
"F-o-r-t-h."

Like a flash a score of hands went up, and the
teacher began saying: "No snapping of fingers,
no snapping of fingers."

This was the first word missed, and it seemed
to me that some of the scholars were about to
lose their senses. Some were dancing up and down
on one foot with a hand above their heads, the
fingers working furiously and joy beaming all
over their faces; others stood still, their hands
raised not so high, their fingers working less
rapidly and their faces expressing not quite so
much happiness; there were still others who did
not move or raise their hands, but stood with
great wrinkles on their foreheads, looking very
thoughtful.

The whole thing was new to me, and I did not
raise my hand but slyly whispered the letter *u* to
Red Head several times. "Second chance," said
the teacher.

The hands went down and the class became
quiet. Red Head, his face now red, after looking
beseechingly at the ceiling, then pitiably at the
floor, began very haltingly: "F-u——" Immediately an impulse to raise hands went through the
class, but the teacher checked it, and poor Red
Head, though he knew that each letter he added
only took him farther out of the way, went dog-
gedly on and finished: "——r-t-h."

The hand-raising was now repeated with more
hubbub and excitement than at first. Those who
before had not moved a finger were now waving
their hands above their heads. Red Head felt that
he was lost. He looked very big and foolish, and
some of the scholars began to snicker. His helpless condition went straight to my heart and
gripped my sympathies. I felt that if he failed,
it would in some way be my failure. I raised my
hand, and under cover of the excitement and the
teacher's attempts to regain order, I hurriedly
shot up into his ear twice, quite distinctly:
"F-o-u-r-t-h, f-o-u-r-t-h."

The teacher tapped on her desk and said:
"Third and last chance."

The hands came down; the silence became
oppressive. Red Head began: "F——" Since that
day I have waited anxiously for many a turn of
the wheel of fortune, but never under greater
tension than when I watched for the order in
which those letters would fall from Red's lips—
"o-u-r-t-h."

A sigh of relief and disappointment went up
from the class. Afterwards, through all our
schooldays, Red Head shared my wit and quick-
ness and I benefited by his strength and dogged
faithfulness.

There were some black and brown boys and
girls in the school, and several of them were in
my class. One of the boys strongly attracted my
attention from the first day I saw him. His face
was as black as night but shone as though it
were polished; he had sparkling eyes, and when
he opened his mouth he displayed glistening
white teeth. It struck me at once as appropriate
to call him "Shiny Face," or "Shiny Eyes," or
"Shiny Teeth," and I spoke of him often by one
of these names to the other boys. These terms
were finally merged into "Shiny," and to that
name he answered good-naturedly during the
balance of his public school days.

Shiny was considered without question to be
the best speller, the best reader, the best penman
—in a word, the best scholar, in the class. He
was very quick to catch anything, but nevertheless studied hard; thus he possessed two powers
very rarely combined in one boy. I saw him year
after year, on up into the high school, win the
majority of the prizes for punctuality, deportment, essay writing and declamation. Yet it did
not take me long to discover that, in spite of his
standing as a scholar, he was in some way looked
down upon.

The other black boys and girls were still more
looked down upon. Some of the boys often spoke
of them as "niggers." Sometimes on the way
home from school a crowd would walk behind
them repeating:

> Nigger, nigger, never die,
> Black face and shiny eye.

On one such afternoon one of the black boys

turned suddenly on his tormentors and hurled a slate. It struck one of the white boys in the mouth, cutting a slight gash in his lip. At sight of the blood the boy who had thrown the slate ran, and his companions quickly followed. We ran after them pelting them with stones until they separated in several directions. I was very much wrought up over the affair, and went home and told my mother how one of the "niggers" had struck a boy with a slate. I shall never forget how she turned on me.

"Don't you ever use that word again," she said, "and don't you ever bother the colored children at school. You ought to be ashamed of yourself."

I did hang my head in shame, not because she had convinced me that I had done wrong, but because I was hurt by the first sharp word she had ever given me.

My schooldays ran along very pleasantly. I stood well in my studies, not always so well with regard to my behavior. I was never guilty of any serious misconduct, but my love of fun sometimes got me into trouble. I remember, however, that my sense of humor was so sly that most of the trouble usually fell on the head of the other fellow. My ability to play on the piano at school exercises was looked upon as little short of marvelous in a boy of my age. I was not chummy with many of my mates but, on the whole, was about as popular as it is good for a boy to be.

One day near the end of my second term at school the principal came into our room and, after talking to the teacher, for some reason said, "I wish all of the white scholars to stand for a moment."

I rose with the others. The teacher looked at me and, calling my name, said: "You sit down for the present, and rise with the others."

I did not quite understand her, and questioned, "Ma'm?" She repeated, with a softer tone in her voice, "You sit down now, and rise with the others."

I sat down dazed. I saw and heard nothing. When the others were asked to rise, I did not know it. When school was dismissed I went out in a kind of stupor. A few of the white boys jeered me, saying, "Oh, you're a nigger too." I

heard some black children say, "We knew he was colored." Shiny said to them, "Come along, don't tease him," and thereby won my undying gratitude.

I hurried on as fast as I could and had gone some distance before I perceived that Red Head was walking by my side. After a while he said to me: "Le' me carry your books." I gave him my strap without being able to answer. When we got to my gate, he said as he handed me my books, "Say, you know my big red agate? I can't shoot with it any more. I'm going to bring it to school for you tomorrow." I took my books and ran into the house.

As I passed through the hallway, I saw that my mother was busy with one of her customers; I rushed up into my own little room, shut the door and went quickly to where my looking glass hung on the wall. For an instant I was afraid to look, but when I did, I looked long and earnestly. I had often heard people say to my mother, "What a pretty boy you have!" I was accustomed to hear remarks about my beauty, but now, for the first time, I became conscious of it and recognized it.

I noticed the ivory whiteness of my skin, the beauty of my mouth, the size and liquid darkness of my eyes and how the long black lashes that fringed and shaded them produced an effect that was strangely fascinating even to me. I noticed the softness and glossiness of my dark hair that fell in waves over my temples, making my forehead appear whiter than it really was.

How long I stood there gazing at my image I do not know. When I came out and reached the head of the stairs, I heard the lady who had been with my mother going out. I ran downstairs and rushed to where my mother was sitting with a piece of work in her hands. I buried my head in her lap and blurted out: "Mother, mother, tell me, am I a nigger?" I could not see her face, but I knew the piece of work dropped to the floor and I felt her hands on my head. I looked up into her face and repeated, "Tell me, mother, am I a nigger?"

There were tears in her eyes and I could see that she was suffering for me. And then it was that I looked at her critically for the first time. I had thought of her in a childish way only as the most beautiful woman in the world; now I looked at her searching for defects. I could see that her skin was almost brown, that her hair was not so soft as mine and that she did differ in some way from the other ladies who came to the house. Yet, even so, I could see that she was very beautiful, more beautiful than any of them. She must have felt that I was examining her, for she hid her face in my hair and said with difficulty: "No, my darling, you are not a nigger." She went on, "You are as good as anybody; if anyone calls you a nigger, don't notice them."

But the more she talked, the less was I reassured, and I stopped her by asking, "Well, mother, am I white? Are you white?" She answered tremblingly, "No, I am not white, but you—your father is one of the greatest men in the country—the best blood of the South is in you—"

This suddenly opened up in my heart a fresh chasm of misgiving and fear, and I almost fiercely demanded: "Who is my father? Where is he?" She stroked my hair and said, "I'll tell you about him some day." I sobbed, "I want to know now." She answered, "No, not now."

Perhaps it had to be done, but I have never forgiven the woman who did it so cruelly. It may be that she never knew that she gave me a sword-thrust that day in school which was years in healing.

—1912

From *The Autobiography of an Ex-Colored Man*

James Weldon Johnson

O Black and Unknown Bards

O BLACK and unknown bards of long ago,
How came your lips to touch the sacred fire?
How, in your darkness, did you come to know
The power and beauty of the minstrel's lyre?
Who first from midst his bonds lifted his eyes?
Who first from out the still watch, lone and long,
Feeling the ancient faith of prophets rise
Within his dark-kept soul, burst into song?

Heart of what slave poured out such melody
As "Steal away to Jesus"? On its strains
His spirit must have nightly floated free,
Though still about his hands he felt his chains.
Who heard great "Jordan roll"? Whose starward eye
Saw chariot "swing low"? And who was he
That breathed that comforting, melodic sigh,
"Nobody knows de trouble I see"?

What merely living clod, what captive thing,
Could up toward God through all its darkness grope,
And find within its deadened heart to sing
These songs of sorrow, love and faith, and hope?
How did it catch that subtle undertone,
That note in music heard not with the ears?
How sound the elusive reed so seldom blown,
Which stirs the soul or melts the heart to tears?

Not that great German master in his dream
Of harmonies that thundered amongst the stars
At the creation, ever heard a theme
Nobler than "Go down, Moses." Mark its bars,
How like a mighty trumpet-call they stir
The blood. Such are the notes that men have sung
Going to valorous deeds; such tones there were
That helped make history when Time was young.

There is a wide, wide wonder in it all,
That from degraded rest and servile toil
The fiery spirit of the seer should call
These simple children of the sun and soil.
O black slave singers, gone, forgot, unfamed,
You—you alone, of all the long, long line
Of those who've sung untaught, unknown, unnamed,
Have stretched out upward, seeking the divine.

You sang not deeds of heroes or of kings;
No chant of bloody war, no exulting paean
Of arms-won triumphs; but your humble strings
You touched in chord with music empyrean.
You sang far better than you knew; the songs
That for your listeners' hungry hearts sufficed
Still live—but more than this to you belongs:
You sang a race from wood and stone to Christ.

—1917

Lift Every Voice and Sing

LIFT every voice and sing
Till earth and heaven ring,
Ring with the harmonies of Liberty;
Let our rejoicing rise
High as the listening skies,
Let it resound loud as the rolling sea.
Sing a song full of the faith that the dark past has
    taught us,
Sing a song full of the hope that the present has
    brought us;
Facing the rising sun of our new day begun,
Let us march on till victory is won.

Stony the road we trod,
Bitter the chastening rod,
Felt in the days when hope unborn had died;
Yet with a steady beat,
Have not our weary feet
Come to the place for which our fathers sighed?

We have come over a way that with tears has been
        watered,
We have come, treading our path through the blood
        of the slaughtered;
Out from the gloomy past,
Till now we stand at last
Where the white gleam of our bright star is cast.

God of our weary years,
God of our silent tears,
Thou who hast brought us thus far on the way,
Thou who hast by Thy might
Led us into the light,
Keep us forever in the path, we pray,
Lest our feet stray from the places, our God, where
        we met Thee,
Lest, our hearts drunk with the wine of the world, we
        forget Thee.
Shadowed beneath Thy hand,
May we forever stand;
True to our God,
True to our native land.

                                            —1900

The Creation

AND God stepped out on space,
And He looked around and said:
"I'm lonely—
I'll make me a world."

And far as the eye of God could see
Darkness covered everything,
Blacker than a hundred midnights
Down in a cypress swamp.

Then God smiled,
And the light broke,
And the darkness rolled up on one side,
And the light stood shining on the other,
And God said: "That's good!"

Then God reached out and took the light in His
        hands,
And God rolled the light around in His hands
Until He made the sun;
And He set that sun a-blazing in the heavens.
And the light that was left from making the sun
God gathered it up in a shining ball
And flung it against the darkness,
Spangling the night with the moon and stars.
Then down between
The darkness and the light
He hurled the world;
And God said: "That's good!"

Then God Himself stepped down—
And the sun was on His right hand,
And the moon was on His left;
The stars were clustered about His head,
And the earth was under His feet.
And God walked, and where He trod
His footsteps hollowed the valleys out
And bulged the mountains up.

Then He stopped and looked and saw
That the earth was hot and barren.
So God stepped over to the edge of the world
And He spat out the seven seas—
He batted His eyes, and the lightnings flashed—
He clapped His hands, and the thunders rolled—
And the waters above the earth came down,
The cooling waters came down.

Then the green grass sprouted,
And the little red flowers blossomed,
The pine tree pointed his finger to the sky,
And the oak spread out his arms,
The lakes cuddled down in the hollows of the
        ground,
And the rivers ran down to the sea;
And God smiled again,
And the rainbow appeared
And curled itself around His shoulder.

Then God raised His arm and He waved His hand
Over the sea and over the land,
And He said: "Bring forth! Bring forth!"
And quicker than God could drop His hand,
Fishes and fowls
And beasts and birds
Swam the rivers and the seas,
Roamed the forests and the woods,
And split the air with their wings.
And God said: "That's good!"

Then God walked around,
And God looked around
On all that He had made.
He looked at His sun,
And He looked at His moon,
And He looked at His little stars;
He looked on His world
With all its living things,
And God said: "I'm lonely still."

Then God sat down
On the side of a hill where He could think;
By a deep, wide river He sat down;
With His head in His hands,
God thought and thought,
Till He thought: "I'll make me a man!"

Up from the bed of the river
God scooped the clay;
And by the bank of the river
He kneeled Him down;
And there the great God Almighty,
Who lit the sun and fixed it in the sky,
Who flung the stars to the most far corner of the
    night,
Who rounded the earth in the middle of His hand,
This great God,
Like a mammy bending over her baby,
Kneeled down in the dust
Toiling over a lump of clay
Till He shaped it in His own image;

Then into it He blew the breath of life,
And man became a living soul.
Amen. Amen.

—1927

Work Songs

Pick a Bale of Cotton

JUMP down, turn around to pick a bale of cotton,
Jump down, turn around, pick a bale a day.
Jump down, turn around to pick a bale of cotton,
Jump down, turn around, pick a bale a day.

Oh, Lordy, pick a bale of cotton!
Oh, Lordy, pick a bale a day!

Me and my gal can pick a bale of cotton,
Me and my gal can pick a bale a day.
Me and my gal can pick a bale of cotton,
Me and my gal can pick a bale a day.

Oh, Lordy, pick a bale of cotton!
Oh, Lordy, pick a bale a day!

Me and my wife can pick a bale of cotton,
Me and my wife can pick a bale a day.
Me and my wife can pick a bale of cotton,
Me and my wife can pick a bale a day.

Oh, Lordy, pick a bale of cotton!
Oh, Lordy, pick a bale a day!

Me and my poppa can pick a bale of cotton,
Me and my poppa can pick a bale a day.
Me and my poppa can pick a bale of cotton,
Me and my poppa can pick a bale a day.

Oh, Lordy, pick a bale of cotton!
Oh, Lordy, pick a bale a day!

South Carolina Chain Gang Song

LAWD, I'm goin' away for the summer,
An' I won't be, won't be back till fall.
I'm goin' to bring so much money,
That your apron strings won't hold.

Don't talk about it, 'bout it, if you do I'll cry;
Don't talk about it, 'bout it, if you do I'll die.

Lawd, I'm goin' down to Columbia,
Goin' to fall down, fall down on my knees;
I'm goin' to ax the hardhearted governor
Will he pardon me, pardon me, if he please.
"No pardon for you, partner, got to make your time,
No pardon for you, partner, got to make your time."

Don't talk about it, 'bout it, if you do I'll cry;
Don't talk about it, 'bout it, if you do I'll die.

Good Morning, Captain

GOOD morning, captain." "Good morning, son."
"Good morning, captain." "Good morning, son."
"Do you need another mule skinner out on your new
    road line?"

Well I like to work, I'm rolling all the time,
Yes, I like to work, I'm rolling all the time,
I can pop my initials on a mule's behind.

Well it's "Hey little water boy bring your water
    'round,"
It's "Hey little water boy bring your water 'round,
If you don't like your job set that water bucket
    down."

Well I'm working on that new road at a dollar and a
    dime a day,
Working on that new road at a dollar and a dime a
    day,
I got three women waiting on a Saturday night just
    to draw my pay.

Ballads

De Ballit of de Boll Weevil

OH, have you heard de lates',
De lates' of de songs?
It's about dem little boll weevils,
Dey's picked up bofe feet an' gone
A-lookin' for a home,
Jes' a-lookin' for a home.

De boll weevil is a little bug
F'um Mexico, dey say;
He come to try dis Texas soil,
An' thought he better stay,
A-lookin' for a home,
Jes' a-lookin' for a home.

De picker say to de boll weevil,
"What makes yo' head so red?"
"I's been wanderin' de whole worl' ovah
Till it's a wonder I ain't dead,
A-lookin' for a home,
Jes' a-lookin' for a home."

Fus' time I saw Mr. Boll Weevil,
He wuz on de western plain;
Nex' time I saw him,
He wuz' ridin' on a Memphis train,
A-lookin' for a home,
Jes' a-lookin' for a home.

De fus' time I saw de boll weevil,
He wuz settin' on de square;
De nex' time I saw de boll weevil
He had all his family dere—
Dey's lookin' for a home,
Jes' a-lookin' for a home.

John Henry

SOME say he's from Georgia,
Some say he's from Alabam',
John Henry's a east Virginia man,
John Henry's a east Virginia man.
But it's wrote on the rock at the Big Ben Tunnel,

John Henry he could hammah,
He could whistle, he could sing;
He went to the mountain early in the mornin'
To hear his hammah ring,
To hear his hammah ring.

John Henry went to the section boss;
Says the section boss, "What kin you do?"
Says, "I kin line a track, I kin histe a jack,
I kin pick an' shovel, too,
I kin pick an' shovel, too."

John Henry went to the tunnel,
And they put him in lead to drive;
The rock was so tall and John Henry so small
That he laid down his hammah and he cried,
That he laid down his hammah and he cried.

The steam drill was on the right-han' side,
John Henry was on the left;

Says, "Before I let this steam drill beat me down,
I'll hammah myself to death,
I'll hammah myself to death."

Oh, the cap'n said to John Henry,
"I b'leeve this mountain's sinkin' in."
John Henry said to the cap'n, "Oh my!
'Tain't nothin' but my hammah suckin' wind,
'Tain't nothin' but my hammah suckin' wind."

John Henry had a pretty liddle wife,
She come all dressed in blue,
And the last words she said to him,
"John Henry I been true to you,
John Henry I been true to you."

John Henry was on the mountain,
The mountain was so high,
He called to his pretty liddle wife,
Said, "I kin almos' touch the sky,"
Said, "I kin almos' touch the sky.

"Who gonna shoe yoh pretty liddle feet,
Who gonna glove yoh han',
Who gonna kiss yoh rosy cheeks,
An' who gonna be yoh man,
An' who gonna be yoh man?"

"Papa gonna shoe my pretty liddle feet,
Mama gonna glove my han',
Sistah gonna kiss my rosy cheeks,
An' I ain't gonna have no man,
An' I ain't gonna have no man."

Then John Henry he did hammah,
He did make his hammah soun';
Says, "Now one more lick before quittin' time,
An' I'll beat this steam drill down,
An' I'll beat this steam drill down."

The hammah that John Henry swung,
It weighed over nine poun';
He broke a rib in his left-han' side,
And his intrels fell on the groun',
And his intrels fell on the groun'.

All the women in the West
That heard of John Henry's death,
Stood in the rain, flagged the eastbound train,
Goin' where John Henry dropped dead,
Goin' where John Henry dropped dead.

They took John Henry to the White House,
And buried him in the san',
And every locomotive come roarin' by,
Says, "There lays that steel-drivin' man,"
Says, "There lays that steel-drivin' man."

Stackalee

IT was in the year of eighteen hundred and sixty-one,
In St. Louis on Market Street where Stackalee was
    born.
Everybody's talkin' 'bout Stackalee.
It was on one cold and frosty night,
When Stackalee and Billy Lyons had one awful fight;
Stackalee got his gun; boy, he got it fast!
He shot poor Billy through and through;
Bullet broke a lookin' glass.
Lord, O Lord, O Lord!
Stackalee shot Billy once; his body fell to the floor,
He cried out, "Oh, please, Stack, please don't shoot
    me no more."

The White Elephant Barrel House was wrecked that
    night;
Gutters full of beer and whiskey; it was an awful
    sight.
Jewelry and rings of the purest solid gold
Scattered over the dance and gamblin' hall.
The can-can dancers they rushed for the door
When Billy cried, "Oh, please, Stack, don't shoot me
    no more;
Have mercy," Billy groaned, "Oh, please spare my
    life."

Stack says, "God bless your children, damn your
    wife!
You stole my magic Stetson; I'm gonna steal your
    life."
"But," says Billy, "I always treated you like a man;
'Tain't nothin' to that old Stetson but the greasy
    band."
He shot poor Billy once, he shot him twice,
And the third time Billy pleaded, "Please go tell my
    wife."
Yes, Stackalee, the gambler, everybody knowed his
    name;
Made his livin' hollerin' "High, low, jack and the
    game."

Meantime the sergeant strapped on his big forty-five,
Says, "Now we'll bring in this bad man, dead or
    alive."
And brass-buttoned policemen tall, dressed in blue,
Came down the sidewalk marchin' two by two.
Sent for the wagon and it hurried and come,
Loaded with pistols and a big Gatlin' gun.
At midnight on that stormy night there came an
    awful wail,
Billy Lyons and a graveyard ghost outside the city
    jail.

"Jailer, jailer," says Stack, "I can't sleep,
For around my bedside poor Billy Lyons still creeps.
He comes in shape of a lion with a blue steel in his
    hand,
For he knows I'll stand and fight if he comes in shape
    of man."
Stackalee went to sleep that night by the city clock
    bell,
Dreamin' the Devil had come all the way up from
    hell.
Red Devil was sayin', "You better hunt your hole;
I've hurried here from hell just to get your soul."

Stackalee told him, "Yes, maybe you're right,
But I'll give even you one hell of a fight."
When they got into the scuffle, I heard the Devil
    shout,
"Come and get this bad man 'fore he puts my fire
    out!"
The next time I seed the Devil he was scramblin' up
    the wall,
Yellin', "Come and get this bad man 'fore he mops
    up with us all."

Then here come Stack's woman runnin', says,
    "Daddy, I love you true;
See what beer, whiskey and smokin' hop has brought
    you to.
But before I'll let you lay in there, I'll put my life in
    pawn."
She hurried and got Stackalee out on a five thousand
    dollar bond.
Stackalee said, "Ain't but one thing that grieves my
    mind,
When they take me away, babe, I leave you behind."
But the woman he really loved was a voodoo queen
From Creole French market, way down in New
    Orleans.

He laid down at home that night, took a good night's
    rest;
Arrived in court at nine o'clock to hear the coroner's
    inquest.
Crowds jammed the sidewalk, far as you could see,
Tryin' to get a good look at tough Stackalee.
Over the cold, dead body Stackalee he did bend,
Then he turned and faced those twelve jury men.
The judge says, "Stackalee, I would spare your life,
But I know you're a bad man; I can see it in your
    red eyes."
The jury heard the witnesses, and they didn't say no
    more;
They crowded into the jury room, and the messenger
    closed the door.

The jury came to agreement, the clerk he wrote it
 down,
And everybody was whisperin', "He's penitentiary
 bound."
When the jury walked out, Stackalee didn't budge;
They wrapped the verdict and passed it to the judge.
Judge looked over his glasses, says, "Mr. Bad Man
 Stackalee,
The jury finds you guilty of murder in the first
 degree."
Now the trial's come to an end, how the folks gave
 cheers;
Bad Stackalee was sent down to Jefferson pen for
 seventy-five years.

Now late at night you can hear him in his cell,
Arguin' with the Devil to keep from goin' to hell.
And the other convicts whisper, "Whatcha know
 about that?
Gonna burn in hell forever over an old Stetson hat!"
Everybody's talkin' 'bout Stackalee,
That bad man, Stackalee!

Blues

Southern Blues

HOUSE catch on fire,
And ain't no water around;
If your house catch on fire,
Ain't no water around,
Throw yourself out the window,
Let it burn on down.

I went to the gypsy
To have my fortune told;
I went to the gypsy
To have my fortune told;
She said, "Doggone you, girlie,
Doggone your hard-luck soul!"

I turned around and
Went to that gypsy next door;
I turned around and
Went to that gypsy next door;
She said, "You can get a man
Anywhere you go."

Let me be your rag doll
Until your china comes;
Let me be your rag doll
Until your china comes;
If he keeps me ragged,
He's got to rag it some.

How Long Blues

How long, baby, how long
Has that evenin' train been gone?
How long, how long, I say, how long?
Standin' at the station watchin' my baby leave town,
Sure am disgusted—for where could she be gone?
For how long, how long, I say, how long?

I can hear the whistle blowin' but I cannot see no
 train,
And deep down in my heart I got an ache and pain;
For how long, how long, I say, how long?

Sometimes I feel so disgusted and I feel so blue
That I hardly know what in this world it's best to do;
For how long, how long, how long?

If I could holler like I was a mountain jack,
I'd go up on the mountain and call my baby back;
For how long, how long, how long?

If some day she's gonna be sorry that she done me
 wrong,
Baby, it will be too late then—for I'll be gone,
For so long, so long, so long!

My mind gets to rattlin', I feel so bad,
Thinkin' 'bout the bad luck that I have had
For so long, so long, so long.

How long, baby, how long?
Baby, how long?
How long?

Good Mornin' Blues

GOOD mornin', blues,
Blues, how do you do?
Good mornin', blues,
Blues, how do you do?
Good mornin', how are you?

I laid down last night,
Turnin' from side to side;
Yes, I was turnin' from side to side;
I was not sick,
I was just dissatisfied.

When I got up this mornin',
Blues walkin' round my bed;
Yes, the blues walkin' round my bed;
I went to eat my breakfast,
The blues was all in my bread.

I sent for you yesterday, baby,
Here you come a-walkin' today;
Yes, here you come a-walkin' today;
Got your mouth wide open,
You don't know what to say.

Good mornin', blues,
Blues, how do you do?
Yes, blues, how do you do?
I'm doin' all right,
Good mornin', how are you?

Street Cries

Sweet Potato Man

SEE dese gread big sweet pertaters
Right chere by dis chicken's side?
Ah'm de one what bakes dese taters,
Makes dem fit to suit yo' pride.

Dere is taters an' mo' taters,
But de ones Ah sells is fine;
Yo' kin go fum hyeah to yondah,
But yo' won't get none lak mine,
'Cause Ah'm de tater man!
(Ah mean!)
De sweet pertater man!

Crab Man

Ho! cra-ab man!
Ho! cra-ab man!
Ho! crabs, I say!

Fresh crabs! hyeah!
Fresh crabs! hyeah!
Fresh crabs, today!

Watermelon Vendor's Cry

WATERMELON! watermelon! red to the rind;
If you don't believe me jest pull down your blind!
I sell to the rich,
I sell to the po';
I'm gonna sell the lady
Standin' in that do'.
Watermelon, lady!
Come and get your nice red watermelon, lady!
Red to the rind, lady!
Come on, lady, and get 'em!
Gotta make the picnic fo' two o'clock,
No flat tires today.
Come on, lady!
I got water with the melon, red to the rind;
If you don't believe it jest pull down your blind!
You eat the watermelon and preee-serve the rind!

Cala Vendor's Cry

WE sell it to the rich, we sell it to the poor,
We give it to the sweet brownskin, peepin' out the
    door.
Tous chauds, madame, tous chauds!
Git 'em while they're hot! Hot calas!

One cup of coffee, fifteen cents calas,
Make you smile the livelong day.
Calas, *tous chauds, madame, tous chauds!*
Git 'em while they're hot! Hot calas!

Oyster Man's Cry

OYSTER man! oyster man!
Get your fresh oysters from the oyster man!
Bring out your pitcher, bring out your can,
Get your nice fresh oysters from the oyster man!

The Negro Renaissance: Jean Toomer and the Harlem Writers of the 1920's

Arna Bontemps

THAT STORY from one of the old countries about the man with the marriageable daughter comes to mind when I think of a leading literary pundit in the second decade of this century. In a land where brides were bartered it was, of course, not uncommon for subtle salesmanship to flourish. Sometimes it could become high-pressured. In this old yarn the eager parent of the bride had recited so many of his daughter's excellent qualities, the prospective husband began to wonder whether she had any human faults at all. "Well, yes," the father finally acknowledged. "A tiny one. She is just a little bit pregnant."

Similarly, in the twenties the man whose comments on writing by or about Negroes were most respected was just a little bit Negro. He was William Stanley Braithwaite, literary critic for the *Boston Transcript* and editor of an annual series, "Anthologies of Magazine Verse, 1913–1929." In "Braithwaite's Anthologies," as they were commonly known, Spoon River poems by Edgar Lee Masters, chants by Vachel Lindsay, free verse by Carl Sandburg and the early works of many other important American poets were recognized and published before the authors had received general acceptance or acclaim.

But Braithwaite did not completely disassociate himself from Negroes, as he might have. Indeed, he was awarded the Spingarn medal in 1917 as "the Negro who, according to a committee appointed by the board [of the NAACP], has reached the highest achievement in his field of activity."

His occasional observations on Negro writing in the decade preceding Harlem's golden era are therefore useful as prologue. In 1913, for ex-ample, Braithwaite took note of James Weldon Johnson's "Fiftieth Anniversary Ode" on the Emancipation and suggested that it represented a move by the Negro poet to disengage himself. A decade of near silence had followed Paul Laurence Dunbar's last lyrics, and Braithwaite's language created an image of the Negro poet in chains, seeking to free himself.

The reappearance of this Johnson poem in a collection called *Fifty Years and Other Poems*, in 1917—the same year that Braithwaite was awarded the Spingarn medal, incidentally—prompted Braithwaite to remark, in effect, that this could be the beginning of something big, like a new awakening among Negro writers, perhaps. But, actually, Johnson's most significant poetic achievement was still a decade in the future, when his collection of folk sermons in verse was to be published as *God's Trombones*, in 1927. Nevertheless, Braithwaite appears to have picked the right year for the first sign of "disengagement" or "awakening" or whatever it was. The year 1917 now stands out, where Negro poetry in the United States is concerned, as the year in which Claude McKay's poem "The Harlem Dancer" appeared in the *Seven Arts* magazine under the pen name of Eli Edwards. You may know the poem. It was in sonnet form:

Applauding youths laughed with young prostitutes
And watched her perfect, half-clothed body sway;
Her voice was like the sound of blended flutes
Blown by black players upon a picnic day.
She sang and danced on gracefully and calm,
The light gauze hanging loose about her form;
To me she seemed a proudly-swaying palm
Grown lovelier for passing through a storm.

Upon her swarthy neck black, shiny curls
Profusely fell; and, tossing coins in praise,
The wine-flushed bold-eyed boys, and even the girls,
Devoured her with their eager, passionate gaze;
But looking at her falsely-smiling face,
I knew her self was not in that strange place.

Now this I submit was the anticipation and the theme of an early outburst of creativity later described as the Negro or Harlem Renaissance. When McKay's "The Harlem Dancer" reappeared in his collection *Harlem Shadows* in 1922, along with other poems so fragrant and fresh they almost drugged the senses, things immediately began to happen. Here was poetry written from experience, differing from poetry written from books and other cultural media in somewhat the same way that real flowers differ from artificial ones.

A chorus of other new voices led by Jean Toomer, Langston Hughes and Countee Cullen promptly began to make the twenties a decade which *Time* magazine has described as Harlem's "golden age."

Interestingly, Braithwaite recognized McKay as the first voice in this new chorus, but he spoke of him as "a genius meshed in [a] dilemma." It bothered Braithwaite that McKay seemed to "waver between the racial and the universal notes." In some of his poems, Braithwaite felt, McKay was clearly "contemplating life and nature with a wistful sympathetic passion," but in others the poet became what Braithwaite called a "strident propagandist, using his poetic gifts to clothe arrogant and defiant thoughts." Braithwaite thought this was bad. He cited McKay's "The Harlem Dancer" and his "Spring in New Hampshire" as instances of the former, his "If We Must Die" as a shameless instance of the latter.

But, ironically, a generation later it was "If We Must Die," a poem that would undoubtedly stir the blood of almost any Black Muslim, that Sir Winston Churchill quoted as climax and conclusion of his oration before the joint houses of the American Congress when he was seeking to draw this nation into the common effort in World War II. McKay had written it as the Negro American's defiant answer to lynching and mob violence in the Southern states. Churchill made

it the voice of the embattled Allies as he read aloud McKay's poem "If We Must Die."

Obviously neither Churchill nor McKay had at that time considered the possibilities of non-violence. The poem does show, however, how a short span of years and certain historical developments can alter the meaning of a literary work. It also demonstrates the risk of trying to separate too soon the local or special subject from the universal.

But if Braithwaite's attitude toward Claude McKay was ambivalent, it was certainly unequivocal with respect to the second, and in some ways the most inspiring, of the writers who made the Harlem Renaissance significant in the long-range development of the Negro writer in the United States.

"In Jean Toomer, the author of *Cane*," Braithwaite wrote in 1925, "we come upon the very first artist of the race, who with all an artist's passion and sympathy for life, its hurts, its sympathies, its desires, its joys, its defeats and strange yearnings, can write about the Negro without the surrender or compromise of the artist's vision. So objective is it, that we feel that it is a mere accident that birth or association has thrown him into contact with the life he has written about. He would write just as well, just as poignantly, just as transmutingly, about the peasants of Russia, or the peasants of Ireland, had experience brought him in touch with their existence. *Cane* is a book of gold and bronze, of dusk and flame, of ecstasy and pain, and Jean Toomer is a bright morning star of a new day of the race in literature."

Cane was published in 1923, after portions of it had first appeared in *Broom*, the *Crisis, Double Dealer, Liberator, Little Review, Modern Review, Nomad, Prairie* and *S 4 N*. But *Cane* and Jean Toomer, its gifted author, presented an enigma— an enigma which has, if anything, deepened in the forty-three years since its publication. Given such a problem, perhaps one may be excused for not wishing to separate the man from his work. Indeed, so separated, Toomer's writing could scarcely be understood at all, and its significance would escape us now as it has escaped so many others in the past.

In any case, *Who's Who in Colored America*

listed Toomer in 1927 and gave the following vita:

> b. Dec. 26, 1894, Washington, D.C.; s. Nathan and Nina (Pinchback) Toomer; educ. Public Scho., Washington, D.C.; Dunbar High Scho.; Univ. of Wisconsin, 1914–15; taught schools, Sparta, Ga., for four months, traveled, worked numerous occupations; auth. *Cane*, pub. Boni and Liveright, 1923; Short Stories and Literary Criticisms in various magazines; address, c/o Civic Club, 439 W. 23rd St., New York, N.Y.

Needless to say, no subsequent listing of Toomer is to be found in this or any other directory of conspicuous Negro Americans. Judging by the above, however, Toomer had always been elusive, and the interest that *Cane* awakened did nothing to change this. Several years later Toomer faded completely into white obscurity, leaving behind a literary mystery almost as intriguing as the disappearance of Ambrose Bierce into Mexico in 1913.

Why did he do it? What did it mean?

Concerned with writing, as we are, we automatically turn to Toomer's book for clues. This could be difficult, because copies are scarce. *Cane*'s two printings were small, and the few people who went quietly mad about the strange book were evidently unable to do much toward enlarging its audience. But among these few was practically the whole generation of young Negro writers then just beginning to appear, and their reaction to Toomer's *Cane* marked an awakening that soon thereafter began to be called a Negro renaissance.

Cane's influence was not limited to the happy band that included Langston Hughes, Countee Cullen, Eric Walrond, Zora Neale Hurston, Wallace Thurman, Rudolph Fisher and their contemporaries of the twenties. Subsequent writing by Negroes in the United States as well as in the West Indies and Africa has continued to reflect its mood and often its method, and, one feels, it also has influenced the writing about Negroes by others. And certainly no earlier volume of poetry or fiction or both had come close to expressing the ethos of the Negro in the Southern setting as *Cane* did.

There are many odd and provocative things about *Cane*, and not the least is its form. Re-

viewers who read it in 1923 were generally stumped. Poetry and prose were whipped together in a kind of frappé. Realism was mixed with what they called mysticism, and the result seemed to many of them confusing. Still, one of them could conclude that "*Cane* is an interesting, occasionally beautiful and often queer book of exploration into old country and new ways of writing." Another noted, "Toomer has not interviewed the Negro, has not asked opinions about him, has not drawn conclusions about him from his reactions to outside stimuli, but has made the much more searching, and much more self-forgetting effort of seeing life with him, through him."

Such comment was cautious, however, compared to the trumpetings of Waldo Frank in the foreword he contributed:

> A poet has arisen among our American youth who has known how to turn the essence and materials of his Southland into the essences and materials of literature. A poet has arisen in that land who writes, not as a Southerner, not as a rebel against Southerners, not as a Negro, not as apologist or priest or critic: who writes as a *poet*. The fashioning of beauty is ever foremost in his inspiration: not forcedly but simply, and because these ultimate aspects of his world are to him more real than all its specific problems. He has made songs and lovely stories of his land. . . .
>
> The gifted Negro has been too often thwarted from becoming a poet because his world was forever forcing him to recollect that he was a Negro. The artist must lose such lesser identities in the great well of life. . . . The whole will and mind of the creator must go below the surfaces of race. And this has been an almost impossible condition for the American Negro to achieve, forced every moment of his life into a specific and superficial plane of consciousness. . . .
>
> It seems to me, therefore, that this is a first book in more ways than one. It is a harbinger of the South's literary maturity: of its emergence from the obsession put upon its minds by the unending racial crisis. . . . It marks the dawn of direct and unafraid creation. And, as the initial work of a man of twenty-seven [*sic*], it is the harbinger of a literary force of whose incalculable future I believe no reader of this book will doubt.

It is well to keep in mind the time of these remarks. Of the novels by which T. S. Stribling is remembered, only *Birthright* had been published. Julia Peterkin had not yet published a book. DuBose Heyward's *Porgy* was still two years away. William Faulkner's first novel was three years away. His Mississippi novels were six or more years in the future. Robert Penn Warren, a student at Vanderbilt University, was just beginning his association with the Fugitive poets. His first novel was still more than a decade and a half ahead. Tennessee Williams was just nine years old.

A chronology of Negro writers is equally revealing. James Weldon Johnson had written lyrics for popular songs, some of them minstrel style, and a sort of documentary novel obscurely published under a pseudonym, but *God's Trombones* was a good four years in the offing. Countee Cullen's *Color* was two and Langston Hughes's *The Weary Blues* three years away, though both of these poets had become known to readers of the Negro magazine *Crisis* while still in their teens, and Hughes at twenty-one, the year of *Cane*'s publication, could already be called a favorite.

The first fiction of the Negro Renaissance required apologies. It was not first-rate. But it was an anticipation of what was to come later. Even so, it followed *Cane* by a year or two, and Eric Walrond's *Tropic Death* did not come for three. Zora Neale Hurston's first novel was published in 1934, eleven years after *Cane*. Richard Wright made his bow with *Uncle Tom's Children* in 1938, fifteen years later. *Invisible Man* by Ralph Ellison followed Toomer's *Cane* by just twenty-nine years. James Baldwin was not born when Toomer began to publish.

Waldo Frank's use of "harbinger" as the word for *Cane* becomes both significant and ironic when we recognize the debt most of these individuals owe Toomer. Consciously or unconsciously, one after another they picked up his cue and began making the "more searching" effort to see life *with* the Negro, "through him." *Cane* heralded an awakening of artistic expression by Negroes that brought to light in less than a decade a surprising array of talents, and these in turn made way for others. An equally significant change in the writing about Negroes paralleled this awakening. Strangely, however, *Cane* was

not at all the harbinger Frank seemed to imagine. Despite his promise—a promise which must impress anyone who puts this first book beside the early writings of either Faulkner or Hemingway, Toomer's contemporaries—Jean Toomer rejected his prospects and turned his back on greatness.

The book by which we remember this writer is as hard to classify as its author. At first glance it appears to consist of assorted sketches, stories and a novelette interspersed with poems. Some of the prose is poetic, and often Toomer slips from one form into the other almost imperceptibly. The novelette is constructed like a play.

His characters, always evoked with effortless strength, are as recognizable as they are unexpected in the fiction of that period. Fern is a "creamy brown" beauty so complicated men take her "but get no joy from it." Becky is a white outcast beside a Georgia road who bears two Negro children. Laymon, a preacher-teacher in the same area, "knows more than would be good for anyone other than a silent man." The name character in the novelette "Kabnis" is a languishing idealist finally redeemed from cynicism and dissipation by the discovery of underlying strength in his people.

It doesn't take long to discover that *Cane* is not without design, however. A world of black peasantry in Georgia appears in the first section. The scene changes to the Negro community of Washington, D.C., in the second. Rural Georgia comes up again in the third. Changes in the concerns of Toomer's folk are noted as the setting moves from the Georgia pike to the bustling Negro section in the nation's capital. The change in the level of awareness that the author discloses is more subtle, but it is clearly discernible when he returns to the Georgia background.

A young poet-observer moves through the book. Drugged by beauty "perfect as dusk when the sun goes down," lifted and swayed by folk song, arrested by eyes that "desired nothing that *you* could give," silenced by "corn leaves swaying, rusty with talk," he recognized that "the Dixie Pike has grown from a goat path in Africa." A native richness is here, he concluded, and the poet embraces it with the passion of love.

This was the sensual power most critics noticed and most readers remembered about *Cane*.

It was the basis for Alfred Kreymborg's remark in *Our Singing Strength* that "Jean Toomer is *one* of the finest artists among the dark people, if not *the* finest." The reviewer for the *New York Herald Tribune* had the rich imagery of *Cane* in mind when he said, "Here are the high brown and black and half-caste colored folk of the cane fields, the gin hovel and the brothel realized with a sure touch of artistry." But there remained much in the book that he could not understand or appreciate. Speaking of Toomer's "sometimes rather strident reactions to the Negro," he added that "at moments his outbursts of emotion approach the inarticulately maudlin," though he had to admit that *Cane* represented "a distinct achievement wholly unlike anything of this sort done before."

Others found "obscurity" and "mysticism" in the novelette which comprises the last third of the book. This is not surprising, for in Toomer's expressed creed, "A symbol is as useful to the spirit as a tool is to the hand," and his fiction is full of them. Add to puzzling symbols an itch to find "new ways of writing" that led him to bold experimentation, and one may begin to see why Toomer baffled as he pleased readers interested in writing by or about Negroes in the early twenties.

Kreymborg spoke of Toomer as "a philosopher and a psychologist by temperament" and went on to say that "the Washington writer is now fascinated by the larger, rather than the parochial interest of the human race, and should some day compose a book in the grand manner."

Of course, Toomer didn't, or at least he has not published one up to now, and to this extent Kreymborg has failed as a prophet, but his reference to Toomer as philosopher and psychologist was certainly on the mark, and his rather large estimate of this writer's capacities was significant, considering its date. The "new criticism," as we have come to recognize it, had scarcely been heard from then, and apparently it has still not discovered Toomer, but the chances are it may yet find him challenging. He would have comforted them, I am almost sorry to say, incarnating, as he does, some of their favorite attitudes. But at the same time, he could have served as a healthy corrective for others. Whether or not he would

prove less complex or less rewarding than Gertrude Stein or James Joyce, for example, remains to be determined.

Saunders Redding gave *Cane* a close reading fifteen years after its publication and saw it as an unfinished experiment, "the conclusion to which we are fearful of never knowing, for since 1923 Toomer has published practically nothing." He meant, one assumes, that Toomer had published little poetry or fiction, or anything else that seemed closely related to *Cane* or to *Cane*'s author. Toomer had published provocative articles here and there, as well as a small book of definitions and aphorisms during that time, and since then he has allowed two of his lectures to be published semi-privately. But Redding must be included in the small group who recognized a problem in *Cane* that has yet to be explained.

To him Toomer was a young writer "fresh from the South," who found a paramount importance in establishing "racial kinship" with Negroes in order to treat them artistically. He was impressed by Toomer's "unashamed and unrestrained" love for the race and for the soil and setting that nourished it. He saw a relationship between the writer's "hot, colorful, primitive" moods and the "naive hysteria of the spirituals," which he held in contrast to "the sophistic savagery of jazz and the blues." *Cane*, he concluded, was "a lesson in emotional release and freedom."

Chapters about Toomer were included in Paul Rosenfeld's *Men Seen*, in 1925, and in Gorham B. Munson's *Destinations*, in 1928, and elsewhere there are indications that Toomer continued to write and to experiment for at least a decade after the publication of *Cane*. Long stories by him appeared in the second and third volumes of the *American Caravan*. A thoughtful essay on "Race Problems and Modern Society" became part of a volume devoted to *Problems of Civilization*, in Baker Brownell's series on "Man and His World." Seven years later, in the *New Caravan* of 1936, Toomer presented similar ideas in the long poem "Blue Meridian." Meanwhile, contributing a chapter to the book *America and Alfred Stieglitz*, in 1934, Toomer was explicit about his own writing as well as several other matters.

The rumor that Toomer had crossed the color line began circulating when his name stopped appearing in print. But a reasonable effort to find out what it was Toomer was trying to say to us subsequently makes it hard to accept "passing" as the skeleton key to the Jean Toomer mystery. He seemed too concerned with truth to masquerade. One wants to believe that Toomer's mind came at last to reject the myth of race as it is fostered in our culture. A man of fair complexion, indistinguishable from the majority of white Americans, he had always had a free choice as to where he would take his place in a color-caste scheme. Having wandered extensively and worked at odd jobs in a variety of cities before he began contributing to little magazines, as he has stated, he could scarcely have escaped being taken at face value by strangers who had no way of knowing that the youth, who looked like Hollywood's conception of an Ivy League basketball star, but who spoke so beautifully, whose very presence was such an influence upon them, was not only a product of the Negro community but a grandson of the man whom the *Dictionary of American Biography* describes as "the typical Negro politician of the Reconstruction."

Men of this kind, such as Walter White of the NAACP or Adam Clayton Powell of the U.S. Congress, sometimes called voluntary Negroes when they elect to remain in the fold, so to speak, have in other circumstances been discovered in strange places in our society—in neo-Fascist organizations in the United States, among big-city bosses, on movie screens, in the student body at "Ole Miss"—but seldom if ever before in an organization working "for understanding between people." Yet Jean Toomer's first publication, following the rumors and the silence, was "An Interpretation of Friends Worship," published by the Committee on Religious Education of Friends General Conference, 1515 Cherry Street, Philadelphia, 1947. It was followed two years later by a pamphlet, *The Flavor of Man*. The writing is eloquent with commitment. It reflects unhurried reading and contemplation, as was also true of his piece on "Race Problems and Modern Society." Toomer did not fail to remind his readers that certain racial attitudes could not be condoned. He certainly did not speak as a Negro

bent on escaping secretly into white society. Jean Toomer, who, like his high-spirited grandfather, had exuberantly published his pride in his Negro heritage, appears to have reached a point in his thinking at which categories of this kind tend to clutter rather than classify. The stand he appears to have taken at first involved nothing more clandestine than the closing of a book or the changing of a subject.

Yet he is on record as having denied later that he was a Negro. That is a story in itself. Nevertheless, at that point, it seems, Jean Toomer stepped out of American letters. Despite the richness of his thought, his gift of expression, he ceased to be a writer and, as I have suggested, turned his back on greatness. His choice, whatever else may be said about it, reflects the human sacrifices in the field of the arts exacted by the racial myth on which so much writing in the United States is based. While he may have escaped its strictures and inconveniences in his personal life, he did not get away from the racial problem in any real sense. His dilemmas and frustrations as a writer are equally the dilemmas and frustrations of the Negro writers who have since emerged. The fact that most of them have not been provided with his invisible cloak makes little difference. He is their representative man. He stands as their prototype.

What, then, ordinarily happened to the Negro writer of Toomer's time in America after his first phase, after he had been published and taken his first steps? Encouraged by reviewers, assured that his talent was genuine, that he was not *just* a Negro writer but an American writer who happened to be a Negro, that his first book had broken new ground and that his next would be awaited with keen interest unrelated to any exotic qualities he may have shown but simply as arresting art, he was readily convinced. The "American writer" tag was especially appealing. It stuck in his mind, and when he got the bad news from the sales department, he coupled it with remarks he had heard from his publishers about a certain "resistance" in bookstores to books about "the problem." Obviously, the solution for him, as an American writer, was not to write narrowly about Negroes but broadly about people.

So sooner or later he did it: a novel not intended to depict Negro life. The results may be examined: Paul Laurence Dunbar's *The Love of Landry*, Richard Wright's *Savage Holiday*, Chester B. Himes's *Cast the First Stone*, Ann Petry's *Country Place*, Zora Neale Hurston's *Seraph on the Suwanee*, James Baldwin's *Giovanni's Room*, along with Jean Toomer's *York Beach*. While the implication that books about whites are about people while those about Negroes are *not* should have provoked laughter, the young Negro writer was too excited to catch it. The discovery which followed was that the bookstore resistance was not removed by this switch. Moreover, he found to his dismay that friendly reviewers had in most instances become cool. In any case, none of these writers seemed sufficiently encouraged by the results to continue in the same direction. Whatever it was that blocked the Negro writer of fiction, that denied him the kind of acceptance accorded the Negro maker of music, for example, was clearly not just the color of his characters.

Southern white novelists, from T. S. Stribling to Julia Peterkin to DuBose Heyward to William Faulkner to Robert Penn Warren, had thronged their novels with Negroes of all descriptions without appearing to meet reader resistance or critical coolness. So now it could be seen that the crucial issue was not the choice of subject but the author's attitude toward it. With this knowledge the young Negro writers pondered and then made their decisions. Dunbar chose drink. Wright and Himes went to Paris to think it over, as did James Baldwin, at first. Toomer disappeared into Bucks County, Pennsylvania. Frank Yerby, on the basis of a short story in *Harper's Magazine* and a manuscript novel that went the rounds without finding a publisher, took the position that "an unpublished writer, or even one published but unread, is no writer at all." He chose "entertainment" over "literature," and worked his way out of the segregated area of letters in the costume of a riverboat gambler. His book *The Foxes of Harrow*, about the Mississippi riverboat gambler, became the first successful non-Negro novel by a Negro American writer.

A curious historical irony is suggested. The memoirs of George H. Devol, published in 1887

under the title *Forty Years a Gambler on the Mississippi*, relates the following about a cabin boy called Pinch:

> I raised him and trained him. I took him out of a steamboat barber shop. I instructed him in the mysteries of card-playing, and he was an apt pupil. . . .

Devol recalled with much amusement a night they left New Orleans on the steamer *Doubloon*:

> There was a strong team of us—Tom Brown, Holly Chappell, and the boy Pinch. We sent Pinch and staked him to open a game of chuck-aluck with the Negro passengers on deck, while we opened up monte in the cabin. The run of luck that evening was something grand to behold. I do not think there was a solitary man on the boat that did not drop around in the course of the evening and lose his bundle. When about thirty miles from New Orleans a heavy fog overtook us, and it was our purpose to get off and walk about six miles to Kennersville, where we could take the cars to the city.
>
> Pinchback got our valises together, and a start was made. A drizzling rain was falling, and the darkness was so great that one could not see his hand before his face. Each of us grabbed a valise except Pinch, who carried along the faro tools. The walking was so slippery that we were in the mud about every ten steps, and poor Pinch he groaned under the load that he carried. At last he broke out:
>
> "Tell you what it is, Master Devol, I'll be dumbed if this aint rough on Pinch. Ise going to do better than this toting along old faro tools."
>
> "What's that, Pinch? What you going to do?"
>
> "Ise going to get into that good old Legislature and I'll make Rome howl if I get there."
>
> Of course I thought at the time that this was all bravado and brag; but the boy was in earnest, and sure enough he got into the Legislature, became Lieutenant Governor, and by the death of the Governor he slipped into the gubernatorial chair, and at last crawled into the United States Senate.

Without necessarily accepting the gambler Devol as an authority on Reconstruction history, we may still take his account as substantially factual. P. B. S. Pinchback himself often referred to his career on the river. He was still a prominent public figure when these memoirs were published. He could have denied them had he wished. That Frank Yerby, who became a teacher in a Negro college in Louisiana after his graduation from Fisk University, should center the story of *The Foxes of Harrow* around a Mississippi riverboat gambler is not an odd coincidence. But that Jean Toomer should be the grandson of Pinchback, and one of the two people to accompany his body back to New Orleans for burial in 1921, suggests another historical irony.

The behavior pattern known sociologically as "passing for white," then, has its literary equivalent, and the question it raises is whether or not this is proper in the arts. The writer's desire to widen his audience by overcoming what has been called resistance to racial material is certainly understandable, but sooner or later the Negro novelist realizes that what he has encountered, as often critical as popular, is more subtle than that. What annoys some readers of fiction, it seems, is not so much that characters in a book are Negro or white or both as the *attitude of the writer* toward these characters. Does he accept the status quo with respect to the races? If so, any character or racial situation can be taken in stride, not excluding miscegenation. But rejection of traditional status, however reflected, tends to alienate these readers.

On the other hand, the Negro reader has little taste for any art in which the racial attitudes of the past are condoned or taken for granted. Since this is what he has come to expect in the fiction in which he sees himself, he too has developed resistance.

His is a wider resistance to the whole world of the contemporary novel. To him literature means poetry, by and large. He knows Phillis Wheatley and Paul Laurence Dunbar far better than he knows any prose writers of the past.

James Weldon Johnson and Countee Cullen are familiar and honored names. There is seldom a sermon in a Negro church, a commencement, a banquet, a program, in which one of these, or a contemporary poet like Hughes or Margaret Walker or Gwendolyn Brooks, is not quoted. But the Negro novelists, aside from Richard Wright, possibly, are lumped with the whole questionable lot in the mind of this reader. When he is not offended by the image of himself that modern fiction has projected, he is at least embarrassed.

The Negro writer, like the white writer of the South, is a product of the Southern condition. Whether he wills it or not, he reflects the tensions and cross-purposes of that environment. Just as the myth of the Old South weakens under close examination, the myth of literature divorced from what have been called sociological considerations dissolves in a bright light.

The fictional world on which most of us first opened our eyes, where the Negro is concerned, is epitomized by a remark made by a character in William Faulkner's *Sartoris*. "What us niggers want ter be free fer, anyhow?" asks old Uncle Simon. "Ain't we got es many white folks now es we kin suppo't?"

The elusiveness of Jean Toomer in the face of complexities like these can well stand for the elusiveness of Negro writers from Charles W. Chesnutt to Frank Yerby. What Toomer was trying to indicate to us by the course he took still intrigues, but I suspect he realizes by now that there is no further need to *signify*. The secrets are out. As the song says, "There's no hiding place down here."

—1966

Esther

Jean Toomer

Nine

ESTHER'S hair falls in soft curls about her high-cheekboned chalk-white face. Esther's hair would be beautiful if there were more gloss to it. And if her face were not prematurely serious, one would call it pretty. Her cheeks are too flat and dead for a girl of nine. Esther looks like a little white child, starched, frilled, as she walks slowly from her home towards her father's grocery store. She is about to turn in Broad from Maple Street. White and black men loafing on the corner hold no interest for her. Then a strange thing happens. A clean-muscled, magnificent black-skinned Negro, whom she had heard her father mention as King Barlo, suddenly drops to his knees on a spot called the Spittoon. White men, unaware of him, continue squirting tobacco juice in his direction. The saffron fluid splashes on his face. His smooth black face begins to glisten and to shine. Soon, people notice him and gather round. His eyes are rapturous upon the heavens. Lips and nostrils quiver. Barlo is in a religious trance. Town folks know it. They are not startled. They are not afraid. They gather round. Some beg boxes from the grocery stores. From old McGregor's notion shop. A coffin case is pressed into use. Folks line the curbstones. Businessmen close shop. And Banker Warply parks his car close by. Silently, all await the prophet's voice. The sheriff, a great florid fellow whose leggings never meet around his bulging calves, swears in three deputies. "Wall, y cant never tell what a nigger like King Barlo might be up t." Soda bottles, five fingers full of shine, are passed to those who want them. A couple of stray dogs start a fight. Old Good-low's cow comes flopping up the street. Barlo, still as an Indian fakir, has not moved. The town bell strikes six. The sun slips in behind a heavy mass of horizon cloud. The crowd is hushed and expectant. Barlo's underjaw relaxes, and his lips begin to move.

"Jesus has been awhisperin strange words deep down, O way down deep, deep in my ears."

Hums of awe and of excitement.

"He called me to His side an said, 'Git down on your knees beside me, son, Ise gwine t whisper in your ears.'"

An old sister cries, "Ah, Lord."

" 'Ise agwine t whisper in your ears,' He said, an I replied, 'Thy will be done on earth as it is in heaven.'"

"Ah, Lord. Amen. Amen."

"An Lord Jesus whispered strange good words deep down, O way down deep, deep in my ears. An He said, 'Tell em till you feel your throat on fire.' I saw a vision. I saw a man arise, an he was big an black an powerful—"

Someone yells, "Preach it, preacher, preach it!"

"—but his head was caught up in th clouds. An while he was agazin at th heavens, heart filled up with th Lord, some little white-ant biddies came an tied his feet to chains. They led him t th coast, they led him t th sea, they led him across th ocean an they didnt set him free. The old coast didnt miss him, an th new coast wasnt free, he left the old-coast brothers, t give birth t you an me. O Lord, great God Almighty, t give birth t you an me."

Barlo pauses. Old gray mothers are in tears. Fragments of melodies are being hummed. White folks are touched and curiously awed. Off to themselves, white and black preachers confer as to how best to rid themselves of the vagrant, usurping fellow. Barlo looks as though he is struggling to continue. People are hushed. One can hear weevils work. Dusk is falling rapidly, and the customary store lights fail to throw their feeble glow across the gray dust and flagging of the Georgia town. Barlo rises to his full height. He is immense. To the people he assumes the outlines of his visioned African. In a mighty voice he bellows:

"Brothers an sisters, turn your faces t th sweet face of the Lord, an fill your hearts with glory. Open your eyes an see th dawnin of th mornin light. Open your ears—"

Years afterwards Esther was told that at that very moment a great, heavy, rumbling voice actually was heard. That hosts of angels and of demons paraded up and down the streets all night. That King Barlo rode out of town astride a pitch-black bull that had a glowing gold ring in its nose. And that old Limp Underwood, who hated niggers, woke up next morning to find that he held a black man in his arms. This much is certain: an inspired Negress, of wide reputation for being sanctified, drew a portrait of a black Madonna on the courthouse wall. And King Barlo left town. He left his image indelibly upon the mind of Esther. He became the starting point of the only living patterns that her mind was to know.

Sixteen

Esther begins to dream. The low evening sun sets the windows of McGregor's notion shop aflame. Esther makes believe that they really are aflame. The town fire department rushes madly down the road. It ruthlessly shoves black and white idlers to one side. It whoops. It clangs. It rescues from the second-story window a dimpled infant which she claims for her own. How had she come by it? She thinks of it immaculately. It is a sin to think of it immaculately. She must dream no more. She must repent her sin. Another dream comes. There is no fire department. There

are no heroic men. The fire starts. The loafers on the corner form a circle, chew their tobacco faster, and squirt juice just as fast as they can chew. Gallons on top of gallons they squirt upon the flames. The air reeks with the stench of scorched tobacco juice. Women, fat chunky Negro women, lean scrawny white women, pull their skirts up above their heads and display the most ludicrous underclothes. The women scoot in all directions from the danger zone. She alone is left to take the baby in her arms. But what a baby! Black, singed, woolly, tobacco-juice baby—ugly as sin. Once held to her breast, miraculous thing: its breath is sweet and its lips can nibble. She loves it frantically. Her joy in it changes the town folks' jeers to harmless jealousy, and she is left alone.

Twenty-two

Esther's schooling is over. She works behind the counter of her father's grocery store. "To keep the money in the family," so he said. She is learning to make distinctions between the business and the social worlds. "Good business comes from remembering that the white folks dont divide the niggers, Esther. Be just as black as any man who has a silver dollar." Esther listlessly forgets that she is near white, and that her father is the richest colored man in town. Black folk who drift in to buy lard and snuff and flour of her, call her a sweet-natured, accommodating girl. She learns their names. She forgets them. She thinks about men. "I dont appeal to them. I wonder why." She recalls an affair she had with a little fair boy while still in school. It had ended in her shame when he as much as told her that for sweetness he preferred a lollipop. She remembers the salesman from the North who wanted to take her to the movies that first night he was in town. She refused, of course. And he never came back, having found out who she was. She thinks of Barlo. Barlo's image gives her a slightly stale thrill. She spices it by telling herself his glories. Black. Magnetically so. Best cotton picker in the county, in the state, in the whole world for that matter. Best man with his fists, best man with dice, with a razor. Promoter of church benefits. Of colored fairs. Vagrant preacher.

Lover of all the women for miles and miles around. Esther decides that she loves him. And with a vague sense of life slipping by, she resolves that she will tell him so, whatever people say, the next time he comes to town. After the making of this resolution which becomes a sort of wedding cake for her to tuck beneath her pillow and go to sleep upon, she sees nothing of Barlo for five years. Her hair thins. It looks like the dull silk on puny corn ears. Her face pales until it is the color of the gray dust that dances with dead cotton leaves.

Twenty-seven

Esther sells lard and snuff and flour to vague black faces that drift in her store to ask for them. Her eyes hardly see the people to whom she gives change. Her body is lean and beaten. She rests listlessly against the counter, too weary to sit down. From the street someone shouts, "King Barlo has come back to town." He passes her window, driving a large new car. Cutout open. He veers to the curb and steps out. Barlo has made money on cotton during the War. He is as rich as anyone. Esther suddenly is animate. She goes to her door. She sees him at a distance, the center of a group of credulous men. She hears the deep-bass rumble of his talk. The sun swings low. McGregor's windows are aflame again. Pale flame. A sharply dressed white girl passes by. For a moment Esther wishes that she might be like her. Not white; she has no need for being that. But sharp, sporty, with getup about her. Barlo is connected with that wish. She mustnt wish. Wishes only make you restless. Emptiness is a thing that grows by being moved. "Ill not think. Not wish. Just set my mind against it." Then the thought comes to her that those purposeless, easygoing men will possess him, if she doesnt. Purpose is not dead in her, now that she comes to think of it. That loose women will have their arms around him at Nat Bowle's place tonight. As if her veins are full of fired, sun-bleached Southern shanties, a swift heat sweeps them. Dead dreams, and a forgotten resolution, are carried upward by the flames. Pale flames. "They shant have him. Oh, they shall not. Not if it kills me they shant have him." Jerky, aflutter,

she closes the store and starts home. Folks lazing on store windowsills wonder what on earth can be the matter with Jim Crane's gal, as she passes them. "Come to remember, she always was a little off, a little crazy, I reckon." Esther seeks her own room, and locks the door. Her mind is a pink mesh-bag filled with baby toes.

Using the noise of the town clock striking twelve to cover the creaks of her departure, Esther slips into the quiet road. The town, her parents, most everyone is sound asleep. This fact is a stable thing that comforts her. After sundown a chill wind came up from the west. It is still blowing, but to her it is a steady, settled thing like the cold. She wants her mind to be like that. Solid, contained, and blank as a sheet of darkened ice. She will not permit herself to notice the peculiar phosphorescent glitter of the sweet-gum leaves. Their movement would excite her. Exciting too, the recession of the dull familiar homes she knows so well. She doesnt know them at all. She closes her eyes, and holds them tightly. Wont do. Her being aware that they are closed recalls her purpose. She does not want to think of it. She opens them. She turns now into the deserted business street. The corrugated iron canopies and mule- and horse-gnawed hitching posts bring her a strange composure. Ghosts of the commonplaces of her daily life take stride with her and become her companions. And the echoes of her heels upon the flagging are rhythmically monotonous and soothing. Crossing the street at the corner of McGregor's notion shop, she thinks that the windows are a dull flame. Only a fancy. She walks faster. Then runs. A turn into a side street brings her abruptly to Nat Bowle's place.

The house is squat and dark. It is always dark. Barlo is within. Quietly she opens the outside door and steps in. She passes through a small room. Pauses before a flight of stairs down which people's voices, muffled, come. The air is heavy with fresh tobacco smoke. It makes her sick. She wants to turn back. She goes up the steps. As if she were mounting to some great height, her head spins. She is violently dizzy. Blackness rushes to her eyes. And then she finds that she is in a large room. Barlo is before her.

"Well, I'm sholy damned—skuse me, but what, what brought you here, lil milk-white gal?"

"You." Her voice sounds like a frightened child's that calls homeward from some point miles away.

"Me?"

"Yes, you Barlo."

"This aint th place fer y. This aint th place fer y."

"I know. I know. But Ive come for you."

"For me for what?"

She manages to look deep and straight into his eyes. He is slow at understanding. Guffaws and giggles break out from all around the room. A coarse woman's voice remarks, "So thats how th dictie niggers does it." Laughs. "Mus give em credit fo their gall."

Esther doesnt hear. Barlo does. His faculties are jogged. She sees a smile, ugly and repulsive to her, working upward through thick licker fumes. Barlo seems hideous. The thought comes suddenly, that conception with a drunken man must be a mighty sin. She draws away, frozen. Like a somnambulist she wheels around and walks stiffly to the stairs. Down them. Jeers and hoots pelter bluntly upon her back. She steps out. There is no air, no street, and the town has completely disappeared.

—1923

From *Cane*

The Return

Zora Neale Hurston

SHIPS AT A DISTANCE have every man's wish on board. For some they come in with the tide. For others they sail forever on the horizon, never out of sight, never landing until the Watcher turns his eyes away in resignation, his dreams mocked to death by Time. That is the life of men.

Now, women forget all those things they don't want to remember, and remember everything they don't want to forget. The dream is the truth. Then they act and do things accordingly.

So the beginning of this was a woman and she had come back from burying the dead. Not the dead of sick and ailing with friends at the pillow and the feet. She had come back from the sodden and the bloated; the sudden dead, their eyes flung wide open in judgment.

The people all saw her come because it was sundown. The sun was gone, but he had left his footprints in the sky. It was the time for sitting on porches beside the road. It was the time to hear things and talk. These sitters had been tongueless, earless, eyeless conveniences all day long. Mules and other brutes had occupied their skins. But now the sun and the bossman were gone, so the skins felt powerful and human. They became lords of sounds and lesser things. They passed nations through their mouths. They sat in judgment.

Seeing the woman as she was made them remember the envy they had stored up from other times. So they chewed up the back parts of their minds and swallowed with relish. They made burning statements with questions, and killing tools out of laughs. It was mass cruelty. A mood come alive. Words walking without masters; walking all together like harmony in a song.

"What she doin' comin' back here in dem overhalls? Can't she find no dress to put on?—Where's dat blue satin dress she left here in?—Where all dat money her husband took and died and left her?—What dat ole forty-year-ole 'oman doin' wid her hair swingin' down her back lak some young gal?—Where she left dat young lad of a boy she went off here wid?—Thought she was going to marry—Where he left *her*?—What he done wid all her money?—Betcha he off wid some gal so young she ain't even got no hairs—Why she don't stay in her class?—"

When she got to where they were she turned her face . . . and spoke. They scrambled a noisy "Good evenin'" and left their mouths setting open and their ears full of hope. Her speech was pleasant enough, but she kept walking straight on to her gate. The porch couldn't talk for looking.

The men noticed her firm buttocks like she had grapefruits in her hip pockets; the great rope of black hair swinging to her waist and unraveling in the wind like a plume; then her pugnacious breasts trying to bore holes in her shirt. They, the men, were saving with the mind what they lost with the eye. The women took the faded shirt and muddy overalls and laid them away for remembrance. It was a weapon against her strength, and if it turned out of no significance, still it was a hope that she might fall to their level some day.

But nobody moved, nobody spoke, nobody even thought to swallow spit until after her gate slammed behind her.

Pearl Stone opened her mouth and laughed

real hard because she didn't know what else to do. She fell all over Mrs. Sumpkins while she laughed. Mrs. Sumpkins snorted violently and sucked her teeth.

"Humph! Y'all let her worry yuh. You ain't like me. Ah ain't got her to study 'bout. If she ain't got manners enough to stop and let folks know how she been makin' out, let her g'wan!"

"She ain't even worth talkin' after," Lulu Moss drawled through her nose. "She sits high, but she looks low. Dat's what Ah say 'bout dese ole women runnin' after young boys."

Pheoby Watson hitched her rocking chair forward before she spoke. "Well, nobody don't know if it's anything to tell or not. Me, Ah'm her best friend, and *Ah* don't know."

"Maybe us don't know into things lak you do, but we all know how she went 'way from here and us sho seen her come back. 'Tain't no use in your tryin' to cloak no ole woman lak Janie Starks, Pheoby, friend or no friend."

"At dat she ain't so ole as some of y'all dat's talkin'."

"She's 'way past forty to my knowledge, Pheoby."

"No more'n forty at de outside."

"She's 'way too old for a boy like Tea Cake."

"Tea Cake ain't been no boy for some time. He's round thirty his ownself."

"Don't keer what it was, she could stop and say a few words with us. She act like we done done somethin' to her," Pearl Stone complained. "She de one been doin' wrong."

"You mean, you mad 'cause she didn't stop and tell us all her business. Anyhow, what you ever know her to do so bad as y'all make out? De worst thing Ah ever knowed her to do was takin' a few years offa her age and dat ain't never harmed nobody. Y'all makes me tired. De way you talkin' you'd think de folks in dis town didn't do nothin' in de bed 'cept praise de Lawd. You have to 'scuse me, 'cause Ah'm bound to go take her some supper." Pheoby stood up sharply.

"Don't mind us," Lulu smiled, "just go right ahead; us can mind yo' house for you till you git back. Mah supper is done. You bettah go see how she feel. You kin let de rest of us know."

"Lawd," Pearl agreed, "Ah done scorched up dat li'l meat and bread too long to talk about.

Ah kin stay 'way from home long as Ah please. Mah husband ain't fussy."

"Oh, er, Pheoby, if youse ready to go, Ah could walk over dere wid you," Mrs. Sumpkins volunteered. "It's sort of duskin' down dark. De booger man might ketch yuh."

"Naw, Ah thank yuh. Nothin' couldn't ketch me dese few steps Ah'm goin'. Anyhow mah husband tell me say no first-class booger would have me. If she got anything to tell yuh, you'll hear it."

Pheoby hurried on off with a covered bowl in her hands. She left the porch pelting her back with unasked questions. They hoped the answers were cruel and strange.

When she arrived at the place, Pheoby Watson didn't go in by the front gate and down the palm walk to the front door. She walked around the fence corner and went in the intimate gate with her heaping plate of mulatto rice. Janie must be round that side.

She found her sitting on the steps of the back porch, with the lamps all filled and the chimneys cleaned.

"Hello, Janie, how you comin'?"

"Aw, pretty good; Ah'm tryin' to soak some uh de tiredness and de dirt outa mah feet." She laughed a little.

"Ah see you is. Gal, you sho looks *good*. You looks like youse yo' own daughter." They both laughed. "Even wid dem overhalls on, you shows yo' womanhood."

"G'wan! G'wan! You must think Ah brought yuh somethin'. When Ah ain't brought home a thing but mahself."

"Dat's a gracious plenty. Yo' friends wouldn't want nothin' better."

"Ah takes dat flattery offa you, Pheoby, 'cause Ah know it's from de heart." Janie extended her hand. "Good Lawd, Pheoby! ain't you never goin' tuh gimme dat li'l rations you brought me? Ah ain't had a thing on mah stomach today exceptin' mah hand." They both laughed easily. "Give it here and have a seat."

"Ah knowed you'd be hongry. No time to be huntin' stove wood after dark. Mah mulatto rice ain't so good dis time. Not enough bacon grease, but Ah reckon it'll kill hongry."

"Ah'll tell you in a minute," Janie said, lifting

the cover. "Gal, it's *too* good! You switches a mean fanny round in a kitchen."

"Aw, dat ain't much to eat, Janie. But Ah'm liable to have somethin' sho 'nuff good tomorrow, 'cause you done come."

Janie ate heartily and said nothing. The varicolored cloud dust that the sun had stirred up in the sky was settling by slow degrees.

"Here, Pheoby, take yo' ole plate. Ah ain't got a bit of use for a empty dish. Dat grub sho come in handy."

Pheoby laughed at her friend's rough joke. "Youse just as crazy as you ever was."

"Hand me dat washrag on dat chair by you, honey. Lemme scrub mah feet." She took the cloth and rubbed vigorously. Laughter came to her from the big road.

"Well, Ah see Mouth-Almighty is still sittin' in de same place. And Ah reckon they got *me* up in they mouth now."

"Yes indeed. You know if you pass some people and don't speak tuh suit 'em they got tuh go 'way back in yo' life and see whut you ever done. They know mo' 'bout yuh than you do yo'self. An envious heart makes a treacherous ear. They done 'heard' 'bout you just what they hope done happened."

"If God don't think no mo' 'bout 'em than Ah do, they's a lost ball in de high grass."

"Ah hears what they say 'cause they just will collect round mah porch 'cause it's on de big road. Mah husband git so sick of 'em sometime he makes 'em all git for home."

"Sam is right, too. They just wearin' out yo' sittin' chairs."

"Yeah, Sam say most of 'em goes to church so they'll be sure to rise in Judgment. Dat's de day dat every secret is s'posed to be made known. They wants to be there and hear it *all*."

"Sam is *too* crazy! You can't stop laughin' when youse round him."

"Uuh-hunh. He says he aims to be there hisself so he can find out who stole his corncob pipe."

"Pheoby, dat Sam of yourn just won't quit! Crazy thing!"

"Most of dese zigaboos is so het up over yo' business till they liable to hurry theyself to Judgment to find out about you if they don't soon know. You better make haste and tell 'em 'bout you and Tea Cake gittin' married, and if he taken all yo' money and went off wid some young gal, and where at he is now and where at is all yo' clothes, dat you got to come back here in overhalls."

"Ah don't mean to bother wid tellin' 'em nothin', Pheoby. 'Tain't worth de trouble. You can tell 'em what Ah say if you wants to. Dat's just de same as me 'cause mah tongue is in mah friend's mouf."

"If you so desire Ah'll tell 'em what you tell me to tell 'em."

"To start off wid, people like dem wastes up too much time puttin' they mouf on things they don't know nothin' about. Now they got to look into me lovin' Tea Cake and see whether it was done right or not! They don't know if life is a mess of cornmeal dumplings, and if love is a bed-quilt!"

"So long as they get a name to gnaw on they don't care whose it is, and what about, 'specially if they can make it sound like evil."

"If they wants to see and know, why they don't come kiss and be kissed? Ah could then sit down and tell 'em things. Ah been a delegate to de big 'ssociation of life. Yessuh! De Grand Lodge, de big convention of livin' is just where Ah been dis year and a half y'all ain't seen me."

They sat there in the fresh young darkness close together. Pheoby eager to feel and do through Janie, but hating to show her zest for fear it might be thought mere curiosity. Janie full of that oldest human longing—self-revelation.

Pheoby held her tongue for a long time, but she couldn't help moving her feet. So Janie spoke.

"They don't need to worry about me and my overhalls long as Ah still got nine hundred dollars in de bank. Tea Cake got me into wearin' 'em—followin' behind him. Tea Cake ain't wasted up no money of mine, and he ain't left me for no young gal, neither. He give me every consolation in de world. He'd tell 'em so, too, if he was here. If he wasn't gone."

Pheoby dilated all over with eagerness, "Tea Cake gone?"

"Yeah, Pheoby, Tea Cake is gone. And dat's de only reason you see me back here—'cause Ah ain't got nothin' to make me happy no more where Ah was at. Down in de Everglades there, down on de muck."

"It's hard for me to understand what you mean, de way you tell it. And then again Ah'm hard of understandin' at times."

"Naw, 'tain't nothin' lak you might think. So 'tain't no use in me tellin' you somethin' unless Ah give you de understandin' to go 'long wid it. Unless you see de fur, a mink skin ain't no different from a coon hide. Looka heah, Pheoby, is Sam waitin' on you for his supper?"

"It's all ready and waitin'. If he ain't got sense enough to eat it, dat's his hard luck."

"Well then, we can set right where we is and talk. Ah got de house all opened up to let dis breeze get a little catchin'.

"Pheoby, we been kissin'-friends for twenty years, so Ah depend on you for a good thought. And Ah'm talkin' to you from dat standpoint."

Time makes everything old, so the kissing, young darkness became a monstropolous old thing while Janie talked.

—1937

From *Their Eyes Were Watching God*

Salvation

Langston Hughes

I WAS SAVED from sin when I was going on thirteen. But not really saved. It happened like this. There was a big revival at my Auntie Reed's church. Every night for weeks there had been much preaching, singing, praying and shouting, and some very hardened sinners had been brought to Christ, and the membership of the church had grown by leaps and bounds. Then just before the revival ended, they held a special meeting for children, "to bring the young lambs to the fold." My aunt spoke of it for days ahead. That night I was escorted to the front row and placed on the mourners' bench with all the other young sinners who had not yet been brought to Jesus.

My aunt told me that when you were saved you saw a light, and something happened to you inside! And Jesus came into your life! And God was with you from then on! She said you could see and hear and feel Jesus in your soul. I believed her. I had heard a great many old people say the same thing and it seemed to me they ought to know. So I sat there calmly in the hot, crowded church, waiting for Jesus to come to me.

The preacher preached a wonderful rhythmical sermon, all moans and shouts and lonely cries and dire pictures of hell, and then he sang a song about the ninety and nine safe in the fold, but one little lamb was left out in the cold. Then he said: "Won't you come? Won't you come to Jesus? Young lambs, won't you come?" And he held out his arms to all us young sinners there on the mourners' bench. And the little girls cried. And some of them jumped up and went to Jesus right away. But most of us just sat there.

A great many old people came and knelt around us and prayed, old women with jet-black faces and braided hair, old men with work-gnarled hands. And the church sang a song about the lower lights are burning, some poor sinners to be saved. And the whole building rocked with prayer and song.

Still I kept waiting to *see* Jesus.

Finally all the young people had gone to the altar and were saved, but one boy and me. He was a rounder's son named Westley. Westley and I were surrounded by sisters and deacons praying. It was very hot in the church, and getting late now. Finally Westley said to me in a whisper: "God damn! I'm tired o' sitting here. Let's get up and be saved." So he got up and was saved.

Then I was left all alone on the mourners' bench. My aunt came and knelt at my knees and cried, while prayers and songs swirled all around me in the little church. The whole congregation prayed for me alone, in a mighty wail of moans and voices. And I kept waiting serenely for Jesus, waiting, waiting—but He didn't come. I wanted to see Him, but nothing happened to me. Nothing! I wanted something to happen to me, but nothing happened.

I heard the songs and the minister saying: "Why don't you come? My dear child, why don't you come to Jesus? Jesus is waiting for you. He wants you. Why don't you come? Sister Reed, what is this child's name?"

"Langston," my aunt sobbed.

"Langston, why don't you come? Why don't you come and be saved? Oh, Lamb of God! Why don't you come?

Now it was really getting late. I began to be ashamed of myself, holding everything up so long. I began to wonder what God thought about

Westley, who certainly hadn't seen Jesus either but who was now sitting proudly on the platform, swinging his knickerbockered legs and grinning down at me, surrounded by deacons and old women on their knees praying. God had not struck Westley dead for taking His name in vain or for lying in the temple. So I decided that maybe to save further trouble I'd better lie too, and say that Jesus had come, and get up and be saved.

So I got up.

Suddenly the whole room broke into a sea of shouting, as they saw me rise. Waves of rejoicing swept the place. Women leaped in the air. My aunt threw her arms around me. The minister took me by the hand and led me to the platform.

From *The Big Sea*

When things quieted down, in a hushed silence, punctuated by a few ecstatic "Amens," all the new young lambs were blessed in the name of God. Then joyous singing filled the room.

That night, for the last time in my life but one —for I was a big boy twelve years old—I cried. I cried, in bed alone, and couldn't stop. I buried my head under the quilts, but my aunt heard me. She woke up and told my uncle I was crying because the Holy Ghost had come into my life, and because I had seen Jesus. But I was really crying because I couldn't bear to tell her that I had lied, that I had deceived everybody in the church, that I hadn't seen Jesus and that now I didn't believe there was a Jesus any more, since He didn't come to help me.

—1940

Color Problems

Langston Hughes

TWO THINGS I would hate to be in Harlem right now is a light-skin Negro and a black cop," said Simple. "If it is true what the downtown papers said about some Black Blood Brotherhood out to kill white folks, how can a near-white Negro the complexion of Adam Powell be sure that the brotherhood might not make a mistake and kill him too?"

"What a thought!" I cried.

"Yes," said Simple. "And as to the colored polices in these days and times with civil rights at the boiling point, if a Negro cop tries to arrest somebody doing wrong to get his rights, that cop is liable to be taken as a traitor to his race, to integration, freedom and also equality. Yes, sir! In fact, any colored cop who has to arrest a civil rights demonstrator these days must feel bad, because I know that cop wants his rights the same as any other Negro. I would feel bad, too, wouldn' you?"

"Indeed, the position of the colored policemen in the civil rights battle must be difficult," I said. "I saw a photograph in the papers of a colored policeman in a Southern town arresting some colored teen-agers who were picketing a white movie theatre to which that colored policeman himself could not buy a ticket. I wonder what would you do if you were a Negro policeman in such a case?"

"I would refuse to make an arrest," said Simple. "I would not be a traitor to my race just in order to be a cop. In most Southern towns which have Negroes on the police forces, colored polices do not dare to arrest a white person. Colored cops is limited to making colored arrests."

"The police force, whatever the nationality of its individuals, should be color-blind," I said.

"What is and what *should be* is two different things," said Simple. "Harlem is so full of white cops with white faces and white viewpoints that when some of them see me, they see red because I am *not* white. So when a black cop sees me, he should not look through white eyes. I am his brother—even when I am walking on a picket line and do not move fast enough to satisfy the police commissioner. Colored cops should know why I do not move any faster—because I have been so slow in getting my rights to belong to that white union I am picketing which bars me from earning a living even on a project built by the city with my tax money. A colored cop ought not to be so quick to arrest me when that cop's own son cannot get into the union, either. That cop knows his tax money and mine is being spent to build government buildings where colored plumbers cannot even install a toilet."

"I admit the dilemma of Negro police in the face of the civil rights struggle is tough. In fact, they face a *double* dilemma."

"I would not like to be a colored cop in the face of no such double," said Simple. "It would break my heart to have to arrest my own teen-age son or his friends, or to arrest these young white students who is fighting and picketing and marching with us for civil rights. Fact is, I would not arrest any of them."

"Are you advocating disobedience to law on the part of Negro policemen?"

"When the law is not on the side of civil rights, then the law is not right, it's white," said Simple. "And if I was a light-complexioned Negro—instead of being dark as I am—I would be afraid some of these kids in Harlem that the papers is calling American Mau Maus might take *me* as being white. And these mixed couples living in Harlem, colored mens married to white womens, and white mens married to colored womens? Suppose Sammy Davis lived in Harlem? or Lena Horne?—and both of them are married white. I met a light-skin Negro friend of mine, a man, the other night who looks white. Some dark Negro he did not even know said to him in a bar, 'What are you doing up here in Harlem?'

"The light-skin man said, 'I was born in Harlem, and I live in Harlem, and I am as black as you.'

"The dark fellow said, 'You better show it then, and get a suntan.'

From *Simple's Uncle Sam*

"My friend said that for the first time in his life he was scared of his own people. He said Adam Powell better come back home from Washington and make a speech about how black Negroes should not bother light Negroes in Harlem, since we is *all* blood brothers. Do you reckon them stories in the papers was true about the Blood Brothers being out to do white folks in?"

"Newspaper headlines make things seem many times worse than they are in reality," I said. "But whites in Harlem are apprehensive, that's sure. It's regrettable."

"Maybe that old saying, 'A dark man shall see dark days,' ought to be changed to include dark cops, *light* Negroes, and white mens. Me, I am glad I am neither," said Simple.

—1965

Contemporary Negro Poetry: 1914—1936

Sterling A. Brown

THE EXTENSIVE migrations from the South, quickened by the devastations of the boll weevil, the growing resentment at injustice and the demand of Northern industries; the advance of the Negro in labor, wealth and education; the World War with its new experiences in camp and battle; the Garvey movement with its exploitation of "race"—all of these contributed to the growth of the "New Negro."

In 1935 Alain Locke, editor of [the book] *The New Negro*, wrote:

> The intelligent Negro of today is resolved not to make discrimination an extenuation for his shortcomings in performance, individual or collective; he is trying to hold himself at par, neither inflated by sentimental allowances nor depreciated by current social discounts. For this he must know himself and be known for precisely what he is, and for that reason he welcomes the new scientific rather than the old sentimental interest. . . . Now we rejoice and pray to be delivered both from self-pity and condescension.

The New Negro was marked by self-respect (which, admittedly at times, became self-preening) and by self-reliance. He asked for less charity and more justice. Negro poetry reflected all of this.

Coincidentally in the postwar years the "New Poetry" appeared in American literature, and New Negro poets naturally shared in this movement's reaction against sentimentality, didacticism, optimism and romantic escape. They learned to shun stilted "poetic diction," to use fresher more original language and to humanize poetry. Race was no longer to be caricatured or neglected; they did not plead "for a race" but

attempted to express it. At their best they belonged with the renascent American poets who "in the tones of ordinary speech rediscovered the strength, the dignity, the vital core of the commonplace."

The resulting poetry had five major concerns: (1) a discovery of Africa as a source for race pride, (2) a use of Negro heroes and heroic episodes from American history, (3) propaganda of protest, (4) a treatment of the Negro masses (frequently of the folk, less often of the workers) with more understanding and less apology, and (5) franker and deeper self-revelation. Some of this subject matter called for a romantic approach, some for a realistic. . . .

Fenton Johnson

Fenton Johnson's works show the two extremes of Negro poetry after 1914. Some of his poems are conventional in form and substance; others, patterned upon his fellow Chicagoan, Sandburg, are striking departures in Negro poetry. With Sandburg's technique and Edgar Lee Masters' outlook, Johnson included in *African Nights* snapshots of bitter experience such as "Aunt Hannah Jackson," "The Banjo Player," "The Minister," "The Scarlet Woman" and "Tired." Unfortunately Johnson, like so many of his Negro contemporaries, fell silent shortly after these poems.

Perhaps there was little audience for their pessimism, either within a race whose optimism is proverbial, or without, where the Negro's brooding over his lot is generally unwelcome. "The Scarlet Woman," educated for more than a white man's kitchen, is driven by poverty to streetwalking, and gin is her only way of forgetfulness. "Tired" indicts civilization:

> I am tired of building up somebody else's civilization. . . . Let the old shanty go to rot, the white people's clothes turn to dust, and the Calvary Baptist Church sink to the bottomless pit. . . .
> Throw the children into the river; civilization has given us too many.

Negro "leaders" who direct the race into optimism condemned this view of life, but it is tonic after such frequent insistence on "a good time coming by and by." Like so many modern poets, Fenton Johnson held to the words of Thomas Hardy, that

> If way to the better there be, it exacts a full look at the worst.

Women Poets

Georgia Douglas Johnson continues in the main the tradition. According to a sponsoring critic, Mrs. Johnson has "set herself the task of documenting the feminine heart . . . and in a simple declarative style engages with ingenuous directness the moods and emotions of her themes." The poems in *The Heart of a Woman* (1918), *Bronze* (1922) and *An Autumn Love Cycle* (1928) are written to appeal to the heart, and are generally autumnal in tone. *Bronze* contains "Hegira," "The Octoroon" and "Aliens," upon race themes; one section, "Motherhood," at times goes deeply into the tragic problems of Negro mothers aware of what faces their children. Though conventional in phrase and meter, her poems are skillful and fluent.

Angelina Weld Grimké is the author of many musical lyrics, frequently in a carefully worded and cadenced free verse. Intellectual, and sensitive to injustice, she has written poems of irony and quiet despair; a puppet player twitches "the strings with slow sardonic grin":

> Let us forget the past unrest—
> We ask for peace.

She is influenced by Imagism, but her images are of the twilight or of winter.

Alice Dunbar Nelson, wife of Paul Laurence

Dunbar, in addition to her better-known sketches of Creole life, wrote many poems. These echo the romantic themes, some being concerned with descriptions of Nature, "the perfect loveliness that God has made," in contrast with man-made imperfections. "I Sit and Sew" laments a woman's enforced inactivity in time of war.

Voices of Protest

More forthright, but done with less artistic care, are the poems of Walter Everette Hawkins. His book is called *Chords and Discords*; the "chords" are conventional lyrics about love or duty, but the "discords" foreshadow New Negro poetry. "The Iconoclast" and "To Prometheus" are self-consciously radical, but the theme was new for Negro poets. "A Festival in Christendom" describes a lynching, but since literary diction is used for lurid details, it does not succeed as poetry:

> Then from his side they tore his heart
> And watched its quivering fibres start.

In "Thus Speaks Africa" Hawkins combines race pride and race history in a manner favored by many contemporary Negro poets:

> I am Africa:
> Wild is the wail of my waters,
> Deep is the cry of my Congo.
> I laid down my life at Fort Pillow. . . .
> I died on the flag at Fort Wagner,
> My bones lie bleaching in Flanders.
> I was burned at the stake down in Georgia,
> I was fuel for the mob in Texas.

After such a catalogue, he states less convincingly:

> And then like the Phoenix of Egypt,
> I rose from the ashes immortal.

Carrie W. Clifford in *The Widening Light* likewise looks forward anxiously to the bursting "full-flowered into life" of black folk choked into a death stupor. Many of her sonnets are race conscious, like "The Black Draftee from Dixie," which tells of one of the many soldiers who were lynched upon their return from overseas.

One of the many Negro poets who died young, Roscoe Jamison is best known for his poem "The Negro Soldiers," beginning:

These truly are the Brave,
These men who cast aside
Old memories, to walk the blood-stained pave
Of Sacrifice, joining the solemn tide
That moves away, to suffer and to die
For Freedom—when their own is yet denied!

Similarly cut off at the outset of his career, Joseph Seamon Cotter [Jr.], gifted son of a gifted father, left behind him a sheaf of poems, *The Band of Gideon and Other Lyrics*. Cotter had a definite lyrical facility, seen in the title poem, "Supplication" and "Rain Music." Closer to the New Negro concern for social themes, done with quiet persuasiveness, is:

Brother, come!
And let us go unto our God.
And when we stand before Him
I shall say—
"Lord, I do not hate,
I am hated.
I scourge no one,
I am scourged.
I covet no lands,
My lands are coveted.
I mock no peoples,
My people are mocked."
And, brother, what shall you say?

Claude McKay

Claude McKay's voice was the strongest in the immediate postwar years. Born in the West Indies, McKay, soon after his arrival in America, discovered the shams of "democracy." With Floyd Dell and Max Eastman he became one of the editors of the *Liberator*, a magazine dedicated to social justice. In the epidemic of race riots occurring shortly after the War, a much-quoted cry of defiance was McKay's

If we must die—let it not be like hogs
Hunted and penned in an inglorious spot . . .
Like men we'll face the murderous, cowardly
   pack,
Pressed to the wall, dying, but fighting back!

"The Lynching," with its crowd where men were jostled by steely-eyed women and "little lads, lynchers that were to be," and "America," which "feeds me bread of bitterness," contain desperate truth. Africa is called, with point and power:

The harlot, now thy time is done,
Of all the mighty nations of the sun.

Streetwalkers of Harlem, cabaret dancers and urban workers are treated with understanding. McKay looks searchingly at reality and reveals its harshness.

But there is a McKay other than the hater, the rebel and the realist—there is the dreamer, nostalgic for the sights and sounds of his native West Indies. "The Tropics in New York" is a poem of memory stirred by the sight of West Indian fruits in a store window. "My Mother" is a simply, tenderly phrased reminiscence. "Flame-Heart," a listing of the delights of youth in Jamaica, is one of the best lyrics in Negro poetry. "Two-an'-Six" is a charming pastoral of Jamaican life, closer to Burns than to Dunbar. When McKay turned almost completely to prose fiction, Negro poetry suffered a real loss.

Anne Spencer

Anne Spencer is the most original of all Negro women poets. Her devotion to Browning, attested by one of her best poems "Life-Long, Poor Browning," results in a closely woven style that is at times cryptic, but even more often richly rewarding. She makes use of poetic tradition without being conventional, and of new styles with a regard for form; her vision and expression are those of a wise, ironic but gentle woman of her times. She is sensitive to natural beauty, praising her home state, Virginia:

Here canopied reaches of dogwood and hazel,
Beech tree and redbud fine-laced in vines,
Fleet clapping rills by lush fern and basil,
Drain blue hills to lowlands scented with pines.

"Neighbors," "I Have a Friend" and "Innocence" convey a great deal, in the deceptively simple manner of Emily Dickinson. "Before the Feast of Shushan" is a poem of vivid sensuous beauty, telling an old story in modern terms. "At the Carnival" has a bitter wisdom; Mrs. Spencer sets before us graphically the drab cheapness: the blind crowd, the sausage and garlic booth, the dancing-tent where "a quivering female-thing gestured assignations," the "Limousine-Lady" and the "bull-necked man"—in contrast to the gleaming beauty of the "Girl-of-the-Tank," but

> Little Diver, Destiny for you,
> Like as for me, is shod in silence;
> Years may seep into your soul
> The bacilli of the usual and the expedient;
> I implore Neptune to claim his child today!

Original, sensitive and keenly observant, the poems of Anne Spencer should be collected for a wider audience.

Jessie Fauset

Though better known as a novelist, Jessie Fauset is likewise a poet. Her interest in French literature is apparent in many titles of her poems and in her translations of poets of the French West Indies—who should be better known. Most of Miss Fauset's personal poems are about love, written with a care for form and an ironic disillusionment. "La Vie C'est la Vie," the best of these, sets forth a triangle of lovers, loving and unbeloved:

> But he will none of me. Nor I
> Of you. Nor you of her. 'Tis said
> The world is full of jests like these—
> I wish that I were dead.

"Oriflamme" celebrates Sojourner Truth, making her symbolic of the Negro mother, bereft of her children, "still visioning the stars."

Jean Toomer

Jean Toomer is best as a poet in the beautiful prose of *Cane* (1923). His few poems in the same volume, however, are original and striking. Jean Toomer has written that Georgia opened him up; "Reapers" and "Cotton Song" show this awakening to folk material. In "Georgia Dusk" there is a sense of the ominous mystery of the Southland:

> The sawmill blows its whistle, buzz-saws stop,
> And silence breaks the bud of knoll and hill . . .
> Smoke from the pyramidal sawdust pile
> Curls up, blue ghosts of trees, . . .
>   . . . the chorus of the cane
> Is caroling a vesper to the stars.

With a mastery of the best rhythmical devices

of Negro folk music, "Song of the Son" expresses the return of the younger Negro to a consciousness of identity with his own, a return to folk sources, to the "caroling softly souls of slavery":

> O land and soil, red soil and sweet-gum tree,
> So scant of grass, so profligate of pines,
> Now just before an epoch's sun declines,
> Thy son, in time, I have returned to thee,
> Thy son, I have in time returned to thee.
>
> In time, for though the sun is setting on
> A song-lit race of slaves, it has not set.

In spite of the small number of his poems, Toomer remains one of the finest and most influential of Negro poets. His long silence has been broken with the publication of "Blue Meridian," a rather long poem calling for a "new America, to be spiritualized by each new American." In it there are only occasional references to Negro life:

> The great African races sent a single wave
> And singing riplets to sorrow in red fields,
> Sing a swan song, to break rocks
> And immortalize a hiding water boy.

James Weldon Johnson

James Weldon Johnson has also felt the need of recording the lives and thoughts of those "leaving, soon gone." After collecting and editing two volumes of spirituals, he turned to the task —attempted in an earlier poem, "The Creation" —of fixing something of the rapidly passing old-time Negro preacher. *God's Trombones: Seven Negro Sermons in Verse* (1927) was widely acclaimed. Material which is usually made ludicrous is here invested with dignity, power and beauty. Convinced that dialect smacks too much of the minstrel stage, Johnson attempts to give truth to folk idiom rather than mere misspellings. The rhythms of these chants have true poetic quality. The advance from his earlier dialect "Jungles and Croons" is a great one; *God's Trombones* is a truthful and sincere rendition of a belief and a way of life. There is the occasional grotesqueness of the folk preacher:

> Wash him with hyssop inside and out,
> Hang him up and drain him dry of sin.

But there is the tenderness of the reference to

Sister Caroline, down in Yamacraw, who had borne the burden of the heat of the day and to whom Death "looked like a welcome friend," and the intimacy of telling a novice in the mad, bad Babylon of scarlet women, dancing and drinking:

> Young man, young man,
> Your arm's too short to box with God.

If the hell-border city of Babylon recalls Memphis, New Orleans and Harlem, "The Crucifixion" and "Let My People Go" recall other Negro experiences:

> Listen!—Listen!
> All you sons of Pharaoh;
> Who do you think can hold God's people
> When the Lord God himself has said,
> "Let my people go"?

The visionary qualities of the spirituals are seen throughout, especially in "The Judgment Day":

> The sun will go out like a candle in the wind,
> The moon will turn to dripping blood,
> The stars will fall like cinders,
> And the sea will burn like tar.

The same visionary type of imagination is to be seen in *Saint Peter Relates an Incident of the Resurrection Day* (1930), a caustic satire of the treatment accorded Negro Gold Star Mothers. The Unknown Soldier, arriving in heaven, is discovered to be a Negro; the GAR, the DAR, the Legion, the Klan, the trustees of the patriotism of the nation, are astounded and want him buried again. In these later poems both the interpretation and the protest are less rhetorical and more dramatic than in *Fifty Years [and Other Poems* (1922)], and consequently more persuasive.

Countee Cullen

Most precocious of contemporary Negro poets is Countee Cullen, who was winner of many nation-wide poetry contests in high school and college, and who published his first volume when he was only twenty-two. This volume, *Color* (1925), is by many critics considered Cullen's best. Like Dunbar's standard English poems, and

Braithwaite's, Cullen's work is marked by technical skill; it is the most polished lyricism of modern Negro poetry. Cullen is a follower of tradition in English verse, of what he calls "the measured line and the skillful rhyme." His chief models are Keats and Edna St. Vincent Millay. But he has poured new wine into the old bottles. His gifts are fluency and brilliant imagery; he can convey deep emotion and concise irony. He writes of the gay abandon of lovely brown girls in Harlem "whose walk is like the replica of some barbaric dance," but he is impressed with the transiency of happiness, "the winter of sure defeat." He is capable of the tenderness of "A Brown Girl Dead":

> Her mother pawned her wedding ring
> To lay her out in white;
> She'd be so proud she'd dance and sing,
> To see herself tonight;

and of the epigrammatic:

> She even thinks that up in heaven
> Her class lies late and snores,
> While poor black cherubs rise at seven
> To do celestial chores.

Cullen insists, as any poet should, that he wants "no racial consideration to bolster up" his reputation, and (a different thing, this) does not wish to be confined to "racial" themes:

> What shepherd heart would keep its fill
> For only the darker lamb?

It is nevertheless true, as James Weldon Johnson points out, that his best poems are those motivated by race. "The Shroud of Color" celebrates a mystical experience in which the poet turns from despair to identity with his people:

> Lord, I will live persuaded by mine own.
> I cannot play the recreant to these;
> My spirit has come home, that sailed the
>   doubtful seas.

"Heritage" is a statement of the atavism that was a cardinal creed of New Negro poetry, of "old remembered ways" from Africa persisting in civilization:

> I can never rest at all
> When the rain begins to fall;
> Like a soul gone mad with pain
> I must match its weird refrain.

But the Africa is "literary" and romanticized,

and the theme is too close to Lindsay's "Congo, creeping through the black." "Heritage," for all of its color and facility, does not quite convince. Cullen has also written sonnets of protest. "The Black Christ" (1929) is a narrative poem about lynching but, like others of his late poems, relies more upon literature than life.

Langston Hughes

Langston Hughes is like Cullen in productivity and wide popularity. These two poets are about the same age; Hughes's *The Weary Blues* (1926) appeared the year after *Color*. Where Cullen is traditional in form, Hughes is experimental, substituting Sandburg for Keats, and going as far in metrical revolt as "The Cat and the Saxophone, 2 A.M." Cullen is subjective, whereas Hughes is frequently objective and dramatic, concerned with the Negro masses. Cullen has most recently translated the *Medea* of Euripides; Hughes's most recent work is communist propaganda. Both poets have strains of pessimism, at times met stoically, but Hughes has now turned to a cause that he believes will usher in social justice.

In *The Weary Blues*, Hughes helped to celebrate jazz-mad Harlem, but a note of sadness intrudes, as in "To Midnight Nan at Leroy's" and "Song for a Banjo Dance." He believes that

> We should have a land of sun. . . .
> And not this land where life is cold.

He, too, sings atavistically of Africa, of the boy in whose blood "all the tom-toms of the jungle beat." But, aware that the dark peoples are caged in "the circus of civilization," he turns realistically to description of his people. His folk portraits are good in "The Weary Blues," "Aunt Sue's Stories" and the tender, stoical "Mother to Son," one of the best Negro poems:

> Well, son, I'll tell you:
> Life for me ain't been no crystal stair.

This interest is continued in *Fine Clothes to the Jew* (1927), in which he combines the melancholy and irony of the folk blues. An abandoned woman sings:

> Don't know's I'd mind his goin',
> But he left me when de coal was low.

He gives dramatic sketches of city workers—elevator boys and porters "climbing up a great big mountain of yes, sirs!" "Ruby Brown," like Fenton Johnson's acid sketches, and "A Ruined Gal" have shocked those who wish poetry to be confined to the pretty and sweet, but they ring true and sympathetic. Another side of Negro experience is made real in "Feet o' Jesus," "Prayer" and "Angel's Wings." "Cross" is a quizzical and "Mulatto" a direct commentary upon the bitter social fruit of race mixture.

Generalized interpretation of the race appears in "I, Too, Sing America" and in "A Negro Speaks of Rivers," one of his finest poems. He calls his people "loud-mouthed laughers in the hands of fate," but is convinced that their "soul has grown deep like the rivers." "Minstrel Man" takes an old concept and reveals a new truth:

> Because my mouth
> Is wide with laughter,
> And my throat
> Is deep with song,
> You do not think
> I suffer after
> I have held my pain
> So long.

Hughes's awakened interest in communism has resulted in such poems as "Good-Bye, Christ," "Letter to the Academy," "Elderly Race Leaders" (which closes with twenty-four dollar signs), the "Ballad of Lenin," "Ballad of Ozzie Powell" and the better "To the Kids Who Die," "America" and the "Ballad of Roosevelt":

> The pot was empty,
> The cupboard was bare.
> I said, "Papa
> What's the matter here?"
> "I'm waitin' on Roosevelt, son,
> Roosevelt, Roosevelt,
> Waitin' on Roosevelt, son."

Other New Negro Poets

Waring Cuney likewise absorbed something of the spirit of the blues and spirituals, and his poems, like those of Hughes, have a deceptive simplicity. "I Think I See Him There," "Troubled Jesus," "Crucifixion" and "Wake Cry" deal gently and truthfully with folk religion. "Burial of the Young Love," "The Death Bed," "Threnody" and "Finis" attain a true melancholy with economy of phrase. "No Images" tells of the girl who thinks "her brown body has no glory":

> If she could dance
> Naked,
> Under palm trees
> And see her image in the river
> She would know.
>
> But there are no palm trees
> On the street,
> And dishwater gives back no images.

Helene Johnson also writes with pride of race. Her "Sonnet to a Negro in Harlem" praises him for his magnificent disdain, his arrogant and bold laughter.

Like Hughes, she believes his setting should be palm trees and mangoes. She writes in Harlemese a sketch of a jazz prince, with his shoulders "jerking the jig-wa." "Bottled" is a semi-humorous lament for a Negro "in trick clothes . . . yaller shoes and yaller gloves and a swallow-tail coat," who would be beautiful back in pagan Africa.

Gwendolyn Bennett's poems are generally race conscious; like most of the New Negro school, she writes in "To a Dark Girl":

> Something of old forgotten queens
> Lurks in the lithe abandon of your walk.

Gladys May Casely Hayford, a native African, writes with a conscious desire to imbue her own people "with the idea of their own beauty, superiority and individuality, with a love and admiration for our own country which has been systematically suppressed." Her "Rainy Season Love Song" is colorful and warm, but the verse form is traditional in cadence and phrasing.

One of the best Negro novelists, Arna Bontemps, is likewise a poet of distinction. His work is meditative, couched in fluent but subdued rhythms.

It is poetry of the twilight, of reverie, as so much of Negro poetry, but the artistry is of high order. "Nocturne," "Nocturne at Bethesda," "Gethsemane," "Golgotha Is a Mountain" and "Return" are his best works, and their titles are indicative. Whether writing in the traditional forms or in free verse, Bontemps' concern seems to be music above all else. The symbolism is at times successful; "Nocturne at Bethesda" has racial import:

> . . . and why
> Do our black faces search the empty sky?
> Is there something we have forgotten? some
>   precious thing
> We have lost, wandering in strange lands?

One of the New Negro poets, Bontemps makes frequent reference to Africa, now grieving over the lost glory, now insisting upon his heritage and now writing:

> Those mountains should be ours.

Something of the attitude of the Garvey movement is to be seen in Lewis Alexander's poems to Africa: there is the allegiance to the "motherland," and a romantic faith in her resurgence:

> And rise from out thy charnel house to be
> Thine own immortal, brilliant self again!

This type of idealization of Africa was an attempted corrective to the typical undervaluation, but was more poetic dreaming than understanding. "The Dark Brother" pleads rhetorically for brotherhood. Lewis Alexander has also experimented with all types of poetry, from the Japanese *tanka* and *hokku* to the blues.

Intellectual irony is in the free-verse poetry of Frank Horne. "To a Persistent Phantom" and "More Letters Found Near a Suicide" are modern portraiture, vivid, racy and unhackneyed. "Nigger—a Chant for Children" is a recital of Negro heroism with the race pride of the New Negro movement. One of the finest poetic recreations of slavery days and characters was "Dead and Gone" by Allison Davis. . . .

Clarissa Scott Delany wrote poems that bore witness to a spirit sensitive and in love with life. "The Mask" is a well-done portrait. Sensitivity likewise marks the poems of Esther Popel Shaw. "Salute to the Flag" departs from her usual Nature description; it attacks the shams of democracy by placing the patriotic teachings of the schools side by side with the newspaper report of a lynching.

George Leonard Allen, a poet-musician of North Carolina, was awarded a prize for the best sonnet in a state-wide contest conducted by the

United Daughters of the Confederacy. He wrote fluently of Nature and music; before his untimely death he was attempting as well to deal with folk experiences. Another Southern poet, Jonathan Brooks, writes with quiet surety. His poems, generally religious in nature or in imagery, are thoughtful and moving. Simple in phrasing and rhythm, they are unobtrusively symbolic. A collection of them would reveal that Brooks has a talent of distinction. *Negrito* (1933), by J. Mason Brewer, is commendable in its purpose of recording Negro experience in the Southwest, but the shadow of Dunbar lies heavy, and there is little reference to anything but the happier side of life.

Sterling Brown

Southern Road, by Sterling A. Brown (1932), is chiefly an attempt at folk portraiture of Southern characters. Brown sought to convey the tragedy of the Southern Negro, as in his title poem, "Children of the Mississippi," "King Cotton" and "Sam Smiley," and the comedy, in the Slim Greer series and "Sporting Beasley." The wandering roustabout is recorded in "Long Gone" and "Odyssey of Big Boy." The irony to be found in Negro folk song appears in "Mr. Samuel and Sam." "Strong Man," making use of a refrain found in Sandburg—"The strong men keep coming on"—is an expression of the dogged stoicism Brown has found in Negro experience. He has made a fairly close study of folkways and folk songs, and has used this in interpreting folk experience and character, which he considers one of the important tasks of Negro poetry. He is not afraid of using folk speech, refusing to believe dialect to be "an instrument of only two stops— pathos and humor." He uses free verse and the traditional forms as well as folk forms, and many of his poems are subjective. His second volume, to be called *No Hiding Place*, re-explores the Southern scene with more emphasis on social themes.

Realism and Protest

"Trumpet in the New Moon," by Welborn Victor Jenkins (1934), is a panoramic picture of the Negro in American life. It recalls Whitman in its patriotism (and its cataloguing), and Sandburg, but has an original place in Negro poetry:

Remember the service:

Come Susie, rock the baby—Go Hannah, get
  the dinner—
Uncle Jim, go plow the new ground—
Here Sambo, grab my satchel and get to hell—

Remember the sweat, the cotton fields, the
  lumber logs, the brick yards, the sawmills
  and turpentine plantation—all black labor.

Realistic and novel in detail, the poem repeats a pattern dear to Negro poets, from [James] Whitfield through Dunbar and James Weldon Johnson: the recording of Negro service will effect

. . . the joys of Rebirth and Regeneration,
At the solemn Love-Feast of Brotherhood and
  Democracy.

Frank Marshall Davis is likewise panoramic in *Black Man's Verse* (1935). "What Do You Want, America," like "Trumpet in the New Moon," lists the services of Negroes, but comments more sardonically on the abuses of democracy.

Davis is at times a mystic escapist, but at his best he is bitterly realistic. "Chicago's Congo," "Jazz Band," "Mojo Mike's Beer Garden," "Cabaret" and "Georgia's Atlanta" are forthright transcripts of reality. "Lynched" is a powerful protest. Davis is satiric about Negro "society": Robert Whitmore, ruler of the local Elks,

died of apoplexy
when a stranger from Georgia
mistook him
for a former Macon waiter.

Davis at times leans heavily upon Masters and Sandburg, but his gift of realistic portraiture, his irony and his knowledge of Negro life should stand him in very good stead.

Richard Wright, likewise of Chicago, is not content with either listing Negro achievement or registering the abuses of American life. He believes in poetry as a weapon, and in his driving rhythms urges Negro workers to rise up like men, side by side with white workers, to establish communism in America:

I am black and I have seen black hands
Raised in fists of revolt, side by side with the
    white fists of white workers,
And some day—and it is only this which
    sustains me—
Some day there shall be millions and millions
    of them,
On some red day in a burst of fists on a
    new horizon!

Romantic Escapes

Quite a few books of verse have been produced by Negro poets within recent years which are romantic escapes for the sensitive authors from depressing actualities. *Make Way for Happiness* (1932), by Alpheus Butler, promises, "I will bring you pretty things measure for measure," and the resulting "prettiness" is trite. J. Harvey L. Baxter bewails the fallen estate of noble poetry. . . .

That Which Concerneth Me (1934) is unconcerned with race experience or the revelation of a personality; what concerns the poet, according to Baxter, is "the song of rose and bee." "Eve Lynn" 's *No Alabaster Box* is praised by her sponsor because "not once does she refer to the peculiar problem of her own group." Marion Cuthbert's *April Grasses* is generally escapist; the interesting subject matter Miss Cuthbert is acquainted with she seems to consider unfit for poetic expression. Mae Cowdery's *We Lift Our Voices* contains too often vague yearning and the romantic worship of Nature, but at times has poetic drive. These poets, by denying racial or even personal experience, pretend to touch "universality" which, according to one Negro critic, means a concern with the universe.

Summary

Contemporary Negro poets are too diverse to be grouped into schools. Certain chief tendencies, however, are apparent. More than Albery Whitman, Dunbar and Braithwaite, the contemporary poets . . . when writing subjective lyrics, are more frankly personal, less restrained and, as a general rule, less conventional. They have been influenced by modern American poetry, of course, as their elders were by post-Victorian, but one of the cardinal lessons of modern poetry is that the poet should express his own view of life in his own way. It has been pointed out, however, that "bookishness" still prevails, that the so-called New Poetry revival has left many versifiers untouched.

Secondly, more than the older poets who hesitantly advanced defenses of the Negro, the contemporary Negro poet is more assured, more self-reliant. He seems less taken in by American hypocrisy and expresses his protest now with irony, now with anger, seldom with humility. The poets who have taken folk types and folk life for their province no longer accept the stereotyped view of the traditional dialect writers, nor, lapsing into gentility, do they flinch from an honest portrayal of folk life. Their laughter has more irony in it than buffoonery. They are ready to see the tragic as well as the pitiful. They are much closer to the true folk product than to the minstrel song.

It is not at all advanced that the contemporary poetry of the American Negro is to be ranked with the best of modern poetry. Too many talented writers have stopped suddenly after their first, sometimes successful, gropings. The Negro audience is naturally small, and that part devoted to poetry much smaller. Few Negro poets have the requisite time for maturing, for mastering technique, for observation of the world and themselves. Negro poets have left uncultivated many fields opened by modern poetry. Many still confine their models to the masters they learned about in school, to the Victorians and the Pre-Raphaelites. Almost as frequently, they have been unaware of the finer uses of tradition. The reading world seems to be ready for a true interpretation of Negro life from within, and poets with a dramatic ability have before them an important task. And the world has always been ready for the poet who in his own manner reveals his deepest thoughts and feelings. What it means to be a Negro in the modern world is a revelation much needed in poetry. But the Negro poet must write so that whosoever touches his book touches a man. Too often, like other minor poets, he has written so that whosoever touches his book touches the books of other and greater poets.

—1944

Georgia Douglas Johnson

I Want To Die While You Love Me

I WANT to die while you love me,
    While yet you hold me fair,
While laughter lies upon my lips
    And lights are in my hair.

I want to die while you love me.
    I could not bear to see
The glory of this perfect day
    Grow dim—or cease to be.

I want to die while you love me.
    Oh! who would care to live
Till love has nothing more to ask,
    And nothing more to give?

I want to die while you love me,
    And bear to that still bed
Your kisses, turbulent, unspent,
    To warm me when I'm dead.

                              —1919

Common Dust

AND who shall separate the dust
    Which later we shall be:
Whose keen discerning eye will scan
    And solve the mystery?

The high, the low, the rich, the poor,
    The black, the white, the red,
And all the chromatique between,
    Of whom shall it be said:

"Here lies the dust of Africa;
    Here are the sons of Rome;
Here lies one unlabeled,
    The world at large his home"?

Can one then separate the dust,
    Will mankind lie apart,
When life has settled back again
    The same as from the start?

                              —1962

Anne Spencer

Letter to My Sister

IT is dangerous for a woman to defy the gods;
To taunt them with the tongue's thin tip,
Or strut in the weakness of mere humanity,
Or draw a line daring them to cross;
The gods who own the searing lightning,
The drowning waters, the tormenting fears,
The anger of red sins.
Oh, but worse still if you mince along timidly—
Dodge this way or that, or kneel, or pray,
Or be kind, or sweat agony drops,
Or lay your quick body over your feeble young,
If you have beauty or plainness, if celibate,
Or vowed—the gods are Juggernaut,
Passing over each of us.
        Or this you may do:
Lock your heart, then, quietly,
And, lest they peer within,
Light no lamp when dark comes down.
Raise no shade for sun;
Breathless must your breath come through,
If you'd die and dare deny
The gods their godlike fun!

                              —1949

Lines to a Nasturtium: A Lover Muses

FLAME-FLOWER, day-torch, Mauna Loa,
I saw a daring bee, today, pause, and soar
        Into your flaming heart;
Then did I hear crisp crinkled laughter
As the furies after tore him apart?
        A bird, next, small and humming,
Looked into your startled depths and fled.
Surely, some dread sight, and dafter
        Than human eyes as mine can see,
Set the stricken air waves drumming
        In his flight.

Day-torch, flame-flower, cool-hot beauty,
I cannot see, I cannot hear your fluty
Voice lure your loving swain,
But I know one other to whom you are in beauty
Born in vain;
Hair like the setting sun,
Her eyes a rising star,
Motions gracious as reeds by Babylon, bar
All your competing;
Hands like, how like, brown lilies sweet,
Cloth of gold were fair enough to touch her feet.
Ah, how the senses flood at my repeating,
As once in her fire-lit heart I felt the furies
Beating, beating.

—1949

Claude McKay

The White House

Your door is shut against my tightened face,
And I am sharp as steel with discontent;
But I possess the courage and the grace
To bear my anger proudly and unbent.
The pavement slabs burn loose beneath my feet,
A chafing savage, down the decent street,
And passion rends my vitals as I pass,
Where boldly shines your shuttered door of glass.
Oh I must search for wisdom every hour,
Deep in my wrathful bosom sore and raw,
And find in it the superhuman power
To hold me to the letter of your law!
Oh I must keep my heart inviolate
Against the potent poison of your hate.

—1937

Outcast

For the dim regions whence my fathers came
My spirit, bondaged by the body, longs.
Words felt, but never heard, my lips would frame;
My soul would sing forgotten jungle songs.
I would go back to darkness and to peace,
But the great Western world holds me in fee,
And I may never hope for full release
While to its alien gods I bend my knee.
Something in me is lost, forever lost,
Some vital thing has gone out of my heart,
And I must walk the way of life a ghost
Among the sons of earth, a thing apart.
For I was born, far from my native clime,
Under the white man's menace, out of time.

—1922

Flame-Heart

So much have I forgotten in ten years,
    So much in ten brief years! I have forgot
What time the purple apples come to juice,
    And what month brings the shy forget-me-not.
I have forgot the special, startling season
    Of the pimento's flowering and fruiting;
What time of year the ground doves brown the fields
    And fill the noonday with their curious fluting,
I have forgotten much, but still remember
The poinsettia's red, blood-red in warm December.

I still recall the honey-fever grass,
    But cannot recollect the high days when
We rooted them out of the ping-wing path
    To stop the mad bees in the rabbit pen.
I often try to think in what sweet month
    The languid painted ladies used to dapple
The yellow by-road mazing from the main,
    Sweet with the golden threads of the rose-apple.
I have forgotten—strange—but quite remember
The poinsettia's red, blood-red in warm December.

What weeks, what months, what time of the mild year
    We cheated school to have our fling at tops?
What days our wine-thrilled bodies pulsed with joy
    Feasting upon blackberries in the copse?
Oh, some I know! I have embalmed the days,
    Even the sacred moments when we played,
All innocent of passion, uncorrupt,
    At noon and evening in the flame-heart's shade.
We were so happy, happy, I remember,
Beneath the poinsettia's red in warm December.

—1920

Jean Toomer

Harvest Song

I am a reaper whose muscles set at sundown. All my
    oats are cradled.
But I am too chilled, and too fatigued to bind them.
    And I hunger.

I crack a grain between my teeth. I do not taste it.
I have been in the fields all day. My throat is dry.
    I hunger.

My eyes are caked with dust of oatfields at harvest-
    time.
I am a blind man who stares across the hills, seeking
    stack'd fields of other harvesters.

It would be good to see them . . . crook'd, split, and iron-ring'd handles of the scythes. It would be good to see them, dust-caked and blind. I hunger.

(Dusk is a strange fear'd sheath their blades are dull'd in.)

My throat is dry. And should I call, a cracked grain like the oats . . . eoho—

I fear to call. What should they hear me, and offer me their grain, oats, or wheat, or corn? I have been in the fields all day. I fear I could not taste it. I fear knowledge of my hunger.

My ears are caked with dust of oatfields at harvest-time.

I am a deaf man who strains to hear the calls of other harvesters whose throats are also dry.

It would be good to hear their songs . . . reapers of the sweet-stalk'd cane, cutters of the corn . . . even though their throats cracked and the strangeness of their voices deafened me.

I hunger. My throat is dry. Now that the sun has set and I am chilled, I fear to call. (Eoho, my brothers!)

I am a reaper. (Eoho!) All my oats are cradled. But I am too fatigued to bind them. And I hunger. I crack a grain. It has no taste to it. My throat is dry . . .

O my brothers, I beat my palms, still soft, against the stubble of my harvesting. (You beat your soft palms, too.) My pain is sweet. Sweeter than the oats or wheat or corn. It will not bring me knowledge of my hunger.

—1923

Conversion

AFRICAN Guardian of Souls,
Drunk with rum,
Feasting on a strange cassava,
Yielding to new words and a weak palabra
Of a white-faced sardonic god—
Grins, cries
Amen,
Shouts hosanna.

—1923

Prayer

MY body is opaque to the soul.
Driven of the spirit, long have I sought to temper it
unto the spirit's longing,
But my mind, too, is opaque to the soul.

A closed lid is my soul's flesh-eye.
O Spirits of whom my soul is but a little finger,
Direct it to the lid of its flesh-eye.
I am weak with much giving.
I am weak with the desire to give more.
(How strong a thing is the little finger!)
So weak that I have confused the body with the soul,
And the body with its little finger.
(How frail is the little finger.)
My voice could not carry to you did you dwell in stars,
O Spirits of whom my soul is but a little finger. . . .

—1923

Frank Horne

Kid Stuff
(December, 1942)

THE wise guys
tell me
that Christmas
is Kid Stuff . . .
Maybe they've got
something there—

Two thousand years ago
three wise guys
chased a star
across a continent
to bring
frankincense and myrrh
to a Kid
born in a manger
with an idea in His head . . .

And as the bombs
crash
all over the world
today
the real wise guys
know
that we've all
got to go chasing stars
again
in the hope
that we can get back
some of that
Kid Stuff
born two thousand years ago.

—1942

Countee Cullen

Yet Do I Marvel

I DOUBT not God is good, well-meaning, kind,
And did He stoop to quibble could tell why
The little buried mole continues blind,
Why flesh that mirrors Him must someday die,
Make plain the reason tortured Tantalus
Is baited by the fickle fruit, declare
If merely brute caprice dooms Sisyphus
To struggle up a never-ending stair.

Inscrutable His ways are, and immune
To catechism by a mind too strewn
With petty cares to slightly understand
What awful brain compels His awful hand;
Yet do I marvel at this curious thing:
To make a poet black, and bid him sing!

—1925

Incident

ONCE riding in old Baltimore,
    Heart-filled, head-filled with glee,
I saw a Baltimorean
    Keep looking straight at me.

Now I was eight and very small,
    And he was no whit bigger,
And so I smiled, but he poked out
    His tongue and called me, "Nigger."

I saw the whole of Baltimore
    From May until December:
Of all the things that happened there
    That's all that I remember.

—1925

Simon the Cyrenian Speaks

HE never spoke a word to me,
And yet He called my name;
He never gave a sign to me,
And yet I knew and came.

At first I said, "I will not bear
His cross upon my back;
He only seeks to place it there
Because my skin is black."

But He was dying for a dream,
And He was very meek,
And in His eyes there shone a gleam
Men journey far to seek.

It was Himself my pity bought;
I did for Christ alone
What all of Rome could not have wrought
With bruise of lash or stone.

—1925

Langston Hughes

Harlem

WHAT happens to a dream deferred?

    Does it dry up
    like a raisin in the sun?
    Or fester like a sore—
    And then run?
    Does it stink like rotten meat?
    Or crust and sugar over—
    like a syrupy sweet?

    Maybe it just sags
    like a heavy load.

    Or does it explode?

—1951

Merry-Go-Round
(Colored child at carnival)

WHERE is the Jim Crow section
On this merry-go-round,
Mister, cause I want to ride?
Down South where I come from
White and colored
Can't sit side by side.
Down South on the train
There's a Jim Crow car.
On the bus we're put in the back—
But there ain't no back
To a merry-go-round!
Where's the horse
For a kid that's black?

—1942

When Sue Wears Red

WHEN Susanna Jones wears red
Her face is like an ancient cameo
Turned brown by the ages.

Come with a blast of trumpets,
    Jesus!

When Susanna Jones wears red
A queen from some time-dead Egyptian night
Walks once again.

Blow trumpets, Jesus!

And the beauty of Susanna Jones in red
Burns in my heart a love-fire sharp like pain.

Sweet silver trumpets,
    Jesus!

               —1926

Feet o' Jesus

AT the feet o' Jesus,
Sorrow like a sea.
Lordy, let yo' mercy
Come driftin' down on me.

At the feet o' Jesus,
At yo' feet I stand.
O, ma little Jesus,
Please reach out yo' hand.

               —1927

My People

THE night is beautiful,
So the faces of my people.

The stars are beautiful,
So the eyes of my people.

Beautiful, also, is the sun.
Beautiful, also, are the souls of my people.

               —1932

Troubled Woman

SHE stands
In the quiet darkness,
This troubled woman
Bowed by
Weariness and pain
Like an
Autumn flower
In the frozen rain,
Like a
Windblown autumn flower
That never lifts its head
Again.

               —1926

The Negro Speaks of Rivers

I'VE known rivers:
I've known rivers ancient as the world and older than
    the flow of human blood in human veins.

My soul has grown deep like the rivers.

I bathed in the Euphrates when dawns were young.
I built my hut near the Congo and it lulled me to
    sleep.
I looked upon the Nile and raised the pyramids
    above it.
I heard the singing of the Mississippi when Abe
    Lincoln went down to New Orleans, and I've
    seen its muddy bosom turn all golden in the
    sunset.

I've known rivers:
Ancient, dusky rivers.

My soul has grown deep like the rivers.

               —1926

One-Way Ticket

I PICK up my life
And take it with me
And I put it down in
Chicago, Detroit,
Buffalo, Scranton,
Any place that is
North and East—
And not Dixie.

I pick up my life
And take it on the train
To Los Angeles, Bakersfield,
Seattle, Oakland, Salt Lake,
Any place that is
North and West—
And not South.

I am fed up
With Jim Crow laws,
People who are cruel
And afraid,
Who lynch and run,
Who are scared of me
And me of them.

I pick up my life
And take it away
On a one-way ticket—
Gone up North,
Gone out West,
Gone!

—1942

Mother to Son

WELL, son, I'll tell you:
Life for me ain't been no crystal stair.
It's had tacks in it,
And splinters,
And boards torn up,
And places with no carpet on the floor—
Bare.
But all the time
I'se been a-climbin' on,
And reachin' landin's,
And turnin' corners,
And sometimes goin' in the dark
Where there ain't been no light.
So, boy, don't you turn back.
Don't you set down on the steps
'Cause you finds it's kinder hard.
Don't you fall now—
For I'se still goin', honey,
I'se still climbin',
And life for me ain't been no crystal stair.

—1926

Border Line

I USED to wonder
About living and dying—
I think the difference lies
Between tears and crying.

I used to wonder
About here and there—
I think the distance
Is nowhere.

—1943

I, Too, Sing America

I, TOO, sing America.

I am the darker brother.
They send me to eat in the kitchen
When company comes,
But I laugh,
And eat well,
And grow strong.

Tomorrow,
I'll sit at the table
When company comes.
Nobody'll dare
Say to me,
"Eat in the kitchen,"
Then.

Besides,
They'll see how beautiful I am
And be ashamed—

I, too, am America.

—1926

Waring Cuney

Threnody

ONLY quiet death
Brings relief
From the wearisome
Interchange
Of hope and grief.
O body
(Credulous heart
And dream-torn head),
What will wisdom be
Or folly—
When you lie dead?
Life-beaten body
Bruised and sore—
Neither hunger nor satiety
Are known beyond death's door.

—1930

Finis

Now that our love has drifted
To a quiet close,
Leaving the empty ache
That always follows when beauty goes;
Now that you and I,
Who stood tiptoe on earth
To touch our fingers to the sky,
Have turned away
To allow our little love to die—
Go, dear, seek again the magic touch.
But if you are wise,
As I shall be wise,
You will not again
Love overmuch.

—1930

Arna Bontemps

A Black Man Talks of Reaping

I HAVE sown beside all waters in my day.
I planted deep, within my heart the fear
That wind or fowl would take the grain away.
I planted safe against this stark, lean year.

I scattered seed enough to plant the land
In rows from Canada to Mexico,
But for my reaping only what the hand
Can hold at once is all that I can show.

Yet what I sowed and what the orchard yields
My brother's sons are gathering stalk and root,
Small wonder then my children glean in fields
They have not sown, and feed on bitter fruit.

—1926

Southern Mansion

POPLARS are standing there still as death,
And ghosts of dead men
Meet their ladies walking
Two by two beneath the shade,
And standing on the marble steps.

There is a sound of music echoing
Through the open door,
And in the field there is
Another sound tinkling in the cotton:
Chains of bondmen dragging on the ground.

The years go back with an iron clank,
A hand is on the gate,
A dry leaf trembles on the wall.
Ghosts are walking.
They have broken roses down,
And poplars stand there still as death.

—1926

Idolatry

YOU have been good to me, I give you this:
The arms of lovers empty as our own,
Marble lips sustaining one long kiss,
And the hard sound of hammers breaking stone.

For I will build a chapel in the place
Where our love died and I will journey there
To make a sign and kneel before your face,
And set an old bell tolling on the air.

—1926

Sterling A. Brown

Challenge

I SAID, in drunken pride of youth and you,
That mischief-making Time would never dare
Play his ill-humored tricks upon us two,
Strange and defiant lovers that we were.
I said that even Death, Highwayman Death,
Could never master lovers such as we,
That even when his clutch had throttled breath,
My hymns would float in praise, undauntedly.

I did not think such words were bravado.
Oh, I think honestly we knew no fear
Of Time or Death. We loved each other so.
And thus, with you believing me, I made
My prophecies, rebellious, unafraid . . .
And that was foolish, wasn't it, my dear?

—1932

Return

I HAVE gone back in boyish wonderment
To things that I had foolishly put by . . .
Have found an alien and unknown content
In seeing how some bits of cloud-filled sky
Are framed in bracken pools; through chuckling hours
Have watched the antic frogs, or curiously
Have numbered all the unnamed, vagrant flowers
That fleck the unkempt meadows, lavishly.

Or where a headlong toppling stream has stayed
Its racing, lulled to quiet by the song
Bursting from out the thick-leaved oaken shade,
There I have lain while hours sauntered past—
I have found peacefulness somewhere at last,
Have found a quiet needed for so long.

—1932

Fate and Bigger Thomas

Richard Wright

NEVER AGAIN did he want to feel anything like hope. That was what was wrong; he had let that preacher talk to him until somewhere in him he had begun to feel that maybe something could happen. Well, something *had* happened: the cross the preacher had hung round his throat had been burned in front of his eyes.

When his hysteria had passed, he got up from the floor. Through blurred eyes he saw men peering at him from the bars of other cells. He heard a low murmur of voices and in the same instant his consciousness recorded without bitterness—like a man stepping out of his house to go to work and noticing that the sun is shining—the fact that even here in the Cook County Jail Negro and white were segregated into different cell-blocks. He lay on the cot with closed eyes and the darkness soothed him some. Occasionally his muscles twitched from the hard storm of passion that had swept him. A small hard core in him resolved never again to trust anybody or anything. Not even Jan. Or Max. They were all right, maybe; but whatever he thought or did from now on would have to come from him and him alone, or not at all. He wanted no more crosses that might turn to fire while still on his chest.

His inflamed senses cooled slowly. He opened his eyes. He heard a soft tapping on a nearby wall. Then a sharp whisper:

"Say, you new guy!"

He sat up, wondering what they wanted.

"Ain't you the guy they got for that Dalton job?"

His hands clenched. He lay down again. He did not want to talk to them. They were not his kind. He felt that they were not here for crimes such

as his. He did not want to talk to the whites because they were white and he did not want to talk to Negroes because he felt ashamed. His own kind would be too curious about him. He lay a long while, empty of mind, and then he heard the steel door open. He looked and saw a white man with a tray of food. He sat up and the man brought the tray to the cot and placed it beside him.

"Your lawyer sent this, kid. You got a good lawyer," the man said.

"Say, can I see a paper?" Bigger asked.

"Well, now," the man said, scratching his head. "Oh, what the hell. Yeah; sure. Here, take mine. I'm through with it. And say, your lawyer's bringing some clothes for you. He told me to tell you."

Bigger did not hear him; he ignored the tray of food and opened out the paper. He paused, waiting to hear the door shut. When it clanged, he bent forward to read, then paused again, wondering about the man who had just left, amazed at how friendly he had acted. For a fleeting moment, while the man had been in his cell, he had not felt apprehensive, cornered. The man had acted straight, matter-of-fact. It was something he could not understand. He lifted the paper close and read: NEGRO KILLER SIGNS CONFESSIONS FOR TWO MURDERS. SHRINKS AT INQUEST WHEN CONFRONTED WITH BODY OF SLAIN GIRL. ARRAIGNED TOMORROW. REDS TAKE CHARGE OF KILLER'S DEFENSE. NOT GUILTY PLEA LIKELY. His eyes ran over the paper, looking for some clue that would tell him something of his fate.

. . . slayer will undoubtedly pay supreme penalty for his crimes . . . there is no doubt of his guilt . . . what is doubtful is how many other crimes he has committed . . . killer attacked at inquest. . . .

Then:

Expressing opinions about Communists' defending the Negro rapist and killer, Mr. David A. Buckley, State's Attorney, said: "What else can you expect from a gang like that? I'm in favor of cleaning them out lock, stock, and barrel. I'm of the conviction that if you got to the bottom of red activity in this country, you'd find the root of many an unsolved crime."

When questioned as to what effect the Thomas trial would have upon the forthcoming April elections, in which he is a candidate to succeed himself, Mr. Buckley took his pink carnation from the lapel of his morning coat and waved the reporters away with a laugh.

A long scream sounded and Bigger dropped the paper, jumped to his feet, and ran to the barred door to see what was happening. Down the corridor he saw six white men struggling with a brown-skinned Negro. They dragged him over the floor by his feet and stopped directly in front of Bigger's cell door. As the door swung in, Bigger backed to his cot, his mouth open in astonishment. The man was turning and twisting in the white men's hands, trying desperately to free himself.

"Turn me loose! Turn me loose!" the man screamed over and over.

The men lifted him and threw him inside, locked the door, and left. The man lay on the floor for a moment, then scrambled to his feet and ran to the door.

"Give me my papers!" he screamed.

Bigger saw that the man's eyes were blood-red; the corners of his lips were white with foam. Sweat glistened on his brown face. He clutched the bars with such frenzy that when he yelled his entire body vibrated. He seemed so agonized that Bigger wondered why the men did not give him his belongings. Emotionally, Bigger sided with the man.

"You can't get away with it!" the man yelled.

Bigger went to him and placed a hand on his shoulder.

"Say, what they got of yours?" he asked.

The man ignored him, shouting:

"I'll report you to the President, you hear? Bring me my papers or let me out of here, you white bastards! You want to destroy all my evidence! You can't cover up your crimes! I'll publish them to the whole world! I know why you're putting me in jail! The professor told you to! But he's not going to get away with it . . ."

Bigger watched, fascinated, fearful. He had the sensation that the man was too emotionally wrought up over whatever it was that he had lost. Yet the man's emotions seemed real; they affected him, compelling sympathy.

"Come back here!" the man screamed. "Bring me my papers or I'll tell the President and have you dismissed from office . . ."

What papers did they have of his? Bigger wondered. Who was the president the man yelled about? And who was the professor? Over the man's screams Bigger heard a voice calling from another cell.

"Say, you new guy!"

Bigger avoided the frenzied man and went to the door.

"He's balmy!" a white man said. "Make 'em take 'im outta your cell. He'll kill you. He went off his nut from studying too much at the university. He was writing a book on how colored people live and he says somebody stole all the facts he'd found. He says he's got to the bottom of why colored folks are treated bad and he's going to tell the President and have things changed, see? He's *nuts*! He swears that his university professor had him locked up. The cops picked him up this morning in his underwear; he was in the lobby of the Post Office building, waiting to speak to the President . . ."

Bigger ran from the door to the cot. All of his fear of death, all his hate and shame vanished in face of his dread of this insane man turning suddenly upon him. The man still clutched the bars, screaming. He was about Bigger's size. Bigger had the queer feeling that his own exhaustion formed a hairline upon which his feelings were poised, and that the man's driving frenzy would suck him into its hot whirlpool. He lay on the cot and wrapped his arms about his head, torn with a nameless anxiety, hearing the man's screams in spite of his need to escape them.

"You're afraid of me!" the man shouted. "That's why you put me in here! But I'll tell the President anyhow! I'll tell 'im you make us live in such crowded conditions on the South Side that one out of every ten of us is insane! I'll tell 'im that you dump all the stale foods into the Black Belt and sell them for more than you can get anywhere else! I'll tell 'im you tax us, but you won't build hospitals! I'll tell 'im the schools are so crowded that they breed perverts! I'll tell 'im you hire us last and fire us first! I'll tell the President and the League of Nations!"

Then men in other cells began to holler.

"Pipe down, you nut!"

"Take 'im away!"

"Throw 'im out!"

"The hell with you!"

"You can't scare me!" the man yelled. "I know you! They put you in here to watch me!"

The men set up a clamor. But soon a group of men dressed in white came running with a stretcher. They unlocked the cell and grabbed the yelling man, faced him in a straitjacket, flung him onto the stretcher and carted him away. Bigger sat up and stared before him, hopelessly. He heard voices calling from cell to cell.

"Say, what they got of his?"

"Nothing! He's nuts!"

Finally, things quieted. For the first time since his capture, Bigger felt that he wanted someone near him, something physical to cling to. He was glad when he heard the lock in his door click. He sat up; a guard loomed over him.

"Come on, boy. Your lawyer's here."

He was handcuffed and led down the hall to a small room where Max stood. He was freed of the steel links on his wrists and pushed inside; he heard the door shut behind him.

"Sit down, Bigger. Say, how do you feel?"

Bigger sat down on the edge of the chair and did not answer. The room was small. A single yellow electric globe dropped from the ceiling. There was one barred window. All about them was profound silence. Max sat opposite Bigger, and Bigger's eyes met his and fell. Bigger felt that he was sitting and holding his life helplessly in his hands, waiting for Max to tell him what to do with it; and it made him hate himself. An organic wish to cease to be, to stop living, seized him. Either he was too weak, or the world was too strong; he did not know which. Over and over he had tried to create a world to live in, and over and over he had failed. Now, once again, he was waiting for someone to tell him something; once more he was poised on the verge of action and commitment. Was he letting himself in for more hate and fear? What could Max do for him now? Even if Max tried hard and honestly, were there not thousands of white hands to stop Max? Why not tell him to go home?

His lips trembled to speak, to tell Max to leave; but no words came. He felt that even in speaking in that way he would be indicating how hopeless he felt, thereby disrobing his soul to more shame.

"I bought some clothes for you," Max said. "When they give 'em to you in the morning, put 'em on. You want to look your best when you come up for arraignment."

Bigger was silent; he glanced at Max again, and then away.

"What's on your mind, Bigger?"

"Nothing," he mumbled.

"Now, listen, Bigger. I want you to tell me all about yourself."

"Mr. Max, it ain't no use in you doing nothing!" Bigger blurted.

Max eyed him sharply.

"Do you really feel that way, Bigger?"

"There ain't no way else to feel."

"I want to talk to you honestly, Bigger. I see no way out of this but a plea of guilty. We can ask for mercy, for life in prison . . ."

"I'd rather die!"

"Nonsense. You want to live."

"For what?"

"Don't you want to fight this thing?"

"What can I do? They got me."

"You don't want to die that way, Bigger."

"It don't matter which way I die," he said; but his voice choked.

"Listen, Bigger, you're facing a sea of hate now that's no different from what you've faced all your life. And because it's that way, you've *got* to fight. If they can wipe you out, then they can wipe others out, too."

"Yeah," Bigger mumbled, resting his hands

upon his knees and staring at the black floor.
"But I can't win."

"First of all, Bigger. Do you trust me?"

Bigger grew angry.

"You can't help me, Mr. Max," he said, looking straight into Max's eyes.

"But do you trust me, Bigger?" Max asked
again.

Bigger looked away. He felt that Max was
making it very difficult for him to tell him to
leave.

"I don't know, Mr. Max."

"Bigger, I know my face is white," Max said.
"And I know that almost every white face you've
met in your life had it in for you, even when that
white face didn't know it. Every white man considers it his duty to make a black man keep his
distance. He doesn't know why most of the time,
but he acts that way. It's the way things are,
Bigger. But I want you to know that you can
trust me."

"It ain't no use, Mr. Max."

"You want me to handle your case?"

"You can't help me none. They got me."

Bigger knew that Max was trying to make him
feel that he accepted the way he looked at things,
and it made him as self-conscious as when Jan
had taken his hand and shaken it that night in
the car. It made him live again in that hard and
sharp consciousness of his color and feel the
shame and fear that went with it, and at the same
time it made him hate himself for feeling it. He
trusted Max. Was Max not taking upon himself
a thing that would make other whites hate him?
But he doubted if Max could make him see things
in a way that would enable him to go to his
death. He doubted that God Himself could give
him a picture for that now. As he felt at present,
they would have to drag him to the chair, as they
had dragged him down the steps the night they
captured him. He did not want his feelings tam-
pered with; he feared that he might walk into
another trap. If he expressed belief in Max, if he
acted on that belief, would it not end just as all
other commitments of faith had ended? He
wanted to believe, but was afraid. He felt that he
should have been able to meet Max halfway; but,
as always, when a white man talked to him, he
was caught out in No Man's Land. He sat

slumped in his chair with his head down and he
looked at Max only when Max's eyes were not
watching him.

"Here; take a cigarette, Bigger." Max lit Bigger's and then lit his own; they smoked awhile.
"Bigger, I'm your lawyer. I want to talk to
you honestly. What you say is in strictest confidence."

Bigger stared at Max. He felt sorry for the
white man. He saw that Max was afraid that he
would not talk at all. And he had no desire to
hurt Max. Max leaned forward determinedly.
Well, tell him. Talk. Get it over with and let
Max go.

"Aw, I don't care what I say or do now."

"Oh, yes, you *do!*" Max said quickly.

In a fleeting second an impulse to laugh rose
up in Bigger, and left. Max was anxious to help
him and he had to die.

"Maybe I do care," Bigger drawled.

"If you don't care about what you say or do,
then why didn't you re-enact that crime out at
the Dalton home today?"

"I wouldn't do nothing for *them.*"

"Why?"

"They hate black folks," he said.

"*Why*, Bigger?"

"I don't know, Mr. Max."

"Bigger, don't you know they hate others,
too?"

"Who they hate?"

"They hate trade unions. They hate folks who
try to organize. They hate Jan."

"But they hate black folks more than they
hate unions," Bigger said. "They don't treat union
folks like they do me."

"Oh, yes, they do. You think that because
your color makes it easy for them to point you
out, segregate you, exploit you. But they do that
to others, too. They hate me because I'm trying
to help you. They're writing me letters, calling
me a 'dirty Jew.' "

"All I know is that they hate me," Bigger said
grimly.

"Bigger, the state's attorney gave me a copy
of your confession. Now, tell me, did you tell
him the truth?"

"Yeah. There wasn't nothing else to do."

"Now, tell me this, Bigger. Why did you do it?"

Bigger sighed, shrugged his shoulders and sucked his lungs full of smoke.

"I don't know," he said; smoke eddied slowly from his nostrils.

"Did you plan it?"

"Naw."

"Did anybody help you?"

"Naw."

"Had you been thinking about doing something like that for a long time?"

"Naw."

"How did it happen?"

"It just happened, Mr. Max."

"Are you sorry?"

"What's the use of being sorry? That won't help me none."

"You can't think of any reason why you did it?"

Bigger was staring straight before him, his eyes wide and shining. His talking to Max had evoked again in him that urge to talk, to tell, to try to make his feelings known. A wave of excitement flooded him. He felt that he ought to be able to reach out with his bare hands and carve from naked space the concrete, solid reasons why he had murdered. He felt them that strongly. If he could do that, he would relax; he would sit and wait until they told him to walk to the chair; and he would walk.

"Mr. Max, I don't know. I was all mixed up. I was feeling so many things at once."

"Did you rape her, Bigger?"

"Naw, Mr. Max. I didn't. But nobody'll believe me."

"Had you planned to before Mrs. Dalton came into the room?"

Bigger shook his head and rubbed his hands nervously across his eyes. In a sense he had forgotten Max was in the room. He was trying to feel the texture of his own feelings, trying to tell what they meant.

"Oh, I don't know. I was feeling a little that way. Yeah, I reckon I was. I was drunk and she was drunk and I was feeling that way."

"But, did you rape her?"

"Naw. But everybody'll say I did. What's the use? I'm black. They say black men do that. So it don't matter if I did or if I didn't."

"How long had you known her?"

"A few hours."

"Did you like her?"

"*Like* her?"

Bigger's voice boomed so suddenly from his throat that Max started. Bigger leaped to his feet; his eyes widened and his hands lifted midway to his face, trembling.

"No! No! Bigger . . ." Max said.

"*Like* her? I *hated* her! So help me God, I hated her!" he shouted.

"Sit down, Bigger!"

"I hate her now, even though she's dead! God knows, I hate her right now . . ."

Max grabbed him and pushed him back into the chair.

"Don't get excited, Bigger. Here; take it easy!"

Bigger quieted, but his eyes roved the room. Finally, he lowered his head and knotted his fingers. His lips were slightly parted.

"You say you hated her?"

"Yeah; and I ain't sorry she's dead."

"But what had she done to you? You say you had just met her."

"I don't know. She didn't do nothing to me." He paused and ran his hand nervously across his forehead. "She . . . it was . . . Hell, I don't know. She asked me a lot of questions. She acted and talked in a way that made me hate her. She made me feel like a dog. I was so mad I wanted to cry. . . ." His voice trailed off in a plaintive whimper. He licked his lips. He was caught in a net of vague, associative memory: he saw an image of his little sister, Vera, sitting on the edge of a chair crying because he had shamed her by "looking" at her; he saw her rise and fling her shoe at him. He shook his head, confused. "Aw, Mr. Max, she wanted me to tell her how Negroes live. She got into the front seat of the car where I was . . ."

"But, Bigger, you don't hate people for that. She was being kind to you."

"Kind, hell! She wasn't kind to me!"

"What do you mean? She accepted you as another human being."

"Mr. Max, we're all split up. What you say is kind ain't kind at all. I didn't know nothing about that woman. All I knew was that they kill us for women like her. We live apart. And then she comes and acts like that to me."

"Bigger, you should have tried to understand. She was acting toward you only as she knew how."

Bigger glared about the small room, searching for an answer. He knew that his actions did not seem logical and he gave up trying to explain them logically. He reverted to his feelings as a guide in answering Max.

"Well, I acted toward her only as I know how. She was rich. She and her kind own the earth. She and her kind say black folks are dogs. They don't let you do nothing but what they want."

"But, Bigger, *this* woman was trying to help you!"

"She didn't act like it."

"How *should* she have acted?"

"Aw, I don't know, Mr. Max. White folks and black folks is strangers. We don't know what each other is thinking. Maybe she was trying to be kind; but she didn't act like it. To me she looked and acted like all other white folks."

"But she's not to be blamed for that, Bigger."

"She's the same color as the rest of 'em," he said defensively.

"I don't understand, Bigger. You say you hated her and yet you say you felt like having her when you were in the room and she was drunk and you were drunk."

"Yeah," Bigger said, wagging his head and wiping his mouth with the back of his hand. "Yeah; that's funny, ain't it?" He sucked at his cigarette. "Yeah; I reckon it was because I knew I oughtn't've wanted to. I reckon it was because they say we black men do that anyhow. Mr. Max, you know what some white men say we black men do? They say we rape white women when we got the clap and they say we do that because we believe that if we rape white women then we'll get rid of the clap. That's what some white men *say*. They *believe* that. Jesus, Mr. Max, when folks says things like that about you, you whipped before you born. What's the use? Yeah; I reckon I was feeling that way when I was in the room with her. They say we do things like that and they say it to kill us. They draw a line and say for you to stay on your side of the line. They don't care if there's no bread over on your side. They don't care if you die. And then they say

things like that about you and when you try to come from behind your line they kill you. They feel they ought to kill you then. Everybody wants to kill you then. Yeah; I reckon I was feeling that way and maybe the reason was because they say it. Maybe that was the reason."

"You mean you wanted to defy them? You wanted to show them that you dared, that you didn't care?"

"I don't know, Mr. Max. But what I got to care about? I knew that some time or other they was going to get me for something. I'm black. I don't have to do nothing for 'em to get me. The first white finger they point at me, I'm a goner, see?"

"But, Bigger, when Mrs. Dalton came into that room, why didn't you stop right there and tell her what was wrong? You wouldn't've been in all this trouble then."

"Mr. Max, so help me God, I couldn't do nothing when I turned around and saw that woman coming to that bed. Honest to God, I didn't know what I was doing . . ."

"You mean you went blank?"

"Naw; naw . . . I knew what I was doing, all right. But I couldn't help it. That's what I mean. It was like another man stepped inside of my skin and started acting for me."

"Bigger, tell me, did you feel more attraction for Mary than for the women of your own race?"

"Naw. But they say that. It ain't true. I hated her then and I hate her now."

"But why did you kill Bessie?"

"To keep her from talking. Mr. Max, after killing that white woman, it wasn't hard to kill somebody else. I didn't have to think much about killing Bessie. I knew I had to kill her and I did. I had to get away . . ."

"Did you hate Bessie?"

"Naw."

"Did you love her?"

"Naw. I was just scared. I wasn't in love with Bessie. She was just my girl. I don't reckon I was ever in love with nobody. I killed Bessie to save myself. You have to have a girl, so I had Bessie. And I killed her."

"Bigger, tell me, when did you start hating Mary?"

"I hated her as soon as she spoke to me, as soon as I saw her. I reckon I hated her before I saw her."

"But, *why?*"

"I told you. What her kind ever let us do?"

"What, exactly, Bigger, did you want to do?"

Bigger sighed and sucked at his cigarette.

"Nothing, I reckon. Nothing. But I reckon I wanted to do what other people do."

"And because you couldn't, you hated her?"

Again Bigger felt that his actions were not logical, and again he fell back upon his feelings for a guide in answering Max's questions.

"Mr. Max, a guy gets tired of being told what he can do and can't do. You get a little job here and a little job there. You shine shoes, sweep streets, anything. You don't make enough to live on. You don't know when you going to get fired. Pretty soon you get so you can't hope for nothing. You just keep moving all the time, doing what other folks say. You ain't a man no more. You just work day in and day out so the world can roll on and other people can live. You know, Mr. Max, I always think of white folks . . ."

He paused. Max leaned forward and touched him.

"Go on, Bigger."

"Well, they own everything. They choke you off the face of the earth. They like God." He swallowed, closed his eyes and sighed. "They don't even let you feel what you want to feel. They after you so hot and hard you can only feel what they doing to you. They kill you before you die."

"But, Bigger, I asked you what it was that you wanted to do so badly that you had to hate them."

"Nothing. I reckon I didn't want to do nothing."

"But you said that people like Mary and her kind never let you do anything."

"Why should I want to do anything? I ain't got a chance. I don't know nothing. I'm just black and they make the laws."

"What would you like to have been?"

Bigger was silent for a long time. Then he laughed without sound, without moving his lips; it was three short expulsions of breath forced upward through his nostrils by the heaving of his chest.

"I wanted to be an aviator once. But they wouldn't let me go to the school where I was suppose' to learn it. They built a big school and then drew a line around it and said that nobody could go to it but those who lived within the line. That kept all the colored boys out."

"And what else?"

"Well, I wanted to be in the Army once."

"Why didn't you join?"

"Hell, it's a Jim Crow Army. All they want a black man for is to dig ditches. And in the Navy all I can do is wash dishes and scrub floors."

"And was there anything else you wanted to do?"

"Oh, I don't know. What's the use now? I'm through, washed up. They got me. I'll die."

"Tell me the things you *thought* you'd have liked to do."

"I'd like to be in business. But what chance has a black guy got in business? We ain't got no money. We don't own no mines, no railroads, no nothing. They don't want us to. They make us stay in one little spot."

"And you didn't want to stay there?"

Bigger glanced up; his lips tightened. There was a feverish pride in his bloodshot eyes.

"I *didn't*," he said.

Max stared and sighed.

"Look, Bigger. You've told me the things you could not do. But you did something. You committed these crimes. You killed two women. What on earth did you think you could get out of it?"

Bigger rose and rammed his hands into his pockets. He leaned against the wall, looking vacantly. Again he forgot that Max was in the room.

"I don't know. Maybe this sounds crazy. Maybe they going to burn me in the electric chair for feeling this way. But I ain't worried none about them women I killed. For a little while I was free. I was doing something. It was wrong, but I was feeling all right. Maybe God'll get me for it. If He do, all right. But I ain't worried. I killed 'em 'cause I was scared and mad. But I been scared and mad all my life, and after I killed that first woman I wasn't scared no more for a little while."

"What were you afraid of?"

"Everything," he breathed and buried his face in his hands.

"Did you ever hope for anything, Bigger?"

"What for? I couldn't get it. I'm black," he mumbled.

"Didn't you ever want to be happy?"

"Yeah; I guess so," he said, straightening.

"How did you think you could be happy?"

"I don't know. I wanted to do things. But everything I wanted to do I couldn't. I wanted to do what the white boys in school did. Some of 'em went to college. Some of 'em went to the Army. But I couldn't go."

"But still, you wanted to be happy?"

"Yeah; sure. Everybody wants to be happy, I reckon."

"Did you think you ever would be?"

"I don't know. I just went to bed at night and got up in the morning. I just lived from day to day. I thought maybe I would be."

"How?"

"I don't know," he said in a voice that was almost a moan.

"What did you think happiness would be like?"

"I don't know. It wouldn't be like this."

"You ought to have some idea of what you wanted, Bigger."

"Well, Mr. Max, if I was happy I wouldn't always be wanting to do something I know I couldn't do."

"And why did you always want to?"

"I couldn't help it. Everybody feels that way, I reckon. And I did, too. Maybe I would've been all right if I could've done something I wanted to do. I wouldn't be scared then. Or mad, maybe. I wouldn't be always hating folks; and maybe I'd feel at home, sort of."

"Did you ever go to the South Side Boys' Club, the place where Mr. Dalton sent those Ping-Pong tables?"

"Yeah; but what the hell can a guy do with Ping-Pong?"

"Do you feel that that club kept you out of trouble?"

Bigger cocked his head.

"Kept me out of trouble?" he repeated Max's words. "Naw; that's where we planned most of our jobs."

"Did you ever go to church, Bigger?"

"Yeah; when I was little. But that was a long time ago."

"Your folks were religious?"

"Yeah; they went to church all the time."

"Why did you stop going?"

"I didn't like it. There was nothing in it. Aw, all they did was sing and shout and pray all the time. And it didn't get 'em nothing. All the colored folks do that, but it don't get 'em nothing. The white folks got everything."

"Did you ever feel happy in church?"

"Naw. I didn't want to. Nobody but poor folks get happy in church."

"But you are poor, Bigger."

Again Bigger's eyes lit with a bitter and feverish pride.

"I ain't that poor," he said.

"But Bigger, you said that if you were where people did not hate you and you did not hate them, you could be happy. Nobody hated you in church. Couldn't you feel at home there?"

"I wanted to be happy in this world, not out of it. I didn't want that kind of happiness. The white folks like for us to be religious; then they can do what they want to with us."

"A little while ago you spoke of God 'getting you' for killing those women. Does that mean you believe in Him?"

"I don't know."

"Aren't you afraid of what'll happen to you after you die?"

"Naw. But I don't want to die."

"Didn't you know that the penalty for killing that white woman would be death?"

"Yeah; I knew it. But I felt like she was killing me, so I didn't care."

"If you could be happy in religion now, would you want to be?"

"Naw. I'll be dead soon enough. If I was religious, I'd be dead now."

"But the church promises eternal life."

"That's for whipped folks."

"You don't feel like you've had a chance, do you?"

"Naw; but I ain't asking nobody to be sorry for me. Naw; I ain't asking that at all. I'm black. They don't give black people a chance, so I took a chance and lost. But I don't care none now. They got me and it's all over."

"Do you feel, Bigger, that somehow, somewhere, or sometime or other you'll have a chance to make up for what you didn't get here on earth?"

"Hell, naw! When they strap me in that chair and turn on the heat, I'm through, for always."

"Bigger, I want to ask you something about your race. Do you love your people?"

"I don't know, Mr. Max. We all black and the white folks treat us the same."

"But Bigger, your race is doing things for you. There are Negroes leading your people."

"Yeah; I know. I heard about 'em. They all right, I guess."

"Don't you know any of 'em?"

"Naw."

"Bigger, are there many Negro boys like you?"

"I reckon so. All of 'em I know ain't got nothing and ain't going nowhere."

"Why didn't you go to some of the leaders of your race and tell them how you and other boys felt?"

"Aw, hell, Mr. Max. They wouldn't listen to me. They rich, even though the white folks treat them almost like they do me. They almost like white people, when it comes to guys like me. They say guys like me make it hard for them to get along with white folks."

"Did you ever hear any of your leaders make speeches?"

"Yeah, sure. At election time."

"What did you think of them?"

"Aw, I don't know. They all the same. They wanted to get elected to office. They wanted money, like everybody else. Mr. Max, it's a game and they play it."

"Why didn't you play it?"

"Hell, what do I know? I ain't got nothing. Nobody'll pay any attention to me. I'm just a black guy with nothing. I just went to grammar school. And politics is full of big shots, guys from colleges."

"Didn't you trust them?"

"I don't reckon they wanted anybody to trust 'em. They wanted to get elected to office. They paid you to vote."

"Did you ever vote?"

"Yeah; I voted twice. I wasn't old enough, so I put my age up so I could vote and get the five dollars."

"You didn't mind selling your vote?"

"Naw; why should I?"

"You didn't think politics could get you anything?"

"It got me five dollars on election day."

"Bigger, did any white people ever talk to you about labor unions?"

"Naw; nobody but Jan and Mary. But she oughtn't done it. . . . But I couldn't help what I did. And Jan. I reckon I did him wrong by signing 'Red' to that ransom note."

"Do you believe he's your friend now?"

"Well, he ain't against me. He didn't turn against me today when they was questioning him. I don't think he hates me like the others. I suppose he's kind of hurt about Miss Dalton, though."

"Bigger, did you think you'd ever come to this?"

"Well, to tell the truth, Mr. Max, it seems sort of natural-like, me being here facing that death chair. Now I come to think of it, it seems like something like this just had to be."

They were silent. Max stood up and sighed. Bigger watched to see what Max was thinking, but Max's face was white and blank.

"Well, Bigger," Max said. "We'll enter a plea of not guilty at the arraignment tomorrow. But when the trial comes up we'll change it to a plea of guilty and ask for mercy. They're rushing the trial; it may be held in two or three days. I'll tell the judge all I can of how you feel and why. I'll try to get him to make it life in prison. That's all I can see under the circumstances. I don't have to tell you how they feel toward you, Bigger. You're a Negro; you know. Don't hope for too much. There's an ocean of hot hate out there against you and I'm going to try to sweep some of it back. They want your life; they want revenge. They felt they had you fenced off so that you could not do what you did. Now they're mad, because deep down in them they believe that they made you do it. When people feel that way, you can't reason with 'em. Then, too, a lot depends upon what judge we have. Any twelve white men in this state will have already condemned you; we can't trust a jury. Well, Bigger, I'll do the best I can."

They were silent. Max gave him another cigarette and took one for himself. Bigger watched Max's head of white hair, his long face, the deep-gray, soft, sad eyes. He felt that Max was kind, and he felt sorry for him.

"Mr. Max, if I was you I wouldn't worry none. If all folks was like you, then maybe I wouldn't be here. But you can't help that now. They going to hate you for trying to help me. I'm gone. They got me."

"Oh, they'll hate me, yes," said Max. "But I can take it. That's the difference. I'm a Jew and they hate me, but I know why and I can fight. But sometimes you can't win no matter how you fight; that is, you can't win if you haven't got time. And they're pressing us now. But you need not worry about their hating me for defending you. The fear of hate keeps many whites from trying to help you and your kind. Before I can fight your battle, I've got to fight a battle with them." Max snuffed out his cigarette. "I got to go now," Max said. He turned and faced Bigger. "Bigger, how do you feel?"

"I don't know. I'm just setting here waiting for 'em to come and tell me to walk to that chair. And I don't know if I'll be able to walk or not."

Max averted his face and opened the door. A guard came and caught Bigger by the wrist.

From *Native Son*

"I'll see you in the morning, Bigger," Max called.

Back in his cell, Bigger stood in the middle of the floor, not moving. He was not stoop-shouldered now, nor were his muscles taut. He breathed softly, wondering about the cool breath of peace that hovered in his body. It was as though he were trying to listen to the beat of his own heart. All round him was darkness and there were no sounds. He could not remember when he had felt as relaxed as this before. He had not thought of it or felt it while Max was speaking to him; it was not until after Max had gone that he discovered that he had spoken to Max as he had never spoken to anyone in his life; not even to himself. And his talking had eased from his shoulders a heavy burden. Then he was suddenly and violently angry. Max had tricked him! But no. Max had not compelled him to talk; he had talked of his own accord, prodded by excitement, by a curiosity about his own feelings. Max had only sat and listened, had only asked questions. His anger passed and fear took its place. If he were as confused as this when his time came, they really *would* have to drag him to the chair. He had to make a decision: in order to walk to that chair he had to weave his feelings into a hard shield of either hope or hate. To fall between them would mean living and dying in a fog of fear. . . .

—1940

Prologue of an Invisible Man

Ralph Ellison

I AM AN invisible man. No, I am not a spook like those who haunted Edgar Allan Poe; nor am I one of your Hollywood-movie ectoplasms. I am a man of substance, of flesh and bone, fiber and liquids—and I might even be said to possess a mind.

I am invisible, understand, simply because people refuse to see me. Like the bodiless heads you see sometimes in circus sideshows, it is as though I have been surrounded by mirrors of hard, distorting glass. When they approach me they see only my surroundings, themselves, or figments of their imagination—indeed, everything and anything except me.

Nor is my invisibility exactly a matter of a biochemical accident to my epidermis. That invisibility to which I refer occurs because of a peculiar disposition of the eyes of those with whom I come in contact. A matter of the construction of their *inner* eyes, those eyes with which they look through their physical eyes upon reality. I am not complaining, nor am I protesting either. It is sometimes advantageous to be unseen, although it is most often rather wearing on the nerves. Then too, you're constantly being bumped against by those of poor vision. Or again, you often doubt if you really exist. You wonder whether you aren't simply a phantom in other people's minds. Say, a figure in a nightmare which the sleeper tries with all his strength to destroy.

It's when you feel like this that, out of resentment, you begin to bump people back. And, let me confess, you feel that way most of the time. You ache with the need to convince yourself that you do exist in the real world, that you're a part of all the sound and anguish, and you strike out with your fists, you curse and you swear to make them recognize you. And, alas, it's seldom successful.

One night I accidentally bumped into a man, and perhaps because of the near darkness he saw me and called me an insulting name. I sprang at him, seized his coat lapels and demanded that he apologize. He was a tall blond man, and as my face came close to his he looked insolently out of his blue eyes and cursed me, his breath hot in my face as he struggled. I pulled his chin down sharp upon the crown of my head, butting him as I had seen the West Indians do, and I felt his flesh tear and the blood gush out, and I yelled, "Apologize! Apologize!" But he continued to curse and struggle, and I butted him again and again until he went down heavily, on his knees, profusely bleeding. I kicked him repeatedly, in a frenzy because he still uttered insults though his lips were frothy with blood. Oh yes, I kicked him!

And in my outrage I got out my knife and prepared to slit his throat, right there beneath the lamplight in the deserted street, holding him by the collar with one hand, and opening the knife with my teeth—when it occurred to me that the man had not *seen* me, actually; that he, as far as he knew, was in the midst of a walking nightmare! And I stopped the blade, slicing the air as I pushed him away, letting him fall back to the street. I stared at him hard as the lights of a car stabbed through the darkness. He lay there, moaning on the asphalt; a man almost killed by a phantom. It unnerved me. I was both disgusted and ashamed. I was like a drunken man myself, wavering about on weakened legs. Then I was amused. Something in this man's thick head had sprung out and beaten him within an inch of his life.

I began to laugh at this crazy discovery. Would he have awakened at the point of death? Would Death himself have freed him for wakeful living? But I didn't linger. I ran away into the dark, laughing so hard I feared I might rupture myself. The next day I saw his picture in the *Daily News*, beneath a caption stating that he had been "mugged." Poor fool, poor blind fool, I thought with sincere compassion, mugged by an invisible man!

Most of the time (although I do not choose as I once did to deny the violence of my days by ignoring it) I am not so overtly violent. I remember that I am invisible and walk softly so as not to awaken the sleeping ones. Sometimes it is best not to awaken them; there are few things in the world as dangerous as sleepwalkers. I learned in time though that it is possible to carry on a fight against them without their realizing it. For instance, I have been carrying on a fight with Monopolated Light and Power for some time now. I use their service and pay them nothing at all, and they don't know it. Oh, they suspect that power is being drained off, but they don't know where. All they know is that according to the master meter back there in their power station a hell of a lot of free current is disappearing somewhere into the jungle of Harlem. The joke, of course, is that I don't live in Harlem but in a border area. Several years ago (before I discovered the advantage of being invisible) I went through the routine process of buying service and paying their outrageous rates. But no more. I gave up all that, along with my apartment and my old way of life: that way based upon the fallacious assumption that I, like other men, was visible. Now, aware of my invisibility, I live rent-free in a building rented strictly to whites, in a section of the basement that was shut off and forgotten during the nineteenth century, which I discovered when I was trying to escape in the night from Ras the Destroyer. But that's getting too far ahead of the story, almost to the end, although the end is in the beginning and lies far ahead.

The point now is that I found a home—or a hole in the ground, as you will. Now don't jump to the conclusion that because I call my home a "hole" it is damp and cold like a grave; there are cold holes and warm holes. Mine is a warm hole. And remember, a bear retires to his hole for the winter and lives until spring; then he comes strolling out like the Easter chick breaking from its shell. I say all this to assure you that it is incorrect to assume that, because I'm invisible and live in a hole, I am dead. I am neither dead nor in a state of suspended animation. Call me Jack-the-Bear, for I am in a state of hibernation.

My hole is warm and full of light. Yes, *full* of light. I doubt if there is a brighter spot in all New York than this hole of mine, and I do not exclude Broadway. Or the Empire State Building on a photographer's dream night. But that is taking advantage of you. Those two spots are among the darkest of our whole civilization—pardon me, our whole *culture* (an important distinction, I've heard)—which might sound like a hoax, or a contradiction, but that (by contradiction, I mean) is how the world moves: Not like an arrow, but a boomerang. (Beware of those who speak of the *spiral* of history; they are preparing a boomerang. Keep a steel helmet handy.) I know; I have been boomeranged across my head so much that I now can see the darkness of lightness.

And I love light. Perhaps you'll think it strange that an invisible man should need light, desire light, love light. But maybe it is exactly because I *am* invisible. Light confirms my reality, gives birth to my form. A beautiful girl once told me of a recurring nightmare in which she lay in the center of a large dark room and felt her face expand until it filled the whole room, becoming a formless mass while her eyes ran in bilious jelly up the chimney. And so it is with me. Without light I am not only invisible, but formless as well; and to be unaware of one's form is to live a death. I myself, after existing some twenty years, did not become alive until I discovered my invisibility.

That is why I fight my battle with Monopolated Light and Power. The deeper reason, I mean: it allows me to feel my vital aliveness. I also fight them for taking so much of my money before I learned to protect myself. In my hole in the basement there are exactly 1,369 lights. I've wired the entire ceiling, every inch of it. And not with fluorescent bulbs, but with the older, more-expensive-to-operate kind, the filament type. An act of sabotage, you know. I've already begun to wire the wall. A junk man I know, a man of vision, has supplied me with wire and sockets. Nothing, storm or flood, must get in the way of our need for light and ever more and brighter light. The truth is the light and light is the truth. When I finish all four walls, then I'll start on the floor. Just how that will go, I don't know. Yet when you have lived invisible as long as I have you develop a certain ingenuity. I'll solve the problem. And maybe I'll invent a gadget to place my coffeepot on the fire while I lie in bed, and even invent a gadget to warm my bed—like the fellow I saw in one of the picture magazines who made himself a gadget to warm his shoes! Though invisible, I am in the great American tradition of tinkers. That makes me kin to Ford, Edison and Franklin. Call me, since I have a theory and a concept, a "thinker-tinker." Yes, I'll warm my shoes; they need it, they're usually full of holes. I'll do that and more.

Now I have one radio-phonograph; I plan to have five. There is a certain acoustical deadness in my hole, and when I have music I want to *feel* its vibration, not only with my ear but with my whole body. I'd like to hear five recordings of Louis Armstrong playing and singing "What Did I Do To Be So Black and Blue"—all at the same time. Sometimes now I listen to Louis while I have my favorite dessert of vanilla ice cream and sloe gin. I pour the red liquid over the white mound, watching it glisten and the vapor rising as Louis bends that military instrument into a beam of lyrical sound. Perhaps I like Louis Armstrong because he's made poetry out of being invisible. I think it must be because he's unaware that he *is* invisible. And my own grasp of invisibility aids me to understand his music. Once when I asked for a cigarette, some jokers gave me a reefer, which I lighted when I got home and sat listening to my phonograph. It was a strange evening.

Invisibility, let me explain, gives one a slightly different sense of time; you're never quite on the beat. Sometimes you're ahead and sometimes behind. Instead of the swift and imperceptible flowing of time, you are aware of its nodes, those points where time stands still or from which it leaps ahead. And you slip into the breaks and look around. That's what you hear vaguely in Louis' music.

Once I saw a prizefighter boxing a yokel. The fighter was swift and amazingly scientific. His body was one violent flow of rapid rhythmic action. He hit the yokel a hundred times while the yokel held up his arms in stunned surprise. But suddenly the yokel, rolling about in the gale of boxing gloves, struck one blow and knocked science, speed and footwork as cold as a welldigger's posterior. The smart money hit the canvas. The long shot got the nod. The yokel had simply stepped inside of his opponent's sense of time.

So under the spell of the reefer I discovered a new analytical way of listening to music. The unheard sounds came through, and each melodic line existed of itself, stood out clearly from all the rest, said its piece, and waited patiently for the other voices to speak. That night I found myself hearing not only in time, but in space as well. I not only entered the music but descended, like Dante, into its depths. And *beneath the swiftness of the hot tempo there was a slower tempo and a cave and I entered it and looked around and heard an old woman singing a spiritual as full of Weltschmerz as flamenco, and beneath that lay a still lower level on which I saw a beautiful girl the color of ivory pleading in a voice like my mother's as she stood before a group of slave-owners who bid for her naked body, and below that I found a lower level and a more rapid tempo and I heard someone shout:*

"Brothers and sisters, my text this morning is the 'Blackness of Blackness.' "

And a congregation of voices answered: "That blackness is most black, brother, most black . . ."

"In the beginning . . ."

"At the very start," they cried.

". . . there was blackness . . ."

"Preach it . . ."

". . . and the sun . . ."

"The sun, Lawd . . ."

"... was bloody red ..."

"Red ..."

"Now black is ..." the preacher shouted.

"Bloody ..."

"I said black is ..."

"Preach it, brother ..."

"... an' black ain't ..."

"Red, Lawd, red. He said it's red!"

"Amen, brother ..."

"Black will git you ..."

"Yes, it will ..."

"... an' black won't ..."

"Naw, it won't!"

"It do ..."

"It do, Lawd ..."

"... an' it don't."

"Halleluiah ..."

"... It'll put you, glory, glory, oh my Lawd, in the WHALE'S BELLY."

"Preach it, dear brother ..."

"... an' make you tempt ..."

"Good God A-mighty!"

"Old Aunt Nelly!"

"Black will make you ..."

"Black ..."

"... or black will unmake you."

"Ain't it the truth, Lawd?"

And at that point a voice of trombone timbre screamed at me, "Git out of here, you fool! Is you ready to commit treason?"

And I tore myself away, hearing the old singer of spirituals moaning, "Go curse your God, boy, and die."

I stopped and questioned her, asked her what was wrong.

"I dearly loved my master, son," she said.

"You should have hated him," I said.

"He gave me several sons," she said, "and because I loved my sons I learned to love their father though I hated him too."

"I too have become acquainted with ambivalence," I said. "That's why I'm here."

"What's that?"

"Nothing, a word that doesn't explain it. Why do you moan?"

"I moan this way 'cause he's dead," she said.

"Then tell me, who is that laughing upstairs?"

"Them's my sons. They glad."

"Yes, I can understand that too," I said.

"I laughs too, but I moans too. He promised to set us free but he never could bring hisself to do it. Still I loved him ..."

"Loved him? You mean ...?"

"Oh yes, but I loved something else even more."

"What more?"

"Freedom."

"Freedom," I said. "Maybe freedom lies in hating."

"Naw, son, it's in loving. I loved him and give him the poison and he withered away like a frost-bit apple. Them boys woulda tore him to pieces with they homemake knives."

"A mistake was made somewhere," I said, "I'm confused." And I wished to say other things, but the laughter upstairs became too loud and moan-like for me and I tried to break out of it, but I couldn't. Just as I was leaving I felt an urgent desire to ask her what freedom was and went back. She sat with her head in her hands, moaning softly; her leather-brown face was filled with sadness.

"Old woman, what is this freedom you love so well?" I asked around a corner of my mind.

She looked surprised, then thoughtful, then baffled. "I done forgot, son. It's all mixed up. First I think it's one thing, then I think it's another. It gits my head to spinning. I guess now it ain't nothing but knowing how to say what I got up in my head. But it's a hard job, son. Too much is done happen to me in too short a time. Hit's like I have a fever. Ever' time I starts to walk my head gits to swirling and I falls down. Or if it ain't that, it's the boys; they gits to laughing and wants to kill up the white folks. They's bitter, that's what they is ..."

"But what about freedom?"

"Leave me 'lone, boy; my head aches!"

I left her, feeling dizzy myself. I didn't get far.

Suddenly one of the sons, a big fellow six feet tall, appeared out of nowhere and struck me with his fist.

"What's the matter, man?" I cried.

"You made Ma cry!"

"But how?" I said, dodging a blow.

"Askin' her them questions, that's how. Git outa here and stay, and next time you got questions like that, ask yourself!"

He held me in a grip like cold stone, his fingers fastening upon my windpipe until I thought I would suffocate before he finally allowed me to go. I stumbled about dazed, the music beating hysterically in my ears. It was dark. My head cleared and I wandered down a dark narrow passage, thinking I heard his footsteps hurrying behind me. I was sore, and into my being had come a profound craving for tranquillity, for peace and quiet, a state I felt I could never achieve. For one thing, the trumpet was blaring and the rhythm was too hectic. A tom-tom beating like heartthuds began. drowning out the trumpet, filling my ears. I longed for water and I heard it rushing through the cold mains my fingers touched as I felt my way, but I couldn't stop to search because of the footsteps behind me.

"Hey, Ras," I called. "Is it you, Destroyer? Rinehart?"

No answer, only the rhythmic footsteps behind me. Once I tried crossing the road, but a speeding machine struck me, scraping the skin from my leg as it roared past.

Then somehow I came out of it, ascending hastily from this underworld of sound to hear Louis Armstrong innocently asking,

> What did I do
> To be so black
> And blue?

At first I was afraid; this familiar music had demanded action, the kind of which I was incapable, and yet had I lingered there beneath the surface I might have attempted to act. Nevertheless, I know now that few really listen to this music.

I sat on the chair's edge in a soaking sweat, as though each of my 1,369 bulbs had every one become a klieg light in an individual setting for a third degree with Ras and Rinehart in charge. It was exhausting—as though I had held my breath continuously for an hour under the terrifying serenity that comes from days of intense hunger. And yet, it was a strangely satisfying experience for an invisible man to hear the silence of sound. I had discovered unrecognized compulsions of my being—even though I could not answer "yes" to their promptings. I haven't

smoked a reefer since, however; not because they're illegal, but because to *see* around corners is enough (that is not unusual when you are invisible). But to hear around them is too much; it inhibits action. And despite Brother Jack and all that sad, lost period of the Brotherhood, I believe in nothing if not in action.

Please, a definition: a hibernation is a covert preparation for a more overt action.

Besides, the drug destroys one's sense of time completely. If that happened, I might forget to dodge some bright morning and some cluck would run me down with an orange and yellow streetcar, or a bilious bus! Or I might forget to leave my hole when the moment for action presents itself.

Meanwhile I enjoy my life with the compliments of Monopolated Light and Power. Since you never recognize me even when in closest contact with me, and since, no doubt, you'll hardly believe that I exist, it won't matter if you know that I tapped a power line leading into the building and ran it into my hole in the ground. Before that I lived in the darkness into which I was chased, but now I see. I've illuminated the blackness of my invisibility—and vice versa. And so I play the invisible music of my isolation. The last statement doesn't seem just right, does it? But it is; you hear this music simply because music is heard and seldom seen, except by musicians. Could this compulsion to put invisibility down in black and white be thus an urge to make music of invisibility? But I am an orator, rabble-rouser—Am? I *was*, and perhaps shall be again. Who knows? All sickness is not unto death, neither is invisibility.

I can hear you say, "What a horrible, irresponsible bastard!" And you're right. I leap to agree with you. I am one of the most irresponsible beings that ever lived. Irresponsibility is part of my invisibility; any way you face it, it is a denial. But to whom can I be responsible, and why should I be, when you refuse to see me? And wait until I reveal how truly irresponsible I am. Responsibility rests upon recognition, and recognition is a form of agreement. Take the man whom I almost killed. Who was responsible for that near murder—I? I don't think so, and I refuse it. I won't buy it. You can't give it to me.

He bumped *me*, *he* insulted *me*. Shouldn't he, for his own personal safety, have recognized my hysteria, my "danger potential"? He, let us say, was lost in a dream world. But didn't *he* control that dream world—which, alas, is only too real! —and didn't *he* rule me out of it? And if he had yelled for a policeman, wouldn't *I* have been taken for the offending one? Yes, yes, yes! Let me agree with you, I was the irresponsible one; for I should have used my knife to protect the higher interests of society. Some day that kind of foolishness will cause us tragic trouble. All dreamers and sleepwalkers must pay the price, and even the invisible victim is responsible for the fate of all. But I shirked that responsibility; I became too snarled in the incompatible notions that buzzed within my brain. I was a coward . . .

But what did *I* do to be so blue? Bear with me.

—1952

From *Invisible Man*

The Revolt of the Evil Fairies

Ted Poston

THE GRAND dramatic offering of the Booker T. Washington Colored Grammar School was the biggest event of the year in our social life in Hopkinsville, Kentucky. It was the one occasion on which they let us use the old Cooper Opera House, and even some of the white folks came out yearly to applaud our presentation. The first two rows of the orchestra were always reserved for our white friends, and our leading colored citizens sat right behind them—with an empty row intervening, of course.

Mr. Ed Smith, our local undertaker, invariably occupied a box to the left of the house and wore his cutaway coat and striped breeches. This distinctive garb was usually reserved for those rare occasions when he officiated at the funerals of our most prominent colored citizens. Mr. Thaddeus Long, our colored mailman, once rented a tuxedo and bought a box too. But nobody paid him much mind. We knew he was just showing off.

The title of our play never varied. It was always *Prince Charming and the Sleeping Beauty*, but no two presentations were ever the same. Miss H. Belle LaPrade, our sixth-grade teacher, rewrote the script every season, and it was never like anything you read in the storybooks.

Miss LaPrade called it "a modern morality play of conflict between the forces of good and evil." And the forces of evil, of course, always came off second best.

The Booker T. Washington Colored Grammar School was in a state of ferment from Christmas until February, for this was the period when parts were assigned. First there was the selection of the Good Fairies and the Evil Fairies. This was very important, because the Good Fairies wore white costumes and the Evil Fairies black. And strangely enough most of the Good Fairies usually turned out to be extremely light in complexion, with straight hair and white folks' features. On rare occasions a dark-skinned girl might be lucky enough to be a Good Fairy, but not one with a speaking part.

There never was any doubt about Prince Charming and the Sleeping Beauty. They were always light-skinned. And though nobody ever discussed those things openly, it was an accepted fact that a lack of pigmentation was a decided advantage in the Prince Charming and Sleeping Beauty sweepstakes.

And therein lay my personal tragedy. I made the best grades in my class, I was the leading debater and the scion of a respected family in the community. But I could never be Prince Charming, because I was black.

In fact, every year when they started casting our grand dramatic offering my family started pricing black cheesecloth at Franklin's Department Store. For they knew that I would be leading the forces of darkness and skulking back in the shadows—waiting to be vanquished in the third act. Mamma had experience with this sort of thing. All my brothers had finished Booker T. before me.

Not that I was alone in my disappointment. Many of my classmates felt it too. I probably just took it more to heart. Rat Joiner, for instance, could rationalize the situation. Rat was not only black; he lived on Billy Goat Hill. But Rat summed it up like this:

"If you black, you black."

I should have been able to regard the matter

calmly too. For our grand dramatic offering was only a reflection of our daily community life in Hopkinsville. The yallers had the best of everything. They held most of the teaching jobs in Booker T. Washington Colored Grammar School. They were the Negro doctors, the lawyers, the insurance men. They even had a Blue Vein Society, and if your dark skin obscured your throbbing pulse you were hardly a member of the elite.

Yet I was inconsolable the first time they turned me down for Prince Charming. That was the year they picked Roger Jackson. Roger was not only dumb; he stuttered. But he was light enough to pass for white, and that was apparently sufficient.

In all fairness, however, it must be admitted that Roger had other qualifications. His father owned the only colored saloon in town and was quite a power in local politics. In fact, Mr. Clinton Jackson had a lot to say about just who taught in the Booker T. Washington Colored Grammar School. So it was understandable that Roger should have been picked for Prince Charming.

My real heartbreak, however, came the year they picked Sarah Williams for Sleeping Beauty. I had been in love with Sarah since kindergarten. She had soft light hair, bluish-gray eyes and a dimple which stayed in her left cheek whether she was smiling or not.

Of course Sarah never encouraged me much. She never answered any of my fervent love letters, and Rat was very scornful of my one-sided love affair. "As long as she don't call you a black baboon," he sneered, "you'll keep on hanging around."

After Sarah was chosen for Sleeping Beauty, I went out for the Prince Charming role with all my heart. If I had declaimed boldly in previous contests, I was matchless now. If I had bothered Mamma with rehearsals at home before, I pestered her to death this time. Yes, and I purloined my sister's can of Palmer's Skin Success.

I knew the Prince's role from start to finish, having played the Head Evil Fairy opposite it for two seasons. And Prince Charming was one character whose lines Miss LaPrade never varied much in her many versions. But although I never admitted it, even to myself, I knew I was doomed

from the start. They gave the part to Leonardius Wright. Leonardius, of course, was yaller.

The teachers sensed my resentment. They were almost apologetic. They pointed out that I had been such a splendid Head Evil Fairy for two seasons that it would be a crime to let anybody else try the role. They reminded me that Mamma wouldn't have to buy any more cheesecloth because I could use my same old costume.

They insisted that the Head Evil Fairy was even more important than Prince Charming, because he was the one who cast the spell on Sleeping Beauty. So what could I do but accept?

I had never liked Leonardius Wright. He was a goody-goody, and even Mamma was always throwing him up to me. But, above all, he too was in love with Sarah Williams. And now he got a chance to kiss Sarah every day in rehearsing the awakening scene.

Well, the show must go on, even for little black boys. So I threw my soul into my part and made the Head Evil Fairy a character to be remembered. When I drew back from the couch of Sleeping Beauty and slunk away into the shadows at the approach of Prince Charming, my facial expression was indeed something to behold. When I was vanquished by the shining sword of Prince Charming in the last act, I was a little hammy, perhaps—but terrific!

The attendance at our grand dramatic offering that year was the best in its history. Even the white folks overflowed the two rows reserved for them, and a few were forced to sit in the intervening one. This created a delicate situation, but everybody tactfully ignored it.

When the curtain went up on the last act, the audience was in fine fettle. Everything had gone well for me, too—except for one spot in the second act. That was where Leonardius unexpectedly rapped me over the head with his sword as I slunk off into the shadows. That was not in the script, but Miss LaPrade quieted me down by saying it made a nice touch anyway. Rat said Leonardius did it on purpose.

The third act went on smoothly, though, until we came to the vanquishing scene. That was where I slunk from the shadows for the last time and challenged Prince Charming to mortal combat. The hero reached for his shining sword—a bit unsportsmanlike, I always thought, since Miss LaPrade consistently left the Head Evil Fairy unarmed—and then it happened!

Later I protested loudly—but in vain—that it was a case of self-defense. I pointed out that Leonardius had a mean look in his eye. I cited the impromptu rapping he had given my head in the second act. But nobody would listen. They just wouldn't believe that Leonardius really intended to brain me when he reached for his sword.

Anyway, he didn't succeed. For the minute I saw that evil gleam in his eye—or was it my own?—I cut loose with a right to the chin, and Prince Charming dropped his shining sword and staggered back. His astonishment lasted only a minute, though, for he lowered his head and came charging in, fists flailing. There was nothing yellow about Leonardius but his skin.

The audience thought the scrap was something new Miss LaPrade had written in. They might have kept on thinking so if Miss LaPrade hadn't been screaming so hysterically from the sidelines. And if Rat Joiner hadn't decided that this was as good a time as any to settle old scores. So he turned around and took a sock at the male Good Fairy nearest him.

When the curtain rang down, the forces of Good and Evil were locked in combat. And Sleeping Beauty was wide awake and streaking for the wings.

They rang the curtain back up fifteen minutes later, and we finished the play. I lay down and expired according to specifications but Prince Charming will probably remember my sneering corpse to his dying day. They wouldn't let me appear in the grand dramatic offering at all the next year. But I didn't care. I couldn't have been Prince Charming anyway.

—1945

Health Card

Frank Yerby

JOHNNY stood under one of the street lights on the corner and tried to read the letter. The street lights down in the Bottom were so dim that he couldn't make out half the words, but he didn't need to: he knew them all by heart anyway.

"Sugar," he read, "it took a long time but I done it. I got the money to come to see you. I waited and waited for them to give you a furlough, but it look like they don't mean to. Sugar, I can't wait no longer. I got to see you. I got to. Find a nice place for me to stay—where we can be happy together. You know what I mean. With all my love, Lily."

Johnny folded the letter up and put it back in his pocket. Then he walked swiftly down the street past all the juke joints with the music blaring out and the G.I. brogans pounding. He turned down a side street, scuffing up a cloud of dust as he did so. None of the streets down in Black Bottom was paved, and there were four inches of fine white powder over everything. When it rained the mud would come up over the tops of his army shoes, but it hadn't rained in nearly three months. There were no juke joints on this street, and the Negro shanties were neatly whitewashed. Johnny kept on walking until he came to the end of the street. On the corner stood the little whitewashed Baptist church, and next to it was the neat, well-kept home of the pastor.

Johnny went up on the porch and hesitated. He thrust his hand in his pocket and the paper crinkled. He took his hand out and knocked on the door.

"Who's that?" a voice called.

"It's me," Johnny answered; "It's a sodjer."

The door opened a crack and a woman peered out. She was middle-aged and fat. Looking down, Johnny could see that her feet were bare.

"Whatcha want, sodjer?"

Johnny took off his cap.

"Please, ma'am, lemme come in. I kin explain it t' yuh better settin' down."

She studied his face for a minute in the darkness.

"Aw right," she said, "you kin come in, son."

Johnny entered the room stiffly and sat down on a cornshuck-bottomed chair.

"It's this way, ma'am," he said. "I got a wife up Nawth. I been tryin' an' tryin' t' git a furlough so I could go t' see huh. But they always put me off. So now she done worked an' saved enuff money t' come an' see me. I wants t' ax you t' rent me a room, ma'am. I doan' know nowheres t' ax."

"This ain't no hotel, son."

"I know it ain't. I cain't take Lily t' no hotel, not lak hotels in this heah town."

"Lily yo' wife?"

"Yes'm. She my sho' nuff, honest t' Gawd wife. Married in th' Baptist church in Deetroit."

The fat woman sat back, and her thick lips widened into a smile.

"She a good girl, ain't she? An' you doan' wanta take her t' one o' these heah ho'houses they calls hotels."

"That's it, ma'am."

"Sho' you kin bring huh heah, son. Be glad t' have huh. Reveren' be glad t' have huh too. What yo' name, son?"

"Johnny. Johnny Green. Ma'am—"

"Yas, son?"

"You understands that I wants t' come heah too?"

The fat woman rocked back in her chair and gurgled with laughter.

"Bless yo' heart, chile, I ain't always been a ole woman! And I ain't always been th' preacher's wife neither!"

"Thank you, ma'am. I gotta go now. Time fur me t' be gettin' back t' camp."

"When you bring Lily?"

"Be Monday night, ma'am. Pays you now if you wants it."

"Monday be aw right. Talk it over with th' Reveren', so he make it light fur yuh. Know sodjer boys ain't got much money."

"No, ma'am, sho' Lawd ain't. G'night, ma'am."

When he turned back into the main street of the Negro section the doors of the joints were all open and the soldiers were coming out. The girls were clinging onto their arms all the way to the bus stop. Johnny looked at the dresses that stopped halfway between the pelvis and the knee and hugged the backside so that every muscle showed when they walked. He saw the purple lipstick smeared across the wide full lips, and the short hair stiffened with smelly grease so that it covered their heads like a black lacquered cap. They went on down to the bus stop arm in arm, their knotty bare calves bunching with each step as they walked. Johnny thought about Lily. He walked past them very fast without turning his head.

But just as he reached the bus stop he heard the whistles. When he turned around he saw the four M.P.'s and the civilian policeman stopping the crowd. He turned around again and walked back until he was standing just behind the white men.

"Aw right," the M.P.'s were saying, "you gals git your health cards out."

Some of the girls started digging in their handbags. Johnny could see them dragging out small yellow cardboard squares. But the others just stood there with blank expressions on their faces. The soldiers started muttering, a dark, deep-throated sound. The M.P.'s started pushing their way through the crowd, looking at each girl's card as they passed. When they came to a girl who didn't have a card they called out to the civilian policeman:

"Aw right, mister, take A'nt Jemima for a little ride."

Then the city policeman would lead the girl away and put her in the Black Maria.

They kept this up until they had examined every girl except one. She hung back beside her soldier, and the first time the M.P.'s didn't see her. When they came back through, one of them caught her by the arm.

"Lemme see your card, Mandy," he said.

The girl looked at him, her little eyes narrowing into slits in her black face.

"Tek yo' hands offen me, white man," she said.

The M.P.'s face crimsoned, so that Johnny could see it even in the darkness.

"Listen, black girl," he said, "I told you to lemme see your card."

"An' I tole you t' tek yo' han' offen me, white man!"

"Gawddammit, you little black bitch, you better do like I tell you!"

Johnny didn't see very clearly what happened after that. There was a sudden explosion of motion, and then the M.P. was trying to jerk his hand back, but he couldn't, for the little old black girl had it between her teeth and was biting it to the bone. He drew his other hand back and slapped her across the face so hard that it sounded like a pistol shot. She went over backwards and her tight skirt split, so that when she got up Johnny could see that she didn't have anything on under it. She came forward like a cat, her nails bared, straight for the M.P.'s eyes. He slapped her down again, but the soldiers surged forward all at once. The M.P.'s fell back and drew their guns and one of them blew a whistle.

Johnny, who was behind them, decided it was time for him to get out of there and he did; but not before he saw the squads of white M.P.'s hurling around the corner and going to work on the Negroes with their clubs. He reached the bus stop and swung on board. The minute after he had pushed his way to the back behind all the white soldiers he heard the shots. The bus driver put the bus in gear and they roared off toward the camp.

It was after one o'clock when all the soldiers straggled in. Those of them who could still walk. Eight of them came in on the meat wagon, three with gunshot wounds. The colonel declared the town out of bounds for all Negro soldiers for a month.

"Dammit," Johnny said, "I gotta go meet Lily, I gotta. I cain't stay heah. I cain't!"

"Whatcha gonna do," Little Willie asked, "go AWOL?"

Johnny looked at him, his brow furrowed into a frown.

"Naw," he said, "I'm gonna go see th' colonel!"

"Whut! Man, you crazy! Colonel kick yo' black ass out fo' you gits yo' mouf open."

"I take a chanct on that."

He walked over to the little half-mirror on the wall of the barracks. Carefully he readjusted his cap. He pulled his tie out of his shirt front and drew the knot tighter around his throat. Then he tucked the ends back in at just the right fraction of an inch between the correct pair of buttons. He bent down and dusted his shoes again, although they were already spotless.

"Man," Little Willie said, "you sho' is a fool!"

"Reckon I am," Johnny said; then he went out of the door and down the short wooden steps.

When he got to the road that divided the colored and white sections of the camp his steps faltered. He stood still a minute, drew in a deep breath, and marched very stiffly and erect across the road. The white soldiers gazed at him curiously, but none of them said anything. If a black soldier came over into their section it was because somebody sent him, so they let him alone.

In front of the colonel's headquarters he stopped. He knew what he had to say, but his breath was very short in his throat and he was going to have a hard time saying it.

"Whatcha want, soldier?" the sentry demanded.

"I wants t' see th' colonel."

"Who sent you?"

Johnny drew his breath in sharply.

"I ain't at liberty t' say," he declared, his breath coming out very fast behind the words.

"You ain't at liberty t' say," the sentry mimicked. "Well I'll be damned! If you ain't at liberty t' say, then I ain't at liberty t' let you see tha colonel! Git tha hell outa here, nigger, before I pump some lead in you!"

Johnny didn't move.

The sentry started toward him, lifting his rifle butt, but another soldier, a sergeant, came around the corner of the building.

"Hold on there," he called. "What tha hell is th' trouble here?"

"This here nigger says he wants t' see tha colonel an' when I ast him who sent him he says he ain't at liberty t' say!"

The sergeant turned to Johnny.

Johnny came to attention and saluted him. You aren't supposed to salute N.C.O.'s, but sometimes it helps.

"What you got t' say fur yourself, boy?" the sergeant said, not unkindly. Johnny's breath evened.

"I got uh message fur th' colonel, suh," he said; "I ain't s'posed t' give it t' nobody else but him. I ain't even s'posed t' tell who sont it, suh."

The sergeant peered at him sharply.

"You tellin' tha truth, boy?"

"Yassuh!"

"Aw right. Wait here a minute."

He went into H.Q. After a couple of minutes he came back.

"Aw right, soldier, you kin go on in."

Johnny mounted the steps and went into the colonel's office. The colonel was a lean, white-haired soldier with a face tanned to the color of saddle leather. He was reading a letter through a pair of horn-rimmed glasses which had only one earhook left, so that he had to hold them up to his eyes with one hand. He put them down and looked up. Johnny saw that his eyes were pale blue, so pale that he felt as if he were looking into the eyes of an eagle or some other fierce bird of prey.

"Well?" he said, and Johnny stiffened into a salute. The colonel half smiled.

"At ease, soldier," he said. Then: "The sergeant tells me that you have a very important message for me."

Johnny gulped in the air.

"Beggin' th' sergeant's pardon, suh," he said, "but that ain't so."

"What!"

"Yassuh," Johnny rushed on, "nobody sent me. I come on m' own hook. I had t' talk t' yuh, Colonel, suh! You kin sen' me t' th' guardhouse afterwards, but please, suh, lissen t' me fur jes' a minute!"

The colonel relaxed slowly. Something very like a smile was playing around the corners of his mouth. He looked at his watch.

"All right, soldier," he said. "You've got five minutes."

"Thank yuh, thank yuh, suh!"

"Speak your piece, soldier; you're wasting time!"

"It's about Lily, suh. She my wife. She done worked an' slaved fur nigh onto six months t' git the money t' come an' see me. An' now you give th' order that none of th' cullud boys kin go t' town. Beggin' yo' pahdon, suh, I wasn't in none of that trouble. I ain't neber been in no trouble. You kin ax my cap'n, if you wants to. All I wants is permission to go into town fur one week, an' I'll stay outa town fur two months if yuh wants me to."

The colonel picked up the phone.

"Ring Captain Walters for me," he said. Then: "What's your name, soldier?"

"It's Green, suh. Private Johnny Green."

"Captain Walters? This is Colonel Milton. Do you have anything in your files concerning Private Johnny Green? Oh yes, go ahead. Take all the time you need."

The colonel lit a long black cigar. Johnny waited. The clock on the wall spun its electric arms.

"What's that? Yes. Yes, yes, I see. Thank you, Captain."

He put down the phone and picked up a fountain pen. He wrote swiftly. Finally he straightened up and gave Johnny the slip of paper.

Johnny read it. It said:

> Private Johnny Green is given express permission to go into town every evening of the week beginning August seventh and ending August fourteenth. He is further permitted to remain in town overnight every night during said week, so long as he returns to camp for reveille the following morning. By order of the commanding officer, Colonel H. H. Milton.

There was a hard knot at the base of Johnny's throat. He couldn't breathe. But he snapped to attention and saluted smartly.

"Thank yuh, suh," he said at last. Then: "Gawd bless you, suh!"

"Forget it, soldier. I was a young married man once myself. My compliments to Captain Walters."

Johnny saluted again and about-faced; then he marched out of the office and down the stairs. On the way back he saluted everybody—privates, N.C.O.'s and civilian visitors, his white teeth gleaming in a huge smile.

"That's sure one happy darky," one of the white soldiers said.

Johnny stood in the station and watched the train running in. The yellow lights from the windows flickered on and off across his face as the alternating squares of light and darkness flashed past. Then it was slowing and Johnny was running beside it, trying to keep abreast of the Jim Crow coach. He could see her standing up, holding her bags. She came down the steps the first one, and they stood there holding each other, Johnny's arms crushing all the breath out of her, holding her so hard against him that his brass buttons hurt through her thin dress. She opened her mouth to speak but he kissed her, bending her head backward on her neck until her little hat fell off. It lay there on the ground, unnoticed.

"Sugah," she said, "sugah. It was awful."

"I know," he said. "I know."

Then he took her bags and they started walking out of the station toward the Negro section of town.

"I missed yuh so much," Johnny said, "I thought I lose m' mind."

"Me too," she said. Then: "I brought th' marriage license with me like yuh tole me. I doan' wan' th' preacher's wife t' think we bad."

"Enybody kin look at yuh an' see yuh uh angel!"

They went very quietly through all the dark streets and the white soldiers turned to look at Johnny and his girl.

Lak a queen, Johnny thought, lak a queen. He looked at the girl beside him, seeing the velvety nightshade skin, the glossy black lacquered curls, the sweet, wide hips and the long, clean legs striding beside him in the darkness. I am black, but comely, O ye daughters of Jerusalem!

They turned into the Bottom where the street lights were dim blobs on the pine poles and the dust rose up in little swirls around their feet. Johnny had his head half turned so that he didn't see the two M.P.'s until he had almost bumped into them. He dropped one bag and caught Lily by the arm. Then he drew her aside quickly and the two men went by them without speaking.

They kept on walking, but every two steps Johnny would jerk his head around and look nervously back over his shoulder. The last time he looked the two M.P.'s had stopped and were looking back at them. Johnny turned out the elbow of the arm next to Lily so that it hooked into hers a little and began to walk faster, pushing her along with him.

"What's yo' hurry, sugah?" she said. "I be heah a whole week!"

But Johnny was looking over his shoulder at the two M.P.'s. They were coming toward them now, walking with long, slow strides, their reddish-white faces set. Johnny started to push Lily along faster, but she shook off his arm and stopped still.

"I do declare, Johnny Green! You th' beatines' man! Whut you walk me so fas' fur?"

Johnny opened his mouth to answer her, but the military police were just behind them now, and the sergeant reached out and laid his hand on her arm.

"C'mon, gal," he said, "lemme see it."

"Let you see whut? Whut he mean, Johnny?"

"Your card," the sergeant growled. "Lemme see your card."

"My card?" Lily said blankly. "Whut kinda card, mister?"

Johnny put the bags down. He was fighting for breath.

"Look heah, Sarge," he said, "this girl my wife!"

"Oh yeah? I said lemme see your card, sister!"

"I ain't got no card, mister. I dunno whut you talkin' about."

"Look, Sarge," the other M.P. said, "th' sol-dier's got bags. Maybe she's just come t' town."

"These your bags, gal?"

"Yessir."

"Aw right. You got twenty-four hours to git yourself a health card. If you don't have it by then we hafta run you in. Git goin' now."

"Listen," Johnny shouted, "this girl my wife! She ain't no ho'! I tell you she ain't—"

"What you say, nigger?—" the M.P. sergeant growled. "Whatcha say?" He started toward Johnny.

Lily swung on Johnny's arm.

"C'mon, Johnny," she said, "they got guns. C'mon, Johnny, please! Please, Johnny!"

Slowly she drew away.

"Aw, leave 'em be, Sarge," the M.P. corporal said, "maybe she is his wife."

The sergeant spat. The brown tobacco juice splashed in the dirt not an inch from Lily's foot. Then the two of them turned and started away.

Johnny stopped.

"Lemme go, Lily," he said, "lemme go!" He tore her arm loose from his and started back up the street. Lily leaped, her two arms fastening themselves around his neck. He fought silently but she clung to him, doubling her knees so that all her weight was hanging from his neck.

"No, Johnny! Oh Jesus, no! You be kilt! Oh, Johnny, listen t' me, sugah! You's all I got!"

He put both hands up to break her grip but she swung her weight sidewise and the two of them went down in the dirt. The M.P.'s turned the corner out of sight.

Johnny sat there in the dust staring at her. The dirt had ruined her dress. He sat there a long time looking at her until the hot tears rose up back of his eyelids faster than he could blink them away, so he put his face down in her lap and cried.

"I ain't no man!" he said. "I ain't no man!"

"Hush, sugah," she said. "You's a man aw right. You's my man!"

Gently she drew him to his feet. He picked up the bags and the two of them went down the dark street toward the preacher's house.

—1944

The Almost White Boy

Willard Motley

BY BIRTH he was half Negro and half white. Socially he was all Negro. That is, when people knew that his mother was a brownskin woman with straightened hair and legs that didn't respect the color line when it came to making men turn around to look at them. His eyes were gray. His skin was as white as Slim Peterson's; his blond hair didn't have any curl to it at all. His nose was big and his lips were big—the only tip-off. Aunt Beulah-May said he looked just like "poor white trash." Other people, black and white, said all kinds of things about his parents behind their backs, even if they were married. And these people, when it came to discussing him, shook their heads, made sucking sounds with their tongues and said, "Too bad! Too bad!" And one straggly-haired Irish woman who had taken quite a liking to him had even gone so far as to tell him, blissfully unmindful of his desires in the matter, "I'd have you marry my daughter if you was white."

One thing he remembered. When he was small his dad had taken him up in his arms and carried him to the big oval mirror in the parlor. "Come here, Lucy," his father had said, calling Jimmy's mother. His mother came, smiling at the picture her two men made hugged close together: one so little and dependent, the other so tall and serious-eyed. She stood beside him, straightening Jimmy's collar and pushing his hair out of his eyes. Dad held him in between them. "Look in the mirror, son," he said. And they all looked. Their eyes were serious, not smiling, not staring, just gloom-colored with seriousness in the mirror. "Look at your mother. . . . Look at me." His dad gave the directions gravely. "Look at your

mother's skin." He looked. That was the dear sweet mother he loved. "Look at the color of my skin." He looked. That was his daddy, the best daddy in the world. "We all love each other, son, all three of us," his dad said, and his mother's eyes in the mirror caught and held his father's with something shining and proud through the seriousness; and his mother's arm stole up around him and around his daddy. "People are just people. Some are good and some are bad," his father said. "People are just people. Look—and remember." He had remembered. He would never forget.

Somehow, something of that day had passed into his life. And he carried it with him back and forth across the color line. The colored fellows he palled with called him "the white nigger," and his white pals would sometimes look at him kind of funny but they never said anything. Only when they went out on dates together; then they'd tell him, "Don't let on you're colored." And sometimes when he was around they'd let something slip about "niggers" without meaning to. Then they'd look sheepish. Jim didn't see much difference. All the guys were swell if you liked them; all the girls flirted and necked and went on crying jags now and then. People were just people.

There were other things Jim remembered.

. . . On Fifty-eighth and Prairie. Lorenzo with white eyes in a black face. With his kinky hair screwed down tight on his bald-looking head like flies on flypaper. Ruby with her face all shiny brown and her hair in stiff-standing braids and her pipy brown legs Mom called razor-legs. Lorenzo saying, "You're black just like us." Ruby singing out, "Yeah! Yeah! You're a white nigger—white nigger—white nigger!" Lorenzo taunting, "You ain't no different. My ma says so. You're just a nigger!" Lorenzo and Ruby pushing up close to him with threatening gestures, making faces at him, pulling his straight blond hair with mean fists, both yelling at the same time, "White nigger! White nigger!"

The name stuck.

. . . Women on the sidewalk in little groups. Their lips moving when he walked past with his schoolbooks under his arm. Their eyes lowered but looking at him. "Too bad! Too bad!" He could see them. He knew they were talking about him. "Too bad! Too bad!"

. . . Mom crying on the third floor of the kitchenette flat on Thirty-ninth Street. Mom saying to Dad, "We've got to move from here, Jim. We can't go on the street together without everybody staring at us. You'd think we'd killed somebody."

"What do we care how much they stare or what they say?"

"Even when I go out alone they stare. They never invite me to their houses. They say—they say that I think I'm better than they are—that I had to marry out of my race—that my own color wasn't good enough for me."

Dad saying, "Why can't people mind their own business? The hell with them." Mom crying. No friends. No company. Just the three of them.

. . . Then moving to the slums near Halstead and Maxwell, where all nationalities lived bundled up next door to each other and even in the same buildings. Jews. Mexicans. Poles. Negroes. Italians. Greeks. It was swell there. People changed races there. They went out on the streets together. No more staring. No more name-calling.

He grew up there.

. . . Getting older. And a lot of the white fellows not inviting him to parties at their houses when there were girls from the neighborhood. But they'd still go out of the neighborhood together and pick up girls or go on blind dates or to parties somewhere else. He didn't like to think of the neighborhood parties with the girls and the music and everything, and the door closed to him.

. . . Only once he denied it. He had been go-

ing around with Tony for a couple of weeks over on Racine Avenue. They played pool together, drank beer together on West Madison Street, drove around in Tony's old rattling Chevy. One day Tony looked at him funny and said, point-blank, "Say, what are you anyway?"

Jim got red; he could feel his face burn. "I'm Polish," he said.

He was sorry afterwards. He didn't know why he said it. He felt ashamed.

. . . Then he was finished with school and he had to go to work. He got a job in a downtown hotel, because nobody knew what he really was and Aunt Beulah-May said it was all right to "pass for white" when it came to making money but he'd better never get any ideas in his head about turning his back on his people. To him it was cheating. It was denying half himself. It wasn't a straight front. He knew how hard it was for colored fellows to find decent jobs. It wasn't saying, "I'm a Negro," and taking the same chances they took when it came to getting a job. But he did it.

Jim remembered many of these things; they were tied inside of him in hard knots. But the color line didn't exist for him and he came and went pretty much as he chose. He took the girls in stride. He went to parties on the South Side, on Thirty-fifth and Michigan, on South Park. He went dancing at the Savoy Ballroom—and the Trianon. He went to Polish hops and Italian fiestas and Irish weddings. And he had a hell of a swell time. People were just people.

He had fun with the colored girls. But some of them held off from him, not knowing what he was. These were his people. No—he didn't feel natural around them. And with white people he wasn't all himself either. He didn't have any people.

Then all of a sudden he was madly in love with Cora. This had never happened before. He had sometimes wondered if, when it came, it would be a white girl or a colored girl. Now it was here. There was nothing he could do about it. And he was scared. He began to worry, and to wonder. And he began to wish, although ashamed to admit it to himself, that he didn't have any colored blood in him.

He met Cora at a dance at the Trianon. Cora's

hair wasn't as blond as his but it curled all over her head. Her skin was pink and soft. Her breasts stood erect and her red lips were parted in a queer little loose way. They were always like that. And they were always moist-looking.

Leo introduced them. Then he let them alone and they danced every dance together; and when it was time to go home Leo had disappeared. Jim asked her if he could take her home.

"I think that would be awfully sweet of you," she said. Her eyes opened wide in a baby-blue smile.

She leaned back against him a little when he helped her into her coat. He flushed with the pleasure of that brief touching of their bodies. They walked through the unwinding ballroom crowd together, not having anything to say to each other, and out onto Cottage Grove, still not having anything to say. As they passed the lighted-up plate-glass window of Walgreen's drugstore Jim asked her, "Wouldn't you like a malted milk?" She didn't answer but just smiled up at him over her shoulder and he felt the softness of her arm in the doorway.

She sipped her malted milk. He sat stirring his straw around in his glass. Once in a while she'd look up over her glass and wrinkle her lips or her eyes at him, friendly-like. Neither of them said anything. Then, when Cora had finished, he held the match for her cigarette and their eyes came together and stayed that way longer than they needed to. And her lips were really parted now, with the cigarette smoke curling up into her hair.

In front of her house they stood close together, neither of them wanting to go.

"It was a nice dance," Cora said; and her fingers played in the hedge-top.

"Yes, especially after I met you."

"I'm going to see you again, aren't I?" Cora asked, looking up at him a little.

Jim looked down at the sidewalk. He hoped he could keep the red out of his cheeks. "I might as well tell you before someone else does— I'm a Negro," he said.

There was a catch in her voice, just a little noise not made of words.

"Oh, you're fooling!" she said with a small, irritated laugh.

"No, I'm not. I told you because I like you."

She had stepped back from him. Her eyes were searching for the windows of the house to see that there was no light behind the shades.

"Please, let me see you again," Jim said.

Her eyes, satisfied, came away from the windows. They looked at the sidewalk where he had looked. Her body was still withdrawn. Her lips weren't parted now. There were hard little lines at the corners of her mouth.

"Let me meet you somewhere," Jim said.

Another furtive glance at the house; then she looked at him, unbelievingly. "You didn't mean that—about being colored?"

"It doesn't matter, does it?"

"No—only—"

"Let me meet you somewhere," Jim begged.

Her lips were parted a little. She looked at him strangely, deep into him in a way that made him tremble, then down his body and back up into his eyes. She tossed her head a little. "Well—call me up tomorrow afternoon." She gave him the number.

He watched her go into the house. Then he walked to the corner to wait for his streetcar; and he kicked at the sidewalk and clenched his fists.

Jim went to meet her in Jackson Park. They walked around. She was beautiful in her pink dress. Her lips were pouted a little bit, and her eyes were averted, and she was everything he had ever wanted. They sat on a bench far away from anybody. "You know," she said, "I never liked nig—Negroes. You're not like a Negro at all." They walked to the other end of the park. "Why do you tell people?" she asked.

"People are just people," he told her, but the words didn't sound real any more.

Twice again he met her in the park. Once they just sat talking and once they went to a movie. Both times he walked her to the car line and left her there. That was the way she wanted it.

After that it was sneaking around to meet her. She didn't like to go on dates with him when he had his white friends along. She'd never tell him why. And yet she put her body up close to him when they were alone. It was all right too when she invited some of her friends who didn't know what he was.

They saw a lot of each other. And pretty soon

he thought from the long, probing looks she gave him that she must like him; from the way she'd grab his hand, tight, sometimes; from the way she danced with him. She even had him take her home now and they'd stand on her porch pressed close together. "Cora, I want you to come over to my house," he told her. "My mother and father are swell. You'll like them." He could see all four of them together. "It isn't a nice neighborhood. I mean it doesn't look good, but the people are nicer than—in other places. Gee, you'll like my mother and father."

"All right, I'll go, Jimmy. I don't care. I don't care."

Dad kidded him about his new flame, saying it must be serious, that he had never brought a girl home before. Mom made fried chicken and hot biscuits. And when he went to get Cora he saw Dad and Mom both with dust rags, shining up everything in the parlor for the tenth time; he heard Dad and Mom laughing quietly together and talking about their first date.

He hadn't told them she was a white girl. But they never batted an eye.

"Mom, this is Cora."

"How do you do, dear. Jimmy has told us so much about you." Dear, sweet Mom. Always gracious and friendly.

"Dad, this is Cora." Dad grinning, looking straight at her with eyes as blue as hers, going into some crazy story about "Jimmy at the age of three." Good old Dad. "People are just people."

Dad and Mom were at ease. Only Cora seemed embarrassed. And she was nervous, not meeting Dad's eyes, not meeting Mom's eyes, looking to him for support. She sat on the edge of her chair. "Y-y-yes, sir . . . No, Mrs. Warner." She only picked at the good food Mom had spent all afternoon getting ready. And Jim, watching her, watching Dad and Mom, hoping they wouldn't notice, got ill at ease himself and he was glad when he got her outside. Then they were themselves again.

"Mom and Dad are really swell. You'll have to get to know them," he said, looking at her appealingly, asking for approval. She smiled with expressionless eyes. She said nothing.

On Fourteenth and Halstead they met Slick Harper. Slick was as black as they come. It was sometimes hard, because of his southern dialect and his Chicago black-belt expressions, to know just what he meant in English. He practiced jitterbug steps on street corners and had a whole string of girls—black, brownskin, high yellow. Everybody called him Slick because he handed his bevy of girls a smooth line and because he wore all the latest fashions in men's clothes—high-waisted trousers, big-brimmed hats, bright sports coats, Cuban heels and coconut straws with gaudy bands. Slick hailed Jim; his eyes gave Cora the once-over.

"Whatcha say, man!" he shouted. "Ah know they all goes when the wagon comes but where you been stuck away? And no jive! Man, Ah been lookin' for you. We're throwing a party next Saturday and we want you to come."

Jim stood locked to the sidewalk, working his hands in his pockets and afraid to look at Cora. He watched Slick's big purple lips move up and down as they showed the slices of white teeth. Now Slick had stopped talking and was staring at Cora with a black-faced smirk.

"Cora, this is Slick Harper."

"How do you do." Her voice came down as from the top of a building.

"Ah'm glad to meetcha," Slick said. "You sho' got good taste, Jim." His eyes took in her whole figure. "Why don't you bring her to the party?"

"Maybe I will. Well, we've got to go." He walked fast then to keep up with Cora.

Cora never came over again.

Cora had him come over to her house. But first she prepared him a lot. "Don't ever—ever—tell my folks you're colored. Please, Jimmy. Promise me. . . . Father doesn't like colored people. . . . They aren't broad-minded like me. . . . And don't mind Father, Jimmy," she warned.

He went. There was a cream-colored car outside the house. In the parlor were smoking stands, and knickknack brackets, and a grand piano nobody played. Cora's father smoked cigars, owned a few pieces of stock, went to Florida two weeks every winter, told stories about the "Florida niggers." Cora's mother had the same parted lips Cora had, but she breathed through them heavily as if she were always trying to catch up with herself. She was fat and overdressed. And admonished her husband when he told his Southern stories through the smoke of big cigars: "Now, Harry, you mustn't talk like that. What will this nice young man think of you? There are plenty of fine upright Negroes—I'm sure. Of course I don't know any personally. . . . Now, Harry, don't be so harsh. Don't forget, you took milk from a colored mammy's breast. Oh, Harry, tell them about the little darky who wanted to watch your car—'Two cents a awah, Mistah No'the'nah!' "

Cora sat with her hands in her lap and her fingers laced tightly together. Jim smiled at Mr. Hartley's jokes and had a miserable time. And Jim discovered that it was best not to go to anybody's house. Just the two of them.

Jim and Cora went together for four months. And they had an awful time of it. But they were unhappy apart. Yet when they were together their eyes were always accusing each other. Sometimes they seemed to enjoy hurting each other. Jim wouldn't call her up; and he'd be miserable. She wouldn't write to him or would stand him up on a date for Chuck Nelson or Fred Schultz; then she'd be miserable. Something held them apart. And something pulled them together.

Jim did a lot of thinking. It had to go four revolutions. Four times a part-Negro had to marry a white person before legally you were white. The blood had to take four revolutions. Mulatto—that's what he was—quadroon—octoroon—then it was all gone. Then you were white. His great-grandchildren maybe. Four times the blood had to let in the other blood.

Then one night they were driving out to the forest preserves in Tony's Chevy. "What are you thinking, Jimmy?"

"Oh, nothing. Just thinking."

"Do you like my new dress? How do I look in it?"

"Isn't that a keen moon, Cora?" The car slid along the dark, deserted highway. They came to a gravel road and Jim eased the car over the crushed stone in second gear. Cora put her cheek against the sleeve of his coat. The branches of trees made scraping sounds against the sides of the car. Cora was closer to him now. He could smell the perfume in her hair, and yellow strands tickled the end of his nose. He stopped the motor and switched the lights off. Cora lifted his arm up over head and around her, putting his hand in close to her waist with her hand over his, stroking his. "Let's sit here like this—close and warm," she whispered. Then her voice lost itself in the breast of his coat.

For a long time they sat like that. Then Jim said, "Let's take a walk." He opened the door and, half supporting her, he lifted her out. While she was still in his arms she bit his ear gently.

"Don't do that," he said, and she giggled.

Panting, they walked through the low scrub into the woods. The bushes scratched their arms. Twigs caught in Cora's hair. Their feet sank in the earth. Cora kept putting her fingers in Jim's hair and mussing it. "Don't. Don't," he said. And finally he caught her fingers and held them tight in his. They walked on like this. The moon made silhouettes of them, silhouettes climbing up the slow incline of hill.

Jim found a little rise of land, treeless, grassy. Far to the northeast Chicago sprawled, row on row of dim lights growing more numerous but gentler.

The night was over them.

They sat on the little hillock, shoulder to shoulder; and Cora moved her body close to him. It was warm there against his shirt, open at the neck. They didn't talk. They didn't move. And when Cora breathed he could feel the movement of her body against him. It was almost as if they were one. He looked up at the splash of stars, and the moon clouding over. His arm went around her, shieldingly. He closed his eyes and put his face into her hair. "Cora! Cora!" The only answer she gave was the slight movement of her body.

"Cora, I love you."

"Do you, Jimmy?" she said, snuggling up so close to him that he could feel her heart beat against him.

He didn't move. But after a while she was slowly leaning back until the weight of her carried him back too and they lay full length. They lay like this a long time. He looked at her. Her eyes were closed. She was breathing hard. Her lips were parted and moist.

"Jimmy."

"What?"

"Nothing."

She hooked one of her feet over his. A slow quiver started in his shoulders, worked its way down the length of him. He sat up. Cora sat up.

"There's nobody here but us," she said. Her fingers unbuttoned the first button on his shirt, the second. Her fingers crept in on his chest, playing with the little hairs there.

"There's nobody here but us," she said, and she ran her fingers inside his shirt, over his shoulders and the back of his neck.

"We can't do this, Cora. We can't."

"Do you mean about you being colored? It doesn't matter to me, Jimmy. Honest it doesn't."

"No. Not that. It's because I love you. That's why I can't. That's why I want—"

He sat up straight then. His fingers pulled up some grass. He held it up to the light and looked at it. She had her head in his lap and lay there perfectly still. He could hear her breathing, and her breath was warm and moist on the back of his other hand where it lay on his leg. He threw the grass away, watched how the wind took it and lowered it down to the ground. He lifted her up by the shoulders, gently, until they were close together, looking into each other's eyes.

"I want it to be right for us, Cora," he said. "Will you marry me?"

The sting of red in her cheeks looked as if a blow had left it there; even the moonlight showed that. She sat up without the support of his hands. Her arms were straight and tense under her. Her eyes met his, burning angrily at the softness in his eyes. "You damn dirty nigger!" she said, and jumped up and walked away from him as fast as she could.

When she was gone he lay on his face where he had been sitting. He lay full length. The grass he had pulled stuck to his lips. "People are just people." He said it aloud. "People are just people." And he laughed, hoarsely, hollowly. People are just people." Then it was only a half-laugh with a sob cutting into it. And he was crying, with his arms flung up wildly above his head, with his face pushed into the grass trying to stop the sound of his crying. Off across the far grass Cora was running away from him. The moon, bright now, lacquered the whiteness of his hands lying helplessly above his head; it touched the blondness of his hair.

—1963

Son in the Afternoon

John A. Williams

IT WAS hot. I tend to be a bitch when it's hot. I goosed the little Ford over Sepulveda Boulevard toward Santa Monica until I got stuck in the traffic that pours from L.A. into the surrounding towns. I'd had a very lousy day at the studio.

I was—still am—a writer and this studio had hired me to check scripts and films with Negroes in them to make sure the Negro moviegoer wouldn't be offended. The signs were already clear one day the whole of American industry would be racing pell-mell to get a Negro, show-case a spade. I was kind of a pioneer. I'm a *Negro* writer, you see. The day had been tough because of a couple of verbs—slink and walk. One of those Hollywood hippies had done a script calling for a Negro waiter to slink away from the table where a dinner party was glaring at him. I said the waiter should walk, not slink, because later on he becomes a hero. The Hollywood hippie, who understood it all because he had some colored friends, said that it was essential to the plot that the waiter slink. I said you don't slink one minute and become a hero the next; there has to be some consistency. The Negro actor I was standing up for said nothing either way. He had played Uncle Tom roles so long that he had become Uncle Tom. But the director agreed with me.

Anyway . . . hear me out now. I was on my way to Santa Monica to pick up my mother, Nora. It was a long haul for such a hot day. I had planned a quiet evening: a nice shower, fresh clothes, and then I would have dinner at the Watkins and talk with some of the musicians on the scene for a quick taste before they cut to their gigs. After, I was going to the Pigalle down on Figueroa and catch Earl Grant at the organ, and still later, if nothing exciting happened, I'd pick up Scottie and make it to the Lighthouse on the Beach or to the Strollers and listen to some of the white boys play. I liked the long drive, especially while listening to Sleepy Stein's show on the radio. Later, much later of course, it would be home, back to Watts.

So you see, this picking up Nora was a little inconvenient. My mother was a maid for the Couchmans. Ronald Couchman was an architect, a good one I understood from Nora who has a fine sense for this sort of thing; you don't work in some hundred-odd houses during your life without getting some idea of the way a house should be laid out. Couchman's wife, Kay, was a playgirl who drove a white Jaguar from one party to another. My mother didn't like her too much; she didn't seem to care much for her son, Ronald junior. There's something wrong with a parent who can't really love her own child, Nora thought. The Couchmans lived in a real fine residential section, of course. A number of actors lived nearby, character actors, not really big stars.

Somehow it is very funny. I mean that the maids and butlers knew everything about these people, and these people knew nothing at all about the help. Through Nora and her friends I knew who was laying whose wife; who had money and who *really* had money; I knew about the wild parties hours before the police, and who smoked marijuana, when, and where they got it.

To get to Couchman's driveway I had to go three blocks up one side of a palm-planted center strip and back down the other. The driveway bent gently, then swept back out of sight of the main road. The house, sheltered by slim palms, looked like a transplanted New England Colonial. I parked and walked to the kitchen door, skirting the growling Great Dane who was tied to a tree. That was the route to the kitchen door.

I don't like kitchen doors. Entering people's houses by them, I mean. I'd done this thing most of my life when I called at places where Nora worked to pick up the patched or worn sheets or the half-eaten roasts, the battered, tarnished silver—the fringe benefits of a housemaid. As a teen-ager I'd told Nora I was through with that crap; I was not going through anyone's kitchen door. She only laughed and said I'd learn. One day soon after, I called for her and without knocking walked right through the front door of this house and right on through the living room. I was almost out of the room when I saw feet behind the couch. I leaned over and there was Mr. Jorgensen and his wife making out like crazy. I guess they thought Nora had gone and it must have hit them sort of suddenly and they went at it like the hell-bomb was due to drop any minute. I've been that way too, mostly in the spring. Of course, when Mr. Jorgensen looked over his shoulder and saw me, you know what happened. I was thrown out and Nora right behind me. It was the middle of winter, the old man was sick and the coal bill three months overdue. Nora was right about those kitchen doors: I learned.

My mother saw me before I could ring the bell. She opened the door. "Hello," she said. She was breathing hard, like she'd been running or something. "Come in and sit down. I don't know *where* that Kay is. Little Ronald is sick and she's probably out gettin' drunk again." She left me then and trotted back through the house, I guess to be with Ronnie. I hated the combination of her white nylon uniform, her dark brown face and the wide streaks of gray in her hair. Nora had married this guy from Texas a few years after the old man had died. He was all right. He made out okay. Nora didn't have to work, but she just couldn't be still; she always had to be doing something. I suggested she quit work, but I had as much luck as her husband. I used to tease her

about liking to be around those white folks. It would have been good for her to take an extended trip around the country visiting my brothers and sisters. Once she got to Philadelphia, she could go right out to the cemetery and sit awhile with the old man.

I walked through the Couchman home. I liked the library. I thought if I knew Couchman I'd like him. The room made me feel like that. I left it and went into the big living room. You could tell that Couchman had let his wife do that. Everything in it was fast, dart-like, with no sense of ease. But on the walls were several of Couchman's conceptions of buildings and homes. I guess he was a disciple of Wright. My mother walked rapidly through the room without looking at me and said, "Just be patient, Wendell. She should be here real soon."

"Yeah," I said, "with a snootful." I had turned back to the drawings when Ronnie scampered into the room, his face twisted with rage.

"Nora!" he tried to roar, perhaps the way he'd seen the parents of some of his friends roar at their maids. I'm quite sure Kay didn't shout at Nora, and I don't think Couchman would. But then no one shouts at Nora. "Nora, you come right back here this minute!" the little bastard shouted, and stamped and pointed to a spot on the floor where Nora was supposed to come to roost. I have a nasty temper. Sometimes it lies dormant for ages and at other times, like when the weather is hot and nothing seems to be going right, it's bubbling and ready to explode. "Don't talk to *my* mother like that, you little—!" I said sharply, breaking off just before I cursed. I wanted him to be large enough for me to strike. "How'd you like for me to talk to *your* mother like that?"

The nine-year-old looked up at me in surprise and confusion. He hadn't expected me to say anything. I was just another piece of furniture. Tears rose in his eyes and spilled out onto his pale cheeks. He put his hands behind him, twisted them. He moved backwards, away from me. He looked at my mother with a "Nora, come help me" look. And sure enough, there was Nora, speeding back across the room, gathering the kid in her arms, tucking his robe together. I was too angry to feel hatred for myself.

Ronnie was the Couchman's only kid. Nora loved him. I suppose that was the trouble. Couchman was gone ten, twelve hours a day. Kay didn't stay around the house any longer than she had to. So Ronnie had only my mother. I think kids should have someone to love, and Nora wasn't a bad sort. But somehow when the six of us, her own children, were growing up we never had her. She was gone, out scuffling to get those crumbs to put into our mouths and shoes for our feet and praying for something to happen so that all the space in between would be taken care of. Nora's affection for us took the form of rushing out into the morning's five o'clock blackness to wake some silly bitch and get her coffee; took form in her trudging five miles home every night instead of taking the streetcar to save money to buy tablets for us, to use at school, we said. But the truth was that all of us liked to draw and we went through a writing tablet in a couple of hours every day. Can you imagine? There's not a goddamn artist among us. We never had the physical affection, the pat on the head, the quick, smiling kiss, the "gimmee a hug" routine. All of this Ronnie was getting.

Now he buried his little blond head in Nora's breast and sobbed. "There, there now," Nora said. "Don't you cry, Ronnie. Ol' Wendell is just jealous, and he hasn't much sense either. He didn't mean nuthin'."

I left the room. Nora had hit it of course, hit it and passed on. I looked back. It didn't look so incongruous, the white and black together, I mean. Ronnie was still sobbing. His head bobbed gently on Nora's shoulder. The only time I ever got that close to her was when she trapped me with a bearhug so she could whale the daylights out of me after I put a snowball through Mrs. Grant's window. I walked outside and lit a cigarette. When Ronnie was in the hospital the month before, Nora got me to run her way over to Hollywood every night to see him. I didn't like that worth a damn. All right, I'll admit it: it did upset me. All that affection I didn't get nor my brothers and sisters going to that little white boy who, without a doubt, when away from her called her the names he'd learned from adults. Can you imagine a nine-year-old kid calling Nora a "girl," "our girl"? I spat at the Great Dane.

He snarled and then I bounced a rock off his fanny. "Lay down, you bastard," I muttered. It was a good thing he was tied up.

I heard the low cough of the Jaguar slapping against the road. The car was throttled down, and with a muted roar it swung into the driveway. The woman aimed it for me. I was evil enough not to move. I was tired of playing with these people. At the last moment, grinning, she swung the wheel over and braked. She bounded out of the car like a tennis player vaulting over a net.

"Hi," she said, tugging at her shorts.

"Hello."

"You're Nora's boy?"

"I'm Nora's son." Hell, I was as old as she was; besides, I can't stand "boy."

"Nora tells us you're working in Hollywood. Like it?"

"It's all right."

"You must be pretty talented."

We stood looking at each other while the dog whined for her attention. Kay had a nice body and it was well tanned. She was high, boy, was she high. Looking at her, I could feel myself going into my sexy bastard routine; sometimes I can swing it great. Maybe it all had to do with the business inside. Kay took off her sunglasses and took a good look at me. "Do you have a cigarette?"

I gave her one and lit it. "Nice tan," I said. Most white people I know think it's a great big deal if a Negro compliments them on their tans. It's a large laugh. You have all this volleyball about color and come summer you can't hold the white folks back from the beaches, anyplace where they can get some sun. And of course the blacker they get, the more pleased they are. Crazy. If there is ever a Negro revolt, it will come during the summer and Negroes will descend upon the beaches around the nation and paralyze the country. You can't conceal cattle prods and bombs and pistols and police dogs when you're showing your birthday suit to the sun.

"You like it?" she asked. She was pleased. She placed her arm next to mine. "Almost the same color," she said.

"Ronnie isn't feeling well," I said.

"Oh, the poor kid. I'm so glad we have Nora.

She's such a charm. I'll run right in and look at him. Do have a drink in the bar. Fix me one too, will you?" Kay skipped inside and I went to the bar and poured out two strong drinks. I made hers stronger than mine. She was back soon. "Nora was trying to put him to sleep and she made me stay out." She giggled. She quickly tossed off her drink. "Another, please?" While I was fixing her drink she was saying how amazing it was for Nora to have such a talented son. What she was really saying was that it was amazing for a servant to have a son who was not also a servant.

"Anything can happen in a democracy," I said. "Servants' sons drink with madams and so on."

"Oh, Nora isn't a servant," Kay said. "She's part of the family."

Yeah, I thought. Where and how many times had I heard *that* before?

In the ensuing silence, she started to admire her tan again. "You think it's pretty good, do you? You don't know how hard I worked to get it." I moved close to her and held her arm. I placed my other arm around her. She pretended not to see or feel it, but she wasn't trying to get away either. In fact she was pressing closer and the register in my brain that tells me at the precise moment when I'm in, went off. Kay was very high. I put both arms around her and she put both hers around me. When I kissed her, she responded completely.

—1962

Barbados

Paule Marshall

DAWN, like the night which had preceded it, came from the sea. In a white mist tumbling like spume over the fishing boats leaving the island and the hunched, ghost shapes of the fishermen. In a white, wet wind breathing over the villages scattered amid the tall canes. The cabbage palms roused, their high headdresses solemnly saluting the wind, and along the white beach which ringed the island the casuarina trees began their moaning—a sound of women lamenting their dead within a cave.

The wind, smarting of the sea, threaded a wet skein through Mr. Watford's five hundred dwarf coconut trees and around his house at the edge of the grove. The house, Colonial American in design, seemed created by the mist—as if out of the dawn's formlessness had come, magically, the solid stone walls, the blind, broad windows and the portico of fat columns which embraced the main story. When the mist cleared, the house remained—pure, proud, a pristine white—disdaining the crude wooden houses in the village outside its high gate.

It was not the dawn settling around his house which awakened Mr. Watford, but the call of his Barbary doves from their hutch in the yard. And it was more the feel of that sound than the sound itself. His hands had retained, from the many times a day he held the doves, the feel of their throats swelling with that murmurous, mournful note. He lay abed now, his hands—as cracked and callused as a cane cutter's—filled with the sound, and against the white sheet which flowed out to the white walls he appeared profoundly alone, yet secure in loneliness, contained. His face was fleshless and severe, his black skin

sucked deep into the hollow of his jaw, while under a high brow, which was like a bastion raised against the world, his eyes were indrawn and pure. It was as if, during all his seventy years, Mr. Watford had permitted nothing to sight which could have affected him.

He stood up, and his body, muscular but stripped of flesh, appeared to be absolved from time, still young. Yet each clenched gesture of his arms, of his lean shank as he dressed in a faded shirt and work pants, each vigilant, snapping motion of his head betrayed tension. Ruthlessly he spurred his body to perform like a younger man's. Savagely he denied the accumulated fatigue of the years. Only sometimes when he paused in his grove of coconut trees during the day, his eyes tearing and the breath torn from his lungs, did it seem that if he could find a place hidden from the world and himself he would give way to exhaustion and weep from weariness.

Dressed, he strode through the house, his step tense, his rough hand touching the furniture from Grand Rapids which crowded each room. For some reason, Mr. Watford had never completed the house. Everywhere the walls were raw and unpainted, the furniture unarranged. In the drawing room, with its coffered ceiling, he stood before his favorite piece, an old mantel clock which eked out the time. Reluctantly it whirred five and Mr. Watford nodded. His day had begun.

It was no different from all the days which made up the five years since his return to Barbados. Downstairs in the unfinished kitchen he prepared his morning tea—tea with canned milk and fried bakes—and ate standing at the stove while lizards skittered over the unplastered walls. Then, belching and snuffling the way a child would, he put on a pith helmet, secured his pants legs with bicycle clasps and stepped into the yard. There he fed the doves, holding them so that their sound poured into his hands and laughing gently —but the laugh gave way to an irritable grunt as he saw the mongoose tracks under the hutch. He set the trap again.

The first heat had swept the island like a huge tidal wave when Mr. Watford, with that tense, headlong stride, entered the grove. He had planted the dwarf coconut trees because of their quick yield and because, with their stunted trunks, they always appeared young. Now as he worked, rearranging the complex of pipes which irrigated the land, stripping off the dead leaves, the trees were like cool, moving presences; the stiletto fronds wove a protective dome above him, and slowly, as the day soared toward noon, his mind filled with the slivers of sunlight through the trees and the feel of earth in his hands, as it might have been filled with thoughts.

Except for a meal at noon, he remained in the grove until dusk surged up from the sea; then, returning to the house, he bathed and dressed in a medical doctor's white uniform, turned on the lights in the parlor and opened the tall doors to the portico.

Then the old women of the village on their way to church, the last hawkers caroling, "Fish, flying fish, a penny, my lady," the roistering saga-boys lugging their heavy steel drums to the crossroad where they would rehearse under the street lamp—all passing could glimpse Mr. Watford, stiff in his white uniform and with his head bent heavily over a Boston newspaper. The papers reached him weeks late but he read them anyway, giving a little savage chuckle at the thought that beyond his world that other world went its senseless way. As he read, the night sounds of the village welled into a joyous chorale against the sea's muffled cadence and the hollow, haunting music of the steel band. Soon the moths, lured in by the light, fought to die on the lamp, the beetles crashed drunkenly against the walls and the night—like a woman offering herself to him—became fragrant with the night-blooming cactus.

Even in America Mr. Watford had spent his evenings this way. Coming home from the hospital, where he worked in the boiler room, he would dress in his white uniform and read in the basement of the large rooming house he owned. He had lived closeted like this, detached, because America—despite the money and property he had slowly accumulated—had meant nothing to him. Each morning, walking to the hospital along the rutted Boston streets, through the smoky dawn light, he had known—although it had never been a thought—that his allegiance, his place, lay elsewhere.

Neither had the few acquaintances he had made mattered. Nor the women he had occasionally kept as a younger man. After the first months their bodies would grow coarse to his hand and he would begin edging away. . . . So that he had felt no regret when, the year before his retirement, he resigned his job, liquidated his properties and, his fifty-year exile over, returned home.

The clock doled out eight and Mr. Watford folded the newspaper and brushed the burnt moths from the lamp base. His lips still shaped the last words he had read as he moved through the rooms fastening the windows against the night air, which he had dreaded even as a boy. Something palpable but unseen was always, he believed, crouched in the night's dim recess, waiting to snare him. . . . Once in bed in his sealed room, Mr. Watford fell asleep quickly.

The next day was no different except that Mr. Goodman, the local shopkeeper, sent the boy for coconuts to sell at the racetrack and then came that evening to pay for them and to herald—although Mr. Watford did not know this—the coming of the girl.

That morning, taking his tea, Mr. Watford heard the careful tap of the mule's hoofs and looking out saw the wagon jolting through the dawn and the boy, still lax with sleep, swaying on the seat. He was perhaps eighteen and the muscles packed tightly beneath his lustrous black skin gave him a brooding strength. He came and stood outside the back door, his hands and lowered head performing the small, subtle rites of deference.

Mr. Watford's pleasure was full, for the gestures were those given only to a white man in his time. Yet the boy always nettled him. He sensed a natural arrogance like a pinpoint of light within his dark stare. The boy's stance exhumed a memory buried under the years. He remembered, staring at him, the time when he had worked as a yard boy for a white family, and had had to assume the same respectful pose while their flat, raw, Barbadian voices assailed him with orders. He remembered the muscles in his neck straining as he nodded deeply and a taste like alum on his tongue as he repeated the "Yes, please," as in a litany. But because of their whiteness and wealth, he had never dared hate them. Instead his rancor, like a boomerang, had rebounded, glancing past him to strike all the dark ones like himself, even his mother with her spindled arms and her stomach sagging with a child who was, invariably, dead at birth. He had been the only one of ten to live, the only one to escape. But he had never lost the sense of being pursued by the same dread presence which had claimed them. He had never lost the fear that if he lived too fully he would tire and death would quickly close the gap. His only defense had been a cautious life and work. He had been almost broken by work at the age of twenty, when his parents died, leaving him enough money for the passage to America. Gladly had he fled the island. But nothing had mattered after his flight.

The boy's foot stirred the dust. He murmured, "Please, sir, Mr. Watford, Mr. Goodman at the shop send me to pick the coconut."

Mr. Watford's head snapped up. A caustic word flared, but died as he noticed a political button pinned to the boy's patched shirt with "Vote for the Barbados People's Party" printed boldly on it, and below that the motto of the party: "The Old Order Shall Pass." At this ludicrous touch (for what could this boy, with his splayed and shigoed feet and blunted mind, understand about politics?) he became suddenly nervous, angry. The button and its motto seemed, somehow, directed at him. He said roughly, "Well, come then. You can't pick any coconuts standing there looking foolish!"—and he led the way to the grove.

The coconuts, he knew, would sell well at the booths in the center of the track, where the poor were penned in like cattle. As the heat thickened and the betting grew desperate, they would clamor: "Man, how you selling the water coconuts?" and hacking off the tops they would pour rum into the water within the hollow centers, then tilt the coconuts to their heads so that the rum-sweetened water skimmed their tongues and trickled bright down their dark chins. Mr. Watford had stood among them at the track as a young man, as poor as they were, but proud. And he had always found something unutterably graceful and free in their gestures, something which had roused contradictory feelings in him: admiration, but just as strong, impatience at their easy ways, and shame. . . .

That night, as he sat in his white uniform reading, he heard Mr. Goodman's heavy step and went out and stood at the head of the stairs in a formal, proprietary pose. Mr. Goodman's face floated up into the light—the loose folds of flesh, the skin slick with sweat as if oiled, the eyes scribbled with veins and mottled, bold—as if each blemish there was a sin he proudly displayed or a scar which proved he had met life head-on. His body, unlike Mr. Watford's, was corpulent and, with the trousers caught up around his full crotch, openly concupiscent. He owned the one shop in the village which gave credit and a booth which sold coconuts at the racetrack, kept a wife and two outside women, drank a rum with each customer at his bar, regularly caned his fourteen children, who still followed him everywhere (even now they were waiting for him in the darkness beyond Mr. Watford's gate), and bet heavily at the races, and when he lost gave a loud hacking laugh which squeezed his body like a pain and left him gasping.

The laugh clutched him now as he flung his pendulous flesh into a chair and wheezed, "Watford, how? Man, I near lose house, shop, shirt and all at races today. I tell you, they got some horses from Trinidad in this meet that's making ours look like they running backwards. Be Jese, I wouldn't bet on a Bajan horse tomorrow if Christ Heself was to give me the top. Those bitches might look good but they's nothing 'pon a track."

Mr. Watford, his back straight as the pillar

he leaned against, his eyes unstained, his gaunt face planed by contempt, gave Mr. Goodman his cold, measured smile, thinking that the man would be dead soon, bloated with rice and rum —and somehow this made his own life more certain.

Sputtering with his amiable laughter, Mr. Goodman paid for the coconuts, but instead of leaving then as he usually did, he lingered, his eyes probing for a glimpse inside the house. Mr. Watford waited, his head snapping warily, then, impatient, he started toward the door and Mr. Goodman said, "I tell you, your coconut trees bearing fast enough even for dwarfs. You's lucky, man."

Ordinarily Mr. Watford would have waved both the man and his remark aside, but repelled more than usual tonight by Mr. Goodman's gross form and immodest laugh, he said—glad of the cold edge his slight American accent gave the words—"What luck got to do with it? I does care the trees properly and they bear, that's all. Luck! People, especially this bunch around here, is always looking to luck when the only answer is a little brains and plenty of hard work . . . " Suddenly remembering the boy that morning and the political button, he added in loud disgust, "Look that half-foolish boy you does send here to pick the coconuts. Instead of him learning a trade and going to England where he might find work he's walking about with a political button. He and all in politics now! But that's the way with these down here. They'll do some of everything but work. They don't want work!" He gestured violently, almost dancing in anger. "They too busy spreeing."

The chair creaked as Mr. Goodman sketched a pained and gentle denial. "No, man," he said, "you wrong. Things is different to before. I mean to say, the young people nowadays is different to how we was. They not just sitting back and taking things no more. They not so frighten for the white people as we was. No, man. Now take that said same boy, for an example. I don't say he don't like a spree, but he's serious, you see him there. He's a member of this new Barbados People's Party. He wants to see his own color running the government. He wants to be able to make a living right here in Barbados instead of going to

any cold England. And he's right!" Mr. Goodman paused at a vehement pitch, then shrugged heavily. "What the young people must do, nuh? They got to look to something . . . "

"Look to work!" And Mr. Watford thrust out a hand so that the horned knuckles caught the light.

"Yes, that's true—and it's up to we that got little something to give them work," Mr. Goodman said, and a sadness filtered among the dissipations in his eyes. "I mean to say we that got little something got to help out. In a manner of speaking, we's responsible . . ."

"Responsible!" The word circled Mr. Watford's head like a gnat and he wanted to reach up and haul it down, to squash it underfoot.

Mr. Goodman spread his hands; his breathing rumbled with a sigh. "Yes, in a manner of speaking. That's why, Watford, man, you got to provide little work for some poor person down in here. Hire a servant at least! 'Cause I gon tell you something . . . " And he hitched forward his chair; his voice dropped to a wheeze. "People talking. Here you come back rich from big America and build a swell house and plant 'nough coconut trees and you still cleaning and cooking and thing like some woman. Man, it don't look good!" His face screwed in emphasis and he sat back. "Now, there's this girl, the daughter of a friend that just dead, and she need work bad enough. But I wouldn't like to see she working for these white people 'cause you know how those men will take advantage of she. And she'd make a good servant, man. Quiet and quick so, and nothing a-tall to feed and she can sleep anywhere about the place. And she don't have no boys always around her either . . . " Still talking, Mr. Goodman eased from his chair and reached the stairs with surprising agility. "You need a servant," he whispered, leaning close to Mr. Watford as he passed. "It don't look good, man, people talking. I gon send she."

Mr. Watford was overcome by nausea. Not only from Mr. Goodman's smell—a stench of salt fish, rum and sweat—but from an outrage which was like a sediment in his stomach. For a long time he stood there almost kecking from disgust, until his clock struck eight, reminding him of the sanctuary within—and suddenly his cold laugh dismissed Mr. Goodman and his proposal. Hurrying in, he locked the doors and windows against the night air and, still laughing, he slept.

The next day, coming from the grove to prepare his noon meal, he saw her. She was standing in his driveway, her bare feet like strong dark roots amid the jagged stones, her face tilted toward the sun—and she might have been standing there always, waiting for him. She seemed of the sun, of the earth. The folktale of creation might have been true with her: that along a river bank a god had scooped up the earth—rich and black and warmed by the sun—and molded her poised head with its tufted braids and then with a whimsical touch crowned it with a sober brown felt hat which should have been worn by some stout English matron in a London suburb, had sculptured the passionless face and drawn a screen of gossamer across her eyes to hide the void behind. Beneath her bodice her small breasts were smooth at the crest. Below her waist, her hips branched wide, the place prepared for its load of life. But it was the bold and sensual strength of her legs which completely unstrung Mr. Watford. He wanted to grab a hoe and drive her off.

"What it 'tis you want?" he called sharply.

"Mr. Goodman send me."

"Send you for what?" His voice was shrill in the glare.

She moved. Holding a caved-in valise and a pair of white sandals, her head weaving slightly as though she bore a pail of water there or a tray of mangoes, she glided over the stones as if they were smooth ground. Her bland expression did not change, but her eyes, meeting his, held a vague trust. Pausing a few feet away, she curtsied deeply. "I's the new servant."

Only Mr. Watford's cold laugh saved him from anger. As always, it raised him to a height where everything below appeared senseless and insignificant—especially his people, whom the girl embodied. From this height he could even be charitable. And thinking suddenly of how she had waited in the brutal sun since morning without taking shelter under the nearby tamarind tree, he said, not unkindly, "Well, girl, go back and tell Mr. Goodman for me that I don't need no servant."

"I can't go back."

"How you mean can't?" His head gave its angry snap.

"I'll get lashes," she said simply. "My mother say I must work the day and then if you don't wish me, I can come back. But I's not to leave till night falling, if not I get lashes."

He was shaken by her dispassion. So much so that his head dropped from its disdaining angle and his hands twitched with helplessness. Despite anything he might say or do, her fear of the whipping would keep her there until nightfall, the valise and shoes in hand. He felt his day with its order and quiet rhythms threatened by her intrusion—and suddenly waving her off as if she were an evil visitation, he hurried into the kitchen to prepare his meal.

But he paused, confused, in front of the stove, knowing that he could not cook and leave her hungry at the door, nor could he cook and serve her as though he were the servant.

"Yes, please."

They said nothing more. She entered the room with a firm step and an air almost of familiarity, placed her valise and shoes in a corner and went directly to the larder.

For a time Mr. Watford stood by, his muscles flexing with anger and his eyes bounding ahead of her every move, until feeling foolish and frighteningly useless, he went out to feed his doves.

The meal was quickly done and as he ate he heard the dry slap of her feet behind him—a pleasant sound—and then silence. When he glanced back she was squatting in the doorway, the sunlight aslant the absurd hat and her face bent to a bowl she held in one palm. She ate slowly, thoughtfully, as if fixing the taste of each spoonful in her mind.

It was then that he decided to let her work the day and at nightfall to pay her a dollar and dismiss her. His decision held when he returned later from the grove and found tea awaiting him, and then through the supper she prepared. Afterward, dressed in his white uniform, he patiently waited out the day's end on the portico, his face setting into a grim mold. Then just as dusk etched the first dark line between the sea and sky, he took out a dollar and went downstairs.

She was not in the kitchen, but the table was set for his morning tea. Muttering at her persistence, he charged down the corridor, which ran the length of the basement, flinging open the doors to the damp, empty rooms on either side, and sending the lizards and the shadows long entrenched there scuttling to safety.

He found her in the small slanted room under the stoop, asleep on an old cot he kept there, her suitcase turned down beside the bed, and the shoes, dress and the ridiculous hat piled on top. A loose nightshift muted the outline of her body and hid her legs, so that she appeared suddenly defenseless, innocent, with a child's trust in her curled hand and in her deep breathing. Standing in the doorway, with his own breathing snarled and his eyes averted, Mr. Watford felt like an intruder. She had claimed the room. Quivering with frustration, he slowly turned away, vowing that in the morning he would shove the dollar at her and lead her like a cow out of his house. . . .

Dawn brought rain and a hot wind which set the leaves rattling and swiping at the air like distraught arms.

Dressing in the dawn darkness, Mr. Watford again armed himself with the dollar and, with his shoulders at an uncompromising set, plunged downstairs. He descended into the warm smell of bakes and this smell, along with the thought that she had been up before him, made his hand knot with exasperation on the banister. The knot tightened as he saw her, dust swirling at her feet as she swept the corridor, her face bent solemn to the task. Shutting her out with a lifted hand, he shouted, "Don't bother sweeping. Here's a dollar. G'long back."

The broom paused, and although she did not raise her head, he sensed her groping through the shadowy maze of her mind toward his voice. Behind the dollar which he waved in her face, her eyes slowly cleared. And, surprisingly, they held no fear. Only anticipation and a tenuous trust. It was as if she expected him to say something kind.

"G'long back!" His angry cry was a plea.

Like a small, starved flame, her trust and expectancy died and she said, almost with reproof, "The rain falling."

To confirm this, the wind set the rain stinging across the windows and he could say nothing, even though the words sputtered at his lips. It was useless. There was nothing inside her to comprehend that she was not wanted. His shoulders sagged under the weight of her ignorance, and with a futile gesture he swung away, the dollar hanging from his hand like a small sword gone limp.

She became as fixed and familiar a part of the house as the stones—and as silent. He paid her five dollars a week, gave her Mondays off and in the evenings, after a time, even allowed her to sit in the alcove off the parlor, while he read with his back to her, taking no more notice of her than he did the moths on the lamp.

But once, after many silent evenings together, he detected a sound apart from the night murmurs of the sea and village and the metallic tuning of the steel band—a low, almost inhuman, cry of loneliness which chilled him. Frightened, he turned to find her leaning hesitantly toward him, her eyes dark with urgency, and her face tight with bewilderment and a growing anger. He started, not understanding, and her arm lifted to stay him. Eagerly she bent closer. But as she uttered the low cry again, as her fingers described her wish to talk, he jerked around, afraid that she would be foolish enough to speak and that once she did they would be brought close. He would be forced then to acknowledge something about her which he refused to grant; above all, he would be called upon to share a little of himself. Quickly he returned to his newspaper, rustling it to settle the air, and after a time he felt her slowly, bitterly, return to her silence. . . .

Like sand poured in a careful measure from the hand, the weeks flowed down to August, and on the first Monday, August Bank Holiday, Mr. Watford awoke to the sound of the excursion buses leaving the village for the annual outing, their backfire pelleting the dawn calm and the ancient motors protesting the overcrowding. Lying there, listening, he saw with disturbing clarity his mother dressed for an excursion—the white headtie wound above her dark face and her head poised like a dancer's under the heavy outing basket of food. That set of her head had haunted his years, reappearing in the girl as she walked toward him the first day. Aching with the memory, yet annoyed with himself for remembering, he went downstairs.

The girl had already left for the excursion, and although it was her day off, he felt vaguely betrayed by her eagerness to leave him. Somehow it suggested ingratitude. It was as if his doves were suddenly to refuse him their song or his trees their fruit, despite the care he gave them. Some vital past which shaped the simple mosaic of his life seemed suddenly missing. An alien silence curled like coal gas throughout the house. To escape it he remained in the grove all day and, upon his return to the house, dressed with more care than usual, putting on a fresh, starched uniform and solemnly brushing his hair until it lay in a smooth bush above his brow. Leaning close to the mirror, but avoiding his eyes, he cleaned the white rheum at their corners, and afterward pried loose the dirt under his nails.

Unable to read his papers, he went out on the portico to escape the unnatural silence in the house, and stood with his hands clenched on the balustrade and his taut body straining forward. After a long wait he heard the buses return and voices in gay shreds upon the wind. Slowly his hands relaxed, as did his shoulders under the white uniform; for the first time that day his breathing was regular. She would soon come.

But she did not come and dusk bloomed into night, with a fragrant heat and a full moon which made the leaves glint as though touched with frost.

The steel band at the crossroads began the lilting songs of sadness and seduction, and suddenly—like shades roused by the night and the music—images of the girl flitted before Mr. Watford's eyes. He saw her lost amid the carousings in the village, despoiled; he imagined someone like Mr. Goodman clasping her lewdly or tumbling her in the canebrake. His hand rose, trembling, to rid the air of her; he tried to summon his cold laugh. But, somehow, he could not dismiss her as he had always done with everyone else. Instead, he wanted to punish and protect her, to find and lead her back to the house.

As he leaned there, trying not to give way to the desire to go and find her, his fist striking the balustrade to deny his longing, he saw them. The girl first, with the moonlight like a silver patina on her skin, then the boy whom Mr. Goodman sent for the coconuts, whose easy strength and the political button—"The Old Order Shall Pass"—had always mocked and challenged Mr. Watford. They were joined in a tender battle: the boy in a sport shirt riotous with color was reaching for the girl as he leaped and spun, weightless, to the music, while she fended him off with a gesture which was lovely in its promise of surrender. Her protests were little scattered bursts:

"But, man, why don't you stop, nuh . . . ? But, you know, you getting on like a real-real idiot . . ."

Each time she chided him he leaped higher and landed closer, until finally he eluded her arm and caught her by the waist. Boldly he pressed a leg between her tightly closed legs until they opened under his pressure. Their bodies cleaved into one whirling form, and while he sang she laughed like a wanton, with her hat cocked over her ear. Dancing, the stones moiling underfoot, they claimed the night. More than the night. The steel band played for them alone. The trees were their frivolous companions, swaying as they swayed. The moon rode the sky because of them.

Mr. Watford, hidden by a dense shadow, felt the tendons which strung him together suddenly go limp; above all, an obscure belief which, like rare china, he had stored on a high shelf in his mind began to tilt. He sensed the familiar specter which hovered in the night reaching out to embrace him, just as the two in the yard were embracing.

Utterly unstrung, incapable of either speech or action, he stumbled into the house, only to meet there an accusing silence from the clock, which had missed its eight o'clock winding, and his newspapers lying like ruined leaves over the floor.

He lay in bed in the white uniform, waiting for sleep to rescue him, his hands seeking the comforting sound of his doves. But sleep eluded him and instead of the doves, their throats tremulous with sound, his scarred hands filled with the shape of a woman he had once kept: her skin, which had been almost bruising in its softness; the buttocks and breasts spread under his hands to inspire both cruelty and tenderness. His hands closed to softly crush those forms, and the searing thrust of passion, which he had not felt for years, stabbed his dry groin. He imagined the two outside, their passion at a pitch by now, lying together behind the tamarind tree, or perhaps—and he sat up sharply—they had been bold enough to bring their lust into the house. Did he not smell their taint on the air? Restored suddenly, he rushed downstairs. As he reached the corridor, a thread of light beckoned him from her room and he dashed furiously toward it, rehearsing the angry words which would jar their bodies apart. He neared the door, glimpsed her through the small opening, and his step faltered; the words collapsed.

She was seated alone on the cot, tenderly holding the absurd felt hat in her lap, one leg tucked under her while the other trailed down. A white sandal, its strap broken, dangled from the foot and gently knocked the floor as she absently swung her leg. Her dress was twisted around her body—and pinned to the bodice, so that it gathered the cloth between her small breasts, was the political button the boy always wore. She was dreamily fingering it, her mouth shaped by a gentle, ironic smile and her eyes strangely acute and critical. What had transpired on the cot had not only, it seemed, twisted the dress around her, tumbled her hat and broken her sandal, but had also defined her and brought the blurred forms of life into focus for her. There was a woman's force in her aspect now, a tragic knowing and acceptance in her bent head, a hint about her of Cassandra watching the future wheel before her eyes.

Before those eyes which looked to another world, Mr. Watford's anger and strength failed him and he held to the wall for support. Unreasonably, he felt that he should assume some hushed and reverent pose, to bow as she had the day she had come. If he had known their names, he would have pleaded forgiveness for the sins he had committed against her and the others all his life, against himself. If he could have borne the thought, he would have confessed that it had been love, terrible in its demand, which he had

always fled. And that love had been the reason for his return. If he had been honest, he would have whispered—his head bent and a hand shading his eyes—that unlike Mr. Goodman (whom he suddenly envied for his full life) and the boy with his political button (to whom he had lost the girl), he had not been willing to bear the weight of his own responsibility. . . . But all Mr. Watford could admit, clinging there to the wall, was simply that he wanted to live—and that the girl held life within her as surely as she held the hat in her hands. If he could prove himself better than the boy, he could win it. Only then, he dimly knew, would he shake off the pursuer which had given him no rest since birth. Hopefully, he staggered forward, his step cautious and contrite, his hands quivering along the wall.

She did not see or hear him as he pushed the door wider. And for some time he stood there, his shoulders hunched in humility, his skin stripped away to reveal each flaw, his whole self offered in one outstretched hand. Still unaware of him, she swung her leg, and the dangling shoe struck a derisive note. Then, just as he had turned away that evening in the parlor when she had uttered her low call, she turned away now, refusing him.

Mr. Watford's body went slack and then stiffened ominously. He knew that he would have to wrest from her the strength needed to sustain him.

Slamming the door, he cried, his voice cracked and strangled, "What you and him was doing in here? Tell me! I'll not have you bringing nastiness round here. Tell me!"

She did not start. Perhaps she had been aware of him all along and had expected his outburst. Or perhaps his demented eye and the desperation rising from him like a musk filled her with pity instead of fear. Whatever, her benign smile held and her eyes remained abstracted until his hand reached out to fling her back on the cot. Then, frowning, she stood up, wobbling a little on the broken shoe and holding the political button as if it was a new power which would steady and protect her.

With a cruel flick of her arm she struck aside his hand and, in a voice as cruel, halted him. "But you best move and don't come holding onto me, you nasty, pissy old man. That's all you is, despite yuh big house and fancy furnitures and yuh newspapers from America. You ain't people, Mr. Watford, you ain't people!"

And with a look and a lift of her head which made her condemnation final, she placed the hat atop her braids, and turning aside, picked up the valise which had always lain, packed, beside the cot—as if even on the first day she had known that this night would come and had been prepared against it. . . .

Mr. Watford did not see her leave, for a pain squeezed his heart dry and the driven blood was a bright, blinding cataract over his eyes. But his inner eye was suddenly clear. For the first time it gazed mutely upon the waste and pretense which had spanned his years. Flung there against the door by the girl's small blow, his body slowly crumpled under the weariness he had long denied.

He sensed that dark but unsubstantial figure which roamed the nights searching for him wind him in its chill embrace. He struggled against it, his hands clutching the air with the spastic eloquence of a drowning man. He moaned —and the anguished sound reached beyond the room to fill the house. It escaped to the yard and his doves swelled their throats, moaning with him.

—1961

From *Soul Clap Hands and Sing*

We're the Only Colored People Here

Gwendolyn Brooks

WHEN THEY went out to the car there were just the very finest bits of white powder coming down, with an almost comical little ethereal hauteur, to add themselves to the really important, piled-up masses of their kind.

And it wasn't cold.

Maud Martha laughed happily to herself. It was pleasant out, and tonight she and Paul were very close to each other.

He held the door open for her—instead of going on round to the driving side, getting in, and leaving her to get in at her side as best she might. When he took this way of calling her "lady" and informing her of his love she felt precious, protected, delicious. She gave him an excited look of gratitude. He smiled indulgently.

"Want it to be the Owl again?"

"Oh, no, no, Paul. Let's not go there tonight. I feel too good inside for that. Let's go downtown?"

She had to suggest that with a question mark at the end, always. He usually had three protests. Too hard to park. Too much money. Too many white folks. And tonight she could almost certainly expect a no, she feared, because he had come out in his blue work shirt. There was a spot of apricot juice on the collar, too. His shoes were not shined.

. . . But he nodded!

"We've never been to the World Playhouse," she said cautiously. "They have a good picture. I'd feel rich in there."

"You really wanta?"

"Please?"

"Sure."

It wasn't like other movie houses. People from the Studebaker Theatre which, as Maud Martha whispered to Paul, was "all-locked-arms" with the World Playhouse, were strolling up and down the lobby, laughing softly, smoking with gentle grace.

"There must be a play going on in there and this is probably an intermission," Maud Martha whispered again.

"I don't know why you feel you got to whisper," whispered Paul. "Nobody else is whispering in here." He looked around, resentfully, wanting to see a few, just a few colored faces. There were only their own.

Maud Martha laughed a nervous defiant little laugh; and spoke loudly. "There certainly isn't any reason to whisper. Silly, huh."

The strolling women were cleverly gowned. Some of them had flowers or flashers in their hair. They looked—cooked. Well cared-for. And as though they had never seen a roach or a rat in their lives. Or gone without heat for a week. And the men had even edges. They were men, Maud Martha thought, who wouldn't stoop to fret over less than a thousand dollars."

"We're the only colored people here," said Paul.

She hated him a little. "Oh, hell. Who in hell cares?"

"Well, what I want to know is, where do you pay the damn fares?"

"There's the box office. Go on up."

He went on up. It was closed.

"Well," sighed Maud Martha, "I guess the picture has started already. But we can't have missed much. Go on up to that girl at the candy counter and ask her where we should pay our money."

He didn't want to do that. The girl was lovely and blonde and cold-eyed, and her arms were akimbo, and the set of her head was eloquent. No one else was at the counter.

"Well. We'll wait a minute. And see—"

Maud Martha hated him again. Coward. She ought to flounce over to the girl herself—show him up. . . .

The people in the lobby tried to avoid looking curiously at two shy Negroes wanting desperately not to seem shy. The white women looked at the Negro woman in her outfit with which no special fault could be found, but which made them think, somehow, of close rooms, and wee, close lives. They looked at her hair. They were always slightly surprised, but agreeably so, when they did. They supposed it was the hair that had got her that yellowish, good-looking Negro man without a tie.

An usher opened a door of the World Play-house part and ran quickly down the few steps that led from it to the lobby. Paul opened his mouth.

"Say, fella. Where do we get the tickets for the movie?"

The usher glanced at Paul's feet before answering. Then he said coolly, but not unpleasantly, "I'll take the money."

They were able to go in.

And the picture! Maud Martha was so glad that they had not gone to the Owl! Here was technicolor, and the love story was sweet. And there was classical music that silvered its way into you and made your back cold. And the theatre itself! It was no palace, no such Great Shakes as the Tivoli out south, for instance

From *Maud Martha*

(where many colored people went every night). But you felt good sitting there, yes, good, and as if when you left it you would be going home to a sweet-smelling apartment with flowers on little gleaming tables; and wonderful silver on night-blue velvet, in chests; and crackly sheets; and lace spreads on such beds as you saw at Marshall Field's. Instead of back to your kit'n't apt., with the garbage of your floor's families in a big can just outside your door, and the gray sound of little gray feet scratching away from it as you drag up those flights of narrow complaining stairs.

Paul pressed her hand. Paul said, "We oughta do this more often."

And again. "We'll have to do this more often. And go to plays, too. I mean at that Blackstone, and Studebaker."

She pressed back, smiling beautifully to herself in the darkness. Though she knew that once the spell was over it would be a year, two years, more, before he would return to the World Playhouse. And he might never go to a real play. But she was learning to love moments. To love moments for themselves.

When the picture was over, and the lights revealed them for what they were, the Negroes stood up among the furs and good cloth and faint perfume, looked about them eagerly. They hoped they would meet no cruel eyes. They hoped no one would look intruded upon. They had enjoyed the picture so, they were so happy, they wanted to laugh, to say warmly to the other outgoers, "Good, huh? Wasn't it swell?"

This, of course, they could not do. But if only no one would look intruded upon. . . .

—1953

Malcolm X Is Dead

John Oliver Killens

IT WAS a rough, white, hard and ruthless winter in New York town, the kind of winter that kept your nostrils blowing and your eyes forever full of tears. It was a cold, cruel, white winter, especially for Carrie Louise's roommate. It was a winter when Death grimly stalked the land. Carrie Louise could not get over the fact that her roommate, not quite nineteen years old, would go out each morning to the newsstand on Broadway near the subway and buy the *New York Times*, and come back to the dormitory and turn first of all to the obituary page. After she scanned the bad news, she would usually let a sigh of relief ooze out of her.

"Hooray and hallelujah, everybody who's anybody made it through the night." Then to the other pages.

This ritual began sometime in autumn of the time when Death would stalk the winter months. The trouble with Sherry Kingsley, she really knew almost everybody who was "black-and-anybody" in the Arts and in the Movement. First, there was Sam Cooke, whom she had met just once out at Town House Restaurant on Eastern Parkway in her native Brooklyn. She owned every record he ever made. And she was shaken at the news of his "crazy senseless death. Honeychile, it makes no damn sense at all!" And there was Nat Cole at the ripe old age of forty-five! She sat around and played his records one after another, and her eyes filled, and she sat around and swore to herself, "Goddamn! Goddamn!"

She had very little to say to honeychile that winter. She just studied and played her records and swore softly to herself, as Death grimly stalked the earth. Sometimes she gave Carrie

Louise such devastating looks, the girl from 'Sippi felt like crying out: "Please! Please! You know damn well I'm not to blame for deaths! You can't blame white folks for everything bad that happens on this earth. Even so, you can't blame me for being white!"

She thought she heard Sherry mumble to herself one day, "Death is a goddamn white man!"

When Lorraine Hansberry's new play *The Sign in Sidney Brustein's Window* opened, Sherry and Carrie Lou went to opening night. Sherry laughed and wept throughout the entire play. Afterward Sherry took Carrie Lou with her across the street to Mama Leone's restaurant to an opening-night party for *Brustein's Window*. Sherry went up to Lorraine, who was seated at the head of one of the long tables; she was emaciated and racked with pain—lonely-looking in the midst of a crowd of friends and admirers.

Sherry smiled her widest and most beautiful smile in her whole repertoire of smiles. She did not have many smiles to choose from. She was not a dedicated smiler. She threw her arms around Lorraine.

"Oh, darling! Darling Lorraine, it was so lovely! So beautiful! It was poetry! It was Shakespeare—it was Shaw! It was Hansberry!"

Lorraine said, "Lord have mercy! You really liked it, Sherry?"

Sherry shook her head. "Liked it? I didn't like it—I loved it! And I love you!" And she kissed Lorraine and turned away, almost colliding with her roommate standing behind her, red-faced with compassion. She mumbled, "This is my roommate, Carrie Louise Wakefield." And Carrie

Lou took the great young woman's hand and said, "I'm mighty pleased to meet you. I think the play was just wonderful!"

And bleary-eyed, Sherry led Carrie Lou over to a table in a corner of the room where a crowd of people, black and white and brown, were seated, including some of the members of the *Brustein's Window* cast and also including David Woodson. And of course, Sherry knew Woodson. Woodson got up from the table and took Sherry into his arms.

And "Sherry baby! How's the college girl?"

She introduced Carrie Lou to Woodson and the girl from 'Sippi felt her heart beat faster and a weakness in her knees. He made room for them and they sat there talking about the play and about everything else under the sun, with Carrie Lou staring directly into Woodson's mouth; he did not appear to notice, and Sherry, who rarely drank except on special occasions, began to drink herself into forgetfulness. Carrie Lou got drunk off the atmosphere and the conversation, which she thought to be the most brilliant she had ever heard.

Then one cold white morning a few weeks later, Carrie Lou went instead of Sherry over to Broadway and got the paper, and when she returned she scanned the front page and she said aloud almost unknowingly, "Oh no!"

Sherry said, half-jokingly, "Oh yes, honeychile. You don't expect to rule forever, do you? How many registered in 'Sippi this time? Fannie Hammer is my patron saint. Believe me when I say so."

Carrie Lou said, "Lorraine Hansberry!"

Sherry turned toward her, dropped the hairbrush from her hand. "Oh no! I don't want to hear it! Please! Do not read it to me! Do not read it to me!" She sank into a chair and sat as quietly as death itself.

Carrie Lou knew Sherry was trying her best to cry, to wail and moan and let the ocean flood wash away the sorrow in her soul with tears. But Sherry just sat there, numb and dumb.

Finally the tears began to spill quietly down her cheeks. She didn't bother to wipe her eyes or blow her nose. She looked like a little girl lost and scared and lonely. She uttered not a single sound, not a sob; she just sat there, let the tears spill down her cheeks.

Carrie Lou went with her to the funeral up in Harlem at the Church of the Masters. A cold white spell lay all over New York that Saturday. It had snowed all day and night the day before and all that Saturday morning. The church was packed with somber faces. Carrie Lou saw many famous and familiar faces among the honorary pallbearers. Sammy Davis, David Woodson. A soft-spoken minister, Reverend Callender, gave a quiet funeral oration. The great Paul Robeson spoke and Shelley Winters spoke and Ruby Dee, and Nina Simone played the organ. How she played the organ! People were wiping their eyes all over the church, some of them crying openly.

Outside the church, afterward, the snow still came down. Photographers made a nuisance of themselves taking pictures of celebrities who were in attendance. Sherry introduced Carrie Louise to Paul Robeson, Eslanda Robeson, Ossie Davis, Irving Burgie and a tall rangy handsome red-bearded man by the name of Malcolm X. She called him Brother Malcolm.

The next day, which was Sunday, Sherry did not get dressed. She sat around all day and moped and sank deeper and deeper in a kind of morbid torpor of despair and helplessness. Late that afternoon she looked up and stared at Carrie Lou and said deliberately and slowly, "Death is a goddamn white man! Death is a goddamn white man!"

It was a silly thing to do, but Carrie Lou felt that she must somehow come to the defense of white manhood. "Come on, Sherry, I mean, be reasonable. You can't blame death on white folks, you just can't blame the white man for all the evil on this earth."

It was the bitterest look she had ever seen on Sherry's face. "Well now, honeychile, just like who has been responsible for centuries for the mass murders of mankind? I mean who killed six million Jews? I mean who killed sixty million blacks? I mean who dropped the bombs on Hiroshima and Nagasaki? Who is it spending billions for mass murder and trips to the moon while millions of humans starve all over the earth and others die of cancer?"

Carrie Lou's face reddened like a ripe pomegranate and then turned white as biscuit dough. "But you can't lump—I mean, collective guilt—I mean—"

Sherry's staring at her now was like spitting in her face. She could almost feel the spittle. "I'll tell you what I mean. I mean you white folk have the stench of death all over you."

Then a few weeks later the world stood still. It was a Sunday afternoon, and Sherry had gone to a meeting up at the northern tip of Harlem. She went almost every Sunday afternoon. Carrie Lou had asked her once or twice if she might go along with her. And Sherry's answer had been unequivocal.

"I really think you'd better not." Unemotionally. Just—"I really think you'd better not. I mean, I've tried to expose you to as much blackness as your white soul could absorb, but this would be a little too rich for your blood. I mean, this one is for black folks only."

About three-fifteen that February afternoon, the girl from Wakefield lay on her bed with a book in her lap, listening to music over the radio and staring at the words in the book, seeing nothing.

The girl was miles and miles away from where she was, in the sweet and crazy land of her daydreams. Then it happened.

> We interrupt this program to bring you an important announcement. Black Nationalist leader Malcolm X has just been shot down while he spoke to a group of faithfuls at the Audubon Ballroom in upper Manhattan. It isn't clear yet how serious the wounds are. Stay close to this station for further developments.

She dropped the book and jumped from the bed. She had shaken his hand just two or three weeks ago at Lorraine Hansberry's funeral. She felt a great overwhelming helplessness. And she quaked all over as she remembered that Sherry was at the meeting at the Audubon. She went every Sunday. And Sherry loved Malcolm. Loved him selfishly and selflessly and completely, holding nothing back. Well, maybe, the girl from 'Sippi thought, maybe it isn't serious. Surely it isn't serious. It couldn't possibly be fatal. Malcolm exuded such a sense of indestructibility. She'd felt it when she'd met him at the funeral.

Then the music was interrupted and the flash came that would change the world.

MALCOLM X IS DEAD! MALCOLM X IS DEAD!

Her eyes filled up. It could not be, and yet deep inside of her she knew it was. It was! And always would henceforth and forever be. He was dead.

SHOT DOWN BY BLACK ASSASSINS, ALLEGEDLY MUSLIMS . . .

She was ashamed of the relief she felt that they were black men, the assassins. They were non-white. She was glad they were non-white. The news kept coming every other minute.

THIRTY-TWO BULLETS ENTERED HIS BODY.

She stared at the radio in a hypnotic state of disbelief. Surely it was a dream, a nightmare, and she would wake up after a while and later Sherry would come in and tell her about the meeting and how handsome Malcolm was and how manly and how he was the hope of black America, which was the hope of all America, all humankind. But she knew she was not dreaming. The finality of the statement.

It was as if the radio itself had murdered him. Once announced dead, he was dead forevermore. Eternally dead everlastingly. There was no appeal from death pronounced by radio.

When Sherry came in a few hours later, she was calm, as if nothing had happened at all of a catastrophic nature, as if the sky had not fallen in on her. She said, "Hi, honeychile," and she got into her pajamas. And she got a book and she clicked on her desk lamp, as if she were going to dig for the night into some intensive concentration.

She read for almost an hour. Then she looked up briefly and said to no one in particular, "Book larnin', that's the only salvation for the nigrah." Bitterly. And she looked down at her book again.

There was another spell of silence in their room, a brief spell that seemed like hours to Carrie Lou.

Then she said softly, tenderly, "But, Sherry, I mean, didn't you go to the meeting today? I mean, don't you know—" Her words hung in mid-air and no more words would issue forth from her.

Sherry looked up from her book and turned toward her roommate, her large eyes widening more than ever, like a little frightened girl lost in the Mississippi jungles. She stared at Carrie Lou. "Why don't you keep your damn mouth shut?" And the dam broke loose and the so-called tough one disassembled.

All that had been building up that day, those months, those years, everything in flood tide now. She stood up from her chair. "He's dead! He's dead! The last man on earth is dead! The last man in this land is gone! Everything is dead and dying! Malcolm's gone! Malcolm's gone!"

Carrie Lou stood up as Sherry walked toward her, and Carrie Lou put her arms around her as Sherry came up to her, but Sherry shoved her violently clear across the room and went and fell upon her bed and cried as if it were the last day on this earth.

"He was the very last angry man!" she sobbed. "He was the last man in this land of queers!" She sat up and looked up into the girl from 'Sippi's frightened face. "Don't you understand? He was the last black hope. He was the last hope that black folk could achieve manhood."

She fell on the bed again and cried and laughed and blurted out words interchangeably. "They killed black manhood! Killed black manhood!" Crying, laughing, sobbing. "He was the last man!" She mumbled, "Where is Robeson? Where is Robeson?" She sobbed, she blurted, "What's to become of black folk? What's to become of black folk?"

Every time this tough sophisticated New York lady screamed now, Carrie Lou's belly did a flip-flop. She felt an overwhelming compassion and she went and sat beside the girl and lifted her to a sitting position and put her arms around her, and Sherry could resist her arms no longer. She turned and wept unashamedly in Carrie Lou's arms, as Carrie Lou massaged her shoulders and ran her hand through her short-cropped hair. Girls, hearing the screaming, gathered in the doorway of Carrie Lou's and Sherry's room.

One of them asked, "What's the matter with Sherry, Carrie Lou?"

Sherry stared up at them. "Get out of my room, you murdering bitches! You bloodthirsty bastards!"

Carrie Lou was frightened. She felt her own eyes filling up. "But, darling, the radio said Negroes killed him."

"Yes," Sherry said, almost quietly. "The miserable black contemptible bastards, they did their masters' bidding." The hysteria was almost absent from her voice now, replaced by a tone even more frightening in its quiet understatement. "The poor ignorant sons-of-bitches killed their black Messiah, the only one who could have saved us from our miserable existence. The only one who could have saved America."

Off and on, she cried for more than three weeks, and despite her growing hostility to whiteness (she even loathed the winter snow), she and Carrie Lou drew closer together, even against Sherry's own volition. Sherry was like a person nearing seventy years of age or thereabouts, who had lived a life of waste and felt dear time slipping from her grasp and felt Death's cold white breath panting wildly on her neck. She talked continuously about death and dying. Between Lorraine and Malcolm, another dear friend had died. Lively, vivacious, beautiful Beverly Robinson. Sherry got into a habit of talking to herself.

"I know I'm going to die at a very early age. I'll never see twenty-seven. Something or somebody will strike me down. I know it; I feel it in the very marrow of my bones."

Then one day she came into their room and sat down on her bed and started to cry again. "Malcolm! Malcolm! Brother Malcolm!" She uttered the name reverently, tenderly, helplessly. "Will to us some of your anger, dear Brother Malcolm. And your great strength."

Carrie Lou came and sat beside her and put her arm around her shoulders. She was smiling through her tears now. Sherry was. "He was so beautiful, you know. So manful. An anachronism in this age of fashionable objectivity and cynicism and faggotism. A knight in shining armor. He was a charmer. All the image of him created by the American press and TV was entirely false, deliberately false. He didn't hate white folks, he loved black folks. And that was what was revolutionary about him. He loved black folks. And that's where he was so far ahead of most of the so-called militant colored leaders and writers and artists who expend so much energy hurling dirty words at white folks, whipping sick white folks on their asses with wet towels. Either that, or talking to white folks endlessly about the degradation of the black man. But Malcolm loved black people; he believed their salvation was in their own hands. Therefore he talked directly to them. That's why they ordered his assassination. He's gone now. And

From *'Sippi*

black folks are defenseless. Brother Malcolm was our lover. Our one true only love."

She started to weep again now, silently. She said, "I'm sorry you didn't meet him, honeychile. He was so beautiful."

Carrie Lou said, "But I met him. You introduced us."

Sherry repeated, "I'm really sorry you didn't get a chance to meet him."

And Sherry broke down into weeping again, quiet weeping. And the girl from 'Sippi found herself weeping softly now, as they wept unashamedly in each other's arms.

Because a man had died.

—1967

Journey to Atlanta

James Baldwin

THE PROGRESSIVE PARTY has not, so far as I can gather, made any very great impression in Harlem, and this is not so much despite as because of its campaign promises, promises rather too extravagant to be believed. It is considered a rather cheerful axiom that all Americans distrust politicians. (No one takes the further and less cheerful step of considering just what effect this mutual contempt has on either the public or the politicians, who have, indeed, very little to do with one another.) Of all Americans, Negroes distrust politicians most, or, more accurately, they have been best trained to expect nothing from them; more than other Americans, they are always aware of the enormous gap between election promises and their daily lives. It is true that the promises excite them, but this is not because they are taken as proof of good intentions. They are the proof of something more concrete than intentions: that the Negro situation is not static, that changes have occurred, and are occurring and will occur—this, in spite of the daily, dead-end monotony. It is this daily, dead-end monotony, though, as well as the wise desire not to be betrayed by too much hoping, which causes them to look on politicians with such an extraordinarily disenchanted eye.

This fatalistic indifference is something that drives the optimistic American liberal quite mad; he is prone, in his more exasperated moments, to refer to Negroes as political children, an appellation not entirely just. Negro liberals, being consulted, assure us that this is something that will disappear with "education," a vast, all-purpose term, conjuring up visions of sunlit housing projects, stacks of copybooks and a race

of well-soaped, dark-skinned people who never slur their r's. Actually, this is not so much political irresponsibility as the product of experience, experience which no amount of education can quite efface. It is, as much as anything else, the reason the Negro vote is so easily bought and sold, the reason for that exclamation heard so frequently on Sugar Hill: "Our people never get anywhere."

"Our people" have functioned in this country for nearly a century as political weapons, the trump card up the enemies' sleeve; anything promised Negroes at election time is also a threat leveled at the opposition; in the struggle for mastery the Negro is the pawn. It is inescapable that this is only possible because of his position in this country and it has very frequently seemed at least equally apparent that this is a position which no one, least of all the politician, seriously intended to change.

Since Negroes have been in this country their one major, devastating gain was their emancipation, an emancipation no one regards any more as having been dictated by humanitarian impulses. All that has followed from that brings to mind the rather unfortunate image of bones thrown to a pack of dogs sufficiently hungry to be dangerous. If all this sounds rather deliberately grim, it is not through any wish to make the picture darker than it is; I would merely like to complete the picture usually presented by pointing out that no matter how many instances there have been of genuine concern and goodwill, nor how many hard, honest struggles have been carried on to improve the position of the Negro people, their position has not, in fact, changed so far as most of them are concerned.

Sociologists and historians, having the historical perspective in mind, may conclude that we are moving toward ever-greater democracy; but this is beyond the ken of a Negro growing up in any one of this country's ghettos. As regards Negro politicians, they are considered with pride as *politicians*, a pride much akin to that felt concerning Marian Anderson or Joe Louis: they have proven the worth of the Negro people and in terms, American terms, which no one can negate. But as no housewife expects Marian Anderson's genius to be of any practical aid in her dealings with the landlord, so nothing is expected of Negro representatives. The terrible thing, and here we have an American phenomenon in relief, is the fact that the Negro representative, by virtue of his position, is ever more removed from the people he ostensibly serves. Moreover, irrespective of personal integrity, his position—neatly and often painfully paradoxical —is utterly dependent on the continuing debasement of fourteen million Negroes; should the national ideals be put into practice tomorrow, countless prominent Negroes would lose their *raison d'être*.

Finally, we are confronted with the psychology and tradition of the country; if the Negro vote is so easily bought and sold, it is because it has been treated with so little respect; since no Negro dares seriously assume that any politician is concerned with the fate of Negroes, or would do much about it if he had the power, the vote must be bartered for what it will get, for whatever short-term goals can be managed. These goals are mainly economic and frequently personal, sometimes pathetic: bread or a new roof or five dollars, or, continuing up the scale, schools, houses or more Negroes in hitherto Caucasian jobs. The American commonwealth chooses to overlook what Negroes are never able to forget: they are not *really* considered a part of it. Like Aziz in *A Passage to India* or Topsy in *Uncle Tom's Cabin*, they know that white people, whatever their love for justice, have no love for them.

This is the crux of the matter; and the Progressive party, with its extravagant claims, has, therefore, imposed on itself the considerable burden of proof. The only party within recent memory which made equally strident claims of fellowship were the Communists, who failed to survive this test; and the only politician of similar claims was, of course, Wallace's erstwhile master, Roosevelt, who did not after all, now that the magic of his voice is gone, succeed in raising the darker brother to the status of a citizen. This is the ancestry of the Wallace party, and it does not work wholly in its favor. It operates to give pause to even the most desperate and the most gullible.

It is, however, considered on one level, the level of short-term goals, with approval, since it does afford temporary work for Negroes, particularly those associated in any manner with the arts. The rather flippant question on 125th Street now is: "So? You working for Mr. Wallace these days?" For at least there is that: entertainers, personalities are in demand. To forestall lawsuits, I must explain that I am not discussing "names" —who are in rather a different position, too touchy and complex to analyze here—but the unknown, the struggling, endless armies of Negro boys and girls bent on, and as yet very far from, recognition. A segment of this army, a quartet called the Melodeers, made a trip to Atlanta under the auspices of the Progressive party in August, a trip which lasted about eighteen days and which left them with no love for Mr. Wallace. Since this quartet included two of my brothers, I was given the details of the trip; indeed, David, the younger, kept a sort of journal for me—literally a blow-by-blow account.

Harlem is filled with churches and on Sundays it gives the impression of being filled with music. Quartets such as my brothers' travel from church to church in the fashion of circuit preachers, singing as much for the love of singing and the need for practice as for the rather indifferent sums collected for them which are then divided. These quartets have "battles of song," the winning team adding, of course, immensely to its prestige, the most consistent winners being the giants in this field. The aim of all these quartets, of course, is to branch out, to hit the big time and sing for a livelihood. The Golden Gate Quartet, judging at least from its music, had its roots here, and out of such a background came Sister Rosetta Tharpe, whom I heard, not quite ten years ago, plunking a guitar in a storefront church on Fifth Avenue. The Melodeers have not been singing very long and are very far from well known, and the invitation to sing on tour with the Wallace party in the South seemed, whatever their misgivings about the Mason-Dixon line, too good an opportunity to pass up.

This invitation, by the way, seems to have been the brainstorm of a Clarence Warde, a Negro merchant seaman once employed as a cottage father in a corrective institution upstate; it was he in New York who acted as a go-between, arranging, since the Melodeers are minors, to be their legal guardian and manager on the road. An extended tour, such as was planned, met with some opposition from the parents, an opposition countered by the possible long-term benefits of the tour in so far as the boys' careers were concerned and, even more urgently, by the assurance that, at the very least, the boys would come home with a considerably larger sum of money than any of them were making on their jobs. (The political implications do not seem to have carried much weight.) A series of churches had been lined up for them presumably throughout the South. "The understanding," writes David, "was that we were supposed to sing"; after which the party was to take over to make speeches and circulate petitions. "The arrangement," David notes laconically, "sounded very promising, so we decided to go."

And, indeed, they traveled South in splendor, in a Pullman, to be exact, in which, since what David describes as a "Southern gentleman and wife" took exception to their presence, they traveled alone.

At the Wallace headquarters in Atlanta they were introduced to a Mrs. Branson Price, a gray-haired white woman of incurably aristocratic leanings who seems to have been the directress of the party in that region. The graciousness of her reception was only slightly marred by the fact that she was not expecting singers and thought they were a new group of canvassers. She arranged for them to take rooms on Butler Street at the YMCA. Here the first gap between promise and performance was made manifest, a gap, they felt, which was perhaps too trifling to make

a fuss about. In New York they had been promised comparative privacy, two to a room; but now, it developed, they were to sleep in a dormitory. This gap, in fact, it was the province of Mr. Warde to close, but whether he was simply weary from the trip or overwhelmed by the aristocratic Mrs. Price, he kept his mouth shut and, indeed, did not open it again for quite some time.

When they returned to headquarters, somewhat irritated at having had to wait three hours for the arrival of Louis Burner, who had the money for their rooms, Mrs. Price suggested that they go out canvassing. This was wholly unexpected, since no one had mentioned canvassing in New York and, since, moreover, canvassers are voluntary workers who are not paid. Further, the oldest of them was twenty, which was not voting age, and none of them knew anything about the Progressive party, nor did they care much. On the other hand, it is somewhat difficult to refuse a gray-haired, aristocratic lady who is toiling day and night for the benefit of your people; and Mr. Warde, who should have been their spokesman, had not yet recovered his voice; so they took the petitions, which were meant to put the Wallace party on the ballot, and began knocking on doors in the Negro section of Atlanta. They were sent out in pairs, white and black, a political device which operates not only as the living proof of brotherhood, but which has the additional virtue of intimidating into passive silence the more susceptible beholder, who cannot, after all, unleash the impatient scorn he may feel with a strange, benevolent white man sitting in his parlor.

They canvassed for three days, during which time their expenses—$2.25 per man per day—were paid, but during which time they were doing no singing and making no money. On the third day they pointed out that this was not quite what they had been promised in New York, to be met with another suggestion from the invincible Mrs. Price: how would they like to sing on the sound-truck? They had not the faintest desire to sing on a sound-truck, especially when they had been promised a string of churches; however, the churches, along with Mr. Warde's vigor, seemed unavailable at the moment; they could hardly sit around Atlanta doing nothing; and so long as they worked with the party they were certain, at least, to be fed. "The purpose of our singing," David writes, "was to draw a crowd so the party could make speeches." Near the end of the singing and during the speeches, leaflets and petitions were circulated through the crowd.

David had not found Negroes in the South different in any important respect from Negroes in the North; except that many of them were distrustful and "they are always talking about the North; they have to let you know they know somebody in New York or Chicago or Detroit." Of the crowds that gathered—and, apparently, the Melodeers attracted great numbers—"Many of these people couldn't read or write their names" and not many of them knew anything at all about the Progressive party. But they did divine, as American Negroes must, what was expected of them; and they listened to the speeches and signed the petitions.

Becoming both desperate and impatient, the Melodeers began making engagements and singing on their own, stealing time from canvassing to rehearse. They made more appointments than they were able to keep; partly because the lack of money limited their mobility but also because the party, discovering these clandestine appointments, moved in, demanding to be heard. Those churches which refused to make room for the party were not allowed to hear the quartet, which thus lost its last hope of making any money. The quartet wondered what had happened to Mr. Warde. David's account all but ignores him until nearly the end of the trip, when his position during all this is perhaps given some illumination.

Things now began to go steadily worse. They got into an argument with the manager of the Y, who objected to their rehearsing, and moved to a private home, for which the party paid seventy-five cents per man per day; and the party, which was, one gathers, furiously retrenching, arranged for them to eat at Fraziers' Cafe, a Negro establishment on Hunter Street, for $1.25 per man per day. My correspondent notes that they had no choice of meals—"They served us what they liked"—which seems to have been mainly limp vegetables—and "We were as hungry when we walked out as we were when we walked in." On the other hand, they were allowed to choose their beverage: tea or coffee or soda pop.

Heaven only knows what prompted Mrs. Branson Price to give a party at this point. Perhaps the campaign was going extraordinarily well; perhaps Fraziers' Cafe, where the party was held, was in need of a little extra revenue as well as the knowledge that its adoption of the party would help to bring about a better world; perhaps Mrs. Price merely longed to be a gracious hostess once again. In any case, on a Sunday night she gave a party to which everyone was invited. My brother, who at this point was much concerned with food, observed glumly, "We had ice-cream."

The quartet sat at a table by itself, robbed, however, of the presence of Mr. Warde, who was invited to sit at Mrs. Price's table: "She said it would be an honor," my correspondent notes, failing, however, to say for whom. "There was a man there called a *folk*-singer," says David with venom, "and, naturally, everybody had to hear some *folk* songs." Eventually, the folksy aspect of the evening was exhausted and the quartet was invited to sing. They sang four selections, apparently to everyone's delight for they had to be quite adamant about not singing a fifth. The strain of continual singing in the open air had done their voices no good and it had made one of them extremely hoarse. So they refused, over loud protests, and apologized. "This displeased Mrs. Price."

Indeed, it had. She was not in the least accustomed to having her suggestions, to say nothing of her requests, refused. Early Monday morning she called Mr. Warde to her office to inquire who those black boys thought they were, and determined to ship them all back that same day in a car. Mr. Warde, who, considering the honors of the evening before, must have been rather astounded, protested such treatment, to be warned that she might very well ship them off without a car; the six of them might very well be forced to take to the road. This is not a pleasant mode of traveling for a Negro in the North and no Negro in Atlanta, particularly no Northern Negro, is likely to get very far. Mr. Warde temporized: they could not leave on such short notice; for one thing, the boys had clothes at the cleaners which would not be ready for a while and which they could hardly afford to lose. Mrs. Price, every aristocratic vein pounding, did not wish to be concerned with such plebeian matters and, finally, losing all patience, commanded Mr. Warde to leave her office: Had he forgotten that he was in Georgia? Didn't he know better than sit in a white woman's office?

Mr. Warde, in whose bowels last night's bread of fellowship must have acquired the weight of rock, left the office. Then the quartet attempted to secure an audience: to be met with implacable refusal and the threat of the police. There were, incidentally, according to my brother, five Negro policemen in Atlanta at this time, who, though they were not allowed to arrest whites, would, of course, be willing, indeed, in their position, anxious, to arrest any Negro who seemed to need it. In Harlem, Negro policemen are feared even more than whites, for they have more to prove and fewer ways to prove it. The prospect of being arrested in Atlanta made them a little dizzy with terror: what might mean a beating in Harlem might quite possibly mean death here. "And at the same time," David says, "it was funny"; by which he means that the five policemen were faint prophecies of that equality which is the Progressive party's goal.

They did not see Mrs. Price again; this was their severance from the party, which now refused to pay any expenses; it was only the fact that their rent had been paid in advance which kept them off the streets. Food, however, remained a problem. Mr. Warde brought them a "couple of loaves of bread" and some jam; they sang one engagement. During this week Mrs. Price relented enough to get their clothes from the cleaners and send Mr. Warde, in custody of a white man who had been at the party, to the bus station for tickets. This man, whose resemblance to the Southern Gentleman of the Pullman is in no way diminished by his allegiance to Mr. Wallace, bought the tickets and threw them on the ground at Mr. Warde's feet, advising him not to show his black face in Georgia again.

The quartet, meanwhile, had gotten together six dollars doing odd jobs, which was enough, perhaps, for three of them to eat on the road. They split up, three leaving that Friday and the other two staying on about ten days longer, working for a construction company. Mr. Warde stopped off to visit his family, promising to see the Melodeers in New York, but he had not arrived as this was being written. The Melodeers laugh about their trip now, that good-natured, hearty laughter which is, according to white men, the peculiar heritage of Negroes, Negroes who were born with the fortunate ability to laugh all their troubles away. Somewhat surprisingly, they are not particularly bitter toward the Progressive party, though they can scarcely be numbered among its supporters. "They're all the same," David tells me, "ain't none of 'em gonna do you no good; if you gonna be foolish enough to believe what they say, then it serves you good and right. Ain't none of 'em gonna do a thing for *me*."

—1948

Gwendolyn Brooks

Bronzeville Man with a Belt in the Back

IN such an armor he may rise and raid
The dark cave after midnight, unafraid,
And slice the shadows with his able sword
Of good broad nonchalance, hashing them down.

And come out and accept the gasping crowd,
Shake off the praises with an airiness.
And, searching, see love shining in an eye,
But never smile.

In such an armor he cannot be slain.
—1944

Hunchback Girl: She Thinks of Heaven

MY Father, it is surely a blue place
And straight. Right. Regular. Where I shall find
No need for scholarly nonchalance or looks
A little to the left or guards upon the
Heart to halt love that runs without crookedness
Along its crooked corridors. My Father,
It is a planned place surely. Out of coils,
Unscrewed, released, no more to be marvelous,
I shall walk straightly through most proper halls
Proper myself, princess of properness.
—1944

Piano after War

ON a snug evening I shall watch her fingers,
Cleverly ringed, declining to clever pink,
Beg glory from the willing keys. Old hungers
Will break their coffins, rise to eat and thank.
And music, warily, like the golden rose
That sometimes after sunset warms the west,
Will warm that room, persuasively suffuse
That room and me, rejuvenate a past.

But suddenly, across my climbing fever
Of proud delight—a multiplying cry.
A cry of bitter dead men who will never
Attend a gentle maker of musical joy.
Then my thawed eye will go again to ice.
And stone will shove the softness from my face.
—1944

The Bean Eaters

THEY eat beans mostly, this old yellow pair.
Dinner is a casual affair.
Plain chipware on a plain and creaking wood,
Tin flatware.

Two who are Mostly Good.
Two who have lived their day,
But keep on putting on their clothes
And putting things away.

And remembering . . .
Remembering, with twinklings and twinges,
As they lean over the beans in their rented back
    room that is full of beads and receipts and dolls
    and cloths, tobacco crumbs, vases and fringes.
—1959

We Real Cool
(The Pool Players Seven at the Golden Shovel)

WE real cool. We
Left school. We

Lurk late. We
Strike straight. We

Sing sin. We
Thin gin. We

Jazz June. We
Die soon.
—1959

Melvin B. Tolson

A Hamlet Rives Us

I saw him faltering toward me in the street:
His eyes emptied of living, his grief unshed.
Pain pitted my heart and meshed my doubtful feet,
As memory's alcove revealed his loved one dead.

Our sorrows mated then, for I had lost
The next of kin in the fogland of the year.
And yet a Hamlet rives us when the frost
Of death comes like a specter buccaneer.

I must console him in this awful hour:
It is the wise and decent thing to do.
Embarrassed, helpless, I was thieved of power
To utter the tags tragedy ordained untrue.

My friend passed by, unseeing in his grief;
And the lash of conscience gave me sweet relief.

—1944

Fenton Johnson

The Banjo Player

THERE is music in me, the music of a peasant people.
I wander through the levee, picking my banjo and
singing my songs of the cabin and the field. At
the Last Chance Saloon I am as welcome as the
violets in March; there is always food and drink
for me there, and the dimes of those who love
honest music. Behind the railroad tracks the
little children clap their hands and love me as
they love Kris Kringle.
But I fear that I am a failure. Last night a woman
called me a troubadour. What is a troubadour?

—1930

The Old Repair Man

GOD is the Old Repair Man.
When we are junk in Nature's storehouse he takes us
apart.
What is good he lays aside; he might use it some day.
What has decayed he buries in six feet of sod to
nurture the weeds.
Those we leave behind moisten the sod with their
tears;
But their eyes are blind as to where he has placed
the good.

Some day the Old Repair Man
Will take the good from its secret place
And with his gentle, strong hands will mold
A more enduring work—a work that will defy
Nature—
And we will laugh at the old days, the troubled days,
When we were but a crude piece of craftsmanship,
When we were but an experiment in Nature's
laboratory . . .
It is good we have the Old Repair Man.

—1949

Gwendolyn B. Bennett

Sonnet I

HE came in silvern armor, trimmed with black—
A lover come from legends long ago—
With silver spurs and silken plumes a-blow,
And flashing sword caught fast and buckled back
In a carven sheath of Tamarack.
He came with footsteps beautifully slow,
And spoke in voice meticulously low.
He came and Romance followed in his track . . .

I did not ask his name—I thought him Love;
I did not care to see his hidden face.
All life seemed born in my intaken breath;
All thought seemed flown like some forgotten dove.
He bent to kiss and raised his visor's lace . . .
All eager-lipped I kissed the mouth of Death.

—1949

Sonnet II

SOME things are very dear to me—
Such things as flowers bathed by rain
Or patterns traced upon the sea
Or crocuses where snow has lain . . .
The iridescence of a gem,
The moon's cool opalescent light,
Azaleas and the scent of them,
And honeysuckles in the night.
And many sounds are also dear—
Like winds that sing among the trees,
Or crickets calling from the weir,
Or Negroes humming melodies.
But dearer far than all surmise
Are sudden teardrops in your eyes.

—1949

Margaret Walker

For My People

FOR my people everywhere singing their slave songs
    repeatedly: their dirges and their ditties and their
    blues and jubilees, praying their prayers nightly
    to an unknown god, bending their knees humbly
    to an unseen power;

For my people lending their strength to the years: to
    the gone years and the now years and the maybe
    years, washing ironing cooking scrubbing sewing
    mending hoeing plowing digging planting prun-
    ing patching dragging along never gaining never
    reaping never knowing and never understanding;

For my playmates in the clay and dust and sand of
    Alabama backyards playing baptizing and
    preaching and doctor and jail and soldier and
    school and mama and cooking and playhouse
    and concert and store and hair and Miss
    Choomby and company;

For the cramped bewildered years we went to school
    to learn to know the reasons why and the an-
    swers to and the people who and the places
    where and the days when, in memory of the
    bitter hours when we discovered we were black
    and poor and small and different and nobody
    wondered and nobody understood;

For the boys and girls who grew in spite of these
    things to be man and woman, to laugh and dance
    and sing and play and drink their wine and re-
    ligion and success, to marry their playmates and
    bear children and then die of consumption and
    anemia and lynching;

For my people thronging 47th Street in Chicago and
    Lenox Avenue in New York and Rampart Street
    in New Orleans, lost disinherited dispossessed
    and HAPPY people filling the cabarets and tav-
    erns and other people's pockets needing bread
    and shoes and milk and land and money and
    Something—Something all our own;

For my people walking blindly, spreading joy, losing
    time being lazy, sleeping when hungry, shouting
    when burdened, drinking when hopeless, tied
    and shackled and tangled among ourselves by
    the unseen creatures who tower over us omni-
    sciently and laugh;

For my people blundering and groping and flounder-
    ing in the dark of churches and schools and
    clubs and societies, associations and councils
    and committees and conventions, distressed and
    disturbed and deceived and devoured by money-
    hungry glory-craving leeches, preyed on by
    facile force of state and fad and novelty by false
    prophet and holy believer;

For my people standing staring trying to fashion a
    better way from confusion from hypocrisy and
    misunderstanding, trying to fashion a world that
    will hold all the people all the faces all the adams
    and eves and their countless generations;

Let a new earth rise. Let another world be born. Let
    a bloody peace be written in the sky. Let a
    second generation full of courage issue forth, let
    a people loving freedom come to growth, let a
    beauty full of healing and a strength of final
    clenching be the pulsing in our spirits and our
    blood. Let the martial songs be written, let the
    dirges disappear. Let a race of men now rise
    and take control!

                                                    1937

Margaret Danner

I'll Walk the Tightrope

I'LL walk the tightrope that's been stretched for me,
And though a wrinkled forehead, perplexed why,
Will accompany me, I'll delicately
Step along. For if I stop to sigh
At the earth-propped stride
Of others, I will fall. I must balance high
Without a parasol to tide
A faltering step, without a net below,
Without a balance stick to guide.

                                                    —1967

Robert Hayden

The Rabbi

WHERE I grew up, I used to see
the rabbi, dour and pale
in religion's mourner clothes,
walking to the synagogue.

Once there, did he put on
sackcloth and ashes? Wail?
He would not let me in to see
the gold menorah burning.

Mazuzah, Pesach, Chanukah—
these were timbred words I learned,
were things I knew by glimpses.
And I learned *schwartze* too

And *schnapps*, which *schwartzes* bought
on credit from "Jew Baby."
Tippling ironists laughed and said
he'd soon be rich as Rothschild

From their swinish Saturdays.
Hirschel and Molly and I meanwhile
divvied halveh, polly seeds,
were spies and owls and Fu Manchu.

But the synagogue became
New Calvary.
The rabbi bore my friends off
in his prayer shawl.

—1966

Frederick Douglass

WHEN it is finally ours, this freedom, this liberty, this
    beautiful
and terrible thing, needful to man as air,
usable as earth; when it belongs at last to all,
when it is truly instinct, brain matter, diastole, systole,
reflex action; when it is finally won; when it is more
than the gaudy mumbo jumbo of politicians:
this man, this Douglass, this former slave, this Negro
beaten to his knees, exiled, visioning a world
where none is lonely, none hunted, alien,
this man, superb in love and logic, this man
shall be remembered. Oh, not with statues' rhetoric,
not with legends and poems and wreaths of bronze
    alone,
but with the lives grown out of his life, the lives
fleshing his dream of the beautiful, needful thing.

—1949

Samuel Allen

A Moment Please

W hen I gaze at the sun
    I walked to the subway booth
    for change for a dime.
and know that this great earth
    Two adolescent girls stood there
    alive with eagerness to know
is but a fragment from it thrown
    all in their new found world
    there was for them to know
in heat and flame a billion years ago,
    they looked at me and brightly asked
    "Are you Arabian?"
that then this world was lifeless
    I smiled and cautiously
    —for one grows cautious—
    shook my head.
as, a billion hence,
    "Egyptian?"
it shall again be,
    Again I smiled and shook my head
    and walked away.
what moment is it that I am betrayed,
    I've gone but seven paces now
oppressed, cast down,
    and from behind comes swift the sneer
or warm with love or triumph?
    "Or Nigger?"

    A moment, please
What is it that to fury I am roused?
    for still it takes a moment
What meaning for me
    and now
in this homeless clan
    I'll turn
the dupe of space,
    and smile
the toy of time?
    and nod my head.

—1963

A New Surge in Literature

Allan Morrison

OUT OF the Negro revolt a racial renaissance in the arts is slowly taking place. An embattled younger generation of black artists is emerging, their talent and convictions giving momentum to a clearly definable movement. Triggered by injustice, younger Negroes find expression for their anger in various fine and popular arts. Although the status of Negroes in the arts pretty much reflects the Negro's position in the general society —the pains of discrimination being many—it is a status, nevertheless, that is improving perceptibly.

The past decade, full of the fury and turmoil which accompany any revolution, has demonstrated more vividly than any other era that the frustrations which plagued Negro artists in the past needn't be considered inevitable any longer. Today, as in the past, Negro voices of dissent and discontent are more numerous in literature than in the other art forms. The turbulence produced by the civil rights upsurge, coupled with the rise of the Black Power philosophy, has moved a number of talented young writers to record strong feelings with considerable passion.

In the literary footsteps of a group that includes Paule Marshall, William Melvin Kelley, the late Frank London Brown, Ronald Fair and the explosive LeRoi Jones, the new group asserts itself in the novel, poem, essay, and in short stories. They are inspired by their progenitors (and some say they are even more angry), as indeed those same progenitors were inspired by Wright, Ellison and Baldwin.

The current crop of young writers includes many as yet unpublished talents, like twenty-three-year-old Alice Walker, a graduate of Sarah Lawrence College. Georgia-born Miss Walker has written a number of highly praised short stories and is now finishing her first book, a volume of short stories.

One member of the new literati, Lindsay Patterson, takes exception to the claims of progress. "There are no opportunities for the young Negro writer now," he insists. "The John Hay Whitney Fellowships are no longer given to writers. All of us cannot compete with white writers. There are writers who need nourishing, and there are very few sources of encouragement. Young Negro writers lack a forum where they can express themselves. We need a place to be nurtured. The average white writer has a cultural head start on the Negro. Negro writers have to learn to put their cultural background in the right perspective. That takes time, and time means money. It takes time for any writer to mature." Patterson, who has published short stories, is working on a first novel. *Anthology of the American Negro in the Theatre* and *The Negro in Music and Art* are works he has edited.

The under-twenty-five Negro novelists are few in number, but they are vital and interesting. Outstanding among them is Robert Boles, whose autobiographical novel *The People One Knows* appeared in 1964, when he was twenty-one. The novel's setting is Europe, where the young author lived both while traveling with his father, a member of the State Department's Foreign Service, and while serving in the Air Force. He now lives with his parents on Cape Cod in Massachusetts, where he is working on a second novel.

Jane Phillips' *Mojo Hand* was published last year by Trident Press and though it did not receive critical acclaim was considered unusual. The story describes the abnormal fascination of a young Negro girl for a much older blues singer, for whom she conducts a wide-ranging search which finally ends in North Carolina. Having fallen under the singer's uncanny spell, she lives with him and becomes pregnant. Established author John O. Killens says that twenty-three-year-old Miss Phillips "has tremendous potential as a writer." He notes her feeling for jazz and the blues, and adds: "She has captured the beauty of Negro language and put it down without fear."

Another of the younger writers, Donald Graham, twenty-two, a student at Fisk University, has already published a volume of verse, *Black Songs*, and is at work on a first novel called *Up South*. His style is tough and taut, and his tone is militant. Graham is a member of John Killens' Creative Writers Workshop at Fisk, out of which came also twenty-two-year-old Mignon Holland. Miss Holland, who graduated from Fisk last year, works on the staff of the *New Yorker* and is finishing a novel, *A Dying Time*, which deals with Negro life in a small Southern town similar to the one in which she grew up.

Detroiter Ron Milner is one of a small group of young Negro writers who writes plays and novels. Recipient of both a John Hay Whitney and a Rockefeller Fellowship, he has had plays performed on TV, and his first full-length drama, *Who's Got His Own*, was produced last year in New York by the experimental American Place Theatre. During the 1966–67 term he was writer-in-residence at Lincoln University in Pennsylvania. Sensitive, and conscious of his racial identity, Milner is working on a first novel which his many admirers are eagerly awaiting.

Not since the famous Harlem Renaissance, during which the names Hughes, Cullen and Bontemps emerged, have so many Negroes been writing poetry. The young Negro is taking full advantage of the medium, and in doing so has accepted an obligation to function as both artist and racial spokesman. "In the work of today's Negro poet," notes Pulitzer Prize winner Gwendolyn Brooks, "the reader will discover evidences of double dedication, hints that the artists have accepted a two-headed responsibility." Adds Miss Brooks: "Few have favored a trek without flags or emblems of any racial kind; and even those few in their deliberate 'renunciation' have in effect spoken racially, have offered race-fed testimony of several sorts. At the present time, poets who happen also to be Negroes are twice-tried. They have to write poetry, and they have to remember that they are Negroes."

Some of the new breed of Negro poets deserve a far wider audience than they have thus far reached. Don Allen Johnson, twenty-five, who writes under the pen name Mustafa, wrote poems for the college newspaper at Central State College before he quit school to roam the country in search of experience and understanding. A glimpse into his racial thinking is afforded by these lines from one of his works:

> O white mistress,
> O tangible feeling of superiority,
> Stand if you wish,
> But your child is sleepy;
> Lay him next to me and I
> Will give him warmth. Poor soul,
> Wretched existence, vain life,
> O indoctrinated cattle of an illusion.
> O egoism, pride, Southern mores.

Mance Williams, a young poet from Gary, Indiana, cries out in starkly eloquent brief works such as "For Lover Man, and All the Other Young Men Who Failed To Return from World War II."

Julian Bond is better known for his work as a former leader of the Student Nonviolent Coordinating Committee, and his stormy career as a Georgia State legislator, but he has written poems that prick the consciousness of his contemporaries:

> I, too, hear America singing,
> But from where I stand
> I can only hear Little Richard
> And Fats Domino;
> But sometimes
> I hear Ray Charles
> Drowning in his own tears
> Or Bird
> Relaxin' at Camarillo
> Or Horace Silver, doodling,
> Then, I don't mind standing a little longer.

There are other young poets of promise and power whose work has appeared in little magazines and college publications. They include

Californian Charles L. Anderson, an itinerant poet-worker who has been, among other things, a fruit-picker. David Henderson, twenty-four, a product of the New School for Social Research, in New York, has appeared in small publications like *Umbra, Seventh Street Quarterly* and the *Black American.* Thurmond L. Snyder, a native of Memphis, Tennessee, was first published by the Le Moyne College campus publication and in 1961 won a first prize for poetry in the *Reader's Digest*-United Negro College Fund Creative Writing Contest. Gloria Davis, just eighteen, who has published poetry and a short story in *Negro Digest,* has had poems published in other magazines and is represented in an anthology. Miss Davis lives in Detroit. Twenty-four-year-old Don L. Lee, a college student who is associated with the Museum of African American History, in Chicago, published privately a first volume of poems, *Think Black.*

There are many more young black poets whom critics and contemporaries have rated highly, who promise ultimately to master the technical complexities of an intricate and difficult craft.

An exciting eruption of young Negro literary talent is under way, claims John Killens. "There is a kind of renaissance of Negro writing going on from New York to San Francisco and on many Negro college campuses," says the novelist-essayist. "Compared to ten years ago, there are fifty times as many young Negroes writing well today. I am most impressed with their anger. They are questioning the status quo. Years ago, writers wrote because they wanted to be 'in.' This generation of young Negro writers is working to change the world. The changes brought about by the existence of the Black Power philosophy have had a profound impact on these writers. They are moving away from whiteness and affirming their black identity. I think this is a healthy trend."

James Baldwin bulldozed his way through the racial barriers in U.S. publishing and paved the way for a succeeding generation of Negro writers, but so far, it seems, the openings and opportunities, especially in fiction, exceed the acceptable and publishable writers.

However, in Killens' opinion, publishing opportunities for unrecognized Negro writers have enlarged only slightly, despite civil rights gains. "Every publishing house now wants to have at least one Negro writer," he observes. "Very few want more than one."

In the meantime, the younger writers give reason to believe that they are here to stay—and they undoubtedly will be heard from, because they possess stamina and persistence coupled with drive and dedication.

—1967

The Engagement Party

Robert Boles

SHE WAS not a drinker, for she held her glass too carefully. My eyes fastened to a detail. Her fingernail polish. The red was put into check by its own too-even glaze, was held, suspended.

"Yes. Well, my husband's work is similar to yours," she continued.

"Is it really?" I asked, but not quite politely enough. Had it been the lines of her eyes which projected the effect of my lack of attention? Her makeup, though not overdone, was obvious. Immediately, a sense of having played this scene before.

I turned slightly away from her as a member of the combo walked by, and noticed Helen beckoning me.

"Excuse me, please," I said.

The woman smiled with closed jaws, shifted her weight and pivoted on a heel. Her last name was Nolan. I remembered that then. I had no intention of embarrassing her. One should be accustomed to that sort of thing at a party.

Smiling now, I worked my way towards Helen.

"By God! It's George! It's George himself!" The voice belonged to Helen's younger brother. I clapped him on the shoulder. "And you don't even have to drink!"

"I left it on the mantel."

"Have you had enough already?"

"I've hardly begun," I said.

Helen appeared. Her arms were in front of her as if she were holding an imaginary purse with both hands. "There's someone you have to meet. My father's partner."

"I'm starved," I said.

She took my hand and led me across the room and into another. The people seemed plantlike, rooted in the carpet. Their motions seemed to have been caused by winds and crosswinds. Necks bent, backs; arms gestured in conversation. I had begun to perspire.

"I hope he doesn't get drunk," she confided without moving her lips or looking at me.

"Who?"

"My brother."

I bumped into the woman who wore the brocade dress, the one I had had the conversation with a moment before. Laughter and apologies, far in excess of what was called for. It was a brief bursting of her tension.

"Here he is," Helen announced.

"So, this is the young man who's going to carry you away." The man, in his late forties or early fifties, took my hand and shook it vigorously.

"Yes, sir," I said, assuming the bearing of a lower- responding to an upperclassman.

"It's about time I met you. Engineering, isn't it?"

"Yes, sir. Aeronautical."

"That's fine. You're a good-looking young man."

"Thank you, sir."

Helen moved away from me. I felt her absence as a hollow space beside me. Someone had asked her something and I had heard her say, "Certainly, Marie." That was all. I folded my arms, turned at the waist and followed her with my eyes. She escorted a woman to the foyer. The woman was a politician of some sort, I think. I believe I had seen her picture in the paper in regards to a "Culture March" on the Negro community.

"Wonderful girl, Helen."

"Yes, I agree," I said, and turned to face him again.

"Fine family."

"Yes, sir, I know," I said.

A group of men to my right were involved in a familiar and hearty political discussion. I tried to divide my attention.

"Your family's in . . . ?"

"California."

"Right. Ken told me. I had forgotten. Doctor, is he?"

"Not an M.D. He has a doctorate in education."

"I was in California for two years, you know."

"No, I didn't," I said. It was difficult for me to keep my eyes on him. His complexion was sallow, the color of coffee with heavy cream. I watched someone take a sip of a drink and felt thirsty again.

"I was in L.A.," he continued.

"We're from San Francisco."

"And what do you think of Boston?"

"It's fine. I like it," I said without much enthusiasm.

The music began. Bass throb, brushes on cymbals, then piano, vibes and saxophone in a long chorus. People separated. We stepped back. Some danced the High-Life, others the Bossa Nova.

"I don't intend for us to stay here," I continued. "I've taken a job in Connecticut."

"I'm sure it's best. Best to get the bride away from her parents."

I nodded, then covered my mouth while belching.

I recognized the bellowing of Tommy's voice to my right. He was, perhaps, getting drunk. "Being colored doesn't have anything to do with color! It's a question of attitudes and history and all that crap!"

"It's a good life that's yours to lead," Helen's father's partner said. "When I was your age, I had to struggle. Not like you young people today."

"Yes," I said. "I realize how hard it must have been. I know how hard my father had to work."

The entire conversation was one often repeated. A needless formality. We were knowledgeably secure in the words we spoke. I felt a little disquiet.

"You youngsters have all of the opportunities, you know. And there are new ones opening every day. No worry about finding a job. If you're qualified, you'll get one."

Although it was not altogether true, I could do nothing but nod in solemn agreement and press my lips together in a gesture akin to a pout.

I thought I heard Helen call me, but I could not see her.

"What are your hobbies, son? I heard that you were a fine trackman in school."

"I swim, of course," I said, and struggled to say naturally, "and I'm a bit of a bug on sailing." It was the truth and it seemed to offend him. I had known that it would and that he would enjoy it.

A group of people parted in laughter. Helen entered between them. She came to my side. "Excuse me, Al. I'm going to take him away from you." Her voice sounded remarkably like her mother's.

"I understand." He extended his hand immediately and shook mine again quite vigorously.

Helen's hand was cool, as if it had been in cold water.

"You look fresh," I remarked.

"I just freshened up. I was wilting. It's so warm, and all of these people," she said. "Did you have a good conversation?"

"Yes. I suppose so. He's a very interesting man."

"What time is it?"

Instead of taking my hand away from her, I stood on my toes, stretched myself, and attempted to read the clock on the mantel in the other room. My drink had disappeared from in front of the mirror. "Quarter to eleven, I think."

There was a roar of laughter that was quickly muffled.

"Little brother is acting up again," she said.

"Leave Tommy alone," I said. "He's happy and well adjusted. Let him have some fun."

"You don't know what I go through with him!"

From across the room, a woman's voice calling Helen's name. The tone of it was comparable to the surface of a highly polished piece of wood. All of us, in a dense atmosphere of movements and poses, were beneath and supportive to it. "Helen!"

She looked.

Again, "Helen!"

I saw her at the other end of the room before Helen did. She sipped at a Manhattan and waved from her wrist as women, curiously, always wave.

Between smiles, I managed to repeat myself more forcefully than before. "I am starved, Helen. Famished!"

"You told me."

"I'm beginning to get a headache," I lied. "I didn't get a chance to eat this evening." But the evening was getting to me, the sensuous fugue, the cacophony of voices, the odors and light, the smoke. But something more than that. My disquietude.

"My poor dear," she mouthed, as she stroked my forehead with her fingertips. "I'm sure the caterer has some of those . . . things left. What were those things? Cabbage leaves stuffed with something and baked. Go into the kitchen."

"I think I will."

She had not really expected me to do so. "Dance with me first."

"No," I said. "You're cruel. I'm salivating and starved and you want me to burn more of my energy."

If she had pressed me, I would have danced. But she didn't.

"I'll see you in a few minutes."

We separated. She, it seemed, with misgivings. But I was relieved. I felt at once the dissolution of the effect of the hundred small embarrassments which had occurred between myself and others throughout the evening, the seconds of arbitrary inattentiveness which inflicted wounds, pinpricks, on each of us.

Perhaps I'm lying.

The kitchen door was on spring hinges. It closed itself after I had entered. I let my smile fall and imagined myself making an entrance onto a stage. I, as an actor with a small part in a play with Strindberg overtones.

I was at ease with the noise practically shut out. I hadn't noticed how sweaty I was. With a lot of room and air, it seemed to be present all

at once. The white tiles of the floor and walls, glazed, flat and hard, made me doubly aware of my body and the bodies of the caterer and the girl. All of us were dark mobile beings set into this sterile chamber. The room was filled with the odors of smoke and powder and perfume in the other rooms.

"The groom-to-be is here!" the caterer said.

"You know it, dad," I said, slipping easily into the dialect to let him know that I was a member. "And I want me some f-o-o-d!"

"I hear you talkin', baby," the caterer said.

A metal chair painted white was against one of the walls. I sat in it and stretched out my legs. The caterer took a plate and began filling it. His white uniform was badly fitted. It was large. His arms were lean. The girl stood beside him and waited to help. She was very dark. Her bones were large, her hair coarse and beautiful.

"Get some salad for the man, Celestine," he said to her.

The name was right for her. It suggested fragility. Her bearing in some remarkable way suggested the same thing. She went to the refrigerator. I pretended that I had had slightly too much to drink. Her uniform played on my mind. The name Celestine did also. Her uniform was white. Starched. The material at the seams was doubled. Something easily noticeable for it was whiter there. The cloth played on her hips.

She looked at me briefly. I returned her glance with a smile and wondered, while I was doing so, what she thought of me. My complexion is agreeable with a black or charcoal-gray suit. I am brown in the way a Mexican is brown. I had my jacket open, my vest unbuttoned part of the way.

Celestine put some salad into a wooden bowl. I raised my hand in a political gesture when enough had been placed there. She added a spoonful more and offered the words, "For your health."

"This is my daughter Celestine," the caterer said proudly.

"She's a very attractive girl."

Celestine turned away from me in modesty. It suddenly seemed right to speak of her with her father in this manner, the masculine dominant, the female subservient. I was particularly aware of the roles we had assumed and had heightened.

I noticed that the caterer continued to put food on my plate. "Enough!" I said. "Man, when I want food for next year, I'll let you know."

He accepted my criticism with gentle laughter, but I was vaguely aware that I had overstepped myself.

"And what do you want to drink with that, sir?" he asked.

"Either Scotch or bourbon on the rocks," I said, with the full, coarse American aplomb.

"I'll have to go to the bar to get some." He put the plate on the table near me. The top of the table was porcelain.

Celestine went to a drawer, pulled it open and began to remove a table mat.

"I don't need that," I said with an unintended sharpness. I smiled idiotically afterwards.

Her father left the kitchen.

I pulled my chair to the table and began to eat.

"Sit down," I said to her after a moment. "You make me nervous standing there."

She obeyed me. My voice still had a residue of sharpness. It was her father who had gotten beneath my skin. All of us had accepted Southern attitudes in a minute.

I wanted to speak to her as I ate, but nothing seemed worth saying. It was difficult to cut through the cloth of pretension we had woven together. I ate in silence and she watched me in silence.

My thoughts turned to Helen, but it was clearly an alternative—something to compensate for my failure to communicate normally with the breathing girl seated next to me.

I ate too quickly, and when I was almost done her father returned with a double light Scotch. I thanked him with a full mouth, then finished eating, and drank half of the drink slowly, with my eyes on the walls and ceiling.

I smiled to myself. I almost laughed.

In another moment I was in one of the large rooms again.

"So you're the fiancé!" a woman said, pointing her finger at my chest.

"I am," I said, and smiled.

"Well, dance with me, darling!" All of her *a*'s were broad, and her voice rasped pleasantly.

"Only the High-Life," I said. "I don't want to put my drink down."

We walked into the other room and began the lilting African dance which had gained so much favor. She danced well, if a bit stiffly, but it became her.

"You know, I just learned this," she said. "I think it's marvelous! And you must tell me about Helen. You two go so well together."

The combo ended the song. We had hardly begun. I hoped that I could separate myself from her without appearing to be rude. I excused myself but she gave no indication of having noticed. She continued as we walked to the side of the room, then she met someone I had met previously and introduced us. I slipped quietly away from her.

I wandered through groups of people as if I were looking for someone. I stopped briefly to chat with Helen's mother, and once again near a small group of men centered around a white civil rights worker who had just returned from the South. He emoted before his words as he told a story of an atrocity too vile to be printed in a newspaper.

It all seemed a circus I cared little about. Or a parade. I've never liked parades. I did something idiotic. I stamped my foot. When I did it, a little of the contents of my glass spilled out onto my thumb and fingers. There was no reason for it. Perhaps I wanted to hear the sound of my footstep beneath the carpet. And I didn't know any longer if I loved Helen. I'd marry her in any case, but I wondered if love was possible. It had disappeared in a second. It was like walking out in the middle of one of those romantic screen comedies. Of course, tomorrow I would feel differently. In all likelihood this pattern would stay with me for the next forty or fifty years.

After finishing my drink, I went to the bar and asked for a Scotch-and-quinine. I was slapped on the back.

"By Jove, it's Georgie!" Helen's brother said.

"Hello, Tommy."

"Great party, is it not?"

"It is that," I said.

He posed unwittingly against the bar. There was a serenity in the moment or him. "Who am I going to play tennis with on Saturdays when you're hooked up to Helen and in Connecticut?"

"Where is she, by the way?" I asked.

"Upstairs. Mrs. Williams spilled a drink on her dress . . . well, I kind of knocked her arm a little. You know how those things happen."

"I'll bet Helen has it in for you."

"What the hell! She's getting married in a couple of months," he said, then added: "You lucky son of a . . . So, what's going to happen to tennis and me on Saturdays?"

"You'll find a better player." I feinted a left to his jaw, bent my knees and jabbed at his stomach with my right. He jackknifed a bit. Then I mussed up his hair. "Judging by your reflexes, you haven't had as much to drink as I thought."

The bartender placed my drink on the counter. I didn't really want it but picked it up and returned to the area in which couples danced. I watched without seeing and heard without listening. My preoccupation was with nothing. Maybe only the restlessness which had no outlet.

"Nice combo," someone said.

I tried, but not very hard, to remember his name. "Yes, they're very good."

In another moment I rested my glass and danced again. I found that this woman whose hand I had taken when I had stepped onto the floor was a fervent dancer. After our first words, all conversation stopped.

I danced with her several times. I got warm. My legs perspired. I saw Helen once and waved at her. She smiled obligingly and waved back. Tommy also danced a lot. We stopped when our foreheads and shirts were wet.

"To hell with being sedate!" he said. "I know we're supposed to, but it is a party."

Both of us went to the bar again, ordered and waited. Helen shook a finger of warning at him. I walked to her and kissed her. She recoiled from lack of privacy and said, "Not now, darling. Not here in front of all of these people. Gracious!"

"Leave your brother alone," I said. "That's an order."

"Yes, dear."

I took my glass and began to mingle halfheartedly. The alcohol had worked its miniature wonder. I was dizzy. Still, I hadn't learned anything. I wanted to go swimming. That was all. The idea of it seized me at once. I could envision

and feel it. I stood still in the center of the crowded room, closed my eyes and began a process of complete imagination. The voices, the laughter, the music intruded.

Upon opening my eyes, I walked without hesitation to the French doors that led to the patio and stepped out into the open. The air was much colder than I had expected it to be, and it took me a few seconds to get used to it. I sat in a deck lounge and closed my eyes. Who would be the first to disturb me? I wondered. Helen might come looking for me. Tommy might want to tell me the latest dirty joke.

I felt myself sinking into the pulsating deepness of intoxication that precedes sleep, but pulled myself up and out of it at the sound of footsteps. I did not look behind me. I took a swallow of my drink. I followed the motion of the person behind me with my hearing. After a moment I realized that whoever it was had no interest in me. I closed my eyes again.

The footsteps moved from here to there, stopped, moved from here to there again. There was the sound of one glass touching another. When the sound moved to the side of me and a little in front of me, I opened my eyes. It was the caterer's daughter. I couldn't remember her name right away. Celestine. I should have guessed that it might have been either she or her father. She was putting empty glasses left by guests onto a tray.

I watched her, unnoticed. There was a certain dignity in her manner I find difficult to explain. It was feminine without the feminine embellishments of gesture. It was not decadent. Her uniform, her darkness, and that she worked contributed to it. But there was much more. I was at ease. I decided to finish my drink so that she would have to take my glass.

She heard me move, turned and seemed surprised by my presence. I smiled at her. She returned the smile and continued. She picked up glasses in front and then to the right of me. When she had almost finished, I held up my glass and turned it upside down to demonstrate its emptiness. She came and took it from me.

"Sit down for a while," I said.

She looked to the patio doors before deciding to accept.

I swung my legs over and put them on the ground to make room for her.

"I meant what I said to your father," I told her. My words were sincere. "It's a bit cold out here, don't you think?"

She did not answer.

I said nothing for the next few seconds. I reached for her bare arm. The contact, though brief, was electric. She did not move and was facing away from me. I wanted very much to see her face. I put my hand to her chin and forced her to look at me. I could not read her expression. I let go of her and waited for her to get up. She sat completely still.

"This is where my engagement was announced," I said. "Everyone was assembled here and a toast was made."

The night spun softly. I was not even able to hear her breathe. She sat rigidly, with her eyes fastened to some immobile bit of shadow. My need for her then urged me. I would give her something afterwards. Money. Fifty dollars perhaps. I had that much in my wallet.

The moment seemed to lick us with a broad tongue. I felt strangely like someone from the Southern past of masters and servants. I did love her for the moment. To make love with her once would be all that I needed. I would never have to see her again.

I stood and took her arm. "Let's go into the garden," I whispered.

I pulled her gently. I beckoned. My whispering voice trembled.

She broke away from me. "No," she said firmly. Her head was lowered. Her chin touched the top of her dress, her uniform, and although I could not see her eyes I detected a look of betrayal on her face.

Had I read the moment so inaccurately? She picked up the tray of unclean glasses and walked with quick, sure steps back to the house.

I waited for a decent length of time before returning. I wanted to smoke a cigarette, but had no matches. My disquietude was inert. The guests would begin to leave in an hour or so. Then the evening could be forgotten.

—1967

Direct Action

Mike Thelwell

WE WERE all sitting around the front room the night it started. The front room of the pad was pretty kooky. See, five guys lived there. It was a reconstructed basement and the landlord didn't care what we did, just so he got his rent.

Well, the five guys who lived there were pretty weird, at least so it was rumored about the campus. We didn't care too much. Lee was on a sign kick, and if he thought of anything that appeared profound or cool—and the words were synonymous with him—wham! we had another sign. See, he'd write a sign and put it up. Not only that; he was klepto about signs. He just couldn't resist lifting them, so the pad always looked like the basement of the Police Traffic Department, with all the DANGER NO STANDING signs he had in the john, and over his bed he had a sign that read WE RESERVE THE RIGHT TO DENY SERVICE TO ANYONE. Man, he'd bring in those silly freshman girls who'd think the whole place was "so-o-o bohemian," and that sign would really crack them up.

Anyway, I was telling you about the front room. Lee had put up an immense sign he'd written: IF YOU DON'T DIG KIKES, DAGOS, NIGGERS, HENRY MILLER, AND J. C., YOU AIN'T WELCOME! Across from that he had another of his prize acquisitions; something in flaming red letters issued a solemn WARNING TO SHOPLIFTERS. You've probably seen them in department stores.

Then there was the kid in art school, Lisa, who was the house artist and mascot. Man, that kid was mixed up. She was variously in love with everyone in the pad. First she was going with

Dick—that's my brother. Then she found that he was a "father surrogate"; then it was Lee, but it seems he had been "only an intellectual status symbol." Later it was Doug "the innocent." After Doug it was Art—that's our other roomie—but he had only been an expression of her "urge to self-destruction." So now that left only me. The chick was starting to project that soulful look, but hell, man, there was only one symbol left and I wasn't too eager to be "symbolized." They should ban all psychology books, at least for freshman girls.

Anyway, I was telling you about the room. When Lisa was "in love" with Dick she was in her Surrealist period. She used to bring these huge, blatantly Freudian canvases, which she hung on the walls until the room looked, as Doug said, like "the pigmented expression of a demented psyche." Then Lisa started to down Dick because of his lack of "critical sensitivity and creativity." She kept this up, and soon we were all bugging Dick. He didn't say too much, but one day when he was alone in the pad, he got some tins of black, green, yellow and red house paint, stripped the room, and started making like Jackson Pollock. The walls, the windows, and dig this, even the damn floor was nothing but one whole mess of different-colored paint. Man, we couldn't go in the front room for four days; when it dried, Dick brought home an instructor from art school to "appraise some original works."

I was sorry for the instructor. He was a short, paunchy little guy with a bald patch, and misty eyes behind some of the thickest lenses you ever saw. At first he thought Dick was joking, and he just stood there fidgeting and blinking his watery little eyes. He gave a weak giggle and muttered something that sounded like, "Great . . . uh . . . sense of humor. Hee."

But Dick was giving him this hurt-creative-spirit come-on real big. His face was all pained, and he really looked stricken and intense.

"But, sir, surely you can see some promise, some little merit?"

"Well, uh, one must consider, uh, the limitations of your medium, uh . . . hee."

"Limitations of medium, yes, but surely there must be *some* merit?"

"Well, you must realize—"

"Yes, but not even *some* spark of promise, some faint, tiny spark of promise?" Dick was really looking distraught now. The art teacher was visibly unhappy and looked at me appealingly, but I gave him a don't-destroy-this-poor-sensitive-spirit look. He mopped his face and tried again.

"Abstractionism is a very advanced genre—"

"Yes, yes, advanced," Dick said, cutting him off impatiently, "but not even the faintest glimmer of merit?" He was really emoting now, and then he started sobbing hysterically and split the scene. I gave the poor instructor a cold how-could-you-be-so-cruel look, and he began to stutter. "I had n-no idea, n-no idea. Oh, dear, so strange . . . Do you suppose he is all right? How d-do you explain? . . . Oh, dear."

"Sir," I said, "I neither suppose nor explain. All I know is that my brother is very high-strung and you have probably induced a severe trauma. If you have nothing further to say, would you . . . ?" and I opened the door suggestively. He looked at the messed-up walls in bewilderment and shook his head. He took off his misty glasses, wiped them, looked at the wall, bleated something about "all insane," and scurried out. He probably heard us laughing.

Man, these white liberals are really tolerant. If Dick and I were white, the cat probably would have known right off that we were kidding. But apparently he was so anxious not to hurt our feelings that he gave a serious response to any old crap we said. Man, these people either kill you with intolerance or they turn around and overdo the tolerance bit. However, as Max Shulman says, "I digress."

The cats in our pad were kind of integrated, but we never thought of it that way. We really dug each other, so we hung around together. As Lee would say, "We related to each other in a meaningful way." (That's another thing about Lee. He was always "establishing relationships." Man, if he made a broad or even asked her the time, it was always, "Oh, I established a relationship today.") Like, if you were a cat who was hung up on this race bit, you could get awfully queered up around the pad. The place was about as mixed up as Brooklyn. The only difference, as far as I could see, was that we could all swear in different languages. Lee's folks had come from Milan, Dick and I were Negro, and Art, with his flaming red head and green Viking eyes, was Jewish.

The only cat who had adjustment problems was Doug. He was from sturdy Anglo-Saxon Protestant stock; his folks still had the Mayflower ticket stub and a lot of bread. When he was a freshman in the dorm, some of the cats put him down because he was shy and you could see that he was well off. And those s.o.b.'s would have been so helpful if the cat had been "culturally deprived" and needed handouts. Man, people are such bastards. It's kind of a gas, you know. Doug probably could have traced his family back to Thor, and yet he had thin, almost Semitic features, dark-brown hair, and deep eyes with a dark rabbinical sadness to them.

Anyway, we guys used to really swing in the pad; seems like we spent most of the time laughing. But don't get the idea that we were just kick-crazy or something out of Kerouac, beat-type stuff. All of us were doing okay in school—grades and that jazz. Take Art, for instance: most people thought that because he had a beard and was always playing the guitar and singing, and ready to party, he was just a campus beatnik-in-residence. They didn't know that he was an instructor and was working on his doctorate in anthropology. Actually, we were really more organized than we looked.

Anyway, this thing I'm telling you about happened the summer when this sit-in bit broke out all over. Since Pearl Springs was a Midwestern college town, there was no segregation of any kind around—at least, I didn't see any. But everyone was going out to picket Woolworth's every weekend. At first we went, but since there was this crowd out each week, and nobody was crossing the line anyway, we kind of lost interest. (Actually, they had more people than they needed.)

So we were all sitting around and jiving each other, when I mentioned that a guy we called "The Crusader" had said he was coming over later.

"Oh, no," Dick groaned, "that cat bugs me. Every time he sees me in the cafeteria or the union he makes a point of coming over to talk, and he never has anything to say. Hell, every time I talk to the guy I feel as if he really isn't seeing me, just a cause—a minority group."

"Yeah, I know," Art added. "Once at a party I was telling some broad that I was Jewish and he heard. You know, he just had to steer me into a corner to tell me how sympathetic he was to the 'Jewish cause' and 'Jewish problems.' The guy isn't vicious, only misguided."

Then Lee said, "So the guy is misguided, but, hell, he's going to come in here preaching all this brotherly love and Universal Brotherhood. And who wants to be a brother to bums like you?"

That started it.

Dick was reading the paper, but he looked up. "Hey, those Israelis in Tel Aviv are really getting progressive."

"Yeah, them Israelis don't mess around. What they do now?" Art asked. He was a real gung-ho Zionist and had even spent a summer in a kibbutz in Israel.

"Oh," said Dick, "they just opened a big hydro-electric plant."

Art waded in deeper. "So what?"

"Nothing, only they ain't got no water, so they call it The Adolf Eichmann Memorial Project."

Everybody cracked up. Art said something about "niggers and flies."

"Niggers and kikes," I chimed in. "I don't like them, either, but they got rights . . . in their place."

"Rights! They got too many rights already. After all, this is a free country, and soon a real American like me won't even have breathing room," cracked Lee.

"Hey, Mike," someone shouted, "you always saying some of your best friends are dagos, but would you like your sister to marry one?"

"Hell no, she better marryink der gute Chewish boy," I replied.

"And for niggers, I should of lynched you all when I had the chance . . ." Art was saying when The Crusader entered. This was the cat who organized the pickets—or at least he used to like to think he did. A real sincere crusading-type white cat. He looked with distaste at Lee's sign about kikes and niggers.

"Well, fellas, all ready for the picket on Saturday?"

"Somebody tell him," said Lee.

"Well, you see," I ventured, "we ain't going."

"Ain't going!" The Crusader howled. "But why? Don't you think—?"

"Of course not. We are all dedicated practitioners of non-think. Besides, all our Negrahs are happy. Ain't yuh happy, Mike?" Art drawled.

"Yeah, but I don' like all these immigran's, kikes, dagos an' such. Like, I thinks—"

"And Ah purely hates niggers: they stink so," Lee announced.

The Crusader didn't get the message. "Look, guys, I know you're joking, but . . . I know you guys are awful close—hell, you room together—but you persist in using all these derogatory racial epithets. I should think that you of all people . . . I really don't think it's funny."

"Man," said Dick, "is this cat for real?"

I knew just what he meant: I can't stomach these crusading liberal types, either, who just have to prove their democracy.

"Okay, can it, guys. I think we ought to explain to this gentleman what we mean," Art said. "Look, I don't think I have to prove anything to anyone in this room. We're all in favor of the demonstrations. In fact, nearly half the community is, so we don't think we need to parade our views. Besides, you have enough people as it is. So we're supporting the students in the South, but why not go across the state line into Missouri and really do something? That's where direct action is needed."

"Oho, the same old excuse for doing nothing," The Crusader sneered.

I could see that Lee over in his corner was

getting mad. Suddenly he said, "So you accuse us of doing nothing? Well, we'll show you what we mean by direct action. We mean action calculated to pressure people, to disrupt economic and social functions and patterns, to pressure them into doing something to improve racial relations."

"Very fine, Comrade Revolutionary, and just what do you propose to do, besides staying home and lecturing active people like me?" The Crusader's tone dripped sarcasm.

Lee completely lost control. "What do we propose to do?" he shouted. "We'll go across the state line and in two weeks we'll integrate some institution! That'll show you what direct action means."

"Okay, okay, just make sure you do it," said The Crusader as he left.

Man, next day it was all over campus that we had promised to integrate everything from the state of Georgia to the White House main bedroom—you know how rumors are. We were in a fix. Every time Lee blew his top we were always in a jam. Now we had to put up or shut up.

The pressure was mounting after about a week. We were all sitting around one day when Doug proclaimed to Lee, "We shall disrupt their social functions, we shall disrupt their human functions —You utter nut, what the hell are you going to do?"

Lee was real quiet, like he hadn't heard; then he jumped up. "Human functions! Doug—genius. I love you!" Then he split the scene, real excited-like.

About an hour later Lee came back still excited, and mysterious. "Look," he said, "we're cool. I have it all worked out. You know that big department store in Deershead? Well, they have segregated sanitary facilities."

Dick interrupted, "So? This is a Christian country. You expect men and women to use the same facilities?"

"Oh, shut up, you know what I mean. Anyway, we're going to integrate them. All you guys have to do is get ten girls and five other guys and I'll do the rest."

"Oh, isn't our genius smart," I snarled. "If you think that, hot as it is, I'm going to picket among those hillbillies, you're out of your cotton-chopping little mind."

"Who's going to picket?" Lee said. "Credit me with more finesse than that. I said direct action, didn't I? Well, that's what I meant. All you guys have to do is sit in the white johns and use all the seats. I'll do the rest."

"And the girls?" I asked.

"They do the same over in the women's rest rooms. Oh, is this plan a riot!" The cat cracked up and wouldn't say any more. Nobody liked it much. Lee was so damn wild at times. See, he was a real slick cat. I mean, if he had ten months with a headshrinker he'd probably end up President. But, man, most of the jams we got into were because the cat *hadn't* seen a headshrinker. Anyway, we didn't have any alternative, so we went along.

The morning we were ready to leave, Lee disappeared. Just when everyone was getting real mad, he showed, dragging two guys with him. One was The Crusader and the other cat turned out to be a photographer from the school paper. So we drove to Deershead, a hick town over in Missouri. All the way, Lee was real confident. He kept gloating to The Crusader that he was going to show him how to operate.

When we arrived at the "target," as Lee called it, he told everyone to go in and proceed with stage one. All this means is that we went and sat in the white johns. The girls did the same. Lee disappeared again. We all sat and waited. Soon he showed up grinning all over and said:

"Very good. Now I shall join you and wait for our little scheme to develop." He told The Crusader and the photographer to wait in the store for our plan to take effect. Man, we sat in that place for about an hour. It was real hot, even in there. The guys started to get restless and finally threatened to leave if Lee didn't clue us in on the plan—if he had one.

Just as he decided to tell us, two guys came into the john real quick. We heard one of them say, "Goddamn, the place is full." They waited around for a while, and more guys kept coming in. All of a sudden the place was filled with guys. They seemed real impatient, and one of them said, "Can't you fellas hurry up? There's quite a line out here."

"Wonder why everyone has such urgent business," drawled Lee. "Must be an epidemic."

"Must be something we ate," the guy said. His voice sounded strange and tense. "Hurry up, fellas, will you?"

I peeped through the crack in the door and saw the guys outside all sweating and red in the face. One cat was doubled up, holding his middle and grimacing. I heard Lee say in a tone of real concern, "I tell you what, men, looks like we'll be here for some time. Why don't you just go down to the other rest room?"

"What!" someone shouted. "You mean the nigger john?"

Then Lee said ever so sweetly, "Oh, well . . . there's always the floor." And he started laughing softly.

The guys got real mad. Someone tried my door, but it was locked. I heard one guy mutter, "The hell with this," and he split. For a minute there was silence; then we heard something like everyone rushing for the door.

Lee said, "C'mon, let's follow them." So we all slipped out.

Man, that joint was in an uproar. There was a crowd of whites milling around the door of both colored johns. The Crusader was standing around looking bewildered. Lee went over to the photographer and told him to get some pictures. After that, we got the girls and split the scene.

In the car coming back, Lee was crowing all over the place about what a genius he was. "See," he said, "I got the idea from Doug when he was saying all that bit about 'human functions.' That was the key: all I had to do then was figure out some way to create a crisis. So what do I do? Merely find a good strong colorless laxative and introduce it into the drinking water at the white coolers—a cinch with the old-fashioned open coolers they got here. Dig? That's what I was doing while you guys were sitting in."

Just then The Crusader bleeped, "Hey—would you stop at the next service station?"

The guy did look kinda pale at that. I thought, "And this cat always peddling his brotherhood and dragging his white man's burden behind him all the time." Oh, well, I guess I might have used the cooler, too.

Well, there was quite a furor over the whole deal. The school newspaper ran the shots and a long funny story, and the local press picked it up. Deershead was the laughingstock of the whole state. The management of the store was threatening to sue Lee and all that jazz, but it was too late to prove any "willful mischief or malice aforethought," or whatever it is they usually prove in these matters. The Negro kids in Deershead got hep and started a regular picket of the store. Man, I hear some of those signs were riots: LET US SIT DOWN TOGETHER, and stuff like that. The store held out a couple of months, but finally they took down the signs over the johns. Guess they wanted to forget.

That's the true story as it happened. You'll hear all kinds of garbled versions up on campus, but that's the true story of the "sitting" as it happened. Oh, yeah, one other thing: the Deershead branch of the NAACP wanted to erect a little statue of either me or Dick sitting on the john, the first Negro to be so integrated in Deershead. You know how they dig this first Negro bit. We had to decline. Always were shy and retiring.

—1963

A New Day

Charles Wright

I'M CAUGHT. Between the devil and the deep blue sea." Lee Mosely laughed and made a V for victory sign and closed the front door against a potpourri of family voices shouting good wishes and tokens of warning.

The late, sharp March air was refreshing and helped cool his nervous excitement, but his large hands were tight fists in his raincoat pockets. All morning he had been socking one fist into the other, running around the crowded, small living room like an impatient man waiting for a train, and had even screamed at his mother, who had recoiled as if he had sliced her heart with a knife. Andy, his brother-in-law, with his whine of advice: "Consider . . . Brother . . ."

Consider your five stair-step children. Consider the sweet, brown babe switching down the subway steps ahead of me. What would she say? Lee wondered.

Of course, deep down in his heart he wanted the job, wanted it desperately. The job seemed to hold so much promise, and really he was getting nowhere fast, not a God damn place in the year and seven weeks that he had been shipping clerk at French-American Hats. But that job, too, in the beginning had held such promise. He remembered how everyone had been proud of him.

Lee Mosely was a twenty-five-year-old Negro whose greatest achievement had been the fact that he had graduated twenty-fourth in his high school class of one hundred and twenty-seven. This new job that he was applying for promised the world, at least as much of the world as he expected to get in one hustling lifetime. But he wouldn't wear his Ivy League suits and unloosen his tie at ten in the morning for coffee and doughnuts. He would have to wear a uniform, and mouth a grave "Yes ma'am" and "No ma'am." What was worse, his future boss was a Southern white woman, and he had never said one word to a Southern white woman in his life—had never expected to either.

"It's honest work, ain't it?" his mother had said. "Mrs. Davies ain't exactly a stranger. All our people down home worked for her people. They were mighty good to us and you should be proud to work for her. Why, you'll even be going overseas and none of us ain't been overseas except Joe, and that was during the big War. Lord knows, Mrs. Davies pays well."

Lee had seen her picture once in the *Daily News*, leaving the opera, furred and bejeweled, a waxen little woman with huge gleaming eyes, who faced the camera with pouting lips as if she were on the verge of spitting. He had laughed because it seemed strange to see a society woman posing as if she were on her way to jail.

Remembering, he laughed now and rushed up the subway steps at Columbus Circle.

Mrs. Maude T. Davies had taken a suite in a hotel on Central Park South for the spring, a spring that might well be two weeks or a year. Lee's Aunt Ella in South Carolina had arranged the job, a very easy job. Morning and afternoon drives around Central Park. The hotel's room service would supply the meals, and Lee would personally serve them. The salary was one hundred and fifty dollars a week, and it was understood that Lee could have the old, custom-built Packard on days off.

"Lord," Lee moaned audibly and sprinted into the servants' entrance of the hotel.

Before ringing the doorbell, he carefully wiped his face with a handkerchief that his mother had ironed last night and inspected his fingernails, cleared his throat, and stole a quick glance around the silent, silk-walled corridor.

He rang the doorbell, whispered "Damnit," because the buzzing sound seemed as loud as the sea in his ears.

"Come in," a husky female voice shouted, and Lee's heart exploded in his ears. His armpits began to drip.

But he opened the door manfully, and entered like a boy who was reluctant to accept a gift, his highly polished black shoes sinking into layers of apple-green carpet.

He raised his head slowly and saw Mrs. Davies sitting in a yellow satin wing chair, bundled in a mink coat and wearing white gloves. A flowered scarf was tied neatly around her small, oval head.

"I'm Lee Mosely. Sarah's boy. I came to see about a job."

Mrs. Davies looked at him coldly and then turned toward the bedroom.

"Muffie," she called, and then sat up stiffly, clasping her gloved hands. "You go down to the garage and get the car. Muffie and I will meet you in the lobby."

"Yes ma'am," Lee said, executing a nod that he prayed would serve as a polite bow. He turned smartly like a soldier and started for the door.

Muffie, a Yorkshire terrier bowed in yellow satin, trotted from the bedroom and darted between Lee's legs. His bark was like an old man coughing. Lee moaned, "Lord," and noiselessly closed the door.

He parked the beige Packard ever so carefully and hopped out of the car as Mrs. Davies emerged from the hotel lobby.

Extending his arm, he assisted Mrs. Davies from the curb.

"Thank you," she said sweetly. "Now, I expect you to open and close the car door, but I'm no invalid. Do you understand?"

"Yes ma'am. I'm sorry."

"Drive me through the park."

Muffie barked. Lee closed the door and then they drove off as the sun skirted from behind dark clouds.

There were many people in the park and it was like a spring day except for the chilled air.

"We haven't had any snow in a long time," Lee said, making conversation. "Guess spring's just around the corner."

"I know that," Mrs. Davies said curtly.

And that was the end of their conversation until they returned to the hotel, twenty minutes later.

"Put the car away," Mrs. Davies commanded. "Don't linger in the garage. The waiter will bring up lunch shortly and you must receive him."

Would the waiter ever come? Lee wondered, pacing the yellow and white tiled serving pantry. Should he or Mrs. Davies phone down to the restaurant? The silence and waiting was unbearable. Even Muffie seemed to be barking impatiently.

The servant entrance bell rang and Mrs. Davies screamed, "Lee!" and he opened the door quickly and smiled at the pale, blue-veined waiter, who did not return the smile. He had eyes like a dead fish, Lee thought, rolling in the white-covered tables. There was a hastily scrawled note which read: "Miss Davies food on top. Yours on bottom."

Grinning, Lee took his tray from under the bottom shelf, and was surprised to see two bottles of German beer. He set his tray on the pantry counter and took a quick peep at Mrs. Davies' tossed salad, one baby lamb chop. There was a split of champagne in a small iced bucket.

"Lord," he marveled, and rolled the white-covered table into the living room.

"Where are you eating, ma'am?" Lee asked, pleased because his voice sounded so professional.

"Where?" Mrs. Davies boomed. "In this room, boy!"

"But don't you have a special place?" Lee asked, relieved to see a faint smile on the thin lips.

"Over by the window. I like the view. It's almost as pretty as South Carolina. Put the yellow wing over there too. I shall always dine by the window unless I decide otherwise. Understand?"

"Yes ma'am." Lee bowed and rolled the table in front of the floor-to-ceiling wall of windows. Then he rushed over and picked up the wing chair as if it were a loaf of bread.

He seated Mrs. Davies and asked gravely: "Will that be all, ma'am?"

"Of course!"

Exiting quickly, Lee remembered what his uncle Joe had said about V-day. "Man. When they tell us the War is over, I just sat down in the foxhole and shook my head."

And Lee Mosely shook his head and entered the serving pantry, took a deep breath of relief which might well have been a prayer.

He pulled up a leather-covered fruitwood stool to the pantry counter and began eating his lunch of fried chicken, mashed potatoes, gravy and tossed salad. He marveled at the silver domes covering the hot, tasty food, amused at his distorted reflection in the domes. He thanked God for the food and the good job. True, Mrs. Davies was sharp-tongued, a little funny, but she was nothing like the Southern women he had seen in the movies and on television and had read about in magazines and newspapers. She was not a part of Negro legends, of plots, deeds and mockery. She was a wealthy woman named Mrs. Maude T. Davies.

Yeah, that's it, Lee mused in the quiet and luxury and warmth of the serving pantry.

He bit into a succulent chicken leg and took a long drink of the rich, clear-tasting German beer.

And then he belched. Mrs. Maude T. Davies screamed: "Nigger!"

I still have half a chicken leg left, Lee thought. He continued eating, chewing very slowly, but it was difficult to swallow. The chicken seemed to set on the valley of his tongue like glue.

So there was not only the pain of digesting but the quicksand sense of rage and frustration, and something else, a nameless something that had always started ruefully at the top of his skull like a windmill.

He knew he had heard *that* word, although the second lever of his mind kept insisting loudly that he was mistaken.

So he continued eating with difficulty his good lunch.

"Nigger boy!" Mrs. Davies repeated, a shrill command, strangely hot and tingling like the telephone wire of the imagination, the words entering through the paneled pantry door like a human being.

Lee Mosely sweated very hard summer and winter. Now, he felt his blood congeal, freeze, although his anger, hot and dry, came bubbling to the surface. Saliva doubled in his mouth and his eyes smarted. The soggy chicken was still wedged on his tongue and he couldn't swallow it nor spit it out. He had never cried since becoming a man and thought very little of men who cried. But for the love of God, what could he do to check his rage, helplessness?

"Nigger!" Mrs. Davies screamed again, and he knew that some evil, white trick had come at last to castrate him. He had lived with this feeling for a long time and it was only natural that his stomach and bowels grumbled as if in protest.

And then like the clammy fear that evaporates at the crack of day, Lee's trembling left hand picked up the bottle of beer and he brought it to his lips and drank. He sopped the bread in the cold gravy. He lit a cigarette and drank the other bottle of German beer.

A few minutes later, he got up and went into the living room.

Mrs. Davies was sitting very erect and elegant in the satin chair, and had that snotty *Daily News* photograph expression, Lee thought bitterly.

"Mrs. Davies," he said politely, clearly, "did you call me?"

"Yes," Mrs. Maude T. Davies replied, like a jaded, professional actress. Her smile was warm, pleased, amused. "Lee, you and I are going to get along very well together. I like people who think before they answer."

—1967

Sarah

Martin J. Hamer

IT SNOWED on Thanksgiving Day. With the wonder of all the preparations and the knowledge that a man was coming to visit, the snow was more than Clyde could bear. "It's snowing!" he screamed. "Mama, it's snowing!" In a frenzy he ran into the kitchen to tell his mother the news. He was in the way; he was sent back into the living room. He came sneaking back, frightening his Aunt Bea with a loud "Boo!" He ran out again and opened the window. The snow was falling in great silver flakes. He took what he could catch in his hands and blew it across the room. "Snow! Snow!" he cried. He was placed in a chair and given a magazine.

Bea Boyce had come early to help out. She was a rotund woman, forty-six years of age, with a romantic air and quick brown eyes. As she moved around and around, setting the open-leafed table, her taffeta dress swished and swirled about her and she hummed in a very high key. She placed the silverware with elaborate care and folded the linen napkins into white fluffed caps. When she remembered that the shoes she wore were open at the toes, she said aloud to no one in particular that she hoped Mr. Boyce would think to bring her rubbers. Then she began to whistle "The Twelve Days of Christmas," the wobbly sound coming from between her large, pursed lips, the effort hollowing her cheeks and arching her penciled-in eyebrows. Sarah called from the kitchen that house whistling was bad luck.

"It's not Christmas, anyway," Clyde said. "It's Thanksgiving!" His aunt rolled her eyes at him, and he pushed himself into the farthest corner of the chair and tried to roll his eyes at her.

"You're getting too cute," she said. "Mr. George will fix you, though. He's going to fix your wagon, but good!"

"Don't frighten the boy," said Sarah. She came from the kitchen with the water glasses tinkling in her slender hands, and after placing them on the table she viewed herself solemnly in the mirror. Her hair was drawn straight back from her oval face, and her pierced ears showed tiny pearl earrings to match the necklace hanging in the fullness of her breast. Unlike her sister's, her brown pupils moved slowly. Her expression was apprehensive, and there was the suggestion of a clown's sorrow about her mouth where the lipstick had been drawn boldly onto the dark facial skin of her upper lip. Turning her body from side to side, she smoothed her purple dress about her hips and asked Bea, "How do I look?"

"Like a belle of the ball," said Bea.

Sarah frowned. "A belle of the ball at forty. A real belle of the ball." She placed one leg out in front of her and pressed a hand to its knee. "I think this dress is too short."

"What do you mean, too short? Look at mine!"

"Yours is too short too," Sarah said.

"Well, honey, that's the style these days."

"Dress like this will only put ideas in his head."

"And that ain't what you want?"

"I most certainly do *not*. Getting a man means about as much to me as getting an ice-cream cone."

"Which is why," said Bea, "you're making all this fuss about dinner." She went back to the table and fluffed a fallen napkin. "You just better pray that Ann's not in one of her moods. 'Cause, child, she'll sure mess things up for you."

"She'd better not," said Sarah angrily. "She'd just better be on her *p*'s and *q*'s if she knows what's good for her."

"I can't see why you even invited her. You know how she is."

"I invited her for the same reason I invited you—you're family."

"Well," said Bea, "remember what Papa used to say: 'Ain't nothing worse—ain't nothing worse than family.'"

"I just wish you'd shut up," said Sarah, "for once!"

The doorbell rang, and Clyde scrambled into the hallway calling, "Who is it? Who is it?"

"It's me!"

"It's me!"

"It is I," shouted the final and strongest voice from far below, and his Aunt Ann's three boys came thundering up the four flights to the landing. They swept past him, shaking snow, fists and tongues in his face. When Ann appeared on the landing, she took his small bewildered form in her arms and pressed him deep into the damp fur collar of her coat. Before they were inside, the bell rang again and Mr. Boyce came up the stairs puffing. A great wool muffler swathed his neck, and his moustache sparkled with melting snow. Bea Boyce made it clear to everyone that he had not thought enough to bring her rubbers.

Ann sat near the oil-stove and warmed her bony frame in its shimmering heat. She was dressed in black, and the huge iron cross that hung about her neck made her corner of the room solemnly remote. Mr. Boyce sprawled on the couch, hung one hand on his vest pocket in the manner of a train conductor, and caressed his bushy moustache with the other. His wife fluttered among the children like a bird. "The boys have grown," she said. "They give no trouble," replied Ann. In less than ten minutes, thought Sarah, they've used Clyde's caps, broken his gun, crushed a plastic soldier and rolled most of his marbles under the piano. "Well," she said loudly, "you all just make yourselves comfortable." "Gimme that!" said Ann's oldest. Without looking up, Ann said, "Now, now." Then she reached into her purse and took out her Bible. Sarah picked up a cigarette from the table and started to light it. Mr.

Boyce brought out a fat cigar. "I hope you're not going to light that thing before dinner," said Bea. He glowered at her, rolling the fat cigar between his jaundiced-looking fingers. He harrumphed and placed it back in his pocket. Sarah's match popped loudly, and Mr. Boyce watched as a cloud of smoke obscured her. "Blow a smoke ring. Aunt Sarah! Blow a smoke ring!" Bea frowned, the doorbell rang, and everyone became silent.

When a light rap sounded at the door, Bea crossed her legs and whispered to Mr. Boyce to sit straight. Ann took one hand from her Bible and began to finger her cross. Her boys gaped stupidly at the door, and Clyde moved cautiously toward his mother. Sarah closed her eyes and prayed: Please, Lord, don't let anything go wrong. "Come in!" she called. "Come in!"

A huge man entered, his black coat glistening with melted snow, and immediately a chilled air, heavy with the pungent odor of stale tobacco, spread about the room. "Come in, Mr. George," said Sarah. "Come in and meet the folks." He removed his coat and stood before them in a neat but tattered blue suit, a bright new white shirt and a faded maroon-colored tie. His gaze moved easily from face to face; his slightly graying hair and soft features made him appear calm, but there was the indication of surprise in his manner, and his brow was drawn and deeply furrowed.

Sarah introduced him to Mr. Boyce. "How do you do, sir," said Mr. George. Mr. Boyce was flattered. He pumped the tall man's arm, mumbling that it was a pleasure to meet a gentleman. Bea was squirming on the couch all the while, and by the time she was introduced her skirts were so high you could see where her stockings ended. When Sarah saw that Mr. George had noticed, she said, "Now, you wouldn't think she was the oldest, would you?" Everyone was silent. "And," Sarah went on loudly, "over here's my other sister, Ann."

Ann extended her left hand, holding onto her cross with her right. "I've heard a lot about you," she said.

"Thank you," said Mr. George warmly.

"I wouldn't be so quick to say thank you if I were you. You're not at all what I expected."

Mr. George stopped smiling. Sarah quickly

said, "These are all her boys, except one. This one," she pushed Clyde forward, "this is Clyde. Well," she said to the boy, "what do you say?" Clyde stared at Mr. George and then retreated back behind Sarah.

"Boy sure needs to be taught," said Ann. "I've never seen a child so backward."

The fire could be heard burning in the oil-stove, and Sarah closed her eyes to pray to God. "I brought you these," said Mr. George awkwardly. When Sarah turned, he was handing her two brown-paper-wrapped packages. Embarrassed, she mumbled "Thank you" and looked toward the floor. He was standing in a small puddle of dark water. "One of you boys fetch a piece of newspaper," she said loudly. "And one of you come take the gentleman's coat." Ann's boys moved furiously about the room. "The paper's in there," she screamed. "Take the coat in there, and the rest of you go get washed! Bea! Come help me in the kitchen." Bea rose like a princess, the swishing sound of her dress adding to the confusion. "Hurry up now, you boys," Sarah screamed. "Put those things up! Get washed! Dinner's almost ready." She turned to leave the room; she turned back. "Oh, have a seat, Mr. George. Do have a seat."

"And, dear Lord," droned Ann, asking the blessing, "help those of us who have erred from your path of righteousness and who are even now sittin' in your house, at your table, eatin' your food without your grace." One of her boys snickered. A loud pop echoed in the silence, and as Ann continued the boy whimpered softly, the short, gurgling wheeze of his breath punctuating his sobs. "God, we thank you for this food which we are about to receive, for the nourishin' of the body, and for Christ's sake"—she looked up—"Amen."

"Amen," they all chorused.

"Leg or breast?" asked Sarah. "Just let me know." She carved the turkey, and the plates were passed in silence, filled with turnips, rice, and bread stuffing. Clyde poured the gravy on his plate for so long that Mr. Boyce quipped, "That bird can't swim, son." Everyone laughed; Bea frowned; then she went out of her way to pass Mr. George the bread. Struggling to cut her share

of the bird, Sarah took time to make note. I'm going to have to speak to her before this day is over.

"How many churches, Mr. George," Ann began slowly, "do they have out there in Queens?" She rested her fork on her plate, the effort of the question distracting her from eating.

"What kind of churches?" asked Mr. George.

"Baptist," came the reply.

"Wouldn't know," he said curtly. "I'm Episcopalian."

Mr. Boyce grinned. Ann stiffened her bony frame until it loomed like a cattail over her boys. "How many of those do you have, then?"

Mr. George hesitated and looked toward the ceiling. In the interim Mr. Boyce belched. Sarah waited for him to excuse himself; then she asked Mr. George, "Did you know that the Boyces are business people? They own that candy store at the corner, one of the nicest in the neighborhood."

"Is that so?" said Mr. George.

"You in business too?" asked Mr. Boyce.

"No, not me," he said. "Don't you know I work with Sarah?"

"I thought you met in a dance hall," said Ann.

"I just read in the paper," said Mr. Boyce, "about two people who got married."

"What's that got to do with anything?" asked Bea.

"If you'd let me finish." He wiped his mouth. "I was going to say they got married in a dance hall."

"Couldn't be no worse sin," said Ann. She placed a finger in her mouth, and to Clyde's wonder and Sarah's chagrin removed a small bone covered with masticated food.

"Is that the wishbone?" Clyde asked.

"If it is," chimed Mr. Boyce, "better give it to his mama." He chuckled; Sarah banged her fork onto her plate, rose, and announced that she was going for dessert. In the kitchen she leaned against the cupboard and cried. They were all against her, and Bea was even trying to make time with him. Nothing's worse than family. Nothing's worse. Oh, Papa! Why'd you have to be right? She moved to get the dessert plates and saw the packages on the table. Unwrapping them carefully, she found the first was a bottle of Scotch, the second, a fuzz-covered monkey in a red velvet suit. It played a blue metal drum and raised a plastic bowler while marching to the sound of an unsteady, tinny beat. I don't know what he sees in me. Lord! I sure don't know what he sees in me. But if You let him go on seeing it, I'll treat him well, I swear it. I'll treat him well.

She re-entered the room and was pleased to see that Mr. George had become the center of attention. He had grown up not far from them on St. Nicholas Avenue, and he was telling them how nice Harlem was in those days. "Curtains at all the foyer windows," he said. "And I used to make my money by going around polishing the mailboxes."

"Yeah," said Mr. Boyce, "those were really the days. Really the days . . ."

"Now, out in Queens, where I am now . . ." he went on.

Sarah thought of Queens. Beautiful Queens. That's where she'd like to live. Throw out all this junk and move to Queens. Only thing I'd keep— she looked about the room—is the piano; Clyde will have to learn to play someday. And maybe the couch. It needs a new cover. With a new cover it won't look so bad. She straightened her shoulders, walked to the table and handed Clyde the monkey. "Say thank you to Mr. George," she prompted.

"Is that his father?" asked Ann's youngest.

"Hush!" said Ann.

"That's all right," Mr. George said. "Children don't know any better."

"You sure have a fine sense for the pumps in life," said Bea.

"Bumps!" corrected Mr. Boyce.

"Bumps, pumps!" screamed Bea. "No matter what you call it, you ain't got it!"

Mr. Boyce harrumphed and looked down at the tablecloth.

"Can't get together, get apart," said Ann sweetly. "Man's a worse worry than hell."

"Is that why you ain't got one?"

"Okay, now you all," said Sarah.

"Okay yourself!" screamed Bea. "You ain't much better. Different one every time you turn around!"

"Why don't you shut up!"

"Look to God," said Ann. "You all better learn to look to God for your happiness. Better put your faith in the Lord . . ."

Tears blurred Sarah's vision. I'm going to move to Queens, she thought. Beautiful Queens. And I'm not going to see any of them again.

The dessert was eaten in silence. Afterward, Bea announced that she would do the dishes, and Ann offered to help. Sarah sat with Mr. George on the couch while Ann's boys, who had overeaten, moved more or less circuitously about the room. They stumbled into furniture and relatives like doped flies, until finally the two younger ones crashed into one another and fell to the floor and to sleep. The oldest one continued to traverse the route for about five more minutes, and then, on receiving a sudden call from nature, he departed for the bathroom. He was found some time later, asleep on the stool. Clyde, no longer finding it necessary to protect his monkey, fell asleep near the stove, and in the big chair nearby Mr. Boyce, his belt and shoes undone, began to snore. Soft shadows moved across the cracked plaster walls of the green room. Only an occasional clatter of a dish or piece of silverware from the kitchen interrupted the silence. Mr. George yawned, stretched, and let his big hand fall lightly on Sarah's thigh. She jumped. "What do you think I am?" she said.

"We're finished," said Ann, entering the room. "Well, will you look at this." She motioned toward her boys and Bea's husband. "Child, what did you put in that food? All right now, c'mon"— she clapped her hands. "Everybody up and out! Dinner's over, day's over, time to go home and to bed!"

The confusion began again. Mr. Boyce wanted Mr. George's address; Sarah could not find a pencil. Bea came back from the window with the news that so much snow had fallen none of them would be able to get home. "Then you all better hurry now," said Sarah, "before it gets worse."

She could not find a pencil, so Mr. Boyce stood in the middle of the room and repeated Mr. George's phone number over and over again until all of the boys were shouting it at the top of their lungs. Finally Sarah got them all to the door. "Good-bye." "Good-bye." "Gimme that!" "So long." "You must come by the store sometime."

"Mama! He took my—" "Whenever you stop here, stop there." "Fine dinner, Sarah," said Mr. Boyce. "Why don't you come to church sometime?" "Gimme!" "Will you two behave! Give him back his monkey!" "So long, Mr. George," said Mr. Boyce. "Don't come crying to me," said Ann. "Stop it! You're pulling my clothes off." "Good-bye." "Good-bye." "So long." They left. Sarah watched them from the window, a huddled group of people in the cold night and the snow. "The world is a beautiful place," she said softly.

"What'd you say?" asked Mr. George.

"I said the world is a beautiful place."

"Only sometimes," he said. "Only sometimes."

Sarah sighed, discouraged that he could not feel what she felt, and began to tidy the room. She cleaned around Clyde, who had fallen asleep in a chair. She emptied the ashtrays and picked up bits of paper from the floor. Then she put the lights out, leaving the oil-stove to light the room, and sat down on the couch next to Mr. George. "There's something I'd like to tell you," she said.

"What beats me," he interrupted, "is why you invited your whole family. I thought it was just going to be me, you, and the boy."

"You had to meet them sometime," she said, annoyed. "Anyway, I love my family . . ."

"Do they always act like that?" he asked.

"Like what?"

"Never mind," he said, and was silent.

She leaned back on the couch. "There's something I have to tell you. Mr. George, I have to know how you feel about something I have to tell you."

He drew in his mouth reflectively and slapped a hand to his knee. "Okay," he said, "I'm listening."

"Once I made a mistake," she went on slowly, "of not telling a fellow all about me. When people come to find out things about you later, they sometimes come to hate you. I want to tell you the worst things about me. That way, if you can't understand, we can quit and neither of us will be the worse off for it. If we stay together, I don't want to have any secrets from you."

"Sort of like a test, huh?" said Mr. George.

"Sort of," said Sarah. "I just hope I pass."

"Well, listen now, Sarah, I don't care about—"

"Hush! I've got to tell you this! Just like I had to have you meet my family—no matter how they treat me. You'll just have to understand. I want to tell you about Clyde's father." She paused, and when he remained quiet, she went on. "I met him in a museum five years ago when I was doing day-work on Fifty-seventh Street. I used to walk past that museum every day. They had this fence made out of wooden slats, and inside was a garden, a beautiful garden with a black stone pool and statues and everything. After a while I got to thinking that one day I was going to go there. Can you imagine that? Me, going to that museum? Well, one day I did." She stopped and listened. It was the wind gently rattling the sashes and tapping the snow lightly against the panes. "I'll never forget that day. It was a Sunday in August, and I had on my blue cotton dress, the one with the paisley print, and my white heels and white gloves. I was really dressed to kill. Really dressed to kill. I left my madam at two that afternoon, went straight there, and when I got inside I went to the lunchroom, ordered myself a glass of iced tea and took it straight to the patio. I can't begin to tell you how I felt. There I was inside, sitting down, and I could see the place where I used to look through. Do you understand what I'm trying to say? Do you?"

"Sort of," said Mr. George. He stared steadily into the fire, rubbing the tips of his thumbs together.

"Well," Sarah said, "after a while I felt like I'd been there all my life. In fact, I was even getting a little bored, and then this fellow came up. He came over to my table and sat down. Just like that. He came over, sat down and started to talk. We went together that same afternoon, and we stayed together after, for a year. I was really a fool." She shook her head sadly. "Some fool. But I loved him. I loved him because I could respect him. But I guess I respected him too much. I started being honest with him, and he started to hate me."

"What were you honest about?" asked Mr. George.

"I told him about the men I'd known. I never loved any of them, but I was hurt plenty, and even though it was in the past I had to tell him."

"Why?"

"I don't know. I guess it made me feel better. I don't know. The important thing is that he couldn't stand knowing I'd been with other men. And when I got pregnant, we broke up." She paused. "Ain't you going to say nothing?"

"What's there to say?" said Mr. George. He rested his head on the back of the couch and touched her shoulder with his hand. She stood up. "I'd better get Clyde to bed, and I think I'm getting a little sleepy, too."

"You're—"

"Clyde! Get up and go to bed." He rose, half asleep, leaving his monkey balanced precariously in the chair, and left the room.

"You're sure making it hard for me," said Mr. George.

"Not if you're a man, I ain't making it hard. A man is supposed to understand a woman's weakness."

"That's not what I'm—"

"He's supposed to understand anything."

"Okay!" shouted Mr. George. "I understand. Now, for the love of God, let's talk about something else."

"I wish I could! I wish I could meet somebody who could make me forget about him. Somebody with just a little of his good side. You know, he took me to more places in that one year than I've ever been before—or since! And please, don't get the idea that I'm saying we don't go out. I just mean he took me downtown, to places we can't afford to go to."

Mr. George stood. "Sarah, what do you want?"

She was silent for a while, and then she answered, "I don't know."

"Well," he said, "since you had your say tonight, maybe I'd better have mine." He paused while she sat down on the couch. "I like you." He turned from her and watched the shadows on the wall. "As far as anything else goes, I guess I ain't happy and I ain't sad. I'm sure not rich— but I ain't poor either. I ain't ugly and I ain't good-looking, and I don't like going downtown among white folks. They make me nervous."

The fire in the stove had burned low. The room was almost dark, and he could barely see her face in the remaining light. "Will you look see how much oil's left in the stove?" she asked. He stooped and then kneeled, peering about the hot metal carefully. "Not much," he finally said. "Looks like it's on E."

"Well then, you'd better turn it out." He fumbled about for the knob while she went on talking in a low voice. "I've been on pins and needles all day," she said. "I wanted everything to go right. I even prayed to God." She went over to him. He was still fumbling about the stove, and when she touched him he tried to rise, almost knocking it over. "Damn it! I've never known a man to be so clumsy." His slap sent her crashing into the chair. "Oh, God," she cried, "aren't there any men left anywhere in this world?"

"*Chica, chica, chica, chi—ca, chi—ca, chi—ca.*" The fuzz-covered monkey in his red velvet suit stopped drumming when he bumped into her leg. She reached down, picked it up, and hurled it at him in the darkness.

—1964

Red Bonnet

Lindsay Patterson

GRANMA JO just upped and walked one day. That she did. She never learnt walking like other people, for she hadn't walked a day in her life, that is, till right 'fore she just vanished into thin air. 'Course I know it ain't so, 'cause I see her sometimes, just sittin'.

I was there the day she suddenly popped herself out of her lopsided old black rocker and just walked on down the street as if she had been walking all her life. I scooted in the house to tell Ma and nearly got tore up with the big razor strap she kept handy over the kitchen sink 'fore I persuaded her to go look for herself. She did, and we could see Granma promenading so straight and proud down the street and nodding her head and saying good morning like she did it every day; and people so flabbergasted that they could hardly speak. And then she came back and sat down in her old rocker like she always did and stayed there till her daughter and her husband came from work and picked up chair and all and carried her into the house like they always did about dusk.

When people tole the daughter and her husband about Granma walking the daughter tole 'em they were all crazy and jealous. Jealous she meant of the new car she had sent all the way from across the ocean, and when she passed by in it kicking up dust 'cause she was going so fast and our eyes popping out of our heads; I guess she thought we were jealous all right.

The next morning everybody sat in his yard not minding the sun beaming down so hard it'd dry up a Jersey cow, or that the folks cross town were howling for their breakfasts and dinners, and all mad 'cause they never had to take care

of their brats before and finally getting a taste of how awful their little monsters really were. Nobody had to wait long. Close to an hour after the daughter and her husband went to work, Granma pushed herself up from her old rocker and started walking again. We kids followed after her, and our folks was so busy watching her walk they didn't notice us running behind the old lady shouting, "One-two, one-two, and look at Granma Jo GO!" WHEW! She didn't go slow. She was like Boots Hatcher, the time he came running so hard into home plate that the only thing that could stop him was the big Pea-con tree in Mister Laske's cotton patch cross the road, and if Boots's head hadn't been so goshdang tough it'd kilt him right then and there.

Granma didn't just walk up and down the block like she did the day before, she went over to Peach Street and walked around for a while and then came back to our street and walked. Twenty-seven times she walked up and down Peach Street, and no countin' the times she walked our street. By the time Granma was through walking we kids were all pooped out, but Granma looked as if she didn't want to quit. But she finally did, and got in her rocker just in time, too. Her daughter and her husband came sailing down the road in their new car, kicking up a dust storm the likes of which we never seen in these parts. Even the rich white folks never drive so fast. They hardly raise a speck.

The daughter really got mad when she was tole that Granma was walking again. She threatened to move and she said that we were not genteel people anyways and she didn't know why she lived on this ugly street anyway. I guess the reason she didn't ask Granma had she been walking again was that Granma just sat there with that sweet smile on her face and her big black eyes shining as if they were close to tears. And then they carried her in like they always did about dusk and put her to bed. They didn't haft to change her clothes like Ma did me years ago being that she wore her going-to-bed clothes all the time, but she did, like me, get a change of clean ones every week. Only I got mine every Saturday night. There was never any set day when they'd change Granma's. Just one morning you'd see her sittin' in her rocker looking so fresh and clean you'd think she was an angel down from heaven.

A delegation of women from our street decided to go over and see the daughter 'cause they didn't want anybody calling them liars. Besides, they didn't think much of the daughter anyways. Her and that new car, even if she did work for the richest white family in town she only got five dollars more a week than most of the ladies, and that wouldn't buy a new car like the folks' she worked for, even with her husband working at the sawmill like all the other men.

Well, the delegation didn't get anywhere with the daughter. I know, I heared it all. We lived next door to Granma. Our house being only about ten feet away, and when anybody raised their voice we could hear everything. Shucks, I heared something every night between the daughter and her husband. Ma and Pa had their room on the other side of the house and they couldn't hear a thing. Well, anyways, it seem that the husband didn't know how the daughter could afford the car, either.

Anyways. Mrs. Goodfellow, president of the AME Zion Church Women's Missionary Society, headed the delegation, and if anybody could straighten out Granma's daughter she could. Mrs. Goodfellow could hold her own with anybody. She makes her husband mind her just like Ma makes me mind her. And if he talks back, like I do sometimes to Ma, she paddles him just like Ma paddles me, only she does it with her fist. But the difference is I don't cry as loud as he does.

But Mrs. Goodfellow was no match for the daughter. We found that the daughter could holler just as loud as Mrs. Goodfellow, even louder.

It's a good thing that the daughter belonged to the Baptist church two miles from town, 'cause it's hard enough having to hear Mrs. Goodfellow getting carried away at prayer meetings every Wednesday, with the AME church only two streets over and down a little toward Snakes' Pond.

Well, Mrs. Goodfellow said to the daughter, "You been telling lies on us and that ain't right. We ain't got nothing to lie about. We all love Granma like you do, and we all seen Granma walking. She walks better than I do, like she been walking all her life. Granma been fooling you. She could walk all the time."

At that the daughter called Mrs. Goodfellow "a bald-headed lie," and the two women started pulling out each other's hair, and Mrs. Grover, vice-president of the Missionaries, got bopped on the head a couple of times before she could part them.

After that Mrs. Goodfellow started calling the daughter nasty names and telling her that she was no good and not fittin' to live in a decent neighborhood; and that she must be doing something wrong to get a new car like the folks she worked for had.

The daughter said, "I works hard and I spends my money anyway I Gawddamn please." Several of the ladies put their hands over their mouths when they heared her use the Lawd's name in vain. It was all right for the men to cuss but to hear a lady use that kind of language, and it wasn't even Saturday night, did not set well with the delegation, most of whom belonged to the Sunday Night Bible Study Group, too.

Finally the daughter said she'd stay home tomorrow and see if Granma walked, and then she ordered the delegation out of her house. Some of them didn't want to leave "poor Granma" in the house 'cause they thought the daughter would do somethin' to her. A woman using the Lawd's name like that'll do anything, they said, and them forgetting that all of their husbands met at Benny's Poolroom every Saturday night, and they went dragging them out on Sunday mornings for church, and the husbands cussing and they cussing right back.

The next day our street was like it was at circus time in the fall on the road going out by Mister Silas Adams' farm. Some of the white folks musta heared about Granma. Their big shiny cars, just like the one the daughter had, were parked all up and down the street. They carried Granma out early that morning and she had been washed and had on her clean red going-to-bed clothes, and her hair had been combed and braided just like my sister's pigtails. The street was crammed so full of people that Granma couldn't have walked if she'd wanted to.

You probably guessed it. Granma didn't budge an inch. She just sat there smiling all cherubic, like one of those figures on the big stone white Epistle church or somethin' like that.

Along about dinner time the people waiting for Granma to walk became restless, especially the white folks, and they began to holler at Granma, but she paid them no mind. Just smiling, I guess, at all the excitement she was causing.

At nightfall everybody went away real mad. The ladies on my street could be heared laying out Granma. They said she just had the Devil in her and all the time they thinking her a woman of God. The ladies from the Bible Study Group, of which Granma was a good standing member, talked about putting her out. Mrs. Goodfellow said that Granma did just what the white folks wanted. It just confirms to them, she said, that we all do nothing but lie. "Ain't nothing but the Devil in that woman." Them was her exact words. "The Devil done come to earth in the form of that old lady."

The only body who was happy about Granma not walking was the daughter; she sat on the porch long after dark singin' like a croaked frog, "I tole 'em so and I tole 'em so."

Things just kinda went along for a while and people forgot about Granma and her daughter and her husband. As Ma said, things was duller than dull. But Ma kept saying she smelt some-thin' in the air and she didn't know what it was. I didn't pay that no mind, Ma was always smelling somethin'. She claimed she smelt somethin' when old man Turner got kilt. She never tole exactly what it was she smelt, but she said she smelt it a week before he got cut in two at the sawmill. I tole her if she ever smelt anything about me to keep it to herself, 'cause I didn't want to know about it.

After what Ma said I noticed somethin' about Granma that I guess other people didn't. She smiled now like my sister does when she wants somethin' from Ma and she knows that Ma doesn't want her to have it. Sis just grins and plays up to Ma, and Ma seeing her so happy and lovable gives her what she wants. She never done me like that when I tried it.

Granma had that same smile, like she wanted somethin' and she was set on getting it. In trying to find out what Granma wanted I'd go over and offer her a lick of my ice cream, but she'd never take it. I don't know why I did that 'cause I ain't never offered my ice cream to nobody since I let Choot Sample take a lick and he darn near took it all, and Ma seeing what he did, tole me not to never give anybody my ice cream ag'in or she'd cut off my nickel a day. But Granma wanted somethin' and it wasn't ice cream.

I hate to see August coming, 'cause it's getting too near schooltime, but there's one good thing. Some days it gets a little cool, but then there're lots of bad points about it getting cool. You can't get no ice cream at the little store on Peach Street and it's quite a piece to haft to truck way uptown. 'Course you can ride the bus, but heck, ain't no sense for a fellow like me to ride it, I wouldn't have anything left over for my ice cream, it being a nickel one way.

There was that day I decided to go to town and buy me some vanilla, come hell or high water, as Pa says. It was hot as blazers that day and a fellow just got all wet if he moved a muscle. Outside of the ice cream cooling you off when you got to the place, they had some kind of thing in it that you couldn't see but it made a little humming noise and the place felt like a March wind had come and hit it. Well, anyways, I re-member that day well, 'cause it was near the end of August and I was getting nervous. There had been talk around that old Miss Dalton was going to have the sixth, and I was as scared as a wildcat of her. She made you wear ties to her class and if you forgot one morning and didn't wear one, she made you put on one of her dead pa's ties, which was kinda spooky; and you'd get no peace from the other kids, they being big and crazy-colored. WOW! You could see them for a mile off. My brother wore one once and he couldn't sleep for a week after. He said it was like having a noose around your neck, and you was waiting for old man Dalton to come and choke you any minute. I heared that the father and daughter didn't get along at all.

As I was getting ready to take off for town the mailman came by. It was a good thing. Ma wasn't going to let me go. She said it was too hot and I'd catch sunstroke. Well, anyways, the mailman left a welfare check for Granma like he always did about this time of month.

I put on my big straw hat with the little green men on it. It came from Panama, that's what the man in the store said when Pa bought it. And Pa and the man talked about it, since both said they had passed through it during the War. Pa said he didn't see much of it, it being so near dinner time and his rolls was about to burn and when he finished tending them they was way out in the ocean and all he could see was a little speck. He tole it to the white man so it must've been true, about a big old somethin' like that looking like a speck.

Anyways. As I was about to pass Granma's I saw that she was trying to get up. She was twisting from side to side and then she put both of her hands on the chair arms and lifted herself. HOTDANG! *She was walking again.*

She came straight down the steps and headed for the mailbox without anything on her head; it being so hot and all she could've had a sunstroke right there. Well, she opened the mailbox and took the letter out and went right past me. I caught up and asked her where she was off to. She tole me she was going to town and I tole her it was too hot, that she'd catch sunstroke, and maybe die. And she tole me she wasn't. Not today anyway. I'd never heared Granma talk so clear before. Usually she said things kinda slow like all old people do. Since I couldn't talk no sense to her, I tole her I was going to town, too, and she said I'd better walk fast or I'd get left behind.

When we got to town I was dripping wet and Granma had hardly worked up a sweat. She took the shortcut through Mister Aaron Tobdy's cornfield and that was enough to work up a sweat,

'cause he'd said that if he found any "niggers" passing through his cornfield he'd fill their hide full of buckshots, but I couldn't talk no sense to Granma.

I wanted to hurry to the ice cream place and get cooled off 'fore I drowned, me being so wet and on top of that my skin prickling from the corn leaves, but Granma wanted me to go to the bank with her, telling me that she might need somebody to tell the bank people who she was. She didn't. They must've heared about her there. Pa says that white people know everything.

I left Granma in front of the bank and hurried to my place. It really was good to get inside and I felt just like somebody had poured a big hundred-pound block of ice on me all crushed up. After I got my vanilla I looked around for Granma and I saw her coming out of Herman's where we buy all of our things. She had on a big red bonnet, the reddest color I'd ever seen. Granma was smiling, and she strutted down the street like she did the first day she started walking. I declare. She sure looked swell.

I asked Granma was she ready to walk back and she tole me that she was going to take the bus, for she wasn't going to get her new bonnet all dusty and everything. She said she had always wanted a red one and now that she got it nothing was going to happen to it. I tole her I was going to walk back, and she said she would pay my way on the bus, I being so kind as to go with her to the bank. I ain't never rode a bus before, but Ma always tole me to go to the back of it. The white folks, she said, took up the front, it being their bus and all, they could sit where they please.

We got on the bus all right, but after Granma paid the man our nickels her legs gave out and she couldn't go no further, having to wheel herself on the front seat to keep from hitting the floor. Remembering what Ma had said, I tried to help Granma up. She said she couldn't go no further, and that she done done all the walking she gonna ever do. I begged her, telling her what Ma had said to me. All she could say was that she done walked out. Everybody was frowning at me and Granma, and the bus driver tole us he wasn't going to move a damn inch till we sat where we belonged. But Granma couldn't move.

The driver got all red in the neck, then he got up and grabbed Granma by the arm and started draggin' her off the bus and me startin' to cry all over my vanilla just like I was a little baby, and not fightin' the man back like I was a man. He just let Granma fall on the ground and got back in the bus and drove off without even giving us our money back. Granma was asking for her red bonnet and it was nowhere in sight. She didn't say anything else, but I could see that she felt bad, 'cause I could see the water swell up in her eyes. I tried to get Granma up, but she still said she couldn't walk any more, and I'm startin' to cry ag'in, just like I was a baby, it being so hot and if Granma caught sunstroke and died, somebody'd blame me.

It's a good thing that Sister Mitchell came along with her T-Model, 'cause me and Granma might still be there and me being blamed for her sunstroke and not having anything to do with it. If Sister Mitchell hadn't been a big woman we'd never gotten Granma up those steps and into her rocker. I was scared to death to tell Ma, but she found out anyway.

Well, soon after Ma had finished with me in the kitchen I ran up to my room, and looking out of the window I could see Granma sittin' there and the sun still hot and it shining off her eyes like they was diamonds.

Soon the daughter came rushing down the road in her new car faster than a lunatic mule, and almost wound up in the ditch by the mailbox 'fore she could stop. She hopped out and ran up to Granma and started shoutin' and cryin' and carryin' on so that I couldn't make out a word she was saying. But Granma paid no attention at all. She had sort of a far-off look in her eyes, the kind Pa gets when he talks about going back across the ocean one day and living. After a while the daughter cooled down and I could make out her talk.

"You is been walking, ain't you? Getting on that bus and sittin' down in the front like you ain't had no sense. My own mama getting me in bad before all those white folks. They don't like what you done, Mama. They think I put you up to it and I tole 'em I swear I didn't know you could walk. I ain't never seen you. Lawd knows you done got those folks all riled up ag'in."

Granma iged her like she wasn't being talked to by nobody. She just sat as she did most of the time, only she wasn't smiling like she was most of the time. She had a funny look in her eyes and once she glanced over in my yard and looked at my red wagon.

Stuff really gets around in this town. As Pa says, the white folks know everything. Before I could count to ten our street was filled with big shiny cars full of white folks and they all getting out and standin' in front of Granma's, like they was the day all of 'em came to see her walk. I ain't going to tell you what they said, 'cause I ain't heared nobody say them things to a person before. Mr. Charlie Fairflax says things like that to his mules, but they ought not have said those things to Granma. She didn't do nothing much wrong.

The daughter hearing all that was going on came out and I guess she couldn't stand them talkin' to Granma like a dog, either, and she started saying them things right back and cussing, the likes of which Pa says no black man had ever done before. They soon left. I guess they were scared of the daughter, too.

For the rest of the afternoon, our street was so quiet it seemed like you was walking through a graveyard. Ma come up to my room and tole me not to go out and she gave me a hug and kissed me on the forehead. Somethin' she never did after I got a whipping.

In the early part of the night things were really dull and I was almost screaming mad at nothing to do. My brother ain't no fun, all he does is carves things with the dirk he got for Christmas. Well, I shouldn't have talked too soon, 'cause things really got hot later.

I smelt smoke. I thought it was my brother sneaking a cigarette, but he was fast asleep. I tole myself it was my imagination. Ma says I got too much funny-book stuff in my mind and she believes that one of these days I'll go crazy. She just doesn't understand a feller like me. One of these days I want to go far away like Pa done, where a feller can have some peace and nobody to bother him.

It was smoke I smelt all right. There got to be so much of it in my room that my eyes started burning and I had to go out. I went to Ma and

Pa's room and tole them about the smoke. They didn't seem at all surprised. They rushed out of the house and then rushed back grabbing my brother and sister. I tagged along behind my folks, not knowing what to expect, and there was the smoke, coming from Granma's house. Pa wanted to go in and see what he could do, but Ma held him back and tole 'em that he'd get as-phix—, well, anyways, she wouldn't let him go in. By the time the fire engine got there, the house had burnt up inside and all they could do was watch out for our house and the one on the other side. You could hardly tell from the outside that Granma's house was burnt, but inside there was nothing. They brought out the daughter and her husband and Ma wouldn't let me look. She caught me by the head and buried my face in her thigh.

By this time everybody on my street had come out and they didn't seem to care nothing about the daughter and her husband getting burnt up. They all wanted to find out about Granma. The women were wailin' and carryin' on so about Granma that I thought I'd cry, too. But the men said that there was nobody else in there. They kept looking and looking, but they couldn't find another body there. After a little while they gave up and decided to come back in the day and look, being that their lights were giving out.

They came early in the morning and searched for most of the day, but they still didn't find anything of Granma.

I ain't never tole nobody, but some nights I see Granma sittin' on the porch, her eyes shining in the moonlight and a bonnet on her head.

—1962

Old Blues Singers Never Die

Clifford Vincent Johnson

HERE'S ONE for the books: River Bottom, the blues singer, in Paris, and he isn't just here, but sporting a big fat diamond ring and wearing fine clothes to go with it . . .

I may be a G.I., but I found out a long time ago that this was Paris and I try all the time to tell the other guys there's something else happening outside of Pig Alley but no, they can't see that because goodtiming with those scroungy women is about all they can think of. Killing time, taking stuff's about the extent of their lives. I've got nothing against killing time, mind you, like I said I'm a G.I., but I realize the difference between Paris and Chicago South Side. I also know that these days call for you to have at least a little something in your head; you've got to have been a few places and seen a few things. That's why when they start getting sharped-up and loaded-up with liquor set to go wild, I say no, because me, it's the Latin Quarter, St.-Michel, St.-Germain, as fast as I can get there. Actually, but I don't go into all that with them, I've got my own private philosophy; I don't see any sense in wasting time when Paris is full of all kinds of people to rub shoulders with and learn something from, do you?

Take that restaurant where I ran into Bottom for instance. They've got a lot of places like that stuck up in little streets that wouldn't even make good alleys back home; and if you're not quick you'd miss them altogether. Anyway, those places are always filled up with all kinds of students and artists and every time I go in this one place where I met Bottom I see these Africans black as sin.

Back home, due to the fact that we're so mixed up with Mister Charlie, you hardly ever see anybody that black except down South, like my cousins for instance, in fact those Africans remind me a lot of my cousins—it's mostly the way they laugh and the way they walk and even when they get to talking African—how they're real free about it. Those are some all right guys though, those Africans. I remember one night after I'd been seeing them in there all the time, they started talking to me in that African they were talking to one another. To me, can you picture that?

"Wait a second," I say to them, "if you come on like that we can't get together at all."

"Ah," one of them says, "you are American."

"That's right."

"You are a student?"

"Kind of," I said and I did it smooth although I should have told him I was just a G.I., you see, and anyway I am a kind of student, too. "I'm not a full-time student but I try to pick up what I can."

He turns around and runs off a bunch of stuff in African to the others and they all look at me funny.

"You not go back, I think?" the one who speaks English says, shaking his head.

"Not go back home?" I say, because I don't know exactly what he means to say. "You mean not go to America?"

"Yes, you not go back to America?"

I didn't quite know if I'd understood him right but I told him sure I'd go back. I didn't have nowhere else to go. He told them what I said and they nodded to me and now I really didn't understand. But like I said before, they're good guys; they even said I should come to Africa one day before it was all over, and if they could understand English better we could probably get something even better going between us. And that taught me one thing: that that stuff they put over on you in school is a lot of junk—about how they're so different and act wild, especially since they don't look or act much different from my cousins down South.

They've got these French students, I guess they are. They try to be cool all the time: even talk cool French and not like most of the Frenchmen you see on the street who look like they want to fight every time they talk to one another; these students look as if they want to be colored. That's okay since they only act like that and don't end up getting into a fight like real colored folks back home and whenever one of them sees me he gives me a little nod, pretending to know what's happening which he doesn't really, but all the same it gives you a kick to see somebody imitating your way of life.

Mostly I have to give it to them when they draw things in those big green pads that they carry with them. Some of them are sure weird though, like when this guy sitting across from me all of a sudden started staring me in the face and then he took out a pad and began drawing something and when he finished it, he showed it to me, and he had a big grin on his face. I looked at it and it had a big, flat nose spread across the face and some fat lips sticking about a mile out from the forehead. Another guy might have wanted to fight. . . . Don't get me wrong now, I'm proud as the next person of being colored; that's something I'm tough about. You don't have to be white to make it, like a lot of people think—white doesn't say anything to me —but the truth was that that just didn't look anything like me. And that's where the other guy would have made his mistake. Not me! Me, I shook my head big as you please to show him that I was really getting a kick out of it, especially since the guy himself was so serious about the way he did it and seemed like a kid with something he was real proud of having made himself. So I figured, what the hell, he knows what he's doing and besides, I didn't know too much about that far-out modern stuff anyway. So I kept it,

and even if I don't flash it around where everybody can see it, I still have it.

You can imagine how surprised I was to run into somebody so down-to-earth as Bottom in that place. Everything I know about Bottom came from some very down-to-earth sources. That was before I went into the Army; we were living on Kimbark Avenue, I remember. We had this regular janitor who the only thing regular about was how he would wait until snow got piled up behind-deep to a ten-foot monkey and the hawk would be whipping across the ice on Lake Michigan at about a hundred miles an hour and that's when he'd be regular about disappearing and letting the furnace go to hell. That's the reason why they had to go and look for somebody to come and fill in, usually around the taverns on Forty-seventh Street.

I remember I was watching this shabby-looking guy fighting with a snow shovel out by the back steps.

"That's a man used to be known anywhere he wanted to go," my old man told me, pointing to him as he said it.

It was pretty obvious, by the way he was scuffling, that it couldn't have been for shoveling no snow, so I asked him what did he do.

" 'Course you never heard of 'im," he said, "you was too young, fact, most of that time you wasn't even on nobody's mind, especially with times being so hard as they was. That's River Bottom, one of the greatest blues singers ever was."

I couldn't see how come he didn't sing then, instead of doing what he was doing. My old man said, "He's just down on his luck, that's all."

"How you mean, down on his luck?" I asked him. "He lost his voice or something?"

"No, it ain't that. I suppose he's still got his voice; it's the ears what listened to that voice what's lost."

Now if you had known my old man, you would be used to all kinds of stuff like that. But losing ears! that was too weird for me. But my old man, you see, well, he spent most of his life down South. He knows a lot about colored history, and colored history, I'd learned, is filled with a lot of weird things, so even if it didn't make much sense at the beginning, I'd learned to listen a while longer and he'd usually explain and what he'd be saying wouldn't be so weird after all. He told me about how there had been many singers like Bottom in Bottom's day but Bottom, well, Bottom was the best. Then it wasn't like now; they had good singers, singers who had something to say and not a bunch of crap. He said that any one of them had more music in his little finger than these slickheads of today had underneath those hairdos.

That was because then our folks liked to hear about their troubles and how hard making it was. When they could hear somebody telling about his own life and talking heart to heart about his own problems, right up there before them in flesh and blood like that, they got the strength to keep on going. And that big Depression, what was that? It didn't say nothing to no colored man because he hadn't known nothing but depressions. By the time the people started crying about some depression and white folks was raining out of windows all over the country, colored folks might have been crying too but you'd have never known it and it was the same way with blues singers like Bottom. They could go anywhere, have any price they could name and when they shouted about hard times the people didn't cry for laughing.

Now that was my old man saying all that. I couldn't know about all that because like he said, I wasn't even born and after I was born I had all the advantages of the North (my old man was smart enough to get out when my mother got pregnant). But he made me know. When he went and dug some records out that I'd never seen before from way back in the closet and he handled them so gentle and got so still after he put them on the record player to listen, that's when I began to see what Bottom meant to him. I've got to admit that that was some other stuff, I mean I couldn't have known anything about *that* without hearing it, and even hearing it I still couldn't believe it was really like that. The way Bottom sounded, I wouldn't ever know anything about. . . . All that made me start thinking about the music we young guys had the habit of listening to, and the stuff we did, and how my old man always stayed down on me about it and I never understood why. I was thinking about us scream-

ing and carrying on like we did at the Trianon Ballroom on South Parkway and thinking about the way the girls fought to have a piece of torn clothing, or a kiss or anything they could get from these smooth-tongued, conk-headed crooners with nothing to say but some sugary nonsense with a beat in groups called the Roaches, or the Studs, or the Stone Thrillers, or any of a hundred even more stupid names and it was listening to Bottom made me ashamed of all that.

I am not the kind of guy that likes to say I told you so, but I really did. I said right then and there, "He's going to be known again," but my old man told me no.

"Folks don't want to hear what that's about," he said. "They've got other things on their minds now. They think hard times is dead and buried. They can't get rid of their money fast enough. What Bottom's talking about ain't true for them no more, ain't nothing true for them 'cept spendin' that money and playing life for a fool."

I let him go on, but knowing this is modern times and they've got TV and jets all around the world, somebody was bound to find out about Bottom. . . .

So, here I am sitting in this little restaurant taking in all that good atmosphere, waiting to get waited on, when I hear this real country voice asking for some greens. I heard right away it wasn't G.I. talk and when I looked I couldn't believe it. I went up and asked him to be sure.

"If you can speak French, I'll make myself know you," he said. Then he looked at me kind of suspicious for a second and said, "Where you know me from?"

"Chicago," I told him.

"Then, since you're a home boy—sit down. I don't have to tell you how it is. I'm trying to get me some greens and maybe some ribs, but between you and me, I know that would be asking just a little too much."

"I gave up long time ago," I told him. "If they've got 'em they keep 'em well hid. But why don't you let me take you to this place across town where they sell everything, they've even got chitterlings, good as they had at that place on Forty-seventh and Drexel. . . ."

"Why you want to tell me all that?" he said. "That don't leave me much hope; I've got a show to do around the corner at the Blues Cave."

"You are here now? I mean, you got a gig in Paris?"

"I ain't no tourist, let's put it that way," he said, looking at me as though he were peeking over glasses.

"I know about you," I tried to assure him. "What I didn't know was that they could pick up on the stuff you put down."

"No," he said, making a real serious face like he was thinking about that, "but I tell you what: I don't have no trouble picking up on the stuff they put down for it. But wait a minute, how's a young fellow like you come to be knowing so much about me?"

He made me real proud so I said, "They've still got some young fellows around with some taste."

"No," he said, "it ain't that. I figured you might be knowing some other things that you ought not to be knowing." And we had a good laugh.

About that time I spy this fellow I know calls himself Moses Selassie. He's one of those guys that I'd seen hanging around all the time. I'd heard him speaking French like it was English and he seemed to have a lot of sense, so I called him to come and sit with us.

"Moses, man," I say to him, "you know River Bottom, the blues singer, don't you?"

Bottom looked him in the face and squinted.

"Moses?" he said, looking at me then back at Moses. "I thought you told me your name was Jenkins or something like that?"

"When did I tell you that?"

"You must've forgot."

"I told you my name was something else beside Moses?"

"Listen, don't tell me I'm crazy. The first night I saw you, you told me you'd just come into town and you told me your name was Jenkins Henry or Henry Jenkins, or something like that."

"No, you've got the wrong man," Moses said, pulling at his bristling, black beard. "How long ago was that?"

"I didn't write no notes, but it was a good two months ago."

"I figured you had me wrong. Two months ago I was in Israel picking up my inheritance and

before that I was in Ethiopia, visiting my relatives."

"You told me then, you came from New York," Bottom said laughing, "but that's all right, us folks got to make it best we can."

"Look, my man," I say, because I don't know what to call him now, "I didn't want to put you in the trick, I just wanted you to order some greens for Bottom."

"Greens?" he says to Bottom. "Don't you know you're in Paris, France, and not in Paris, Georgia?"

"I know I'm in Paris, France, better than you."

"You don't act like it," Moses says. "Don't you know that they throw that stuff away over here?"

"Throw it away?" I say.

"They throw it away because those are scraps," Moses says. "All that stuff you call soul food, all that's nothing but scraps. The master threw scraps to the hogs and to the colored folks."

"How you know so much about it?" I asked him, and Bottom broke out laughing and Moses didn't go for that.

"Maybe my folks was throwing the scraps . . ." he says.

Bottom passes him off by saying, "Yeah, man, that's right, your folks was throwin' scraps."

When the waiter comes up Moses commences right off to run down a long spiel in French and when he's through the waiter looks at him and grins and says: "Tell me in English." And Moses mumbles that he wants beef something or other and then Bottom and me order chicken and rice. And while we're sitting and waiting Moses digs in his pocket and pulls out a book and starts reading as if we aren't even there.

"Look, Bottom," I say, "I'd like to know how'd they come to hear about you way over here? I don't mean to be getting into your business but when I left to go into the Army you wasn't doing any good for yourself."

"Seriously, who told you about me? You pretty young to be knowin'."

"My old man."

"They'd have to be pretty old," Moses chimes in, looking up from his book. "Bottom's about as old as water." But Bottom ignores him. "Hey," he goes on anyway, "you should be glad. Aren't you glad?"

"A lot of people have heard of him," I say.

"But there's a whole lot of people dead since then, too," Moses says.

"I just put my trust in God," Bottom says, still ignoring Moses. "He's responsible for me bein' here."

"You can call it God if you want," Moses says.

"What you call it?" Bottom says, turning on him.

"I wouldn't call it God, and you know better yourself."

"I asked you what you'd call it."

"Bottom, don't be crazy."

"I ain't crazy. You crazy if you don't know what I'm talkin' about."

"I don't know nothing about no God. Where is He?"

"You still young, boy," Bottom says. You would have expected him to be mad at Moses or Jenkins or whatever his name was, but he stayed cool—fact, he was talking soft and almost loving. "You got to walk it for yourself. Can't nobody walk it for you."

Moses shakes his head and frowns and goes back to reading and the waiter comes up and while we're eating, everything calms down.

"Yeah, baby," Bottom says after a while, "I put all that religious stuff down when I was up there. All that stuff they used to tell me 'bout. What you talkin' 'bout? I was River Bottom, I could make people laugh and if I wanted, could make 'em cry too, that's right. Had more women than you could shake a stick at. Man, I was up there and I was goin' through the gates of hell and I didn't know it."

Moses looks up from his plate and says, "That's what's kept colored folks behind for so long, all that stuff you're talking about. Why can't you be man enough to admit that you're on your own? Quit talking about hell; that's life, Bottom."

"Yeah," Bottom says, "that's just what I thought; I could make it on Bottom and Bottom knew just how the deal went down. But then, one day, yeah, baby, one day Bottom didn't have nothin', not a cent, no place to go, nothin'. Bottom wasn't sharp no more and he didn't have no

more women; Bottom had him some blues and you better know it and right then and there I got to thinkin' about that stuff I'd put down long time before and I had to see that none of that belonged to Bottom; Bottom wasn't nothin', baby. Bottom wasn't no better than a speck of dirt and I woke up one mornin' and started prayin' and readin' the Bible. Nigger! I said to myself, this earth ain't yours, the earth is the Lord's and the fullness therein. And I knew that the Lord had done sacrificed for the world His Son Jesus Christ, which must have called for a lot of sufferin' on His part, and here I was cryin' 'cause I was broke. I was still livin' and that was somethin'. And who was Bottom anyway? . . ."

"You're a man, aren't you?" Jenkins says.

"I ain't nothin' before the Lord."

"That's the white man that made you believe that."

"Nigger, I ain't talkin' about no white man!" Bottom says, starting to get worked up. "Don't you go gettin' God and the white man mixed up. White man's lost 'fore he starts."

"If you weren't making it, Bottom, that was your folks' fault. Colored folks put you down. You better wake up, Bottom."

"Son, God is in everythin'. God is love, and He is buried so deep you can't see him. . . ."

"O," Moses says and laughs, "so that's how you figure. God got you up off the street back home and dropped you over here."

"You sound stupid. All I'm sayin' is that havin' faith . . ."

"Having faith, shit! Your God and all that crap had thrown you down. Having some white men with money is what you're trying to say. It wasn't any praying that got you here. White people trying to do some good for humanity brought you over here and put you in a museum . . ."

"Museum!" Bottom says. "Museum, you hear that? Nigger, what you talkin' 'bout? I'm workin' at the Blues Cave, that ain't no museum."

This Moses guy should have been cool and I told him so. What'd he want to jump on Bottom for, anyway?

"I'm just trying to straighten Bottom out," he says to me, "and you, do you go for all that stuff?"

"It's no big thing what I go for."

"Don't worry 'bout the mule," Bottom says to me, "he ain't no fool."

"You may not be no fool, but you don't act like you've got good sense. Your soul's in the white man's hands. He left you with a dead horse, something worn out that he'd thrown away, just like he'd thrown away all those scraps you call soul food . . ."

"Yeah, maybe he did throw it down. Yeah, suppose he did. I got it now, you hear me? I got it! Finders keepers, losers weepers. Looka here, I got nothin' to do with him not knowin' what to do with it."

"Aw, man," Moses says, "the hell with it! I don't want to go into all that anyway. You can't hear what I'm saying. You're deaf. But I'll tell you this, you may not want to hear it, but I'll tell you anyway." Moses leans up across the table with a stupid smile on his face and his coat lapels almost dipping in his plate. "You want to see where your God is? I'll tell you how: you just try to go back home with all that old-time rinky-dinky music, if you think God is everywhere. Your big rich white God's gonna get you in His booking office and have a heart-to-heart talk with you. And you know what He's gonna say? He's gonna say Bottom, you better get your black be-hind back in the Blues Cave if you know what's good for you, unless you want to come back and pull down public assistance. When He tells you that, do you think you gonna like it? You think you gonna say Lord goin' take care of me? You think you gonna pawn all them fine clothes you wearing, that diamond ring?—you're too old for that."

What Moses had done to Bottom was no different from if he'd just upped and slapped him smack in the face. Bottom just sat there, looking surprised, with his mouth half open and his lower lip hanging. Honest, it was like as if Moses had gone right upside his head! When Bottom started talking his eyes got as big as half-dollars and the big vein welled up in his forehead.

"I don't have nothin' my way, boy?" he says, "what you mean, my own way? Don't be tellin' me that shit! You think you got somethin' you own way? Do you? Tell me, boy, do you?"

"Forget it, Bottom."

"No, you ain't finished. No, now you listen to me, young boy . . ."

"Bottom, you've got nothing to tell me."

"I do got somethin' to tell you. Damn right I got somethin' to tell you, 'cause you think you know somethin'. I went up against Him, I crossed Him when I was young, but I knew I was crossin' Him and I could feel the evil I was doin' but I could feel Him all the while too, but you . . ."

"Okay, so I'm young, let me be young."

"Me, when I was young I could feel the Devil, but you, you don't feel nothin', that's why you in worse shape, you don't come nowhere close to feelin' nothin'. And you know why? No, you don't know a goddamn thing!"

"I know enough; more than you'll know."

"You don't know nothin'," Bottom spit out, and he almost did because he was choking up on his words and spit was coming out the corners of his mouth, "I say you don't know nothin', don't none of us know nothin'. How we gonna know somethin'? Just when we git a little power in our hands that the most dangerous time. You start to thinkin' you know somethin', figurin' you can do somethin' by yourself. But there ain't no days like that, Lord no. That's evil actin', Lord know it's evil, that's the way he work, evil: sneakin' up and lettin' you get your head up just a li'l bit higher above the trees, lettin' you get some fine clothes on your back and a big, brand-new Stetson on your heads, that's evil, Lord ain't that the truth, and then he just sit back there evil and he be grinnin' 'cause he know once you all dress up you ain't gonna turn back one look at the Lord, ain't that the truth Lord, and he take you and make you walk to where the Lord's light can't shine on you no more, yes Lord, and right there's when he cut out just like that and all them other things you'd been seein' cut out too, 'cause they was all a part of evil—and you's imaginin' it—and that's when you by yourself, Lord know you by yourself, you got to walk that lonesome road back, turn them fine things into somethin' to eat, turn 'em into . . ."

Moses reached over and shook Bottom by the sleeve. "Bottom, you're a bigger, more ignorant fool than I thought. . . ."

And about that time I got mad. I know I should've got mad before, before he'd hurt Bottom so bad. But when I get mad I don't say nothing, that's because I'm a regular guy and I want to wait and try to understand everybody. I learned something long time ago that came back to me while I was sitting up there watching this Moses fellow who was too proud to smell his own shit and even though I had tended to agree with some of the things Moses had said about religion, I had to agree with Bottom when he said that Moses wasn't nothing. And I was thinking how this Moses—and what was that guy's game anyway, calling himself all kinds of names?—who was nobody even, had less of a right to jump on Bottom who was already somebody. . . . One time back home when I was a little kid I used to get some of the other guys and we'd go down on Cottage Grove Avenue where they've got all these storefront churches. We'd get to dancing and laughing because we thought it was really funny the way all those cool jazz musicians, who worked when they could in the Sixty-third Street jazz clubs, would file into those churches the same way, carrying drums and horns and bass, everything. It was mostly funny watching those good sisters and brothers bowing and grinning all dressed in white and black, all holy-like, calling them young boys God's musicians and welcoming them in. When the service would get to rocking and moving with a good swing beat, we'd dance and cut up and even try to get people passing by to join us out on the sidewalk in front.

We'd do it every night without fail until that one night my old man collared me and whipped my head all the way home. I remember a lot of people sitting out on the tenement steps because it was hot and I remember trying to dodge all them blows and them laughing and my old man saying, "Ain't you got no respect?" WOP! "Ain't I taught you no better?" WOP!

And when he got home and got his razor strap he really got to teaching me how nobody had no right to be singing and dancing and cutting up like that when folks was praying, SMACK! and it didn't make no difference if you didn't understand them, SMACK! it was for them to understand, not you, that's what they had to get them through and that had well gotten them through for a long time and as long as I didn't

have nothing no better, SMACK! I ought not to be cutting up when nobody was praying. . . .

I learnt that well and I knew that praying was like what Bottom was doing; he wasn't in any church, but he was praying just the same because he was saying what he believed in; and so the next time Moses opened his mouth, and it didn't make any difference that the two of them had already stopped talking and were ignoring each other, that didn't matter I told him he didn't believe in nothing and the next time he said something to Bottom I was going to put my foot in his behind.

That was about the only thing that seemed to say something to him. He didn't say another word after that; he simply got up and went to look for the waiter and when he found him he paid him and wasted no time leaving.

I swore to Bottom that the next time I saw Moses I'd kick his behind anyway, on general principle, and make him apologize to him. But Bottom said not to worry. Bottom knew how that ass had messed up my night, that's probably why he had me come over to the Blues Cave to hear him play.

Once we got there, after I got a drink of Scotch in front of me and all that good blues in my ear, I had the best night I've had since I've left Stateside. Sitting up there was like me and Bottom had something going between us. All the while he was singing and playing, he kept looking over at me and I'd nod back at him and when the people saw that, I could tell by the way they were smiling that they didn't know what was happening—not really—and that, for them, I was somebody too. But they couldn't begin to imagine how boss all that made me feel.

So he finishes for the night and we go across town where we can find lights and people, and everything going like it was daytime—something like on Sixty-third, if you follow me—and all the while we're drinking good liquor he's telling me stories about all kinds of old-timers he was tight with, stories about Chicago and Kansas City and St. Louis, stories about everything, and they were some good stories too.

I told Bottom the same thing I'd told my old man, I mean how he was so good and all, and how with this modern age, he'd be back up top.

more tired than he'd been in a coon's age and had true, you don't know. I don't care what they say. I wouldn't be surprised if Bottom gets back Stateside before me.

He didn't deny any of that either, Bottom's no fool; he didn't say anything, he just looked at me for a long time and finally flashed me one of those little smiles like he'd been doing in the Blues Cave. He was beat, tired as he could be, more tired than he'd been in a coon's age and had

to go home. But he said I could look him up any time, any time I wanted and I said he didn't have to do all that for me but he said he did and that's when he paid up and we both went home. . . .

No, that was one night I won't forget for a long time! River Bottom, the blues singer, in Paris, France, doing all right for himself, that's something I've got to write my old man about. And you think I'm not going to tell him how for once he was wrong?

—1967

Ruth's Story

Henry Van Dyke

MERIJEAN WALLENSTEIN came out of the bathroom with Pink Ice on her face. Thousands of busy fingers, just as advertised, began to go to work around her tiny chin. "Darling," she said to Ruth, "you know something? I'd like something metaphysical to happen to me; nothing metaphysical's ever happened to me and it's sad-making."

Ruth rolled down a stocking over her heavy leg and looked up at her roommate. Merijean, oh Lord, was going to be pretentious again. Her little pygmy brain was tiresome at any time, but no, not today, not in all this hot weather. And all that Pink Ice was just as bad. Hot-looking, needless.

"Ruth?" Merijean threw *Movie Life* on the sofa and tucked her vain little red lips into a pout. "What's all the gloom for? You've been gloomy ever since you got home."

Stockingless, Ruth Schwartz's feet were cooling. The August heat, always worse on West Seventy-fourth Street than anyplace in town, climbed from the floor to strike her in the face. "Tired," she said, and then, pulling at the thick black hair around her neck, she said, "No, it's not only that entirely, it's that nun, that damned nun."

"*Nun?*"

"Oh, she wasn't fooling anybody, I can tell you that, but what gets me, what really gets me is how she can get away with it."

"Love, the heat's making you terribly cryptic. What's eating you?"

Ruth got out of the chair, in four movements, pulling at the damp brassiere strap wetting her shoulder, and waving her hand in the stubborn air. "The nun, the nun, the false nun begging on Forty-second Street! Merijean, I've never seen anything more disgusting. And I don't think there is. You know what? You could *see* that woman's heels. *High, high* heels, a mile high. Frilly. Except all filthy and old. And toeless! And this awful woman, this vile woman had the nerve, the gall"—Ruth's hand stabbed the hot air, and held it there, and dropped it to her thigh.

She turned sharply when she heard Merijean's silly laughing, bad laughing, like a chorus girl's, all tinsel and cellophane. "You mean the Forty-second Street nuns? Around Eighth Avenue? Oh, really, darling, you mean you've never seen them out before?" Merijean giggled, reached for a cigarette, her Pink Ice drying. "With their grubby habits and grubby nails and grubby little blood-shot eyes? They *are* heaven, aren't they? *Ter*ribly heaven."

Ruth Schwartz stood still; it would have been very easy to slap her, slap Merijean's pampered little vain face. "I don't think it's funny. Not even a little bit. It's . . . it's . . ."

"It's what, darling?" Merijean hopped up from the chair, rolled her body on a mannequin hip, flicked ashes from her cigarette the way she'd seen Bette Davis do it in a movie.

Even in an argument, Merijean had to be dramatic, vain with all that skinniness she tried to make pass as slim. Anybody could be skinny and unhealthy if they wanted to eat salads and take pills and massage flesh half of the day and night. Even in high school, back in Wilkinsburg, years before they met again and became roommates in New York—even *then* Merijean was buying lotion and pills and impractical clothes and frills like every other birdbrain female. Even then she was throwing herself at men just like she did last week with Bernie Kaye who God knows was an intellectual and he'd soon see quick enough what Merijean was made of. She'd manage to spoil him, though. Probably even sleep with him. There certainly wasn't any question about Merijean's being a virgin or not.

"It's *what*, darling?" Merijean had spread her skinny shoulders back into a ridiculous posture she'd seen in a fashion magazine, showing just how little bust she really did have. "Huh? Oh, Ruth, honestly, you'll never get Wilkinsburg out of you, will you?"

Ruth sat down and turned the radio dial to WNCN. "I still say it's wrong."

"Wrong? Wrong?" Merijean nearly danced around the room in her Midgie panties and Playtelle bra. "It may be, darling, but everybody's money-oriented in this town."

Ruth turned up the volume to the Schumann symphony. Money-oriented, indeed; Merijean never heard that word until last week, and she still probably didn't know what it meant.

"*Every*body begs for *something* in one way or the other," she said. "All right, I'll grant you, it's crude, I admit it, but, love, it's part of the scheme of things, I mean, of all the pure, premeditated, distilled *sin* in New York, this is *nothing*. In fact, it's funny."

Schumann whirled around Ruth's dark head as she watched Merijean's Pink Ice drying. On the street, the evening sun stood on the pavement, and in the room it was hot, and August, and hot, so hot. "Merijean," Ruth said, "it is not funny. It's false, Merijean. It's vulgar and it's a disgrace —to the Catholic church.

Merijean picked up *Movie Life*, blew smoke to the ceiling as though she were a little fountain spewing up water. "So you should worry about it, love? Let the Catholics worry about it."

"It's false," Ruth said and walked, without much arch in her feet, from the room. In the kitchen, over a Birdseye package of broccoli, Schumann followed her, and sweat ran down her neck. "It's false," she said.

Bernie Kaye drove up after supper in a little blue MG and his pants were too tight and his jacket was too short and he focused his eyes so *hard* into a person's, but his strawberry hair was good to look at and he was intelligent. Just what he would find to talk about to Merijean was what she'd like to know. "Come in. Merijean'll be ready in a minute, or at least she ought to be ready in a minute. Sit."

His eyes were blue, blue as his MG, and as jaunty. "Cigarette?" he offered. "I'm sorry, but you know, I've forgotten your name. Or maybe I never really caught it—the *noise* in that lobby last week was—"

"Ruth," she said softly but it seemed like a thunderclap, saying it, and standing there in the middle of the floor. Why was she always standing in the middle of the floor?

"Of course, of course," he lied, stretching to reach an ashtray, stretching, smiling, lying to her beautifully. "I'm a dunce on names."

Well, he certainly remembered Merijean's and God knows how loud the theatre crowd was talking in that lobby last week and half the time Merijean mumbled, but on the other hand, the way she threw herself after him with her cigarette holder and silly Greenwich Village earrings in that lobby, with people watching it, too, well it's no wonder he could remember Merijean. "It's Ruth Schwartz," she said to him and sat down quickly. "Bernard Kaye. I remember yours all right, you're Bernie Kaye." She wanted to hit herself with a hard object for sounding—so thick.

With his teeth, he held his cigarette in the center of his mouth and moved his lips dryly around it to speak. "Can I take off this jacket?" he asked, standing to peel off his Wash 'N Wear before she could reply. "I'm about to die in this thing."

"Na, na, na, darling," Merijean said, entering the room in a raspberry dress, with faun steps, and tilting a perfume bottle upside down at the end of her finger. "I'm just about"—she spun around in a half circle, searching the living room for her purse—"ready."

Bernie Kaye's composure wobbled and Ruth saw that he didn't even have the decency to keep his eyes off the thin of Merijean's dress in the rear—even if Merijean was trying to provoke him to look down there. And she *was* trying to provoke Bernie to look down there, down there where her skinny hips were, where the elastics on her panties made a dent in her raspberry dress when she walked. And she walked so it would. You'd think Bernie, or anyone, could see through a trick like that.

Ruth sighed and fanned her face. "You've got too much of that stuff on. Really, Merijean."

"Too much, old groutchie-pooh? It can never be too much. It's very heaven, isn't it? Don't you think it's heaven, Bernie? *Ter*ribly heaven?" Merijean slid a perfume-damp finger down Ruth's neck. "There! 'S good for you. Good as vitamins. And now, *off* we go," she said, pulling Bernie by the arm, faking tiny helpless high heel steps as if she walked that way all the time and had to press into him every now and then for support. The pity of it all was that Bernie had a mind; couldn't Merijean see that Bernie had a mind?

And then . . . giggling . . . floating up from the curb by Bernie's little blue MG . . . "No, no," Merijean's voice came faint, up from the street to Ruth's window on the second floor, "Ruthie's a good kid, actually" . . . then something she couldn't hear . . . "but quite fan*ta*stically drab" . . . the car door whacked shut, and then, from Merijean again, peppermint-candied, "Ooooh, Ber*nie*."

Ruth hurried to the window, face frozen in the evening heat. The car had gone.

After a time, she lifted her hands from the windowsill and lay down in the dark-hot, perfumed bedroom. Her eyes were open and she listened to every sound she could listen to and pushed every thought in her mind out of her mind. Over and over she refused to think of Bernie Kaye. There was no point in thinking about him. Besides, he was smart, he wasn't like the rest of the men Merijean got and dropped, and- he'd soon enough see what Merijean was made of. Yet, maybe he liked falseness and frill. Maybe all men liked falseness and frill. Camouflage. Deception. Maybe. . . . She got up in the dark and went to Merijean's dressing table and turned a small wall lamp on her face. Slowly, step by step she dabbed into Merijean's things; first some cold cream to reach down in the pores for the dirt—it said so on the label; then some foundation cream—over her cheeks, her chin, her nose; now the powder, but why would Merijean have *three* different kinds? . . . well; now a little

pencil line around the edge of the eyes, and at the corners a faint little line out towards the temple; and so many lipsticks—so many! . . . but how really different was one from the other? Her hair. What about all of her hair? If she brushed it a bit upwards, and . . . there. She held a Japanese silk, Merijean's robe, up to her shoulders, but she had not done a good job of it; she needed practice at it; she had not done a good job of it: there was, in the mirror, a—a— "You clown!" she hissed.

The still air began to move and began to cool, but she did not leave the dresser with its thousands of artifices, its false things.

It was late when she scrubbed her face in the unlit bathroom. It was late when she shut her eyes in the black bedroom; Merijean had been back for more than an hour, and she was asleep, snoring, with her red-tipped fingers dripping over the edge of the white sheet, when Ruth Schwartz shut her eyes in the black bedroom.

There was only one thing Ruth loved, really loved without reservation, and loved constantly. Pigeons. Undoubtedly it was a childhood thing, the adoration of pigeons, but she couldn't remember any significant incident, any delightful trauma with pigeons. At times it seemed that all the love she had in her would run out of her as she watched them. And all summer she watched them amidst sun-dried droppings, old people, young people, at lunch time on the steps facing Fifth Avenue at the New York Public Library. Hundreds and hundreds of pigeons played games there and joyously took food from old ladies. On the stone cornices of the library they lodged, and they swooped down in winged clusters at the least provocation; this was their province. Passersby moved out of *their* way. There was a joy in their strut, an aggressive cockiness to their noonday conclave.

Ruth usually packed a fruit lunch and sat on the steps to eat it. Some days she bought it, but on those days she tried to find the speediest lunch possible, for her office was several long Manhattan blocks away from the pigeons, on Forty-second Street, further west than the McGraw-Hill Company. She didn't want to spend *all* of her lunch time looking for a place to eat and then have to wait precious minutes to get served. There were days, in fact, she ran into Stern's for a swift counter-lunch. Of two things she was certain, ever since she found her pigeons congregating around the library steps: unless it was raining to beat the band, her pigeons would be there, *and*, no matter how depressed she might be, they managed to lessen her gloom. It was something about their wobbly jauntiness, something about their perky independence. It certainly wasn't a belief they possessed any great beauty as far as birds go, but she had always loved pigeons and this summer, her first summer in New York, it seemed as though they were more important than ever. There had been times, on a Saturday or Sunday, when she sat in her apartment and wondered: Are the pigeons out in front of the library steps? How are my pigeons this afternoon? Sometimes, especially this summer, when she came out of a movie, or up from a subway—or in any number of a dozen places— she'd think: Are they out there at night? Do they sleep around there? It was painful to her sometimes that she could not *possess* them, but, too, she knew that was foolish pain; it was like being grieved over the inability to possess a landscape, or possess the sound of music.

Only one thing!—and it was a crime, a real crime. There was a disgusting bit of perversion right there in front of all of those exuberant pigeons. Scores of men hung around the steps to look under the dresses of women who sat on the steps. In broad daylight, right in front of God and everybody they'd stand in clusters, some thirty feet away, watching a woman's legs—and more—there on the warm afternoon steps. It was crazy, it was absurd. What could they possibly hope to accomplish? What vicarious energy drove them to such oafish sleuthing? They were like ants: as each woman appeared and sat, with a newspaper or lunch, or just to take in the sun, the men, The Leg Watchers, would saunter slyly in the woman's direction and watch, hardly squinting their eyes in the sun, to see if they could see more than the woman's legs. And on a breezy day! Lord, you could see their nostrils dilate. The poor stupid women, though, with their impractical dresses and skinny legs, hadn't the least idea they were being X-rayed, panted over. In fact, their stupidity merely goaded The Leg Watchers on. It's a wonder the police didn't do something about it.

Every day, every weekday, Ruth saw The Leg Watchers. Three or four of the same ones were there every time she came there and she despised them the most. Her jaw locked when she saw them. One thing, *she* always kept her legs clamped together, from the knees all the way down her calves. Not even a bit was she going to let them see—see anything. She turned to feed a pigeon. She had a pear core and she liked the feel of a pigeon's beak pecking in her palm.

As she dug into her bag for a tissue, the sun stung her big round knee. The noon sun put a pink glaze on her nylon at her knee and she looked at it, exposed; her calves were wet from pressing them together so. Digging in her bag, but with half an eye on—yes! they were watching! The Leg Watchers were watching, which went to prove that if she wanted to be loose like all those skinny, frilly things on the library steps she could attract attention, too. If she wanted to use guile, it was no problem, for God's sake, to draw attention. If she wanted to let the breeze push at the ends of her dress—upwards a bit— as it was doing, it was no problem to draw around her a group of dirty-minded men.

When she decided she didn't have a tissue in her bag, and stopped looking for it, she raised her head alertly, triumphantly, to stare at The Leg Watchers.

All she saw was teeth. One man slapped his thigh. Another punched his eye sockets with the flat of his hands, writhing his vile body. And as plain as day, Ruth saw one of the men mouth a derogation: "Man, that broad's a bona fide dog." Then pigeons flew. Then her scalp stung. Somewhere a siren screamed, but Ruth thought the noise was the noise in her breast, so she held it, her heavy breast, walking down Forty-second Street as noon crowds pushed her towards Eighth Avenue; blankets of cold from open restaurant doors did not jar her, nor did the stale gales from greasy food shops nauseate her; her afternoon daze was broken only by a gentle jab in the rib. By a cup. A tin cup. Of a nun's. One of those grubby nuns.

"What do *you* want?" Ruth asked, trying to

control the urge to grab her shoulders and shake her. *This* nun was old and wore a pince-nez, and her shoes were flat, but she was false just the same.

"A few pennies for charity?" The Nun said, her pince-nez gleaming in the Forty-second Street sun.

"For what? For what did you say? You ought to be put in chains. You know that?"

The Nun began to move away, but Ruth's big thigh blocked her. "Don't you have any shame? Standing on the street in that—in that getup?"

The Nun's eyes shifted from left to right, from right to left, trying to see the street around Ruth's big figure. "Please," The Nun whispered.

"I'll do no such thing. You disgust me. What order do you belong to is what I'd like to know, if you're a nun. Tell me that. What order do you belong to?"

The Nun covered her cup with a wrinkled hand, and drew it to her black habit. "There are begging orders. There are."

"All right then, what's yours? Tell me that. Can you tell me that?"

In a lower voice than before, The Nun said, "The Blessed Sisters of St. Heliotrope."

"The Blessed *what*?" The laugh in Ruth's mouth hit The Nun in the face. "You and your kind ought to be lashed. You know that? False, false, false, that's what you are. All the way through. And *look* at your filthy collar. It's been a week, if ever, if soap's seen that, I bet. I really ought to go to the police."

Freckles of water popped out on The Nun's skin about her lips, but her eyes, old and hooded by the pince-nez, burned into Ruth's face for the first time. "So you're not a woman cop?"

Ruth shook her head and folded her arms beneath the bosom under her white cotton blouse. "But I think I ought to call one. This sort of thing is—"

The smile broke on The Nun's face, as though it had been the strike of cymbals. "Get the goddam hell out of my face, will you?" Her thin, pearl-gray teeth hung in the sun, exposed to the hot of the street. "Go crusade on some other corner, woman. I'm busy." She sidestepped Ruth, rattling her cup, and assumed, without effort, a beatific aura for her customers.

In the phone booth at the corner, Ruth called her office and said she'd become ill, that she wouldn't be in for the afternoon. And she *was* a bit dizzy, unable to think except about derobing The False Nun. She waited, there in the booth, pressing sweat from her neck, and trying to get The Nun out of her mind. She tried. Even as she followed The Nun, blocks, seven blocks, to Thirty-fifth Street, she tried to get The Nun out of her mind, but she kept following her, watching her walk pinch-stepped and pious, cup forward, black gown hanging still in the sun-numbed sunlight.

Several blocks west on Thirty-fifth Street The Nun entered the black hollow of a red-brick building near a warehouse. Ruth stood a block away, leaning on a mailbox, with part of her blouse hanging out of her skirt, then she walked into the building. There was a strong smell of baby's vomit, and a man, a tiny man, with bad skin and beautiful eyes, stood near a door on the ground floor talking in Spanish to a woman.

"The Nun?" Ruth was very much taller than either of them. "Which floor's The Nun's?"

The tiny man looked to the woman beside him, and then unleashed a rivet machine of Spanish. The woman responded with a series of shrugs, and they both stared at her with black eyes.

"The Nun," Ruth said again. She raised her hands to her head and let them fall around her big shoulders, stooping to the linoleum to indicate The Nun's habit. Then, with her hands extended in front of her, she walked like The Nun, mimicking her pious step.

Pistol laughter shot from the Spanish couple, and simultaneously they said, "Ah, *La Monja, La Monja.*"

"Yes, The *Monja*," Ruth said, exhausted.

"Up, up," the woman pointed. "2C."

The man nodded, his eyes blinking mirth. "She live, *La Monja*, she live in 2C. Up. Up."

The Nun was in her underskirt feeding a parakeet. Her hair was thin dry straw, parted neatly in the middle. She turned, her pince-nez gone— replaced with steel-framed hexagonal spectacles —and whispered, as though she dared not believe her old eyes, "*You?*"

"Yes, I'm here. I've come here. I followed you here."

The Nun came forward, in low flat soft shoes, her underskirt sticking to her bottom and to the back of her legs.

Ruth watched the woman, looking for some wicked trick. "You might try to throw me out, but I followed you. I followed you all the way from Forty-second Street. You didn't get away from me. You thought you'd get away from me, didn't you?"

The Nun backed up and looked down at the floor.

"Didn't you? You thought you'd escape me, didn't you?"

"What do you want?" The sun's glare from a window without curtains erased the sight of her eyes through the hexagonal glasses. "What do you want with me?"

"I've come to find out," Ruth said, aware for the first time that her blouse was hanging out of her skirt. "And you're going to tell me," she said, tucking it in.

The Nun turned to a small sewing basket filled with cigarette butts and colored thread and took out the largest of the short, wrinkled cigarettes. "Are you out of your head, girlie? You some sort of fanatic or something?"

Ruth stood in the middle of the floor. She dwarfed The Nun's junky furniture. "I've come to find out," she said, the sun burning into her shoulder and her arms in the furnished room.

"Why I beg?" The Nun asked.

"Why you beg in that false garb," Ruth said, pointing to the lump of black cloth heaped on the woman's unmade bed.

"Why you want to know?" The Nun said.

"I came here to ask why. You tell me why. You could be punished, you know that?"

"Who by?" The Nun laughed and sat on the end of the bed, out of the sun, smoking. "God?"

"The police!" Ruth told her.

"The cops? Neh. Listen, girlie, I've got some things to do. I've some things to do and I've got to go out. Why don't you go pick on somebody else, huh?"

Ruth would not move. Great sweat stains spread across her body but she would not move, move out of the sun. "I've come here to find out

why you do it and I intend to find out why you do it."

The Nun started to smile, and changed her mind. "I do it for money, girlie. M-o-n-e-y. Now, will you get off with you?"

Ruth loosened, moved nearer the bed, out of the sun. "But surely you must be able to—to— aren't there welfare agencies that—?"

"I get money!" The Nun said, standing, grabbing at the sides of her damp underskirt, grasping for dignity. "I get a retirement pension, and I get fifty dollars every two weeks from my brother sometimes. My brother, he's a taxi driver and he makes good money and he sees to it that I wouldn't starve, which I don't."

"But you beg. In *that*. In that thing, you beg."

"Yes, and it's nobody's business if I do. I need a little more now and then, more than Carl can give me. And my pension, it's not always as much as I need. But so what?"

"So *what*? It's disgusting. It's sad and disgusting, you dressing up like a nun. Does your brother know about this?"

"No. He don't have to know."

The sound of trucks and the silence of heat filled the room. Ruth was going to burst. "But *why*? I mean, what do you need the extra money for?"

The Nun stiffened and looked frightened for the first time, and it made Ruth's neck throb as she picked up the scent again. "Why? Tell me why. Tell me why and I'll go."

The Nun shook her head.

"Why can't you tell me why?"

The Nun shook her head again and sat back down.

Ruth advanced, stood over The Nun, over the straw hair at the foot of the bed. "Why? Tell me why!" Ruth wanted so to beat her, to hit her, and afraid that she would, she backed away once again into the sun. The Nun, half undressed, looked like an old child: her feet hardly touched the floor; her hexagonal glasses fell forward on her thin nose, as if she were a child playing Old Lady, and she was breathing hard, through her mouth.

"Why?" Ruth demanded.

"Get out of my room."

"Why, you dirty old woman? You impostor. Why won't you tell me why?"

A cockroach ran across the sunny floor and went into a neglected flower pot, and Ruth waited, but The Nun would not tell her why. The parakeet sang harshly without the sound of singing and The Nun sat, and would not tell her why. In the middle of the parakeet's song, Ruth made a dash for The Nun's habit and began picking at it, shaking it, pushing off The Nun, pulling at the strong seams, ripping it, shouting *why, why, why,* as The Nun beat her small fists in Ruth's fleshy back.

"Leave my clothes alone! Get out of my room and leave my things alone! Please leave my things alone!"

Even after Ruth staggered from the room, The Nun remained huddled over the shredded black heap on the sunny floor, her straw head crying into the black pieces, "Oh, please leave my things alone, please leave my things alone."

Ruth scarcely heard her, though; she could hear only the sound of her tired voice—a voice as tired as her legs were tired going down the stairs—mumbling, "What do you need the money for? Why can't you tell me what you need the money for?"

Although she sat in the sun, Ruth felt cold all over. It was three-thirty, and she was sitting on the library steps, and it puzzled her: she could not remember getting there. In fact her head ached so she couldn't think very clearly about anything, but it did make her happy to think she had come, in spite of everything, to be soothed by the sight of her pigeons. And they swarmed about her, over her, back and forth, strutting, wobbling. They swarmed about her, and they were good to see, but her body was still with a chill in the middle of all the day's heat. An aspirin. She decided she needed an aspirin and walked slowly down the last group of steps, five steps, in front of the library, towards the drugstore. With three aspirins and a large soda she felt better, although the unrealistic cold of the drugstore confused her flesh as she came out onto the street. This time, clearheaded, she went to the library steps,

determined to spend a half hour's rest before going home. As she walked up the five steps, between the smug couchant lions, half-smiling stone lions—who were always near the pigeons, guarding them—she saw . . . no, it would not be . . . it would be her imagination . . . it would be the heat . . . the straw yellow hair in the sun. Hexagonal glasses in the sun. There she was, The Nun, in the same low flat soft shoes, and with a cotton skirt of faded green and beige.

Ruth felt she could choke the woman. Right there on the steps. Before her tongue could move, could demand why she was there, The Nun turned, with a handful of pigeon feed high over her straw head, and screamed above the hum of traffic, "Don't touch me, don't touch me, you crazy woman! You going to follow me all over town? Aren't you *ever* going to leave me alone?"

Ruth looked at the pigeon feed, the huge bag of it at The Nun's feet. "You don't mean to say—you mean, you—?"

"Yes, yes, you crusading little busybody, so now you know. So now you know. Satisfied? It's my business what I do with my money and how I get it, isn't it? Isn't it? Shoo! Shoo!" The Nun kicked in the air towards Ruth, "Get away from here!"—and with dozens of deep lines showing on her face, she threw a handful of feed at Ruth with such force that it stung through her blouse, bit into her hip. She buckled to her knees, there on the pavement of stone, there with her hands before her, all fours, facing the sun over the library roof. Up above her, etched on the library wall, she saw: MDCCCXV ★ THE NEW YORK PUBLIC LIBRARY ★ MDCCCCII, and she saw pigeons, with pulsating feathered necks, tiny red eyes, crinkly feet, there on the stone cornices, twisting their necks, there as she was hunched on all fours; and as they took flight, wings spreading in nervous flight, thousands of them swooping down, down towards her in a winged blanket, blotting out the sun over the library roof, she saw their thousands of tiny red cold eyes in that black feather quilt, quivering winged quilt, and it was then that Ruth Schwartz opened her mouth, on her hands and knees, and croaked as a pigeon would croak, if pigeons croaked.

—1961

Uncle Tom's Cabin: Alternate Ending

LeRoi Jones

"6½" *was* the answer. But it seemed to irritate Miss Orbach. Maybe not the answer—the figure itself, but the fact it should be there, and in such loose possession.

"OH who is he to know such a thing? That's really improper to set up such liberations. And moreso."

What came into her head next she could hardly understand. A breath of cold. She did shudder, and her fingers clawed at the tiny watch she wore hidden in the lace of the blouse her grandmother had given her when she graduated teacher's college.

Ellen, Eileen, Evelyn . . . Orbach. She could be any of them. Her personality was one of theirs. As specific and as vague. The kindly menace of leading a life in whose balance evil was a constant intrigue but grew uglier and more remote as it grew stronger. She would have loved to do something really dirty. But nothing she had ever heard of was dirty enough. So she contented herself with good, i.e., purity, as a refuge from mediocrity. But being unconscious, or largely remote from her own sources, she would only admit to the possibility of grace. Not God. She would not be trapped into *wanting* even God.

So remorse took her easily. For any reason. A reflection in a shop window, of a man looking in vain for her ankles. (Which she covered with heavy colorless woolen.) A sudden gust of warm damp air around her legs or face. Long dull rains that turned her from her books. Or, as was the case this morning, some completely uncalled-for shaking of her silent doctrinaire routines.

"6½" had wrenched her unwillingly to exactly where she was. Teaching the fifth grade, in a grim industrial complex of Northeastern America; about 1942. And how the social doth pain the anchorite.

Nothing made much sense in such a context. People moved around, and disliked each other for no reason. Also, and worse, they said they loved each other, and usually for less reason, Miss Orbach thought. Or would have if she did.

And in this class sat thirty dreary sons and daughters of such circumstance. Specifically, the thriving children of the thriving urban lower middle classes. Postmen's sons and factory-worker debutantes. Making a great run for America, now prosperity and the War had silenced for a time the intelligent cackle of tradition. Like a huge gray bubbling vat the country, in its apocalyptic version of history and the future, sought now, in its equally apocalyptic profile of itself, as it had urged swiftly its own death since the Civil War. To promise. Promise. And that to be that all who had ever dared to live here would die when the people and interests who had been its rulers died. The intelligent poor now were being admitted. And with them a great many Negroes . . . who would die when the rest of the dream died not even understanding that they, like Ishmael, should have been the sole survivors. But now they were being tricked. "6½" the boy said. After the fidgeting and awkward silence. One little black boy raised his hand, and looking at the tip of Miss Orbach's nose said "6½." And then he smiled, very embarrassed and very sure of being wrong.

I would have said "No, boy, shut up and sit down. You are wrong. You don't know anything. Get out of here and be very quick. Have you no idea what you're getting involved in? My God . . . you nigger, get out of here and save yourself, while there's time. Now beat it." But those people had already been convinced. Read Booker T. Washington one day, when there's time. What that led to. The 6½'s moved for power . . . and there seemed no other way.

So three elegant Negroes in light gray suits grin and throw me through the window. They are happy and I am sad. It is an ample test of an idea. And besides "6½" is the right answer to the woman's question.

[The psychological and the social. The spiritual and the practical. Keep them together and you profit, maybe, someday, come out on top. Separate them, and you go along the road to the commonest of hells. The one we Westerners love to try to make art out of.]

The woman looked at the little brown boy. He blinked at her, trying again not to smile. She tightened her eyes, but her lips flew open. She tightened her lips, and her eyes blinked like the boy's. She said, "How do you get that answer?" The boy told her. "Well, it's right," she said, and the boy fell limp, straining even harder to look sorry. The Negro in back of the answerer pinched him, and the boy shuddered. A little white girl next to him touched his hand, and he tried to pull his own hand away with his brain.

"Well, that's right, class. That's exactly right. You may sit down now Mr. McGhee."

Later on in the day, after it had started exaggeratedly to rain very hard and very stupidly against the windows and soul of her fifth-grade class, Miss Orbach became convinced that the little boy's eyes were too large. And in fact they did bulge almost grotesquely white and huge against his bony heavy-veined skull. Also, his head was much too large for the rest of the scrawny body. And he talked too much, and caused too many disturbances. He also stared out the window when Miss Orbach herself would drift off into her sanctuary of light and hygiene even though her voice carried the inanities of arithmetic seemingly without delay. When she came back to the petty social demands of twentieth-century humanism the boy would be watching something walk across the playground. OH, it just would not work.

She wrote a note to Miss Janone, the school nurse, and gave it to the boy, McGhee, to take to her. The note read: "Are the large eyes a sign of ———?"

Little McGhee, of course, could read, and read the note. But he didn't of course understand the last large word which was misspelled anyway. But he tried to memorize the note, repeating to himself over and over again its contents . . . sounding the last long word out in his head, as best he could.

Miss Janone wiped her big nose and sat the boy down, reading the note. She looked at him when she finished, then read the note again, crumpling it on her desk.

She looked in her medical book and found out what Miss Orbach meant. Then she said to the little Negro, "Dr. Robard will be here in five minutes. He'll look at you." Then she began doing something to her eyes and fingernails.

When the doctor arrived he looked closely at McGhee and said to Miss Janone, "Miss Orbach is confused."

McGhee's mother thought that too. Though by the time little McGhee had gotten home he had forgotten the "long word" at the end of the note.

"Is Miss Orbach the woman who told you to say sangwich instead of sammich?" Louise McGhee giggled.

"No, that was Miss Columbe."

"Sangwich, my christ. That's worse than sammich. Though you better not let me hear you saying sammich either . . . like those Davises."

"I don't say sammich, mamma."

"What's the word then?"

"Sandwich."

"That's right. And don't let anyone tell you anything else. Teacher or otherwise. Now I wonder what that word could've been?"

"I donno. It was very long. I forgot it."

Eddie McGhee Sr. didn't have much of an idea what the word could be either. But he had never been to college like his wife. It was one of the most conspicuously dealt with factors of their marriage.

So the next morning Louise McGhee, after calling her office, the Child Welfare Bureau, and telling them she would be a little late, took a trip to the school, which was on the same block as the house where the McGhees lived, to speak to Miss Orbach about the long word which she suspected might be injurious to her son and maybe to Negroes In General. This suspicion had been bolstered a great deal by what Eddie Jr. had told her about Miss Orbach, and also equally by what Eddie Sr. had long maintained about the nature of White People In General. "Oh well," Louise McGhee sighed, "I guess I better straighten this sister out." And that is exactly what she intended.

When the two McGhees reached the Center Street School the next morning Mrs. McGhee took Eddie along with her to the principal's office, where she would request that she be allowed to see Eddie's teacher.

Miss Day, the old, lady principal, would then send Eddie to his class with a note for his teacher, and talk to Louise McGhee, while she was waiting, on general problems of the neighborhood. Miss Day was a very old woman who had despised Calvin Coolidge. She was also, in one sense, exotically liberal. One time she had forbidden old man Seidman to wear his pince-nez anymore, as they looked too snooty. Center Street sold more war stamps than any other grammar school in the area, and had a fairly good track team.

Miss Orbach was going to say something about Eddie McGhee's being late, but he immediately produced Miss Day's note. Then Miss Orbach looked at Eddie again, as she had when she had written her own note the day before.

She made Mary Ann Fantano the monitor and stalked off down the dim halls. The class had a merry time of it when she left, and Eddie won an extra two Nabisco graham crackers by kissing Mary Ann while she sat at Miss Orbach's desk.

When Miss Orbach got to the principal's office and pushed open the door she looked directly into Louise McGhee's large brown eyes, and fell deeply and hopelessly in love.

—1967

Games
A One-Act Play

George Houston Bass

CHARACTERS

BOB
FRANK
JOE
SUE } The Gang
SALLY
ANNA
JANE
CHARLOTTE, The Victim

PLACE: *A Playground, an open field*

Members of THE GANG *enter playing individual games—jump rope, bouncing a ball, hopscotch, walking on cracks, cowboy, etc.—*BOB *enters playing a game of chase with* SALLY. CHARLOTTE *enters dragging a box containing a doll and objects she might use to play house.* CHARLOTTE *settles in a spot and begins playing alone.* THE GANG *stops playing to focus on* CHARLOTTE. *She ignores them and continues her play uninterrupted.* BOB *initiates group activity.*

BOB: Hide spy, mickey-moe-rye, snatch a victim from the sky. Fly to the east. Fly to the west. Trap the victim in her nest.

JANE: Honey-hiney-bee-ball, I can't see y'all. All my black sheep hid?

SALLY: All around my base is spy. All in the house is spy.

FRANK: Here I come with my eyes wide open.

SUE: Ready or not, you shall be caught.

JOE: Hide spy.

BOB: You better be hid by twelve o'clock.

ANNA: Ready or not you shall be caught.

JANE: Hide spy, mickey-moe-rye.

SALLY: All ain't hid just holler I.

BOB: Honey-hiney-bee-ball, I can't see y'all. All my black sheep hid?

JOE: Fly to the east.

ANNA: Fly to the west.

SUE: Trap the victim in her nest.

JANE: One, two, three for Johnny.

SALLY: Home free!

FRANK: Home free!

BOB: One, two, three for Mary.

SUE: All behind my base is spy.

ANNA: Home free!

JOE: Home free!

SALLY: One, two, three for Kootie.

SUE: Hide spy, mickey-moe-rye.

FRANK: Home free!

JANE: Home free!

BOB: I caught you.

SUE: One, two, three.

JOE: Home free!

FRANK: Home free!
ANNA: Home free!
GANG: Home free!
BOB: Home free!
SALLY: Home free!
GANG: Ho-ooo-oo-ome Fre-eee-ee-ee!
BOB: Honey-hiney-bee-ball, I can't see y'all.
SUE: All hi-iii-ii-id.

Members of THE GANG *all run to home base and pile on top of each other, laughing, clowning, tickling each other, engaging in horseplay.* CHAR-LOTTE *watches, eager to participate.*

GANG: Oh, here we go loop-de-loo. Here we go loop-de-la. Here we go loop-de-loo, all on a Saturday night. I put my right foot in, I take my right foot out. I give my right foot a shake, shake, shake, and turn myself about. Oh, here we go loop-de-loo. Here we go loop-de-la. Here we go loop-de-loo, all on a Saturday night.
JANE: Ring around the roses. Pocket full of poses.
SALLY: Ring around the roses. Pocket full of poses.
BOB: Leap frog!
FRANK: Leap frog!
BOB: Leap frog!
FRANK: Leap!
SUE: One, two, three, red light.
JOE: One, two, three, red light.
BOB: Leap frog!
FRANK: Leap!
JOE: One, two, three, red light.
SUE: One, two, three, red light.
ANNA: Here we go loop-de-loo.
JANE: Ring around the roses.
SALLY: Pocket full of poses.
JANE: Ashes.
SALLY: Ashes.
BOB and FRANK: All fall down.
BOB: Last one in the field is an old rotten egg.
ANNA: Here we go loop-de-loo.

GANG *exits;* ANNA, *left behind, discovers herself alone then follows others.* CHARLOTTE, *left alone with her own world, plays with her doll.*

CHARLOTTE: One, two, buckle my shoe. Three,

four, knock at the door. Five, six, pick up sticks. Seven, eight, lay them straight. Nine, ten, start again. One potato, two potato, three potato, four. Five potato, six potato, seven potato more. Out goes the rat. Out goes the cat. Out goes the lady with the seesaw hat. I went to the river and I couldn't get across. I paid five dollars for an old blind horse. The horse wouldn't pull, I swapped it for a bull. The bull wouldn't holler, I swapped it for a dollar. The dollar wouldn't pass, I threw it in the grass. The grass wouldn't grow, I chopped it with a hoe. The hoe wouldn't chop, I put it in the shop. The shop wouldn't fix it, and so I had to nix it. Wish I had my money back.

CHARLOTTE *begins singing to her doll.* THE GANG *returns, playing statue.* BOB *throws the members of* THE GANG *and each freezes in the position he finds himself. They form a tableau around* CHARLOTTE *as if preparing to attack.* CHARLOTTE *is seemingly unaware of them.*

CHARLOTTE: Oh Mary Mack, Mack, Mack all dressed in black, black, black with three gold buttons, buttons, buttons up and down her back, back, back. She asked her mother, mother, mother for fifteen cents, cents, cents to see the elephant, elephant, elephant jump the fence, fence, fence. He jumped so high, high, high that he touched the sky, sky, sky and he never got back, back, back until the Fourth of July, lie, lie. Milk in the pitcher, pitcher, pitcher and butter in the bowl, bowl, bowl, she can't find a sweetheart, sweetheart, sweetheart for to save her soul, soul, soul. She feels very blue, blue, blue but there's nothing she can do, do, do except sit and sigh, sigh, sigh until the day she will die, die, die.
BOB: You moved. You moved. I saw you move.
SUE: I didn't.
BOB: You have now.

SUE *covers her eyes and counts while members of* THE GANG *assume new poses.*

SUE: On your toes, change your pose. One, two, three, four, freeze.

SUE *looks statues over and tries to make them*

break. CHARLOTTE *becomes interested and moves near.*

BOB (*to* CHARLOTTE): Scram! (*Pause, then to* GANG) Raccoon up the 'simmon tree, possum on the ground. Raccoon shakes the 'simmons down, possum pass them round. Little fishes in the brook; Willie catch them with a hook. Mama fry them in a pan and daddy eat them like a man. Now ain't I right?
GANG: Yeah!
BOB: Ain't I right?
GANG: Yeah! Yeah!
BOB: Ain't I right?
GANG: Yeah, yeah, yeah!
BOB: I told you so, I'm right.
FRANK: Old cow died in Tennessee. Sent her jawbone back to me. Jawbone walked. Jawbone talked. Jawbone ate with knife and fork. Now ain't I right?
GANG: Yeah!
FRANK: Now ain't I right?
GANG: Yeah! Yeah!
FRANK: Ain't I right?
GANG: Yeah, yeah, yeah!
FRANK: I told you so. I'm right.
SUE: Too late. Too late. The door is locked and you're too late.
GANG (*except* FRANK): Too late. Too late. The door is locked and you're too late.
FRANK: Whip! Whip!
JANE: Whip! Whip!
SALLY: Whip!
JOE: Whip!
GANG: Whi-iii-ii-ii-ip!
BOB: Whip! Whip!
SUE: Whip! Whip!
GANG: Whi-iii-iii-ii-ii-ip! . . . Oh, this is the way you willow-bee, willow-bee, willow-bee. This is the way you willow-bee, all night long. Step back Sally, Sally, Sally. Step back Sally, all night long. Strolling down the alley, the alley, the alley. Strolling down the alley, all night long. This is the way you willow-bee, willow-bee, willow-bee. This is the way you willow-bee, all night long. Step back Sally, Sally, Sally—
CHARLOTTE: Can I play? Can I play?
SUE: Can't you read? Are you blind? Don't you see you aren't our kind?

BOB: Stink fink not worth a wink, go jump in the lake and sink, sink, sink.
SALLY: Stink fink not worth a wink, go jump in a lake and sink, sink, sink.
GANG: Stink fink not worth a wink, go jump in a lake and sink, sink, sink.
CHARLOTTE: Stink fink not worth a wink, go jump in a lake and sink, sink, sink.
JANE: Monkey see, monkey do, monkey spelled Y–O–U.
BOB: Y–O–U spells O–U–T.
ANNA: O–U–T spells out.
CHARLOTTE: Sticks and stones may break my bones, but words will never hurt me.
BOB: Rain, rain go away. Little Mary wants to play.
GANG: Rain, rain go away. Little Mary wants to play.
CHARLOTTE: You're not bad, you just smell bad.
BOB: Eeny-meany-miny-moe.
SUE: Catch a *victim* by the toe.
FRANK: If she hollers let her go.
ANNA: But what if she won't holler?
BOB: Stamp her!
FRANK: Squeeze her!
SALLY: Squash her!
SUE: Bleed her!
BOB: Stamp her!
JOE: Squeeze her!
JANE: Squash her!
BOB: Bleed her!

THE GANG *forms a line and grabs hold of elbows to become a train, then moves about chanting and making train sounds.*

GANG: Stamp her! Squeeze her! Squash her! Bleed her! Stamp her! Squeeze her! Squash her! Bleed her! Stamp her! Squeeze her! Squash her! Bleed her! Stamp her! Squeeze her! Squash her! Bleed her! Stamp her!

CHARLOTTE *joins the train and begins playing, too.* BOB *sees her.*

BOB: Freeze!

All action stops. BOB *leads* THE GANG *in forming*

a circle around CHARLOTTE. SUE *confronts* CHARLOTTE.

SUE: Put your foot on my foot. (CHARLOTTE *remains still.*) If you don't I'll knock you down.

CHARLOTTE *puts her foot on* SUE's *foot.* SUE *knocks her down.* THE GANG *laughs and makes faces at* CHARLOTTE.

BOB: Last one in the field got two left feet.

CHARLOTTE *is left sprawled on the ground. She gets up, makes an obscene gesture in direction of* THE GANG's *exit, then returns to play with her doll.*

CHARLOTTE: Aunt Dinah's dead. How'd she die? Oh, she died like this and she died like that. She died like this and she died like that. She died like this and she died like that . . . all night long. Hide spy, mickey-moe-rye, snatch a victim from the sky. Fly to the east. Fly to the west. Trap the victim in her nest. Ready or not you shall be caught. Here I come with my eyes wide open. Too late. Too late. The door is locked and you're too late. Stamp her! Squeeze her! Squash her! Bleed her! Stamp her! Squeeze her, Squash her! Bleed her! This is the way you willow-bee, willow-bee, willow-bee. This is the way you willow-bee, all night long. Stamp her! Squeeze her! Squash her! Bleed her! Stamp her! Squeeze her! . . . Stink fink not worth a wink, go jump in a lake and sink, sink, sink.

THE GANG *returns playing follow the leader.* BOB *leads as if they were airplanes.* GANG *makes proper sounds for the game. They move all about the play area making various patterns. Then* BOB *suddenly breaks away from* GANG, *snatches* CHARLOTTE's *doll from her and initiates a game*

of catch with the doll. CHARLOTTE *runs around trying to retrieve her doll. Finally she attacks one of the members of* THE GANG. *The entire* GANG *jumps on her.* THE GANG *moves away from* CHARLOTTE, *leaving her on the ground. They join hands and form a circle about* CHARLOTTE.

CHARLOTTE: My bread is burning.
GANG: You can't get out.
CHARLOTTE: My stove is burning.
GANG: You can't get out.
CHARLOTTE: My house is burning.
GANG: You can't get out.
CHARLOTTE: My baby's in it.
GANG: You can't get out.
CHARLOTTE: She's all alone.
GANG: You can't get out.
CHARLOTTE: She's all alone.
GANG: You can't get out.
CHARLOTTE: She's all alone.
GANG: You can't get out. You can't get out. You can't get out. You can't get out.
CHARLOTTE: Button, button, who's got the button?
GANG: You can't get out. You can't get out.
CHARLOTTE: Eeny-meany-miny-moe.
GANG: You can't get out. You can't get out.
CHARLOTTE: Eeny-meany-miny-moe catch a—
BOB: *Victim* by the toe.
GANG: You can't get out. You can't get out. You can't get out. You can't get out. (GANG *exits, individually, in different directions, leaving* CHARLOTTE *alone.*) You can't get out. You can't get out. You can't get out. You can't get out.

CHARLOTTE *is left alone. She goes to her doll, holds it close to her and weeps.*

CHARLOTTE: I can't get out. I can't get out. I can't get out.

CURTAIN

—1967

LeRoi Jones

Preface to a *Twenty Volume Suicide Note*
(For Kellie Jones, born 16 May 1959)

LATELY, I've become accustomed to the way
The ground opens up and envelops me
Each time I go out to walk the dog.
Or the broad-edged silly music the wind
Makes when I run for a bus . . .

Things have come to that.

And now, each night I count the stars,
And each night I get the same number.
And when they will not come to be counted,
I count the holes they leave.

Nobody sings anymore.

And then last night, I tiptoed up
To my daughter's room and heard her
Talking to someone, and when I opened
The door, there was no one there . . .
Only she on her knees, peeking into

Her own clasped hands.

—1957

Epistrophe

IT's such a static reference; looking
out the window all the time! the eyes' limits . . .
On good days, the sun.

& what you see. (here in New York)
Walls and buildings; or in the hidden gardens
of opulent Queens: profusion, endless stretches of
    leisure.

It's like being chained to some dead actress;
& she keeps trying to tell you something horribly
    maudlin.

e.g. ("the leaves are flat & motionless.")

What I know of the mind
seems to end here;
Just outside my face.

I wish some weird-looking animal
would come along.

—1961

Lines to Garcia Lorca

Climin' up the mountin, chillun,
Didn't come here for to stay,
If I'm ever gonna see you agin,
It'll be on the Judgment Day.
Negro Spiritual

SEND soldiers again to kill you, Garcia.
Send them to quell my escape.
These things mean nothing.
You are dying again, Garcia.
This is all I remember.
Send soldiers again, Garcia.
Hail Mary,
Holy Mother,
Pray for me.

I live near a mountain, green mirror
Of burning paths and a low sun
To measure my growing by.
There is a wind that repeats
A bird's name and near his
Cage is a poem, and a small boy herding
Cattle with diamonds
In their mouths.

Mandolins grow on the high slopes
And orange-robed monks collect songs
Just beyond the last line of fruit trees.
Naked girls pretend they are butterflies,
And a deer tells stories to the twilight.

Garcia, where is my Bible?
I want to read those myths
Again.   No answer.
But, away off, quite close to the daylight,
I hear his voice, and he is laughing, laughing
Like a Spanish guitar.

—1961

Jay Wright

This Morning

THIS morning I threw the windows
of my room open, the light burst
in like crystal gauze and I hung
it on my wall to frame.
And here I am watching it take possession
of my room, watching the obscure love
match of light and shadow—of cold and warmth.
It is a matter of acceptance, I guess.
It is a matter of finding some room
with shadows to embrace, open. Now
the light has settled in, I don't think
I shall ever close my windows again.

—1964

David Henderson

Sketches of Harlem

1

IT was Tiny's habit
To go down to the GREAT WHITE WAY
Without understanding the subway ride.

2

The man asked Bubba to sign
A petition for more fallout shelters.
All Bubba wanted to know was
Which way the bomb was coming—
From Washington Heights
Or Sutton Place.

3

The boy arrived from Mississippi
And got a room on Seventh Avenue the same day.
Right away he wrote to Mama:
    "Dear Ma,
                I got up here safely.
    I got me a room in Harlem
    and everything is all right."

4

Black small boy asking Mama
Why the sun shines at night,
And she answering that it
Ain't shining at all.
"That's a moon."

—1964

Ted Joans

Lester Young

SOMETIMES he was cool like an eternal blue flame
    burning in the old Kansas City nunnery

Sometimes he was happy 'til he'd think about his
    birthplace and its blood-stained clay hills and
    crow-filled trees

Most times he was blowin' on the wonderful tenor
    sax of his, preachin' in very cool tones, shout-
    ing only to remind you of a certain point in
    his blue messages

He was our president as well as the minister of
    soul-stirring Jazz, he knew what he blew, and
    he did what a prez should do, wail, wail, wail.
    There were many of them to follow him and
    most of them were fair—but they never spoke
    so eloquently in so far out a funky air

Our prez done died, he know'd this would come but
    death has only booked him, alongside Bird, Art
    Tatum, and other heavenly wailers

Angels of Jazz—they don't die—they live
they live—in hipsters like you and I

—1963

Mari Evans

When in Rome

MARRIE dear
the box is full . . .
take
whatever you like
to eat . . .

     (an egg
     or soup
     . . . there ain't no meat.)

there's endive there
and
cottage cheese . . .

     (whew! if I had some
     black-eyed peas . . .)

there's sardines
on the shelves
and such . . .
but
don't
get my anchovies . . .

they cost
too much!

     (me get the
     anchovies indeed!
     what she think, she got—
     a bird to feed?)

there's plenty in there
to fill you up . . .

     (yes'm. just the
     sight's
     enough!

     Hope I lives till I get
     home
     I'm tired of eatin'
     what they eats in Rome . . .)

          —1964

Where Have You Gone . . . ?

WHERE have you gone . . .

with your confident
walk . . . with
your crooked smile . . . ?

why did you leave
me
when you took your
laughter
and departed . . . ?
Are you aware that
with you
went the sun
all light
and what few stars
there were . . . ?

where have you gone
with your confident
walk your
crooked smile the
rent money
in one pocket and
my heart
in
another . . . ?

          1963

Tom Dent

Come Visit My Garden

BEETLES,
noisy bumblebees
and yellow jackets too,
rest,
rest awhile.

Come visit my garden,
come sit with me,
come drink with me,
come abide with me,
come think, talk
and relax with me
in my garden.

Look out from my cool abode
into the hot, hot day
and rest.

Come dream with me
while I surgically remove thorns
from my sweet roses.

Enjoy with me
the insulation
of my methodically erected
clean
brick walls.

          —1964

G. C. Oden

Review from Staten Island

THE skyline of New York does not excite me
(ferrying towards it) as mountains do in snow-steeped
                    hostility to sun.
There is something in the view—spewed up from
    water
                        to pure abandonment in air—
                        that snakes my spine with cold
and mouse-tracks over my heart.

Strewn across the meet of wave and wind, it seems
the incompleted play of some helter-skeltering child
    whose
                        hegira (as all
our circles go) has not yet led him back, but will, ripe
                        with that ferocious glee which
                        can boot these building-blocks
to earth, then heel under.

One gets used to dying living. Growth is an
end to many things—even the rose disposes of sum-
    mer—
                        but still I
wince at being there when the relentless foot kicks
    down;
                        and the tides come roaring over
                        to pool within
the unlearned depths of me.
                                        —1963

A Private Letter to Brazil

THE map shows me where it is you are. I
am here, where the words NEW YORK run an inch
out to sea, ending where GULF STREAM flows by.

The coastline bristles with place names. The pinch
in printing space has launched them offshore
with the fish-bone's fine-tooth spread, to clinch

their urban identity. Much more
noticeable it is in the chain
of hopscotching islands that, loosely, moors

your continent to mine. (Already plain
is its eastward drift, and who could say
what would become of it left free!) Again,

the needle-pine alignment round SA,
while where it is you are (or often go),
RIO, spills its subtle phonic bouquet

Farthest seaward of all. Out there I know
the sounding is some deep 2000 feet,
and the nationalized current tours so

pregnant with resacas. In their flux meets
all the subtlety of God's great nature
and man's terse grief. See, Hero, at your feet

is not that slight tossing dead Leander?
                                        1959

Julia Fields

Madness One Monday Evening

LATE that mad Monday evening
I made mermaids come from the sea
As the block sky sat
Upon the waves
And night came
Creeping up to me

            (I tell you I made mermaids
            Come from the sea)

The green waves lulled and rolled
As I sat by the locust tree
And the bright glare of the neon world
Sent gas-words bursting free—
Their spewed splendor fell on the billows
And gaudy it grew to me
As I sat up upon the shore
And made mermaids come from the sea.
                                        —1964

No Time for Poetry

MIDNIGHT is no time for
Poetry—
    The heart is much too
calm
    The spirit too lagging
    and dull—
But the morning!
With the sunshine in one's eyes
and breath—
And all the pink clouds
Like chiffon in a dressing gown
And the orange-white mists
That leap and furl—

Ah, I should greet the morning
   As though I never saw a morning before
And only heard that it
   was this or that,
Gossip that was good either way,
There being nothing derogatory to say.

And in that strange-white mist
I'd be content to go upon the paths
with neither shoes nor hat
winding my way away from home
much like a
   cornerless cat
Holding vibrations of laughter in my
Fur
   That floated from who knows where
   and goes who-less-could-care.

There are no orange-white mists
   at midnight
   They are a world away
   And so
   Midnight is no time for Poetry.

                   —1963

Calvin C. Hernton

Madhouse

HERE is a place that is no place
And here is no place that is a place,
A place somewhere beyond the reaches of time
And beyond the reaches of those who in time
Bring flowers and fruit to this place.
Yet here is a definite place
And a definite time, fixed
In a timelessness of precise vantage
From which to view flowers and view fruit
And those who come bearing them.

Those who come by Sunday's habit are weary
And kiss us, half-foreign but sympathetic,
Spread and eat noisily to crack the unbearable
Silence of this place:
They do not know that something must always come
From something and that nothing must come always
From nothing, and that nothing is always a thing

To drive us mad.

                   —1964

Reclaiming the Lost African Heritage

John Henrik Clarke

THERE IS A school of thought supporting the thesis that the people of African descent in the Western world have no African heritage to reclaim. I am not of that school. The image of Africa was deliberately distorted by imperialists who needed moral justification for their rape, pillage, and destruction of African cultural patterns and ways of life. It was they who said, in spite of voluminous documents in the libraries of Europe proving the contrary, that Africa was a savage and backward land with little history and no golden age.

However, many writers and scholars, both black and white, have pointed to a rich and ancient African heritage, which, in my opinion, must be reclaimed if American Negroes in general and Negro writers in particular are ever to be reconciled with their roots. Let us first note some of those people who have called attention to this inheritance, then consider a few of the more salient facts of African history and civilization, and finally ask how Negro writers can use this material in their historical and creative writing.

A number of white writers, keenly aware of the distorted image of Africa, have expressed amazement at what seems to be the indifference of the black man in the Western world to the glory of his ancient heritage. In the following excerpt from his book *Tom-Tom* (1926), John W. Vandercook speaks unsparingly:

> The civilized Negro must lose his contempt for his "heathen" brethren in Africa and in the jungles of Melanesia and Surinam. He must learn that the fathers of the race had and still possess blessed secrets, wonderful lores, and great philosophies that rank the jungle Negro's civilization as the equal, and in many respects, the superior of any way of life that is to be found anywhere in the world.

In his column of August 8, 1933, Arthur Brisbane, then editor of the *New York American*, had these reproving words to say about "Negro Day" at the Century of Progress Exposition in Chicago:

> Next Saturday is set apart as "Negro Day" at the Century of Progress Exposition in Chicago, with athletic sports including colored Olympic champions, a pageant at Soldier's Field called "The Epic of a Race," and 3,000 Negro voices singing spirituals.
>
> The committee in charge might have reproduced on Soldier's Field the great Sphinx that stands on the Egyptian desert. That Sphinx has an Ethiopian face, proving that the Negro race was important far back in the night of time. Many colored men and women would be more proud of the fact that one of their race once ruled over Egypt than of any modern "spirituals," *Green Pastures*, or athletic records.

In the statements of both John W. Vandercook and Arthur Brisbane, I detect the note of the condescending teacher. They infer that they are revealing something of which we are totally unaware. Of course this is not true. There is a tendency among the recent discoverers of African history to think that they were the first explorers on the scene.

As far back as 1881, the renowned scholar and benefactor of West Africa, Dr. Edward Wilmot Blyden, speaking on the occasion of his inauguration as president of Liberia College, sounded the note for the organized teaching of the culture and civilization of Africa and decried the fact that the world's image of Africa was not in keeping with Africa's true status in world history. I quote from his address on this occasion:

> The people generally are not yet prepared to understand their own interests in the great work to be done for themselves and their children. We shall be obliged to work for some time to come not only without the popular sympathy we ought to have but with utterly inadequate resources.
>
> In all English-speaking countries the mind of the intelligent Negro child revolts against the descriptions of the Negro given in elementary books, geographies, travels, histories. . . .
>
> Having embraced or at least assented to these falsehoods about himself, he concludes that his only hope of rising in the scale of respectable manhood is to strive for what is most unlike himself and most alien to his peculiar tastes. And whatever his literary attainments or acquired ability, he fancies that he must grind at the mill which is provided for him, putting in material furnished to his hands, bringing no contribution from his own field; and of course nothing comes out but what is put in.

A year after this pronouncement by Dr. Blyden, George W. Williams, first Negro member of the Ohio legislature and founder of African studies in the United States, wrote in two volumes his *History of the Negro Race in America*. The first volume contained 464 pages of text, of which 125 pages were devoted to the African background. The field of research in African history was later widened under the leadership of three men: Dr. W. E. B. Du Bois, beginning with his Atlanta studies; Dr. Moorland in Washington, D.C.; and Dr. Carter G. Woodson, founder of the Association for the Study of Negro Life and History. The American Negro writer's mission to reclaim his lost African heritage had begun.

What is this heritage? In the first place, the rich and colorful history, art and folklore of West Africa, the ancestral home of most American Negroes, presents evidence to prove that Negroes built great nations and cultures long before their first appearance in Jamestown, Virginia, in 1619. Contrary to a misconception which still prevails, the African was familiar with literature and art for hundreds of years before his contact with the Western world. Before the breaking up of the social and political structure of the West African states of Ghana, Melle, Songhay, Kanen-Bornu and the Mossi States, and before the internal strife within these nations that made the slave trade possible, the forefathers of the Negroes who eventually became slaves in the Western world lived in a society where university life was highly regarded and scholars were beheld with reverence.

In the years when Timbuktu was the great intellectual nucleus of the Songhay empire, African scholars were enjoying a renaissance that was known and respected throughout most of Africa and in parts of Europe. At this period in African history, the University of Sankore was the educational capital of the Western Sudan. In his book *Timbuctoo the Mysterious*, Felix Du Bois gives us the following picture:

> The scholars of Timbuctoo yielded in nothing to the saints and their sojourns in the foreign universities of Fez, Tunis and Cairo. They astounded the most learned men of Islam by their erudition. That these Negroes were on a level with the Arabian savants is proved by the fact that they were installed as professors in Morocco and Egypt. In contrast to this, we find that the Arabs were not always equal to the requirements of Sankore.

Ahmed Baba, one of the greatest scholars of this period, stands out as a brilliant example of the sweep of Sudanese erudition. An author of more than forty books on such diverse themes as theology, astronomy, ethnography and biography, Baba was a scholar of great depth and inspiration. He was in Timbuktu when it was invaded by the Moroccans in 1592 and protested against their occupation. His collection of sixteen hundred books, one of the richest libraries of his day, was lost during his expatriation from Timbuktu. Ahmed Baba, although the most conspicuous, was only one of the great scholars of the Western Sudan. This is part of the African heritage that must be understood and reclaimed.

In the second place, before the European colonial period, there were already established in Africa independent nations with a long and glorious history. In the fifteenth century, when the

Portuguese established trading posts along the coast of West Africa, Soni Ali—one of the greatest of Africa's empire builders—was ruling Songhay. Soni Ali was followed to the throne by Mohammed Abubaker El-Touré, founder of the Askia dynasty of kings and later called Askia the Great. He came to power in 1493, one year after Columbus discovered America. During the reign of Askia the Great, the nations of West Africa enjoyed a standard of life which was equal to, and often higher than, that of other nations of the world.

By 1884, when the European powers with colonial aspirations in Africa sat down and agreed on a plan to divide and exploit the entire continent of Africa, the colonial period was well under way—and so was Africa's resistance to it.

The British met with continued resistance in many quarters. In West Africa, the Ashanti and other tribal wars against British rule lasted from 1821 until the eve of the First World War. In the Sudan, the Mahdi movement, founded and led by Mohammed Ahmed, cost the British some of their best officers and soldiers, the most famous being General Gordon. When the Mahdi died in 1885, the movement continued under the leadership of Abdullah Khalifa and Osman Digna, commander of the colorful Fuzzy Wuzzy warriors. Osman Digna was not captured and killed until 1928. In Somaliland, a Mohammedan religious reformer, Mohammed Ben Abdullah—later called the Mad Mullah of Somaliland—rose up against British rule in 1899 and was not defeated until 1920. In South Africa, the Zulu wars of resistance lasted from the rise of Chaka in 1800 to the last Zulu rebellion in Natal in 1906.

Nor did the French find the Africans more submissive. Somory Touré, last of the great Mandingo warriors, fought the French in West Africa for seventeen years. He stood astride their path from Senegal to the Niger when the French were trying to extend their control to the source of this great river, then to Timbuktu. He was captured on September 29, 1898, by an African scout in the French army, while he was in the midst of his morning prayers. He died in exile two years later. The King of Dahomey, Gle-Gle, and his son and successor, Behanzin Hassu Bowelle, called "The King Shark," opposed

French rule in their country for over fifty years. Behanzin was defeated by the French mulatto General Alfred A. Dodds, and died in exile in 1906. Thus Africa came bleeding and fighting into the twentieth century.

Then a new type of leader emerged. A well-known Egyptian nationalist of Sudanese descent, Duse Mohammed Ali, editor of the anti-imperialist magazine *African Times and Orient Review*, extended the support of North African nationalism to the rest of the continent. From Morocco, the voice of El-Hadj Thami El-Glaoui, the famous Pasha of Marrakesh, was heard. In West Africa men like Casely-Hayford, John Sarbah and Dr. J. E. K. Aggrey were preparing that area of Africa for eventual independence. From the French-dominated territories, Blaise Diagne, René Maran and Gratien Candace were heard. In East Africa and the Congo, Paul Banda, Daudi Chwa, King of Buganda, and Apolo Kagwa lifted their voices.

In South Africa a missionary-educated native of Nyasaland founded the Industrial and Commercial Union. A few years after its formation, this union had a membership of nearly three hundred thousand. Two able Bantu editors, John Tengo Jabavu and Sol Plaatje, gave the founder of this union, Clements Kadalie, the support he needed to make the ICU the most powerful African trade union on the continent.

The lives of these men, and many others, went into making the emergent Africa we know today. This, too, is part of our African heritage. It is both the responsibility and good fortune of Negro writers to learn that in this heritage there is material for more books than they can write in ten lifetimes. The African story is still untold.

For the last three hundred years Africa and its people have been viewed mainly through European eyes and for European reasons. The entire history of Africa will have to be literally rewritten, challenging and reversing the European concept. It is singularly the responsibility of the Negro writer to proclaim and celebrate the fact that his people have in their ancestry rulers who expanded kingdoms into empires and built great and magnificent armies, scholars whose vision of life showed foresight and wisdom, and priests who told of gods that were strong and kind. The American Negro writer should pay particular attention to the Western Sudan (West Africa), his ancestral home.

The personalities who influenced the rich and colorful history of Africa have been natural attractions for many writers. Material on the rise and fall of the magnificent Ashanti people and their inland kingdom that cast its warlike shadow over the Gold Coast (now Ghana) for over two hundred years is staggering; yet no Negro writer in the Western world has seen fit to write a complete book on the Ashanti people. The life of the first great Ashanti king, Osei Tutu, can be retold by our writers in the form of biography, a historical novel, a grand opera or an epic poem.

This is a scant sampling of the rich material on African life still waiting for our attention.

Countee Cullen's poem "Heritage" begins with the challenging question: "What is Africa to me?" Our writers must expand this question in order to give a more pertinent answer. To the question, "What is Africa to me?" we must add, "What is Africa to the Africans?" and "What is Africa to the world?" In answering these questions let us consider using as a guide the following lines from John W. Vandercook's book *Tom-Tom*:

A race is like a man. Until it uses its own talents, takes pride in its own history, and loves its own memories, it can never fulfill itself completely.

—1959

Writers: Black and White

Langston Hughes

EVEN TO sell *bad* writing you have to be good.

There was a time when, if you were colored, you might sell bad writing a little easier than if you were white. But no more. The days of the Negro's passing as a writer and getting by purely because of his "negritude" are past.

Even white Africans find it hard to get published in the U.S.A. You have to be a Nadine Gordimer or an Alan Paton. For the general public, "the blacker the berry, the sweeter the juice" may be true in jazz, but not in prose. These days I would hate to be a Negro writer depending on race to get somewhere.

To create a market for your writing you have to be consistent, professional, a continuing writer —not just a one-article or a one-story or a one-book man. Those expert vendors, the literary agents, do not like to be bothered with a one-shot writer. No money in them. Agents like to help build a career, not light a flash in the pan. With one-shot writers, literary hucksters cannot pay their income taxes. Nor can publishers get their money back on what they lose on the first book.

Even if you are a good writer, but *not* consistent, you probably will not get far. Color has nothing to do with writing as such. So I would say, in your mind don't be a *colored* writer even when dealing in racial material. Be a *writer* first. Like an egg: first, egg; then an Easter egg, the color applied.

To write about yourself, you should first be outside yourself—objective. To write well about Negroes, it might be wise, occasionally at least, to look at them with white eyes—then the better will you see how distinctive we are. Sometimes I think whites are more appreciative of our *uniqueness* than we are ourselves. The white "black" artists—dealing in Negro material—have certainly been financially more successful than any of us real Negroes have ever been. Who wrote the most famous "Negro" (in quotes) music? George Gershwin, who looked at Harlem from a downtown penthouse, while Duke Ellington still rode the "A" train. Who wrote the best-selling plays and novels and thereby made money's mammy? White Eugene O'Neill, white Paul Green, white Lillian Smith, white Marc Connelly and DuBose Heyward: *Emperor Jones, In Abraham's Bosom, Strange Fruit, Green Pastures, Porgy.* Who originated the longest running Negro radio and TV show? The various white authors of the original "Amos and Andy" scripts, not Negroes. Who wrote all those Negro and interracial pictures that have swept across the Hollywood screen from *Hallelujah* to *Anna Lucasta,* from *Pinky* to *Porgy and Bess?* Not Negroes. Not you, not I, not any colored-body here.

Our eyes are not white enough to look at Negroes clearly in terms of popular commercial marketing. Not even white enough to see as Faulkner sees—through Mississippi-Nobel-Prize-winning-Broadway eyes in his play *Requiem for a Nun.* There his "nigger dope-fiend whore" of a mammy, Nancy Manningoe, "cullud," raises the curtain with three traditional "Yas, Lawd's," and when asked later by a white actor, "What would a person like you be doing in heaven?" humbly replies, "Ah kin work." Since Faulkner repeatedly calls Nancy a "nigger dope-fiend whore," all I can add is she is also a liar—because the *last* thing a Negro thinks of doing in heaven is working. Nancy knows better, even if Faulkner doesn't.

Nigger dope-fiend Nancy, Porgy's immoral Bess, Mamba's immoral daughter, streetwalking Anna Lucasta, whorish Carmen Jones! Lawd, let me be a member of the wedding! "White folks, Ah kin work!" In fact, yas, Lawd, I have to work because—

> You've done taken my blues and gone—
> Sure have! You sing 'em on Broadway,
> And you sing 'em in Hollywood Bowl.
> You mixed 'em up with symphonies,
> And you fixed 'em so they don't sound like me
> Yep, you done taken my blues and gone!
> You also took my spirituals and gone.
> Now you've rocked-an-rolled 'em to death!
> You put me in *Macbeth*,
> In *Carmen Jones* and *Anna Lucasta*,
> And all kinds of *Swing Mikados*
> And in everything but what's about me—
> But someday somebody'll
> Stand up and talk about me,
> And write about me—
> Black and beautiful—
> And sing about me,
> And put on plays about me!
> I reckon it'll be me myself!
> Yes, it'll be me.

Of course, it may be a long time before we finance big Broadway shows or a seven-million-dollar movie like *Porgy and Bess*, on which, so far as I know, not a single Negro writer was employed. The *Encyclopaedia Britannica* declares *Porgy and Bess* "the greatest American musical drama ever written." The *Encyclopaedia Britannica* is white. White is right. So shoot the seven million! 7 come 11! Dice, gin, razors, knives, dope, watermelon, whores—7–11! Come 7!

Yet, surely Negro writing, even when commercial, need not be in terms of stereotypes. The interminable crap game at the beginning of *Porgy and Bess* is just because its authors could not see beyond the *surface* of Negro color. But the author of the original novel did see, with his white eyes, wonderful, poetic human qualities in the inhabitants of Catfish Row that made them come alive in his book, half alive on the stage, and I am sure, bigger than life on the screen. DuBose Heyward was a *writer* first, white second, and this you will have to be, too: *writer* first, *colored* second. That means losing nothing of

your racial identity. It is just that in the great sense of the word, anytime, any place, good art transcends land, race or nationality, and color drops away. If you are a good writer, in the end neither blackness nor whiteness makes a difference to readers.

Greek the writer of *Oedipus* might have been, but *Oedipus* shakes Booker T. Washington High School. Irish was Shaw, but he rocks Fisk University. Scottish was Bobby Burns, but kids like him at Tuskegee. The more regional or national an art is in its origins, the more universal it may become in the end. What could be more Spanish than *Don Quixote*? Yet what is more universal? What more Italian than Dante? Or more English than Shakespeare? Advice to Negro writers: Step *outside yourself*, then look back—and you will see how human, yet how beautiful and black, you are. How very black—even when you're integrated.

As to marketing, however, blackness seen through black eyes may be too black for wide white consumption—unless coupled with greatness or its approximation. What should a Negro writer do, then, in a land where we have no black literary magazines, no black publishers, no black producers, no black investors able to corral seven million dollars to finance a movie? Sell what writing you can, get a job teaching, and give the rest of your talent away. Or else try becoming a good *bad* writer or a black *white* writer, in which case you might, with luck, do as well as white *black* writers do. If you are good enough in a *bad* way, or colored enough in a *good* way, you stand a chance perhaps, maybe, of becoming *even* commercially successful. At any rate, I would say, keep writing. Practice will do you no harm.

Second, be not dismayed! Keep sending your work out, magazine after magazine, publisher after publisher. Collect rejection slips as some people collect stamps. When you achieve a publication or two, try to get a literary agent—who will seek to collect checks for you instead of rejection slips. See along the way how few editors or agents will ask what color you are physically if you have something good to sell. I would say very few or NONE. Basically they do not care about race, if what you write is readable, new, different, exciting, alive on the printed page. Almost nobody knows Frank Yerby is colored. Few think about Willard Motley's complexion. Although how you treat the materials of race may narrow your market, I do not believe your actual race will. Certainly racial or regional subject matter has its marketing limitations. Publishers want only so many Chinese books a year. The same is true of Negro books.

However, if you want a job as a free-lance writer in Hollywood, on radio or in TV, that now is sometimes possible—in contrast to the years before the War. But in the entertainment field, regular full-time staff jobs are still not too easy to come by if you are colored. Positions are valuable in the U.S.A., so commercial white culture would rather allow a colored writer a book than a job, even fame rather than an ordinary, decent, dependable living. But if you are so constituted as to wish a dependable living, with luck you might possibly nowadays achieve that too, purely as a writer. I hope so—because *starving* writers are stereotypes. And a stereotype is the last thing a Negro wants to be.

But you can't be a member of the Beat Generation, the fashionable word at the moment in marketing, *unless* you starve a little. Yet who wants to be "beat"? Not Negroes. . . . So don't worry about beatness. That is easy enough to come by.

Instead, let your talent bloom! You say you are mired in manure? Manure fertilizes. As the old saying goes, "Where the finest roses bloom, there is always a lot of manure around."

Of course, to be highly successful in a white world—commercially successful—in writing or anything else, you really should *be* white. But until you get white, *write*.

—1959

The Negro Writer and His Materials

Loften Mitchell

TWO SOUTHERNERS, one Negro and one white, went hunting together. They shot a turkey and a buzzard. The white man said, "Tell you what, I'll take the turkey and you can have the buzzard." The Negro stared at his companion. The white man rephrased his decision: "Let's put it like this: you take the buzzard and I'll take the other bird." The Negro shook his head and said, "Man, you still ain't talked turkey to me yet!"

This story was related during the panel discussion on "Materials Used by Negro Writers" at the conference sponsored by the American Society of African Culture. The participants agreed that while much has been said about Negro writers, few people have "talked turkey." A conscientious effort was made here. The panel not only discussed materials used by Negro writers but reviewed materials that have been misused, abused, confused and not used.

Of course the plight of the Negro in America from 1619 to the present has markedly affected the materials used in his literature. The African slave, brought unwillingly to these shores, was shorn of his cultural heritage, family ties and traditions. Such action was mandatory for the enslavement of a people. But, contrary to the lies of many historians, the Negro was not happy during slavery. He revolted and sometimes he killed himself rather than submit to the slaver's whip. One group, chained together, marched into the sea and drowned rather than endure a life of slavery. Some rioted openly and were killed. Others tried more subtle approaches. They sang songs of protest, later called spirituals, while they plotted to escape. They created minstrel shows to amuse themselves and to satirize the slavemas-ter. We see here the first of many examples of Negro creativity attempting to "say something" while "not offending" the white group.

Slavery blotted the conscience of the nation and so necessitated a moral justification. The pretense of making "Christians" out of "heathens" was not satisfactory. A "black personality" had to be created. The plan was blueprinted—the plan to portray black people as "savages," "buffoons," or "inferior persons with unclean blood." This portrait was stamped in the pages of history books, in fiction, in drama and in the minds of people. It was the word and the will of God. Black people were inferior, ugly; and slavery was a blessing for them. The rape of the black American had begun!

The rape was evident in Murdock's play *The Triumph of Love* (1795), which portrayed the Negro as a comic servant. It was evident in the 1820's when whites destroyed the African Company's theatre, where Negroes produced Shakespearean plays. It was evident in such well-intentioned plays as *The Branded Hand, Uncle Tom's Cabin, Dred* and *The Octoroon*. These spread the myth of the Negro's submissiveness and the fallacy of the superiority of "mixed" Negroes. And the rape continued when white performers blackened their faces and performed minstrel shows throughout the land. Later, in order to earn a living, Negro performers had to conform to the stereotype that white minstrels had created.

Negroes objected. The portrait was untrue because it did not represent the true intent of the minstrel tradition, nor did it reflect the advances made by the race. A group of men—among them

Bert Williams, George Walker, Ernest Hogan, Jesse Shipp, Sam T. Jack, S. H. Dudley and Bob Cole—deliberately sought to destroy the minstrel pattern. Here, then, was a clear-cut, understandable effort to prove Negroes were not inferior people. Here the Negro writer decided what materials he could *not* use. The Negro writer, therefore, started by trying to prove he was a human being like other human beings.

The minstrel pattern was broken, and Negroes performed on Broadway until 1910, when a wave of reaction evicted them from downtown theatres. *The Clansman*, later filmed as *The Birth of a Nation*, reflected the national attitudes toward the Negro. His activity was largely confined to Harlem until 1917, when Ridgely Torrence's *Three Plays for a Negro Theatre* appeared. This and Eugene O'Neill's *Emperor Jones* demonstrated to white America that the Negro was potential dramatic material. But this material fell into "white hands that wrote with a white point of view," always touching on part of a truth but never on a whole truth about a whole race. Negroes wrote too, and sometimes they wrote what would sell and sometimes they sought the truth; but they were always inhibited by the necessity of not offending whites.

Even in the era of protest writing, society dictated certain terms to the Negro writer. "Negro-white unity" had to be shown at all times. There was always a "good" white who helped the Negro solve his problem. . . . It is difficult to recall an instance of an Englishman "helping" the Irish in one of O'Casey's plays.

To judge from some of the condescending attitudes toward protest writing . . . one would think that Negroes were the only ones who did "agit-prop" writing during the protest era. Actually they were not. And what they did write was no better or worse than the work of their contemporaries. . . .

In reviewing this and other eras, our panel concluded that the Negro writer should protest more than he has. For clearly he is asked to do something no other writer is asked to do, namely, to forget his cultural heritage and write of something else—something "universal." This, of course, implies that the Negro is not human. No one has asked O'Casey to ignore the Irish. No

one has told Odets to forget the Jews. No one has told Tennessee Williams to get out of the South.

As the panel pointed out, the truth is that the very appearance of the Negro is controversial. If the theme isn't "racial," it becomes so when he appears on the scene. Recently someone took fifty plays, among them the Passion play, and put a Negro in the central role. The "problem" immediately arose. The desire of many to see Negroes in "just another play" is understandable, but in the United States in the twentieth century it is naive.

Commercially successful American Negro plays generally fall into two categories. Category one: the play in which a sympathetic white character is assisting "these poor Negroes," as in *Deep Are the Roots*, or as in the films *Home of the Brave*, *Something of Value* and *Intruder in the Dust*. Category two: the play that invites the audience to look down upon "these poor simple souls," as in *The Green Pastures*, *Porgy and Bess* and *Anna Lucasta*. Nowhere in the commercially successful drama—with the exception of *Take a Giant Step* and *A Raisin in the Sun*—do we find an audience *identifying horizontally with a central character who happens to be a Negro*. The following question is raised: Is there a psychological barrier that makes white audiences refuse to identify horizontally with a central Negro character?

Panelists at our session agreed that all the attitudes mentioned above are outgrowths of national attitudes towards Negroes in general—attitudes that have affected the materials used by Negro writers. . . . Alice Childress, author of *Just a Little Simple*, *Gold through the Trees*, *Trouble in Mind* and *Like One of the Family*, declared that the media of communication have, for the most part, promoted the idea that the Negro is not entitled to life, liberty and the pursuit of happiness. "At best," Miss Childress stated, "they believe the Negro deserves pity and charity rather than justice. The 'sympathetic treatment' has been as harmful as the buffoon."

Concerning protest literature Miss Childress said: "We have been assailed with charges of wallowing in the problem, but have the problems of America been truthfully presented? Most of our problems have not seen the light of day in our works, and much has been pruned from our manuscripts before the public has been allowed a glimpse of a finished work. It is ironical that those who oppose us are in a position to dictate the quality and quantity of our contributions. To insult a man is one thing, but to tell him how to react to the insult adds a great and crippling injury."

Miss Childress described the cash prize available for the Negro writer who forsakes the "problem." She stated: "With this prize in mind he may wearily seek to write about general subjects —just people—just human beings. But he finds it rough going because human beings are more than just people. Many of us would rather be writers than Negro writers, and when I get that urge, I look about for the kind of white writer— which is what we mean when we say 'just a writer' —that I would emulate. I come up with Sean O'Casey. Immediately, I am a problem writer. O'Casey writes about the people he knows best and I must—well, there you have it!"

She added that Negro writers have much to say about white society, "and we must say it, but we do not have to obliterate ourselves in order to do so. And there is a new dimension when we write as we see it. For they cannot write what we see." She called attention to the Negro servant whom the white author represents as so greatly concerned about her employers that she works without pay. The servant is sometimes so attentive to the master's health that she ignores her own! Next Miss Childress cited the special problems of one who is "passing" and wondered if anyone really knows the numerous insults awaiting such a person. In short, Miss Childress declared, the flow of white supremacist ideas has made the majority of white Americans incapable of portraying Negro life without prejudice, contempt, or pity.

The general discussion then turned to materials not used by writers. It was noted that there is a paucity of books for children. Love stories, stories of the Negro family and of Negro middle class life are waiting to be written. Works about Negro businessmen, historical figures and professional men are ignored. A visitor to the panel suggested that, based on the evidence outlined, it appears that it may prove more difficult to sell works of this nature than to sell propaganda pieces. This thinking is founded upon the belief that propaganda pieces soothe guilt complexes. A work dealing with human beings may conceivably bring latent prejudices to the fore when white America faces the "black personality" in a portrait contrary to the traditional concept.

Despite all this, defeatism found no welcome at this session. If anything, determination and the ally known as Time hovered over us, assuring us of victory. Integration may be on the march in America, but the fear that the Negro's roots will be obliterated by a white society seems groundless. The rising tide of African nationalism and the uprooting of colonialism have brought reality crashing against the lies of history. The restless stirring in our own Southland is from a people turning *towards* their roots, not seeking to lose this newly found identity. New challenges and new horizons stir the Negro writer towards continued creativity. While it is true that American Negroes are arguing for integration—or more correctly, desegregation—and that they have too long been influenced by a white majority, the majority of the present-day, shrinking world happens to be colored!

The major recommendations of our panel are as follows:

> 1. encouragement of Negro writers to continue writing, using all materials at their command without apology;
> 2. a Negro writers' organization;
> 3. an American counterpart to *Présence Africaine*;
> 4. a bibliography of works on Africa and African writers and one on American Negro writers;
> 5. a larger number of children's books about Negroes; and
> 6. a Negro book publishing business.

In addition, the panel called for an end to the spurious practice of integrating Negro History Week with Brotherhood Week. Since Negro History is excluded from American textbooks, it deserves at least one week a year.

—1959

The Negro Writer and His Relationship to His Roots

Saunders Redding

SINCE MY theme is that the American situation has complex and multifarious sources and that these sources sustain the emotional and intellectual life of American Negro writers, let me take as my starting point a classic oversimplification. This is that the meaning of American society and of the American situation to the Negro is summed up in such works as *Native Son*, *Invisible Man* and *The Ordeal of Mansart*, and in two or three volumes of poetry, notably *Harlem Shadows*, *The Black Christ* and *The Weary Blues*, and that the American Negro writer's entire spirit is represented by such writers as Richard Wright, Ralph Ellison and William Burghardt Du Bois—by realists, Surrealists and romantic idealists.

Please understand me. Wright, Ellison and Du Bois are not mendacious men, and they are doing what writers must always do. They are telling the truth as they see it, which happens to be largely what it is, and they are producing from the examined, or at least the observed causes, the predictable effects; and no one should blame them if the impression they give of the American situation is deplorable. They have been blamed, you know. But let those who blame these writers blame themselves for forgetting that fiction is fiction, and that no novel can pretend to be an exact photographic copy of a country or of the people in a country.

Moreover, dishonor, bigotry, hatred, degradation, injustice, arrogance and obscenity do flourish in American life, and especially in the prescribed and proscriptive American Negro life; and it is the right and the duty of the Negro writer to say so—to complain. He has cause. The temptation of the moral enthusiast is not only strong in him; it is inevitable. He never suspends social and moral judgment. Few actions and events that touch him as a man fail to set in motion his machinery as an artist. History is as personal to him as the woman he loves; and he is caught in the flux of its events, the currents of its opinion and the tides of its emotion; and he believes that the mood is weak which tolerates an impartial presentment of these, and that this weak mood cannot be indulged in a world where the consequences of the actions of a few men produce insupportable calamities for millions of humble folk. He is one of the humble folk. He forages in the cause of righteousness. He forgets that he is also one of Apollo's company.

On the one hand, the jungle; on the other, the resourceful hunter to clear it. The jungle, where lurk the beasts, nourishes the hunter. It is there that he has that sum of relationships that make him what he is. It is where he lives. It is precisely because the jungle is there and is terrible and dangerous that the Negro writer writes and lives at all.

But first, I suppose you must grant me, if only for the sake of this brief exposition, that the American Negro writer is not just an American with a dark skin. . . . This granted, you want to know what the frame of reference is, and about this I shall be dogmatic.

Neither the simplest nor the subtlest scrutiny reveals to an honest man that he has two utterly diverse kinds of experience, that of sense data and that of purpose. Psychology seems to have no difficulty establishing the natural gradation of impulse to purpose. In varying degrees, all our experiences are complications of physical processes.

Shifting from the dogmatic to the apologetic, I must eliminate from view a period of nearly three hundred years, from 1619 to 1900. It was the period that saw the solid establishment here in America of a tradition of race relations and of the concepts that supported the tradition. It was a period that need not be rehearsed. Within the frame of reference thus established, let us look at a certain chain of events.

In 1902 came Thomas Dixon's *The Leopard's Spots*, and three years later *The Clansman*. Both were tremendously popular, and both were included in the repertoires of traveling theatrical companies; and I think it is significant—though we will only imply how—that even a colored company, the Lafayette Players, undertook an adaptation of *The Leopard's Spots*. In 1903 there was a race riot in New York. In 1906 race riots occurred in Georgia and Texas; in 1908 in Illinois. By this latter year, too, all the Southern states had disfranchised the Negro, and color caste was legalized or had legal status everywhere. The Negro's talent for monkeyshines had been exploited on the stage, and some of the music that accompanied the monkeyshines was created by James Weldon Johnson and his brother Rosamond. Meantime, in 1904, Thomas Nelson Page had written the one true canonical book of the law and the prophets, *The Negro: The Southerner's Problem*. And, most cogent fact of all, Booker Washington, having sworn on this bible of reactionism, had been made the undisputed leader of American Negroes because, as he had pledged to do, he advocated a race policy strictly in line with the tradition and the supporting concepts of race relations.

If there had been a time when this tradition seemed to promise the Negro a way out, that time was not now. He had been laughed at, tolerated, amusingly despaired of, but all his own efforts were vain. All the instruments of social progress —schools, churches, lodges—adopted by colored people were the subjects of ribald jokes and derisive laughter. "Mandy, has you studied yo' Greek?" "I's sewing, Ma." "Go naked, gal. Git dat Greek!"

Any objective judgment of Booker Washing-

ton's basic notion must be that it was an extension of the old tradition framed in new terms. Under the impact of social change, the concept was modified to include the stereotype of the Negro as a happy peasant, a docile and satisfied laborer under the stern but kindly eye of the white boss, a creature who had a place and knew it and loved it and would keep it unless he got bad notions from somewhere. The once merely laughable coon had become now also the cheap farm grub or city laborer who could be righteously exploited for his own good and for the greater glory of America. By this addition to the concept, the Negro-white status quo, the condition of inferior-superior race and caste, could be maintained in the face of profound changes in the general society.

What this meant to the Negro writer was that he must, if he wished an audience, adhere to the old forms and the acceptable patterns. It meant that he must create within the limitations of the concept, or that he must dissemble completely, or that he must ignore his racial kinship altogether and leave unsounded the profoundest depths of the peculiar experiences which were his by reason of that kinship. Some chose the first course; at least one—Dunbar—chose the second (as witness his sickly, sticky novels of white love life and his sad epithalamium to death); and a good many chose the third: Braithwaite's anthologies of magazine verse, James Weldon Johnson's contributions to the *Century Magazine* and the writing of Alice Dunbar, Anne Spencer and Angelina Grimké.

But given the whole web of circumstances— empirical, historic, psychological—these writers must have realized that they could not go on and that the damps and fevers, chills and blights, terrors and dangers of the jungle could not be ignored. They must have realized that, with a full tide of race consciousness bearing in upon them, they could not go on forever denying their racehood and that to try to do this at all was a symptom of psychotic strain. Rather perish now than escape only to die of slow starvation.

What had happened was that Booker Washington, with the help of the historic situation and the old concepts, had so thoroughly captured the minds of white people that his was the only Negro voice that could be heard in the jungle. Negro schools needing help could get it only through Booker Washington. Negro social thought wanting a sounding board could have it only on Washington's say-so. Negro political action was weak and ineffective without his strength. Many Negro writers fell silent, and for the writer, silence is death.

Many, but not all. There were stubborn souls and courageous, and the frankly mad among them. There was the Boston *Guardian*, and the Chicago *Defender*, and the Atlanta University Pamphlets, and *The Souls of Black Folk*, and finally the *Crisis*; and this latter quickly developed a voice of multi-range and many tones. It roared like a lion and cooed like a dove and screamed like a monkey and laughed like a hyena. And always it protested. Always the sounds it made were the sounds of revolt in the jungle, and protestation and revolt were becoming—forgive me for changing my figure—powerful reagents in the social chemistry that produced the "New" Negro.

Other factors contributed to this generation, too. The breath of academic scholarship was just beginning to blow hot and steadily enough to wither some of the myths about the Negro. The changes occurring with the onset of war in Europe sloughed off other emotional and intellectual accretions. The Negro might be a creature of "moral debate," but he was also something more. "I ain't a problem," a Negro character was made to say, "I's a person." And that person turned out to be a seeker after the realities in the American dream. When he was called upon to protect that dream with his blood, he asked questions and demanded answers. Whose dream was he protecting, he wanted to know, and why and wherefore? There followed such promises as only the less scrupulous politicians had made to him before. Then came the fighting and the dying, and finally came a thing called peace.

By this time, the Negro was already stirring massively along many fronts. He cracked Broadway wide open. The Garvey movement swept the country like wildfire. *Harlem Shadows, The Gift of Black Folk, Color, Fire in the Flint, The Autobiography of an Ex-Colored Man*. The writers of these and other works were declared to

be irresponsible. A polemical offensive was launched against them, and against such non-artist writers as Philip Randolph, Theophilus Lewis, William Patterson, Angelo Herndon. They were accused of negativism; they were called un-American. Cultural nationalism raised its head and demanded that literature be patriotic, optimistic, positive, uncritical, like *Americans All*, and *American Ideals*, and *America Is Promises*, and *It Takes a Heap o' Living*, which were all written and published in the period of which I speak. But democracy encourages criticism, and it is true that even negative criticism implies certain positive values like veracity, for instance, and these Negro writers had positive allegiances. Their sensibilities were violently irritated, but their faith and imaginations were wonderfully nourished by the very environment which they saw to be and depicted as being bad.

Fortunately there was more than faith and fat imagination in some of these works. There was also talent. Had this not been so, Negro writing would have come to nothing for perhaps another quarter century, for the ground would not have been plowed for the seeds of later talents. But Du Bois, Johnson, McKay, Fisher, Cullen, Hughes, knew what they were about. Their work considerably furthered the interest of white writers and critics. Whatever else O'Neill, Rosenfeld, Connelly, Calverton and Heyward did, they gave validity to the notion that the Negro was material for serious literary treatment.

Beginning then and continuing into the forties, Negro writing had two distinct aspects. The first of these was arty, self-conscious, somewhat precious, experimental, and not truly concerned with the condition of man. Some of the "little reviews" printed a lot of nonsense by Negro writers, including the first chapter of a novel which was to be entirely constructed of elliptical sentences. Then there was *Cane*: sensibility, inwardness, but much of it for the purpose of being absorbed into the universal oneness. Nirvana. Oblivion. Transcendence over one's own personality through the practice of art for art's sake. The appropriate way of feeling and thinking growing out of a particular system of living. And so eventually Gurdjieff.

But the second aspect was more important.

The pathos of man is that he hungers for personal fulfillment and for a sense of community with others. And these writers hungered. There is no American national character. There is only an American situation, and within this situation these writers sought to find themselves. They had always been alienated, not only because they were Negroes but because democracy in America decisively separates the intellectual from everyone else. The intellectual in America is a radically alienated personality, the Negro in common with the white, and both were hungry and seeking, and some of the best of both found food and an identity in communism. But the identity was only partial and, the way things turned out, further emphasized their alienation. So—at least for the Negro writers among them—back into the American situation, the jungle where they could find themselves. A reflex of the natural gradation of impulse to purpose.

Surely this is the meaning of *Native Son.* "Bigger Thomas was not black all the time," his creator says. "He was white too, and there were literally millions of him. . . . Modern experiences were creating types of personalities whose existence ignored racial . . . lines." Identity. Community. Surely this is the meaning of *Invisible Man* and the poignant, pain-filled, pain-relieving humor of simple Jesse B. It is the meaning of *Go Tell It on the Mountain,* and it is explicitly the meaning of four brilliant essays in Part Three of a little book of essays called *Notes of a Native Son.* (How often that word "native" appears, and how meaningful its implications!) Let me quote a short, concluding passage from one of these essays:

. . . since I no longer felt that I would stay in this cell forever, I was beginning to be able to make peace with it for a time. On the 27th I went again to trial and . . . the case . . . was dismissed. The story of the *drap de lit* . . . caused great merriment in the courtroom . . . . I was chilled by their merriment, even though it was meant to warm me. It could only remind me of the laughter I had often heard at home . . . . This laughter is the laughter of those who consider themselves to be at a safe remove from all the wretched, for whom the pain of the living is not real. I had heard it so often in my native land that I had resolved to find a place where I would never hear it any more. In some deep, black, stony, and liberating way, my life, in my own eyes, began during that first year in Paris, when it was borne in on me that this laughter is universal and never can be stilled.

Explicit.

The human condition, the discovery of self. Community. Identity. Surely this must be achieved before it can be seen that a particular identity has a relation to a common identity, commonly described as human. This is the ultimate that the honest writer seeks. He knows that the dilemmas, the perils, the likelihood of catastrophe in the human situation are real and that they have to do not only with whether men understand each other but with the quality of man himself. The writer's ultimate purpose is to use his gifts to develop man's awareness of himself so that he, man, can become a better instrument for living together with other men. This sense of identity is the root by which all honest creative effort is fed, and the writer's relation to it is the relation of the infant to the breast of the mother.

—1959

An Interview with Ralph Ellison

Alfred Chester and Vilma Howard

*I*N THE SUMMER of 1954, Mr. Ellison came abroad to travel and lecture. His visit ended with Paris, where for a very few weeks he mingled with the American expatriate group to whom his work was known and of much interest. The day before he left he talked to us in the Café de la Mairie du VIᵉ about art and the novel.

Ralph Ellison takes both art and the novel seriously. And the Café de la Mairie has a tradition of seriousness behind it, for here was written Djuna Barnes's spectacular novel Nightwood. *There is a tradition, too, of speech and eloquence, for Miss Barnes's hero, Dr. O'Connor, often drew a crowd of listeners to his mighty rhetoric. So here gravity is in the air and rhetoric too. While Mr. Ellison speaks, he rarely pauses, and although the strain of organizing his thought is sometimes evident, his phraseology and the quiet steady flow and development of ideas are overwhelming. To listen to him is rather like sitting in the back of a huge hall and feeling the lecturer's faraway eyes staring directly into your own. The highly emphatic, almost professorial, intonations startle with their distance, self-confidence and warm undertones of humor.*

ELLISON: Let me say right now that my book [*Invisible Man*] is not an autobiographical work.

INTERVIEWERS: You weren't thrown out of school like the boy in your novel?

ELLISON: No. Though, like him, I went from one job to another.

INTERVIEWERS: Why did you give up music and begin writing?

ELLISON: I didn't give up music, but I became interested in writing through incessant reading. In 1935 I discovered Eliot's *The Waste Land*, which moved and intrigued me but defied my powers of analysis—such as they were—and I wondered why I had never read anything of equal intensity and sensibility by an American Negro writer. Later on, in New York, I read a poem by Richard Wright, who, as luck would have it, came to town the next week. He was editing a magazine called *New Challenge* and asked me to try a book review of Waters E. Turpin's *These Low Grounds*. On the basis of this review Wright suggested that I try a short story, which I did. I tried to use my knowledge of riding freight trains.

He liked the story well enough to accept it and it got as far as the galley proofs when it was bumped from the issue because there was too much material. Just after that the mazagine failed.

INTERVIEWERS: But you went on writing . . .

ELLISON: With difficulty, because this was the recession of 1937. I went to Dayton, Ohio, where my brother and I hunted and sold game to earn a living.

At night I practiced writing and studied Joyce, Dostoevski, Stein and Hemingway. Especially Hemingway; I read him to learn his sentence structure and how to organize a story. I guess many young writers were doing this, but I also used his description of hunting when I went into the fields the next day. I had been hunting since I was eleven, but no one had broken down the process of wing-shooting for me, and it was from reading Hemingway that I learned to lead a bird. When he describes something in print, believe him; believe him even when he describes the process of art in terms of baseball or boxing; he's been there.

INTERVIEWERS: Were you affected by the social realism of the period?

ELLISON: I was seeking to learn, and social realism was a highly regarded theory, though I didn't think too much of the so-called "proletarian fiction," even when I was most impressed by Marxism. I was intrigued by Malraux, who at that time was being claimed by the Communists. I noticed, however, that whenever the heroes of *Man's Fate* regarded their condition during moments of heightened self-consciousness, their thinking was something other than Marxist. Actually they were more profoundly intellectual than their real-life counterparts. Of course, Malraux was more of a humanist than most of the Marxist writers of that period—and also much more of an artist. He was the artist-revolutionary rather than a politician when he wrote *Man's Fate*, and the book lives not because of a political position embraced at the time but because of its larger concern with the tragic struggle of humanity. Most of the social realists of the period were concerned less with tragedy than with injustice. I wasn't, and am not, *primarily* concerned with injustice, but with art.

INTERVIEWERS: Then you consider your novel a purely literary work as opposed to one in the tradition of social protest?

ELLISON: Now, mind, I recognize no dichotomy between art and protest. Dostoevski's *Notes from Underground* is, among other things, a protest against the limitations of nineteenth-century rationalism. *Don Quixote, Man's Fate, Oedipus Rex, The Trial*—all these embody protest, even against the limitation of human life itself. If social protest is antithetical to art, what then shall we make of Goya, Dickens and Twain? One hears a lot of complaints about the so-called "protest novel," especially when written by Negroes; but it seems to me that the critics could more accurately complain about the lack of craftsmanship and the provincialism which is typical of such works.

INTERVIEWERS: But isn't it going to be difficult for the Negro writer to escape provincialism when his literature is concerned with a minority?

ELLISON: All novels are about certain minorities: the individual is a minority. The universal in the novel—and isn't that what we're all clamoring for these days?—is reached only through the depiction of the specific man in a specific circumstance.

INTERVIEWERS: But still, how is the Negro writer, in terms of what is expected of him by critics and readers, going to escape his particular need for social protest and reach the "universal" you speak of?

ELLISON: If the Negro, or any other writer, is going to do what is expected of him, he's lost the battle before he takes the field. I suspect that all the agony that goes into writing is borne precisely because the writer longs for acceptance—but it must be acceptance on his own terms. Perhaps, though, this thing cuts both ways: the Negro novelist draws his blackness too tightly around him when he sits down to write—that's what the anti-protest critics believe—but perhaps the white reader draws his whiteness around himself when he sits down to read. He doesn't want to identify himself with Negro characters in terms of our immediate racial and social situation, though, on the deeper human level, identification can become compelling when the situation is revealed artistically. The white reader doesn't want to get too close, not even in an imaginary re-creation of society. Negro writers have felt this, and it has led to much of our failure.

Too many books by Negro writers are addressed to a white audience. By doing this the authors run the risk of limiting themselves to the audience's presumptions of what a Negro is or should be; the tendency is to become involved in polemics, to plead the Negro's humanity. You know, many white people question that humanity, but I don't think that Negroes can afford to indulge in such a false issue. For us the question should be, "What are the specific *forms* of that humanity, and what in our background is worth preserving or abandoning?" The clue to this can be found in folklore, which offers the first drawings of any group's character. It preserves mainly those situations which have repeated themselves again and again in the history of any given group. It describes those rites, manners, customs and so forth which ensure the good life, or destroy it; and it describes those boundaries of feeling, thought and action which that particular group has found to be the limitation of the human condition.

It projects this wisdom in symbols which express the group's will to survive; it embodies those values by which the group lives and dies. These drawings may be crude, but they are nonetheless profound in that they represent the group's attempt to humanize the world. It's no accident that great literature, the product of individual artists, is erected upon this humble base. The hero of Dostoevski's *Notes from Underground* and the hero of Gogol's "The Overcoat" appear in their rudimentary forms far back in Russian folklore. French literature has never ceased exploring the nature of the Frenchman. Or take Picasso . . .

INTERVIEWERS: How does Picasso fit into all this?

ELLISON: Why, he's the greatest wrestler with forms and techniques of them all. Just the same, he's never abandoned the old symbolic forms of Spanish art: the guitar, the bull, daggers, women, shawls, veils, mirrors. Such symbols serve a dual function: they allow the artist to speak of complex experiences and to annihilate time with simple lines and curves; and they allow the viewer an orientation, both emotional and associative, which goes so deep that a total culture may resound in a simple rhythm, an image. It has been said that Escudero could recapitulate the history and spirit of the Spanish dance with a simple arabesque of his fingers.

INTERVIEWERS: But these are examples from homogeneous cultures. How representative of the American nation would you say Negro folklore is?

ELLISON: The history of the American Negro is a most intimate part of American history. Through the very process of slavery came the building of the United States. Negro folklore, evolving within a larger culture which regarded it as inferior, was an especially courageous expression. It announced the Negro's willingness to trust his own experience, his own sensibilities as to the definition of reality, rather than allow his masters to define these crucial matters for him. His experience is that of America and the West, and is as rich a body of experience as one would find anywhere. We can view it narrowly as something exotic, folksy or "low-down," or we may identify ourselves with it and recognize it as an important segment of the larger American experience—not lying at the bottom of it, but intertwined, diffused in its very texture. I can't take this lightly or be impressed by those who cannot see its importance; it is important to *me*. One ironic witness to the beauty and the universality of this art is the fact that the descendants of the very men who enslaved us can now sing the spirituals and find in the singing an exaltation of their own humanity. Just take a look at some of the slave songs, blues, folk ballads; their possibilities for the writer are infinitely suggestive. Some of them have named human situations so well that a whole corps of writers could not exhaust their universality. For instance, here's an old slave verse:

> Ole Aunt Dinah, she's just like me,
> She work so hard she want to be free.
> But ole Aunt Dinah's gittin' kinda ole,
> She's afraid to go to Canada on account of the
>   cold.
>
> Ole Uncle Jack, now he's a mighty "good
>   nigger";
> You tell him that you want to be free for a fac';
> Next thing you know they done stripped the
>   skin off your back.
>
> Now ole Uncle Ned, he want to be free,
> He found his way North by the moss on the
>   tree;
> He cross that river floating in a tub;
> The patateroller [*sic*] give him a mighty close
>   rub.

It's crude, but in it you have three universal attitudes toward the problem of freedom. You can refine it and sketch in the psychological subtleties and historical and philosophical allusions, action and whatnot, but I don't think its basic definition can be exhausted. Perhaps some genius could do as much with it as Mann has done with the Joseph story.

INTERVIEWERS: Can you give us an example of the use of folklore in your own novel?

ELLISON: Well, there are certain themes, symbols and images which are based on folk material. For example, there is the old saying among Negroes: "If you're black, stay back; if you're brown, stick around; if you're white, you're right." And there is the joke Negroes tell on themselves about their being so black they can't be seen in the dark. In my book this sort of thing was merged with the meanings which blackness and light have long had in Western mythology: evil and goodness, ignorance and knowledge, and so on.

In my novel the narrator's development is one through blackness to light, that is, from ignorance to enlightenment: invisibility to visibility. He leaves the South and goes North; this, as you will notice in reading Negro folk tales, is always the road to freedom—the movement upward. You have the same thing again when he leaves his underground cave for the open.

It took me a long time to learn how to adapt such examples of myth into my work—also ritual. The use of ritual is equally a vital part of the creative process. I learned a few things from Eliot, Joyce and Hemingway, but not how to adapt them. When I started writing, I knew that in both *The Waste Land* and *Ulysses* ancient myth and ritual were used to give form and significance to the material; but it took me a few years to realize that the myths and rites which we find functioning in our everyday lives could be used in the same way.

In my first attempt at a novel—which I was unable to complete—I began by trying to manipulate the simple structural unities of *beginning*, *middle* and *end*, but when I attempted to deal with the psychological strata—the images, symbols and emotional configurations—of the experience at hand, I discovered that the unities were simply cool points of stability on which one could suspend the narrative line; but beneath the surface of apparently rational human relationships, there seethed a chaos before which I was helpless. People rationalize what they shun or are incapable of dealing with; these superstitions and their rationalizations become ritual as they govern behavior. The rituals become social forms, and it is one of the functions of the artist to recognize them and raise them to the level of art.

I don't know whether I'm getting this over or not. Let's put it this way: Take the "Battle Royal" passage in my novel, where the boys are blindfolded and forced to fight each other for the amusement of the white observers. This is a vital part of behavior pattern in the South, which both Negroes and whites thoughtlessly accept. It is a ritual in preservation of caste lines, a keeping of taboo to appease the gods and ward off bad luck. It is also the initiation ritual to which all greenhorns are subjected. This passage states what Negroes will see I did not have to invent; the patterns were already there in society, so that all I had to do was present them in a broader context of meaning. In any society there are many rituals of situation which, for the most part, go unquestioned. They can be simple or elaborate, but they are the connective tissue between the work of art and the audience.

INTERVIEWERS: Do you think a reader unacquainted with this folklore can properly understand your work?

ELLISON: Yes, I think so. It's like jazz; there's no inherent problem which prohibits understanding but the assumptions brought to it. We don't all dig Shakespeare uniformly, or even "Little Red Riding-hood." The understanding of art depends finally upon one's willingness to extend one's humanity and one's knowledge of human life. I noticed, incidentally, that the Germans, having no special caste assumptions concerning American Negroes, dealt with my work simply as a novel. I think the Americans will come to view it that way in twenty years—if it's around that long.

INTERVIEWERS: Don't you think it will be?

ELLISON: I doubt it. It's not an important novel. I failed of eloquence, and many of the immediate issues are rapidly fading away. If it does last, it will be simply because there are things going on in its depth that are of more permanent interest than on its surface. I hope so, anyway.

INTERVIEWERS: Have the critics given you any constructive help in your writing, or changed in any way your aims in fiction?

ELLISON: No, except that I have a better idea of how the critics react, of what they see and fail to see, of how their sense of life differs with mine and mine with theirs. In some instances they were nice for the wrong reasons. In the U.S.—and I don't want this to sound like an apology for my own failures—some reviewers did not see what was before them because of this nonsense about protest.

INTERVIEWERS: Did the critics change your view of yourself as a writer?

ELLISON: I can't say that they did. I've been seeing by my own candle too long for that. The critics did give me a sharper sense of a larger audience, yes; and some convinced me that they were willing to judge me in terms of my writing rather than in terms of my racial identity. But there is one widely syndicated critical bankrupt who made liberal noises during the thirties and has been frightened ever since. He attacked my book as a "literary race riot." By and large, the critics and readers gave me an affirmed sense of my identity as a writer. You might know this within yourself, but to have it affirmed by others is of utmost importance. Writing is, after all, a form of communication.

INTERVIEWERS: When did you begin *Invisible Man*?

ELLISON: In the summer of 1945. I had returned from the sea, ill, with advice to get some rest. Part of my illness was due, no doubt, to the fact that I had not been able to write a novel for which I'd received a Rosenwald Fellowship the previous winter. So on a farm in Vermont, where I was reading *The Hero* by Lord Ragland and speculating on the nature of Negro leadership in the U.S., I wrote the first paragraph of *Invisible Man*, and was soon involved in the struggle of creating the novel.

INTERVIEWERS: How long did it take you to write it?

ELLISON: Five years, with one year out for a short novel which was unsatisfactory, ill-conceived and never submitted for publication.

INTERVIEWERS: Did you have everything thought out before you began to write *Invisible Man*?

ELLISON: The symbols and their connections were known to me. I began it with a chart of the three-part division. It was a conceptual frame with most of the ideas and some incidents indicated. The three parts represent the narrator's movement from, using Kenneth Burke's terms, purpose to passion to perception. These three major sections are built up of smaller units of three which mark the course of the action and which depend for their development upon what I hoped was a consistent and developing motivation. However, you'll note that the maximum insight on the hero's part isn't reached until the final section. After all, it's a novel about innocence and human error, a struggle through illusion to reality.

Each section begins with a sheet of paper; each piece of paper is exchanged for another and contains a definition of his identity, or the social role he is to play as defined for him by others. But all say essentially the same thing: "Keep this nigger boy running." Before he could have some voice in his own destiny he had to discard these old identities and illusions; his enlightenment couldn't come until then. Once he recognizes the hole of darkness into which these papers put him, he has to burn them. That's the plan and the intention; whether I achieved this is something else.

INTERVIEWERS: Would you say that the search for identity is primarily an American theme?

ELLISON: It is *the* American theme. The nature of our society is such that we are prevented from knowing who we are. It is still a young society, and this is an integral part of its development.

INTERVIEWERS: A common criticism of "first novels" is that the central incident is either omitted or weak. *Invisible Man* seems to suffer here; shouldn't we have been present at the scenes which are the dividing lines in the book—namely, when the Brotherhood organization moves the narrator downtown, then back uptown?

ELLISON: I think you missed the point. The major flaw in the hero's character is his unquestioning willingness to do what is required of him by others as a way to success, and this was the specific form of his "innocence." He goes where he is told to go; he does what he is told to do; he does not even choose his Brotherhood name. It is chosen for him and he accepts it. He has accepted party discipline, and thus cannot be present at the scene since it is not the will of the Brotherhood leaders. What is important is not the scene but his failure to question their decision.

There is also the fact that no single person can be everywhere at once, nor can a single consciousness be aware of all the nuances of a large social action. What happens uptown while he is downtown is part of his darkness, both symbolic and actual. No; I don't feel that any vital scenes have been left out.

INTERVIEWERS: Why did you find it necessary to shift styles throughout the book, particularly in the Prologue and Epilogue?

ELLISON: The Prologue was written afterwards, really—in terms of a shift in the hero's point of view. I wanted to throw the reader off balance—make him accept certain non-naturalistic effects. It was really a memoir written underground, and I wanted a foreshadowing through which I hoped the reader would view the actions which took place in the main body of the book.

For another thing, the styles of life presented are different. In the South, where he was trying to fit into a traditional pattern and where his sense of certainty had not yet been challenged, I felt a more naturalistic treatment was adequate. The college trustee's speech to the students is really an echo of a certain kind of Southern rhetoric, and I enjoyed trying to re-create it. As the hero passes from the South to the North, from the relatively stable to the swiftly changing, his sense of certainty is lost and the style becomes Expressionistic. Later on, during his fall from grace in the Brotherhood, it becomes somewhat Surrealistic. The styles try to express both his state of consciousness and the state of society. The Epilogue was necessary to complete the action begun when he set out to write his memoirs.

INTERVIEWERS: After four hundred pages you still felt the Epilogue was necessary?

ELLISON: Yes. Look at it this way. The book is a series of reversals. It is the portrait of the artist as a rabble-rouser, thus the various mediums of expression. In the Epilogue the hero discovers what he had not discovered throughout the book: you have to make your own decisions; you have to think for yourself. The hero comes up from underground because the act of writing

and thinking necessitated it. He could not stay down there.

INTERVIEWERS: You say that the book is "a series of reversals." It seemed to us that this was a weakness, that it was built on a series of provocative situations which were canceled by the calling up of conventional emotions.

ELLISON: I don't quite see what you mean.

INTERVIEWERS: Well, for one thing, you begin with a provocative situation of the American Negro's status in society. The responsibility for this is that of the white American citizen; that's where the guilt lies. Then you cancel it by introducing the Communist party, or the Brotherhood, so that the reader tends to say to himself, "Ah, they're the guilty ones. They're the ones who mistreat him; not us."

ELLISON: I think that's a case of misreading. And I didn't identify the Brotherhood as the C.P., but since you do I'll remind you that they too are white.

The hero's invisibility is not a matter of being seen, but a refusal to run the risk of his own humanity, which involves guilt. This is not an attack upon white society! It is what the hero refuses to do in each section which leads to further action. He must assert and achieve his own humanity; he cannot run with the pack and do this: this is the reason for all the reversals. The Epilogue is the most final reversal of all; therefore it is a necessary statement.

INTERVIEWERS: And the love affairs—or almost love-affairs?

ELLISON (laughing): I'm glad you put it that way. The point is that when thrown into a situation which he thinks he wants, the hero is sometimes thrown at a loss; he doesn't know how to act. After he had made this speech about the "Place of the Woman in Our Society," for example, and was approached by one of the women in the audience, he thought she wanted to talk about the Brotherhood and found that she wanted to talk about brother-and-sisterhood. Look, didn't you find the book at all funny? I felt that such a man as this character would have been incapable of a love affair; it would have been inconsistent with his personality.

INTERVIEWERS: Do you have any difficulty controlling your characters? E. M. Forster says that he sometimes finds a character running away with him.

ELLISON: No, because I find that a sense of the ritual understructure of the fiction helps to guide the creation of characters. Action is the thing. We are what we do and do not do. The problem for me is to get from A to B to C. My anxiety about transitions greatly prolonged the writing of my book. The naturalists stick to case histories and sociology and are willing to compete with the camera and the tape recorder. I despise concreteness in writing, but when reality is deranged in fiction, one must worry about the seams.

INTERVIEWERS: Do you have difficulty turning real characters into fiction?

ELLISON: Real characters are just a limitation. It's like turning your own life into fiction: you have to be hindered by chronology and fact. A number of the characters just jumped out, like Rinehart and Ras.

INTERVIEWERS: Isn't Ras based on Marcus Garvey?

ELLISON: No. In 1950 my wife and I were staying at a vacation spot where we met some white liberals who thought the best way to be friendly was to tell us what it was like to be Negro. I got mad at hearing this from people who otherwise seemed very intelligent. I had already sketched Ras, but the passion of his statement came out after I went upstairs that night feeling that we needed to have this thing out once and for all and get it done with; then we could go on living like people and individuals. No conscious reference to Garvey is intended.

INTERVIEWERS: What about Rinehart? Is he related to Rinehart in the blues tradition, or Django Reinhardt, the jazz musician?

ELLISON: There is a peculiar set of circumstances connected with my choice of that name. My old Oklahoma friend, Jimmy Rushing, the blues singer, used to sing one with a refrain that went:

> Rinehart, Rinehart,
> It's so lonesome up here
> On Beacon Hill,

which haunted me, and as I was thinking of a character who was a master of disguise, of coin-

cidence, this name with its suggestion of inner and outer came to my mind. Later I learned that it was a call used by Harvard students when they prepared to riot, a call to chaos. Which is very interesting, because it is not long after Rinehart appears in my novel that the riot breaks out in Harlem. Rinehart is my name for the personification of chaos. He is also intended to represent America and change. He has lived so long with chaos that he knows how to manipulate it. It is the old theme of *The Confidence Man*. He is a figure in a country with no solid past or stable class lines; therefore he is able to move about easily from one to the other. . . .

You know, I'm still thinking of your question about the use of Negro experience as material for fiction. One function of serious literature is to deal with the moral core of a given society. Well, in the United States the Negro and his status have always stood for that moral concern. He symbolizes among other things the human and social possibility of equality. This is the moral question raised in our two great nineteenth-century novels, *Moby Dick* and *Huckleberry Finn*. The very center of Twain's book revolves finally around the boy's relations with Nigger Jim and the question of what Huck should do about getting Jim free after the two scoundrels had sold him. There is a magic here worth conjuring, and that reaches to the very nerve of the American consciousness—so why should I abandon it? Our so-called "race problem" has now lined up with the world problems of colonialism and the struggle of the West to gain the allegiance of the remaining non-white people who have thus far remained outside the communist sphere; thus its possibilities for art have increased rather than lessened.

Looking at the novelist as manipulator and depicter of moral problems, I ask myself how much of the achievement of democratic ideals in the U.S. has been affected by the steady pressure of Negroes and those whites who were sensitive to the implications of our condition; and I know that without that pressure the position of our country before the world would be much more serious than it is even now. Here is part of the social dynamics of a great society. Perhaps the discomfort about protest in books by Negro authors comes because since the nineteenth century American literature has avoided profound moral searching. It was too painful, and besides, there were specific problems of language and form to which the writers could address themselves. They did wonderful things, but perhaps they left the real problems untouched. There are exceptions, of course, like Faulkner, who has been working the great moral theme all along, taking it up where Mark Twain put it down.

I feel that with my decision to devote myself to the novel I took on one of the responsibilities inherited by those who practice the craft in the U.S.: that of describing for all that fragment of the huge diverse American experience which I know best, and which offers me the possibility of contributing not only to the growth of the literature but to the shaping of the culture as I should like it to be. The American novel is in this sense a conquest of the frontier; as it describes our experience, it creates it.

—1954

Bibliography

ALBERT, OCTAVIA V. ROGERS. *The House of Bondage: Or Charlotte Brooks and Other Slaves.* New York, 1890.

ALLEN, RICHARD, and JONES, ABSALOM. *A Narrative of the Proceedings of the Black People during the Late Awful Calamity in Philadelphia in the Year 1793: And a Refutation of Some Censures Thrown upon Them in Some Late Publications.* Philadelphia, 1794.

ALLEN, WILLIAM G. *The American Prejudice against Color: An Authentic Narrative, Showing How Easily the Nation Got into an Uproar.* London, 1853.

BALDWIN, JAMES. *Notes of a Native Son.* Boston, 1955.

BANNEKER, BENJAMIN. *Benjamin Banneker's Pennsylvania, Delaware, Maryland and Virginia Almanack and Ephemeris for the Year of Our Lord, 1792.* Baltimore, 1792.

———. *Copy of a Letter from Benjamin Banneker to the Secretary of State, with His Answer.* Philadelphia, 1792.

BIBB, HENRY. *Narrative of the Life and Adventures of Henry Bibb, an American Slave: Written by Himself.* New York, 1849.

BLACKSON, LORENZO D. *The Rise and Progress of the Kingdoms of Light and Darkness: Or the Reigns of Kings Alpha and Abadon.* Philadelphia, 1867.

BONE, ROBERT A. *The Negro Novel in America.* New Haven, Conn., 1965.

BRAWLEY, BENJAMIN. *Early Negro American Writers.* Chapel Hill, N.C., 1935.

BROWN, HENRY BOX. *Narrative of Henry Box Brown, Who Escaped from Slavery Enclosed in a Box Three Feet Long and Two Feet Wide: Written from a Statement of Facts Made by Himself.* Boston, 1849.

BROWN, STERLING A., DAVIS, ARTHUR P. and LEE, ULYSSES. *The Negro Caravan.* New York, 1941.

BROWN, WILLIAM WELLS. *The American Fugitive in Europe: Sketches of Places and People Abroad, with a Memoir by the Author.* Boston, 1855.

———. *The Black Man: His Antecedents, His Genius and His Achievements.* New York, 1863.

———. *Clotel: Or the President's Daughter. A Narrative of Slave Life in the United States.* London, 1853.

———. *Three Years in Europe: Or Places I Have Seen and People I Have Met. With a Memoir of the Author by William Farmer.* London, 1852.

BUTCHER, MARGARET JUST. *The Negro in American Culture.* New York, 1956.

CAMPBELL, ROBERT. *A Pilgrimage to my Motherland: An Account of a Journey among the Egbas and Yorubas of Central Africa in 1859–60.* New York, 1861.

CANNON, N. C. *The Rock of Wisdom: An Explanation of the Sacred Scriptures, to Which Are Added Several Interesting Hymns.* New York, 1833.

CATTO, WILLIAM T. *A Semi-Centenary Discourse, Delivered in the First African Presbyterian Church, Philadelphia, on the Fourth Sabbath of May, 1857: With a History of the Church from Its First Organization.* Philadelphia, 1857.

CHAPMAN, ABRAHAM (ed.). *Black Voices.* New York, 1968.

CHESNUTT, CHARLES WADDELL. *Frederick Douglass.* Boston, 1899.

CLARK, PETER H. *The Black Brigade of Cincinnati.* Cincinnati, 1864.

CLARKE, JOHN HENRIK (ed.). *American Negro Short Stories.* New York, 1966.

———. *Harlem, U.S.A.* Berlin, 1964.

COFFIN, ALFRED O., and COLEMAN, N. *A List of the Native Plants That Are Found in the Vicinity of Marshall, Texas.* Marshall, Tex., 1895.

COKER, DANIEL. *Journal of Daniel Coker, a Descendant of Africa: From the Time of Leaving New York in the Ship* Elizabeth, *Capt. Sebor . . . for . . . Africa.* Baltimore, 1820.

CORNISH, SAMUEL E., and WRIGHT, THEODORE S. *The Colonization Scheme Considered.* Newark, N.J., 1840.

COTTER, JOSEPH SEAMON. *Links of Friendship.* Louisville, Ky., 1898.

CRAFT, WILLIAM, and CRAFT, ELLEN. *Running a Thousand Miles for Freedom: Or the Escape of William and Ellen Craft from Slavery.* London, 1860.

CRUMMELL, ALEXANDER. *Africa and America: Addresses and Discourses.* Springfield, Mass., 1891.

CUFFE, PAUL. *A Brief Account of the Settlement and Present Situation of the Colony of Sierra Leone, in Africa.* New York, 1812.

DELANY, MARTIN R. *The Condition, Elevation, Emigration and Destiny of the Colored People of the United States, Politically Considered.* Philadelphia, 1852.

———. *Official Report of the Niger Valley Exploring Party.* New York, 1861.

DOUGLASS, WILLIAM. *Annals of the First African Church in the United States of America, Now Styled the African Episcopal Church of St. Thomas, Philadelphia.* Philadelphia, 1862.

DREER, HERMAN. *American Literature by Negro Authors.* New York, 1950.

DU BOIS, W. E. B. *The Philadelphia Negro: A Social Study.* Philadelphia, 1899.

———. *The Souls of Black Folk.* Chicago, 1903.

DUNBAR, PAUL LAURENCE. *Folks from Dixie.* New York, 1898.

———. *Majors and Minors.* Toledo, Ohio, 1896.

———. *Oak and Ivy.* Dayton, Ohio, 1892.

EATON, HOSEA. *A Treatise on the Intellectual Character and Civil and Political Condition of the Colored People of the United States, and the Prejudice Exercised towards Them.* Boston, 1837.

ELLIOTT, ROBERT BROWN. *Oration Delivered April 16, 1872, at the Celebration of the Tenth Anniversary of Emancipation in the District of Columbia.* Washington, 1872.

EMANUEL, JAMES A., and GROSS, THEODORE L. (eds.). *Dark Symphony.* New York, 1968.

EMBRY, JAMES C. *Our Father's House, and Family, Past, Present and Future.* Philadelphia, 1893.

FLIPPER, HENRY OSSIAN. *The Colored Cadet at West Point: Autobiography of Lieutenant Henry Ossian Flipper, U.S.A., First Graduate of Color from the U.S. Military Academy.* New York, 1878.

FORD, N. A. *The Contemporary Negro Novel.* Boston, 1936.

FORTEN, JAMES. *Letters from a Man of Color: On a Late Bill before the Senate of Pennsylvania.* Philadelphia, 1813.

FORTUNE, T. THOMAS. *The Negro in Politics.* New York, 1885.

GREEN, WILLIAM. *Narrative of Events in the Life of William Green, Formerly a Slave: Written by Himself.* Springfield, Mass., 1853.

GRIMKÉ, FRANCIS J. *The Negro: His Rights and Wrongs, the Forces for and against Him.* Washington, 1898.

GROSS, SEYMOUR L., and HARDY, JOHN E. *Images of the Negro in American Literature.* Chicago, 1966.

HAMMON, JUPITER. *An Address to the Negroes in the State of New York.* New York, 1787.

HARPER, FRANCES ELLEN WATKINS. *Moses: A Story of the Nile.* Philadelphia, 1869.

HILL, HERBERT (ed.). *Anger and Beyond.* New York, 1966.

HUGHES, JOHN M. *The Negro Novelist: 1940–1950.* New York, 1953.

HUGHES, LANGSTON (ed.). *Best Short Stories by Negro Writers.* Boston, 1967.

——. *The Book of Negro Humor.* New York, 1966.

——. *New Negro Poets.* Bloomington, Ind., 1964.

HUGHES, LANGSTON, and BONTEMPS, ARNA (eds.). *The Book of Negro Folklore.* New York, 1958.

——. *The Poetry of the Negro: 1746–1949.* New York, 1949.

JASPER, JOHN. *The Sun Do Move! The Celebrated Theory of the Sun's Rotation around the Earth, as Preached by Rev. John Jasper of Richmond, Va.: With a Memoir of His Life.* New York, 1882.

JOHNSON, JAMES WELDON. *Black Manhattan.* New York, 1930.

JONES, THOMAS H. *Experiences and Personal Narrative of Uncle Tom Jones: Who Was for Forty Years a Slave.* Boston, 1858.

KECKLEY, ELIZABETH. *Behind the Scenes: Or Thirty Years a Slave and Four Years in the White House.* New York, 1868.

LANGSTON, JOHN MERCER. *From the Virginia Plantation to the National Capitol: Or the First and Only Negro Representative in Congress from the Old Dominion.* Hartford, Conn., 1894.

LOCKE, ALAIN. *The New Negro.* New York, 1925.

LOGGINS, VERNON. *The Negro Author: His Development in America to 1900.* New York, 1931.

MARRANT, JOHN. *A Narrative of the Lord's Wonderful Dealings with J. Marrant, a Black . . . Taken Down from His Own Relation.* London, 1785.

MEACHUM, JOHN B. *An Address to All the Colored Citizens of the United States.* Philadelphia, 1846.

NELL, WILLIAM C. *The Colored Patriots of the American Revolution, with Sketches of Several Distinguished Colored Persons: To Which Is Added a Brief Survey of the Condition and Prospects of Colored Americans . . . with an Introduction by Harriet Beecher Stowe.* Boston, 1855.

NELSON, ALICE DUNBAR. *The Goodness of St. Rocque, and Other Stories.* New York, 1899.

OFFLEY, G. W. *A Narrative of the Life and Labors of the Rev. G. W. Offley, a Colored Man and Local Preacher.* Hartford, Conn., 1860.

PARROTT, RUSSELL. *An Address on the Abolition of the Slave Trade, Delivered . . . 1st of January, 1816.* Philadelphia, 1816.

PENNINGTON, JAMES W. C. *Covenants Involving Moral Wrong Are Not Obligatory upon Man: A Sermon Delivered in the Fifth Congregational Church, Hartford, on Thanksgiving Day, Nov. 17th, 1842.* Hartford, Conn., 1842.

PLATO, ANN. *Essays: Including Biographies and Miscellaneous Pieces in Prose and Poetry. With an Introduction by the Rev. James W. C. Pennington.* Hartford, Conn., 1841.

PURVIS, ROBERT. *Appeal of Forty Thousand Citizens Threatened with Disfranchisement to the People of Pennsylvania.* Philadelphia, 1838.

RUCHAMES, LOUIS. *The Abolitionists.* New York, 1963.

RUGGLES, DAVID. *The "Extinguisher" Extinguished! Or D. M. Reese, M.D., "Used Up."* New York, 1834.

SMITH, VENTURE. *A Narrative of the Life and Adventures of Venture, a Native of Africa, but Resident above Sixty Years in the United States of America.* New London, Conn., 1789.

STEWARD, AUSTIN. *Twenty-two Years a Slave and Forty Years a Freeman: Embracing a Correspondence of Several Years While President of Wilberforce Colony, London, Canada West.* Rochester, N.Y., 1857.

STILL, JAMES. *Early Recollections and Life.* Philadelphia, 1877.

TROTTER, JAMES M. *Music and Some Highly Musical People.* Boston, 1878.

VASSA, GUSTAVUS. *The Interesting Narrative of the Life of Olaudah Equiano, or Gustavus Vassa, the African: Written by Himself.* London, 1789.

WALDEN, ISLAY. *Walden's Miscellaneous Poems.* Washington, 1873.

WAYMAN, ALEXANDER W. *Cyclopedia of African Methodism.* Baltimore, 1882.

WEBB, FRANK. *The Garies and Their Friends.* London, 1857.

WEGELIN, OSCAR. *Jupiter Hammon, American Negro Poet.* New York, 1915.

WHEATLEY, PHILLIS. *Poems and Letters,* ed. C. F. HEARTMAN. New York, 1915.

——. *Poems on Various Subjects, Religious and Moral.* London, 1773.

WHITEMAN, MAXWELL. *A Century of Fiction by American Negroes: 1853–1952.* Philadelphia, 1955.

WHITMAN, ALBERY A. *An Idyl of the South: An Epic Poem in Two Parts.* New York, 1901.

WILLIAMS, JOHN A. (ed.). *Beyond the Angry Black.* New York, 1966.